ENGLISH
CONSTITUTIONAL IDEAS
IN THE
FIFTEENTH CENTURY

ENGLISH
CONSTITUTIONAL IDEAS
IN THE
FIFTEENTH CENTURY

by

S. B. CHRIMES
M.A. (Lond.), Ph.D. (Camb.), F.R.Hist.S.

*Lecturer in Constitutional History in the University of Glasgow;
Sometime Lindley Student in the University of London
and Rouse Ball Research Student in
Trinity College, Cambridge*

CAMBRIDGE

AT THE UNIVERSITY PRESS

1936

CAMBRIDGE UNIVERSITY PRESS
Cambridge, New York, Melbourne, Madrid, Cape Town,
Singapore, São Paulo, Delhi, Mexico City

Cambridge University Press
The Edinburgh Building, Cambridge CB2 8RU, UK

Published in the United States of America by Cambridge University Press, New York

www.cambridge.org
Information on this title: www.cambridge.org/9781107683334

© Cambridge University Press 1936

First published 1936
First paperback edition 2013

A catalogue record for this publication is available from the British Library

ISBN 978-1-107-68333-4 Paperback

CONTENTS

Contents

Contents

PREFACE

This work could not have been undertaken, completed, or published but for the liberality of the Council of Trinity College, Cambridge. The opportunity to undertake the work was given me by my election to the research studentship offered by that Council to graduates of other Universities, and I was able to continue it as a result of my subsequent election to a Rouse Ball research studentship in the same College. Publication of the work, moreover, was made possible by the Council's vote of a substantial grant-in-aid from the Rouse Ball Fund. My indebtedness to Trinity College is thus very heavy, but it cannot be expressed merely in terms of finance.

I am grateful to the Cambridge University Press for undertaking the remaining costs of publication, and for the courtesy and accurate work of its staff. I have had the advantage of consulting a number of scholars on various points; in particular Professors Sir William Holdsworth, H. F. Jolowicz, F. M. Powicke, M. T. Smiley, C. H. Williams; Miss H. Cam, and Rev. Dr A. J. Carlyle. Professors E. F. Jacob and T. F. T. Plucknett, and Mr K. Pickthorn read my manuscript in its early stages, and made many helpful suggestions.

Several friends have been long-suffering in the toll I have taken of them. Miss Mabel Keyser patiently searched my proofs for misprints. Mr R. R. Page applied his subtle logic to the improvement of the form of the book, and helped to prune away many infelicities. Mr A. S. Gilbert, of University College, London, and the Middle Temple, placed at my disposal his expert legal knowledge, which I have drawn on very freely, to the great benefit of my text. He read my proofs with extreme care, and his criticisms and suggestions have saved me numerous errors and inaccuracies, as well as indicated fresh points for consideration. My most fundamental debt, however, is to a master of early constitutional history. The work was begun under the supervision of Dr Gaillard Lapsley, and his encouragement, criticism, and suggestions at every stage have been of inestimable value. Scarcely a page of the book has not, at one time or another, been improved in form or substance as a result of his comments. Where I have begged to differ from him, I have done so with an uncomfortable feeling that my confidence has probably sprung from ignorance. For the errors and defects that remain, I, of course, am alone responsible.

I have been obliged to the Council of the Royal Historical Society for permission to reprint my paper on 'Sir John Fortescue and his Theory of Dominion' which was published in the Society's *Transactions* for 1934, and to make use of the text of Bishop Russell's parliamentary sermons which was published in 1854 by Mr J. G. Nichols in vol. LX of the Camden Society's publications; also to the Editor of the *English Historical Review* for permission to reproduce my Note on 'The Terms House of Lords and House of Commons in the 15th century' published therein in 1934; also to the Honourable Societies of Lincoln's Inn and the Inner Temple for kind permission to consult the manuscripts in their libraries.

Some words of reservation and caution should be said here regarding the legal materials I have used. The bulk of the fresh material that has been embodied in the text has come from the Black-Letter *Year Books*. The dangers of using this source for the purpose I have had in mind are many, even though they may be obvious only to students who are more expert in the law than I. These dangers are not lessened by the fact that at present only two fifteenth-century *Year Books* are available in modern editions. I have not, however, attempted the task of editing the cases which I cite. Even had I wished to do so, the examination of the manuscripts of a century's *Year Books* would have been an impossible task. Consequently, I have contented myself with printing in an Appendix the most relevant portions of the cases I have cited, and have reproduced them, without comment or amendment, in the form of the Black-Letter 'Vulgate' edition. No doubt corruptions appear in these texts, but on the whole I believe they are adequate for the strictly limited purposes I have had in view. A much more serious matter, to my mind, is the question of the evidential value of the *Year Books* for those very purposes. From one point of view these law reports are of the highest value as authentic evidence of the ideas of the times in which they were composed; they are almost the only *verbatim* reports of the living word that we have coming from the century, and as such possess an actuality which is lacking in nearly all other sources. From other points of view they seem to be of questionable value for the history of ideas: much of the pleading reported is necessarily special pleading; the arts of advocacy were often more ingenious than ingenuous then as they are now; judicial ruling and counsel's argument are two very different things; the one may give us the law, but which best reflects contemporary opinion? Moreover, whatever is said, by whomsoever it is said, in the courts, is necessarily said within the framework of the law, which may have been, and often was, rather out-of-date in matters of constitutional theory. Consequently, the precise value of any *Year Book* case for the history of constitutional ideas, and indeed of constitutional law, is a very delicate and complicated problem. I cannot hope that I have justly assessed the evidential value of each of the hundred odd cases cited in my pages, nor can I offer the reader the compensation of a complete text of each case. Nevertheless, in basing my conclusions on *Year Book* evidence, I have endeavoured to bear in mind the inevitable complications, and to apply the appropriate reservations, and in every instance I refer the reader to the extract printed in the Appendix; where this extract proves inadequate, the Black-Letter edition should be consulted.

I may say, in conclusion, that I had hoped to obtain additional material from some of the Serjeants' Readings to the Inns of Court. I examined, I believe, all the likely manuscripts of these Readings, but found nothing relevant to the purpose.

S. B. C.

University College Hall
Queen's Walk
Ealing, London
10 May 1936

ABBREVIATIONS

Chapters.	Tout's Chapters in Mediaeval Administrative History.
De Laudibus.	Fortescue's De Laudibus Legum Angliae.
Bull. I.H.R.	Bulletin of the Institute of Historical Research, London.
Bull. J.R.L.	Bulletin of John Rylands Library, Manchester.
E.E.T.S.	Early English Text Society.
E.H.R.	English Historical Review.
Hist. Eng. Law.	History of English Law.
Hist. Zeit.	Historische Zeitschrift.
L.Q.R.	Law Quarterly Review.
N.L.N.	Fortescue's De Natura Legis Naturae.
Procs. and Ords.	Proceedings and Ordinances of the Privy Council, ed. Sir Harris Nicolas.
Rot. Parl.	Rotuli Parliamentorum.
T.R.H.S.	Transactions of the Royal Historical Society.
Y.B.	Year Book.

INTRODUCTION

*What men have done and said, and above all what they
have thought—that is history*   MAITLAND

These studies are the outcome of a desire to pursue further the
suggestions that were made by Mr T. F. T. Plucknett in his
essay on 'The Lancastrian Constitution', which was published
in 1924 in the volume of *Tudor Studies* presented to A. F.
Pollard. In that essay, Mr Plucknett, on the basis of four
significant Year Book cases which he was the first to bring into
notice, raised afresh the whole problem of the character of the
Lancastrian and Yorkist constitution. He pointed out that the
'later splendours of the constitution have been reflected back
upon the fifteenth century, throwing certain features of it into
undue relief and enveloping the whole structure with an
appearance of maturity and completeness which is in fact
illusory'.[1] He concluded, in the light of the evidence he adduced, that—though much would have to be done before a
confident judgement could be given—the uneasy feeling which
had long existed about the 'constitutionalism' of the Lancastrians
seemed to be thoroughly justified. Beneath the strange modernity
of its appearance there lay, he suggested, a fundamental
deficiency which made it peculiarly difficult to understand, and
he thought this was, in some measure at least, due to the fact
that however familiar the forms of Lancastrian government
might seem, the spirit within them was completely alien to
modern thought.[2]

To investigate this spirit behind the forms of fifteenth-
century government has been the object of the present writer.
The task has not always been easy, for the materials for such a
study are far from simple, and the *Year Books* in particular do
not lend themselves readily to the purpose in hand. Moreover,

[1] *Loc. cit.* 161.   [2] *Ibid.* 181.

the half-expressed concepts and ideas behind the machinery of government are often elusive and hard to interpret, because of the meagreness with which fifteenth-century people recorded what to them were assumptions that called for no statement. But something has been learned, and of that the reader may judge for himself.

The subject is not one which has greatly attracted the attention of historians. It is perhaps arguable that the whole field of the history of constitutional theory—as distinct from constitutional practice—is one that may with advantage be worked more fully than it has hitherto been, and might, if so worked as a theme in itself, yield some light on many dark places in the history of both political thought and constitutional development. However that may be, the bibliography of our present restricted subject is a very brief one. It begins, and— apart from Mr Plucknett's essay—very nearly, if not quite, ends,[1] with Stubbs's *Constitutional History of England*—the starting-point for all work in English mediaeval constitutional history.

Even Stubbs, however, was little concerned with the history of theory, and his classic exposition is mostly one of constitutional practice. His brief allusions to constitutional ideas no more than confirm his own general view of the constitutional significance of the period. He regarded the Lancastrian régime as having a double interest. It contained, he said, not only the foundation, consolidation, and destruction of a fabric of dynastic power, but, parallel therewith, the trial and failure of a great constitutional experiment, a premature testing of the strength of the parliamentary system.[2] 'The house of Lancaster', he believed, 'had risen by advocating constitutional principles, and on constitutional principles they governed.'[3] The case against the house of York, on the other hand, rested primarily on legal and moral grounds, but also upon an underlying spirit that defied and

---

[1] There is, of course, Plummer's edition of Fortescue's *Governance of England* (1885); but Plummer's views were manifestly dominated by Stubbs, and his erudition is more conspicuous than his insight.

[2] *Op. cit.* 5th ed. III, 5.　　　　　　　　[3] *Ibid.* 8.

ignored constitutional restraints.[1] The period as a whole was one in which constitutional progress had outrun administrative order.[2]

These views of Stubbs, that the Lancastrian period witnessed a conscious constitutional experiment, that this experiment was not maintained under the Yorkists, together with the implication that the spirit of the constitution in the earlier part, at least, of the century was distinctly modern in character, represent, in brief, the essence of the accounts of the matter that have long been purveyed in numerous textbooks and countless lecture-rooms, until a recent date.

In the hands of less subtle and cautious writers than Stubbs, his implicit conclusions have been magnified into explicit and forthright pronouncements. Stubbs himself never actually said that the Lancastrian constitution was modern; but even so well known a scholar as G. B. Adams had no hesitation, as late as 1920, in asserting that the Lancastrian period 'was one of unbroken constitutional government'. It was, he says, startlingly and prematurely modern; and 'though the machinery of constitutional government had as yet been worked out in few details, it was in spirit modern'.[3]

The 'uneasy feeling' mentioned by Mr Plucknett in 1924 has arisen about views of this sort. It is not, perhaps, too much to say that the large amount of original work that has been done in constitutional history—especially in the history of parliament and of the administrative system—since Stubbs's day, has made such extreme views highly improbable, if not impossible. The detection of any notable constitutional experiment under the Lancastrians becomes more and more difficult, and consequently any theory of backsliding on the part of the Yorkists becomes more and more meaningless.

The present writer does not, in these studies, touch specifically upon this matter; but he has not, in the course of his reading

[1] *Ibid.* 281.   [2] *Ibid.* 276.
[3] *Constitutional History of England*, 218. The same statements appear in the revised edition of the work (1935).

of the sources, discerned any such traces, in contemporary ideas, of a conscious constitutional experiment as might have been expected if the older views were justified. It is quite certain that whatever constitutional progress took place during the fifteenth century was not of a sensational character, but was sufficiently quiet and below the surface to escape the comments of contemporaries.

It may, indeed, be taken for granted that no historian to-day would profess to observe any very close resemblance between the constitution of the early fifteenth century and that of the nineteenth, except in a few forms and phrases. But what of the spirit behind those forms? Was that really modern—startlingly and prematurely modern? On this specific question little or no original work has been done in recent years, and there is no bibliography of it to mention. The importance, however, of coming to some conclusions as to the nature of the fifteenth-century constitution has been clearly demonstrated by Mr Kenneth Pickthorn's notable work, *Early Tudor Government* (1934). In this book, which is a contribution to constitutional history from a new angle, Mr Pickthorn found it necessary to analyse the 'constitution' as it was at the accession of Henry VII, and his allusions to it show how far opinion on the matter has travelled since Stubbs's day. Mr Pickthorn, it seems, represents an extreme reaction against the old views of the fifteenth-century constitution. In fact he goes so far as to doubt whether the fifteenth century had anything that can very usefully be called a constitution at all;[1] and if there was one, he thinks it amounted to no more than the mediaeval idea of the supremacy of law.[2] In face of such assertions as these, it is evidently desirable that fifteenth-century people themselves should be consulted as to what they thought about the matter, if anything.

[1] *Op. cit.* I, 101: '...another occasion to remark how far the fifteenth century was from anything which can very usefully be called a constitution.'

[2] *Ibid.* 55: '...the mediaeval idea of the supremacy of the law, an idea of which it is hardly too much to say that before the sixteenth century it was all there was in England in the way of a constitution.'

Now obviously, in all discussions of this nature, much depends upon the definitions of the terms 'constitution' and 'constitutional' adopted. Often—far too often—they are used simply to mean 'parliamentary limited monarchy as understood from the nineteenth century'. Certainly this is Stubbs's usage—unhistorical though it be—and must surely be also Mr Pickthorn's. For it is impossible to conceive of any established government without *some* sort of constitution, however primitive, crude, or unparliamentary. Since Mr Pickthorn analyses the government as established in 1485, at considerable length, we must needs believe that *some* sort of constitution existed even in that deficient century.

Whatever definition of a constitution be adopted, it is most important, in order to avoid endless confusion and question-begging, to adopt one that is not unhistorical. The modern constitutional lawyer and the constitutional historian cannot adopt the same definition, for the simple reason that though the child may be father to the man, 'child' is not a synonym for 'man'. The present writer understands a constitution to be that body of governmental rights and duties[1] which exist in a state at any given time in virtue of their recognition or implication by law, custom, convention, practice, or opinion. By this definition, even the most extreme despotism is a constitution, wherein all governmental rights centre in one person; by it also, Mr Pickthorn's assertion *is* impossible, and Stubbs's, if not meaningless, is quite non-committal; since by it, the expression 'constitutional principles' gives no indication of the *sort* of government meant: by it, the word can justly be applied to any century and any place, and the assumption that only one sort of constitution, namely, the modern, is worth mentioning, is avoided.

---

[1] These words are to be preferred, for purposes of English history at least, to the term 'rules', which appears in many definitions; because whatever constitutional rules may exist, they are never more than statements about somebody or other's rights or duties. Rules may formalise rights, but they are not elemental. Mr Pickthorn himself notes this fact, following Dicey, in *Some Historical Principles of the Constitution*, 120: '...the law of the constitution, the rules which in foreign countries naturally form part of a constitutional code, are not the source, but the consequence, of the rights of individuals.'

The purpose, then, of these studies is to examine and as far as may be to interpret what has been called 'the spirit of the constitution', as it was in the fifteenth century. The four Chapters attempt to analyse the information that has been gleaned on the several subjects relevant to this purpose; and the Conclusion aims at giving an account of the constitution in the form in which an observer at the end of the fifteenth century *could* have given it *if* he had tried. The phrase 'spirit of the constitution' is not, perhaps, altogether satisfactory; but it serves, and by it is meant 'opinions, ideas, and assumptions as to the nature and distribution of governmental rights'. As such, it is a theme necessarily fundamental to the constitutional history of England, whose constitution remains mostly unwritten because at any given time it actually is, in large part, what opinion makes it.

The present writer is not interested in answering specifically the question of the modernity of the constitution in the fifteenth or any other century—a question which he feels is essentially futile. On the contrary, his endeavour is merely to examine the constitution as it actually was, leaving shibboleths and anachronisms aside. In so doing, he is well content to take his stand with the late Professor Tout when he repudiated the aim of seeking in the middle ages what seems important to ourselves, not what was important to them.[1]

---

[1] *Chapters*, i, 2. Cf. *ibid.* 7: 'We investigate the past not to deduce practical lessons, but to find out what really happened.'

Chapter I

THE ESTATE OF KING

The progress of ideas, Maitland taught us in one of his most brilliant generalisations, is not from the simple to the complex, but from the vague to the definite.[1] The truth of this assertion is nowhere more apparent than in the history of the idea of monarchy. The history of monarchy is, in some sense, everywhere the history of its definition. A vast course of evolution, indeed, separates 'the ancient king who was often little more than the chief magician of his tribe'[2] from the kings of the house of Windsor; but the development in the conception of kingship during that course has been continually away from the vague. The English kingship is the oldest now surviving in Europe, if not in the world; and looking back over its thousand and more years of unbroken history, the modern enquirer can discern how complicated are the factors that have gone to make it what it is, and how slow the process of its definition has been.

We can see, dimly perhaps, that early Germanic notions of kingship by right of election and of kingship by right of birth were merged by the pressure of events into the belief in an hereditary right to be elected; and we can see the slow transformation of the king of the English into the king of England.[3] Long before the formal recognition of the territoriality of the English king, the descendant of Woden had become the vicar of Christ. Holy Church had its ideas of what kingship ought to be; and in undertaking to anoint and to crown kings, it learned not only to bless them with sacramental mystery, but also to bind

---

[1] *Domesday Book and Beyond*, 9.
[2] Sir James Frazer, *Lectures on the Early History of Kingship*, 1.
[3] The style *rex Angliae* was first used by Richard I, but only occasionally, in lieu of the traditional *rex Anglorum*. It became the usual form, however, under John. (*V.* J. E. W. Wallis, 'English Regnal Years and Titles', *English Time Books*, 1.)

them with sacred oaths. The time came when an uncrowned
king was no king at all, and in receiving his crown from the
hands of the Church, the king accepted an emblem, not only
of his majesty, but also of the duties of his royal office. His
moral responsibilities were asserted and defined in his coronation oath.

Likewise, we can see, a little more clearly, the process by
which kingship became inextricably mingled with landlordship,
by which *rex* became *dominus*—even, it seems, sometimes more
dominus than *rex*. The fact of the Conquest by the Norman
adventurer made his heirs the universal landlords. They became
each in turn the apex of the feudal pyramid, the ultimate points
in countless tenurial lines, the seigneurs of whom all land, immediately or mediately, was holden. The definition of the rights
involved in such a position, in a world that was not stagnant,
was the work of centuries.

But the history of the English monarchy, as an institution, has
still to be written. The great length of that history, its extreme
complexity, its profound ramifications into the very heart of
English evolution—not to mention the parliamentary pre-
occupations of constitutional historians, and the Whiggish outlook of nearly all historians except the more recent—have
seriously militated against its construction, in all its fullness.
A great theme—one of the very few left—as rich in the play of
personalities as in the subtleties of law and the machinations of
politics, awaits its exponent; and he will need to be something
of a Stubbs, of a Maitland, and of a Tout, all in one.

The contribution of the present study to that theme is in-
finitesimal. It aims merely at making some estimate of the
extent to which the definition of kingship was carried during the
fifteenth century.[1] It attempts to answer questions about the
monarchy of which few, if any, were actually posed during that

[1] Mr Pickthorn's suggestion (*Early Tudor Government*, I, 15) that the 'rights and
powers of the monarchy inherited by Henry VII were unlimited and indefinite'
is surely an exaggeration. Actually, the king's rights were and always had been in
some sense limited, and in part they were certainly defined.

century. At best, it gives an analytical account of the monarchy as an institution, in much the same sense as that in which the description of a slice of brain-tissue under the microscope may be called an account of a man's mental endowment.

§ 1. THE CONCEPTION OF THE KINGSHIP

Contemporary terminology is a matter of great importance when one examines past notions of something still extant, for only by understanding that terminology can our modern intellectual accretions be shorn away. No apology, therefore, is needed for some attention, at the start, to what may seem to be 'mere words'.

The phrase commonly used during the late fourteenth and the fifteenth centuries to designate the mass of traditions, attributes, rights, powers—and perhaps duties also—which were deemed to centre in the monarch was 'estate of king'. Thus, when in 1399 the task fell to Thirning, J., of informing Richard II that his abdication had been accepted by all the estates, he told him that he had been deposed and deprived of the 'Astate of Kyng', and of all the lordship, dignity, worship, and administration belonging thereto.[1] Thomas Hoccleve, the most indefatigable rhymester of the century, was thinking of this occasion when he wrote:

> Me fel to mynde how that, not long ago,
> fortunës strok doun threst estaat royal
> Into myscheef;[2]

The Speaker in the sixth parliament of Henry IV—which to Stubbs seemed 'almost to stand for an exponent of the most advanced principles of mediaeval constitutional life'[3]—protested that he had spoken nothing against the 'prerogative or estate royal'.[4] Furthermore, Henry assented to the various pro-

[1] *Rot. Parl.* III, 424. Richard himself used the word in protesting against the proposal for household reform in 1397. He said (*ibid.* 338) that it was against his regality, estate, and royal liberty.
[2] *The Regement of Princes*, stanza 4, 2.
[3] *Const. Hist.* III, 59. [4] *Rot. Parl.* III, 572.

posals for administrative reform which were put forward during the same parliament, 'sauvant toutfoitz a luy son estat et prerogative de son corone'.[1] It was for the better governance of the very excellent person and estate of their sovereign lord that the lords assembled after receipt of the news of the death of Henry V in 1422.[2] The duke of York in 1452 swore not to attack the 'Roiall Estate'.[3] At the time when the boy king Edward V was still living, his chancellor, Bishop Russell, wrote hopefully: 'who can thynke but that the lordes and commens of thys lande wylle as agreabilly pourvey for the sure maynetenaunce of hys hyghe estate as eny of their predecessours have done to eny other of the kynges of Englonde afore...?'[4] The king's estate, wrote Fortescue, is the highest estate temporal.[5]

There can be no doubt that to English minds in the fifteenth century this estate was a necessity. The idea that monarchy could be dispensed with appears only as the reverse of arguments on its necessity. Thus John Kemp, archbishop of York's parliamentary sermon in 1427, on the text 'Without the royal providence, it is impossible that peace be given',[6] was followed fifty years later by his successor Thomas Rotherham's, on 'The Lord reigns over me and I nothing lack', in which he showed that 'the royal majesty was not only right as if it were the hand and counsel of God, but was also established for the advantage of the kingdom'.[7] Again, in 1470, it was asserted —this time in court—*nem. con.* that 'it is necessary for the realm to have a king under whom the laws shall be held and maintained'.[8]

What the attributes—potent if vague—of this royal estate were thought to be was stated repeatedly but not exhaustively in the various transactions involved in Richard II's abdication

[1] *Rot. Parl.* III, 585.   [2] *Rot. Parl.* IV, 170.   [3] *Rot. Parl.* V, 346.
[4] *Grants of Edward V* (*v. infra*, Chapter II, Excursus VI, p. 176).
[5] *Governance*, viii.   [6] *Rot. Parl.* IV, 316.   [7] *Rot. Parl.* VI, 167.
[8] *Y.B. 9 Edward IV*, Pas. pl. 2 (App. no. 53 (i)). Fortescue's allusions to government without monarchy were very slight (*v.* Chapter IV, *infra*). Cf. Pecock's defence of monarchy, *Repressor*, II, iv, v.

and deposition. The value of these transactions as evidence of
the admitted attributes of regality is enhanced by the fact that
the documents which record them unquestionably represent—
at least in the articles against Richard—the Lancastrian view,
and thus indicate the notions of kingship admitted even by the
party which for long had been in opposition to the Plantagenet
monarchy.[1] Some ten years before those events of 1399, in the
appeal put forward by the Lancastrian lords in the parliament
of 1388, there appeared certain admissions of this kind. Thus,
in the first three articles advanced against the archbishop of
York, the duke of Ireland, and the earl of Suffolk, it was alleged
that they had usurped royal power by 'disenfranchising' the
king of sovereignty, and had degraded his royal prerogative by
causing him to swear to be governed and counselled by them.
They had done this, it was said, notwithstanding that the king
ought not to take any oath unless it were at his coronation or
for the common profit of himself and his realm. Though the
king ought to be in a freer condition than his subjects, they
nevertheless had put him in more subservience, against his
honour, estate, and regality. Moreover, they had not allowed
any of the great men or good counsellors to approach or to
speak to him save in their presence, and thus had encroached
upon the royal power, lordship, and sovereignty, to the great
dishonour and peril of the crown and of the realm.[2]

The deposition documents of 1399, above mentioned, carried
further this disclosure of Lancastrian ideas of regality. In his
renunciation and cession, Richard declared, or was made to
declare,[3] that he absolved all persons of whatsoever condition

---

[1] As Mr Pickthorn justly points out (*op. cit.* 1, 6): 'It is always remembered,
generally in a quite false sense, that the Lancastrian champion was especially
bound to parliament; it should not be forgotten that the traditions of his House
[*i.e.* Henry IV's] inclined him to take high views of kingship no less than of parliaments.'

[2] *Rot. Parl.* III, 230.

[3] *V.* M. V. Clarke and V. H. Galbraith, 'The Deposition of Richard II', *Bull.
J.R.L.* (July 1930), XIV, 125–181; and G. T. Lapsley, 'The Parliamentary Title of
Henry IV', *E.H.R.* (1934), XLIX, 423–449, 577–606. (Cf. *infra*, p. 106.)

from every oath of fealty and homage, and every bond of allegiance, regality, and lordship, by which they were bound to him, and absolved them also from every obligation or oath 'quantum ad suam personam attinet', and from every effect of law ensuing therefrom. He renounced likewise the royal dignity, majesty, and crown—renounced also lordship, power, rule, governance, administration, empire, jurisdiction, and the name, honour, regality, and highness of king.[1]

The ideas embodied in these large and high-sounding words— many of them with a tradition behind them stretching back into the remote origins of kingship—were certainly forces which have to be reckoned with in any assessment of monarchical conceptions during the century. There was little in some of these notions that was amenable to definitive legal ruling. It is possible to define legally such matters as oaths and obligations of fealty, homage, and allegiance; but it would, and did, require a long course of narrowing legal restrictions of 'prerogative' before the vague and ancient amplitude of notions such as majesty, rule, empire, and highness of king could lose their mysterious power and awe-inspiring significance. It was still possible, as late as 1460, for the judges to declare that the king's high estate and regality were above the law and passed their learning.[2] Five years before this, when the exercise of the royal power was for the first time put in commission during Henry's illness, the lords admitted explicitly that the 'high prerogative, pre-eminence, and authority of his majesty royal, and also the sovereignty of them and all the land was resting and always must rest in his most excellent person'.[3] Moile, J., ruled, in 1457, that a certain statute, though general, did not bind the king 'car le roy ne semble a un comon person'.[4] Marowe, in his Reading of the year 1503, thought of the king as the principal Head or Captain of the realm, though, indeed, he agreed that

[1] *Rot. Parl.* III, 417.   [2] *Rot. Parl.* v, 376.
[3] *Ibid.* 290.
[4] *Y.B.* 35 *Henry VI*, Trin. pl. 1 (App. no. 33 (ii)). The expression was of course common form with the lawyers.

treason against his person was to the prejudice of all his subjects.[1]

Despite all the vicissitudes of kingly fortune during the century, the continued tenacity of belief in the sacrosanctity and miraculous powers of regality is apparent. The large space allotted by the chroniclers to the anointing of Henry IV by the holy oil presented to St Thomas of Canterbury by the Virgin Mary during a vision—even if the story of the miracle were a hasty forgery—is a fair tribute to popular notions; and Richard declared that he could not renounce his spiritual honour.[2] Fortescue several times makes a point in the case against female succession to the crown, by insisting that a woman could not be anointed in the hands. This disability, according to him, not only prevented women from exercising power temporal and spiritual, but denied them that thaumaturgical potency which was such striking evidence of the divine favour upon English kings: 'Sithen', he said, 'the Kynges of England been enoynted in theyre hands and by vertue and meane thereof God commonlie healeth sickness, by putting to and touching the maladie, by thenontinge hands, and also gould and silver handled by them and so offred on Good Friday have ben the meane and causes of great cures, as it is knowne, and therefore such gold and silver is desired in all the world.'[3] Thus the most con-

---

[1] Putnam, *Early Treatises*, 331: 'Item, si home commytt ascun treson al person le Roie, serra dit vne enfreindre de le peas et vncore le recognisaunce est: quod ipse geret pacem versus cunctum populum domini Regis et precipue versus J. de T., et ne parle de le Roie. Mes purceo que lact que est fait encountre luy que est le principall Test (Capteyn) de le Roialme, est adiuge en preiudice a toutz ces subgettes et issint encountre le peas.'

[2] *Annales Henrici Quarti*, 286: 'Ubi vero Dominus Willelmus Thirnyng dixit ei quod renunciavit omnibus honoribus et dignitati Regi pertinentibus, respondit quod noluit renunciare spirituali honori characteris sibi impressi, et inunctioni, quibus renunciare nec potuit, nec ab hiis cessare.' Apparently Thirning was obliged tacitly to admit that this spiritual character had not been renounced by the cession.

[3] *Of the Title of the House of York*, Works, 498. Cf. *Defensio Juris Domus Lancastriae*, *ibid.* 508: 'Reges insuper Angliae in ipsa unctione sua talem coelitus gratiam infusam recipiunt quod per tactum manuum suarum unctarum, infestos morbo quodam qui vulgo Regius morbus appellatur, mundant et curant, qui alias dicuntur incurabiles. Item aurum et argentum sacris unctis manibus Regum Angliae in die Parascivae divinorum tempore, quemadmodum Reges Angliae annuatim facere

spicuous publicist of the century believed—or appeared to believe—in a miraculous power conferred by divine grace upon the person of the monarch. But, though unction was necessary to ensure this power for the king, it was effective only when given to the legitimate inheritor.[1] Even if Fortescue made use of the belief only as an argument to discredit the legitimacy of the Yorkist claimant, still it is at least evident that he did deem it an argument. As Lyndwood said, an anointed king is not merely a layman, but is a 'persona mixta'.[2] He is called *Rex et Sacerdos*.[3]

Other admitted attributes of regality may be discerned in the application to the king of the terms 'liberty', 'will', and 'grace'. The kings of England had 'libertas'. Richard, it was said in 1399, had understood the 'libertas' of his progenitors to mean that he could turn all the laws to his own will. The commons, notwithstanding, stated that they wished Henry IV to be 'en auxi graunde libertee roial come ses nobles progenitours furent devant luy'.[4] To this wish Henry replied that it was not his intent nor his will to turn the laws, statutes, or good usages, nor to take advantage by the grant of such liberty, but only to keep ('garder') the ancient laws and statutes ordained and used in the time of his noble progenitors, and to do right to all men in mercy and in truth, according to his oath. The king, then, had

---

solent, tactum devote et oblatum spasmaticos et caducos curant, quemadmodum per annulos ex dicto auro seu argento factos et digitis hominum morbidorum impositos multis in mundi partibus crebro usu expertum est; quae gratia Reginis non confertur, cum ipsae in manibus non ungantur.' On the whole of this subject M. Bloch's *Les Rois Thaumaturges* is exhaustive. (Cf. also F. Kern, *Gottesgnadentum und Widerstandsrecht*.) Bloch observes (111–112): 'Ainsi les Lancastriens refusaient aux princes de la maison d'York le don du miracle. Nul doute que leurs adversaires politiques ne leur rendissent la pareille. Chaque camp cherchait à discréditer le rite pratiqué dans le camp adverse. Comment un peu de ce discrédit n'eût-il pas rejailli sur le rite en général? Le roi légitime pensait-on, savait guérir; mais qui était le roi légitime?'

[1] *De Titulo*, 85.
[2] *Provinciale*, lib. III, tit. 2, cited by Pickthorn (*op. cit.* 6). The learned doctor's inference seems, however, to be distinctly unorthodox. Cf. Brian's observation in *Y.B.* 10 *Henry VII*, Hil. pl. 17 (App. no. 96).
[3] Fortescue, *Declaracion*, 531.
[4] *Rot. Parl.* III, 434. Cf. G. T. Lapsley, *op. cit.* 599.

liberty in order that he might keep the laws and do justice. He had, we may say, a discretionary power. But his discretion was to be used, not for his personal purposes, but in the interests of the laws and of justice.

Moreover, this liberty required will for its exercise. The king must *will*. Archbishop Arundel, in his conciliatory opening address at the first parliament of Henry IV's reign, declared that it was the king's will that the liberties of Holy Church and the liberties and franchises of lords, cities, and boroughs be maintained, and that there be equal justice and equity for all.[1] It was the king's liberty to will the maintenance of the liberties of others.

But the king also had grace. He might accept 'novellerie', not because the maintenance of good usages required it, but because of his good grace. Thus, in 1403, Henry assented to a consultation of the commons with some of the lords, but stated that he 'ne le vorroit faire de deuete ne de custume, mais de sa grace especiale a ceste foitz'.[2] Similarly, the request of the commons to have their petitions engrossed without alteration was assented to by Henry V only of his especial grace.[3]

The manner in which the king's rights were sometimes discussed in the courts obliges us to take account of the extent to which the kingdom was still being regarded as a piece of property belonging to the king. Fortescue has often been supposed to have held constitutional notions of a modern degree of enlightenment; and it is therefore especially significant to notice how deeply the lawyer-publicist was imbued with the real-property idea of kingship. In his writings—the bulk of which was devoted to the discussion of the succession question —this proprietary notion is most marked. The ideas which made this view possible are well illustrated in his work *De Natura*

---

[1] *Rot. Parl.* III, 415. The declaration frequently appears in later opening addresses, and headed the statute roll for many of the years in which there was a statute.

[2] *Ibid.* 486.

[3] *Rot. Parl.* IV, 22. Presumably an act of grace could not form a precedent.

Legis Naturae, the second part of which is by no means so dull as
is sometimes said.[1]

In the long course of the first part of this work, the law of
nature[2] is discussed, and concluded to be the only law in the
light of which the succession to kingdoms can be decided. In
the second part this conclusion is applied to a case in which the
kingdom of a deceased monarch is claimed respectively by his
brother, his daughter, and his daughter's son. The narrations,
replications, and duplications run through more than fifty
thousand words;[3] and the most diverse and unlikely arguments
and authorities are brought to bear on the subject.[4] But it is in
occasional distinctions drawn between different notions of the
kingship that the chief interest of the work lies. Thus the son
rebukes his mother for not recognising the difference between
the rights of succession to a kingdom and those of succession
to a private estate. Human law, he says, does not regulate
an office as it does a field, nor a public office as a private
function.[5]

By such a distinction as this between the king's capacity as
public office-holder and his capacity as private proprietor, the
son attempts to show that his mother might succeed to the
patrimony but could not, as a woman, succeed to the kingship.

The late king's brother, in his argument, adopts this distinction, but turns it against the grandson. If the father's
royalty cannot be inherited by the daughter, then she cannot
be a medium for its inheritance by her son, though she
might inherit and pass on his private estates.[6] The kingdom

---

[1] Cf. Winfield, *Chief Sources*; and Holdsworth, *Hist. Eng. Law*, III.
[2] Cf. Chapters III (§ 1) and IV, *infra*.
[3] Works, 115–248.   [4] *V.* editor's list of quotations, *ibid.* 350–353.
[5] *Ibid.* II, iii: 'Ignorantia juris est non facti quae eam concitat ad hanc litem, non enim sine consule poterit simplicitas pia muliebris diversitatem noscere qualiter in regno, et qualiter in predio differunt jura succedendi. Non ut agrum ita officium, nec ut privatum ministerium, ita et publicum regulat lex humana.'
[6] *Ibid.* xxxvii, 155: 'Sic et in rege defuncto erat jus regni, quod publicum est et non potest ad filiam descendere; residebat etiam in eo jus hereditatis privatae, quam post eum hereditabit filia ejus; in cujus privatae hereditatis descensu ipsa medium est domesticum et naturale.'

is not private, but public, property, and is incapable of inheritance by women, and ought to descend to the nearest male heir of his blood in the male line of descent, *i.e.* to him, the brother. The grandson, in his reply to this argument, enlists the aid of the civil-law principle of guardianship of children. By that law, guardianship was committed to the nearest male relative of the blood, whether agnatic or cognatic,[1] but never to a woman. If, then, by the Roman law, 'tutela' could be acquired through but not by a woman, there is no reason why the kingdom—even though it is public office and not private property—should not be inherited by a similar rule.

The reply of the king's brother to this suggestion is a striking one, and is worth quoting in full.[2] It is based on the sub-

[1] *Ibid.* xlviii, 165: 'Leges Civiles impuberum tutelas proximis de eorum sanguine committunt, agnati fuerint seu cognati. Mulieri tamen, preterquam matri et aviae infantis, leges illae tutelam non concedunt.'

[2] *Ibid.* l, 167: 'Non aliquid statuit lex illa Civilis quod meis directe obviat replicatis; quo si quid contra ea lex illa agere senciatur, per obliquum, ut similitudinis vigore, eam hoc facere necesse est fateri. Quare quam similia sunt illa quae haec lex statuit ad ea quae ego superius exaravi primitus congruit ut queramus. Haec lex tutelam quam matri denegat, filio tribuit; ego regnum quod matri negat lex naturae etiam filio denegavi. Haec lex ad officium oneris vocat filium mulieris; ego mulieris filium ab officio propuli, non tantum oneris sed et honoris. Lex illa judicat quis privatum quoddam ministrabit officium; ego non de privato sed de publico officio disputavi. Illa virum dignum eligit ad alterius obsequium; ego non alterius sed hereditatem propriam, non electionis sed descensionis titulo, indifferenter digno contuli et indigno. Ipsa maturum virum eligit providum et sensatum; ego juvenes admitto, nec naturae defectu respuo insensatos. Ipsa ad ministrandum, ego ad dominandum; ipsa ad alienum, ego ad proprium comodum homines preficimus. Quid plura? Ego ad dignitatem a qua mulieres abigit natura nec earum filios jam admitto; sed lex illa ad humile officium quod mulieres exercere non spernit natura quarumdam earum filios recipit, nec omnes abdicat mulieres. Quare dum ex factis, ut dicunt Leges, jus metimur, tam dissimilia facta nec meriti consimilis jura similia sive jus unum regere non valebunt. Non eodem jure, ut superius est ostensum, officium publicum regitur et privatum; nec sub ejusdem juris ratione cadunt hereditas et officii collatio, dum unam heredi conferat jus descensus, alteram benemerito ratio humana distribuit, ut jam facit haec lex Civilis; quo tutela sepius in Legibus munus appellatur. Sub una vero et eadem juris ratione cadere oportebit singulos casus qui una lege regentur. Quare non lege consimili criminale facinus regitur et transgressio personalis, neque predialium descensus similiter regitur ut contractus. *Reale est quod petimus regnum, descendibile preregnantis heredi*; sed personalis cura est impuberem regere, ejus quoque patrimonium regulare. Quo lex quae rectorem talem eligere novit nescia est juris hereditarii descensus. Sic lex quae criminalia plectit non didicit in personalibus

ordination of the idea of the kingship as public office to the idea of it as property, albeit public property; and this argument proves victorious, in the end, in the imaginary trial.

The brother considers the merits of the Roman analogy put forward by his grand-nephew, and contrasts the nature of the law of 'tutela' with the law of inheritance of the kingdom for which he had argued. The one law, the brother says, concerns a certain private duty, the other a duty not private but public. The one law selects a fit and proper person for the service of another; the other confers on a man, without regard to his merits or demerits, his own inheritance—without title of election, and by descent alone. The one law chooses a man ripe in years and of sound mind; the other admits a man of any age, whether defective in nature or in mind; the one to administer, and the other to rule: the one to care for another's interest, the other to care for his own. But private and public duty are not governed by the same law; nor do conferring of an office, and inheritance, fall under the same principle of law, since human reason disposes of one according to merit, and the other is determined by right of descent alone. The kingdom which they seek is real property, capable of descending to the heir of the preceding king. The king's brother is adjudged, after further discussion, to have proved his case, and the kingdom is awarded him.[1]

The rules on which the judgement was given were the rules of succession to real property, restricted to the agnatic line on the grounds of the public nature of the property in dispute. The fact that it was possible for Fortescue to argue at great

mitigare rigorem; unde tot sunt legum species quot factorum merita sunt diversa. Sic judex in criminibus veritatem extorquet torturis, in personalibus tertii deposicione veritatem agnoscit. Sic realia bona agnatis cognatis que descendunt, mobilia tamen non illi sed legatarii executores ve rapiunt et disponunt. Quare dum casus legis illius Civilis et casus quem disputamus tam dispares sunt in meritis dissimiles et in factis, quo nec sub unius juris cadunt ratione, nec lex una, nec lex similis ambos poterit regere casus. Lex illa Civilis sicut non directe, sic nec oblique, ut similitudinis ratione, replicatis meis officit, nec aliquibus derogat quae suasi.' (Italics mine.)

[1] *Ibid.* lxix, 182.

length the case for such a rule of succession as this (in support of the Lancastrian house) testifies to the absence of any accepted legal principles of royal succession. Even if real-property notions were uppermost in his mind, still he was able to exclude women altogether from the succession only by distinguishing between private and public property, and so designating the kingdom as real property of a public character. The prince was a public person:[1] his office was public because the kingship was office and had duty attached to it. There were, however, no available legal rules for acquiring the duties of that office, except in so far as the office itself was an object of the law of property.

The extent to which the idea of the king as proprietor could be carried is well illustrated by the views sometimes held by lawyers other than Fortescue upon what constituted the royal inheritance. Thus to Chief Baron Fray, in 1441, it seemed that the law-courts, including the court of parliament, were the king's inheritance, and that the law itself was a part of that inheritance. The money grants in the parliament were the revenues of his court and equally an hereditament.[2] As late as 1482, Nottingham, CB., asserted of a tenth granted in convocation that it was an inheritance and duty to the king;[3] and it could be argued—though not very conclusively, perhaps—whether or not collectors of tenths were the king's debtors.[4]

But though the kingdom was property, the kingship was

---

[1] *A Dialogue between Understanding and Faith*, Works, 489: 'The iniquite of a prince which is a publike persone thorowe whoes dedes falleth oftetymes unyversal slaundre and gret hurt to the people, causeth hym to have generalite of payne above all others.' Clearly much of Fortescue's thought had its roots in feudal theory. For example, an heritable fief might be both 'officium' and 'beneficium', and in such a case, although the public interest would necessarily be involved, private law alone would determine both office and benefice.

[2] *Y.B. 19 Henry VI*, Pas. pl. 1 (App. no. 25).

[3] *Y.B. 21 Edward IV*, Mich. pl. 6 (App. no. 63). Another instance of the application to the king of purely private-law principles is to be found in the opinion of all the justices that a safe-conduct granted by the king to an alien was a covenant between him and the king (*v. Y.B. 13 Edward IV*, Pas. pl. 5 (App. no. 58)).

[4] *Y.B. 1 Henry VII*, Hil. pl. 5 (App. no. 76).

office. The golden and jewelled crown of an anointed king was the symbol of his honour and his office:[1]

> What doth a kynges crowne signifye,
> Whan stones and floures on sercle is bent?
> Lordis, comouns, and clergye
> To ben all at on assent.
> To kepe that crowne, take good tent.
> In wode, in feld, in dale, and downe,
> The leste lyge-man, with body and rent,
> He is a parcel of the crowne.[2]

The king's office was temporal,[3] and by reason of office he was keeper of the peace,[4]

> ffirst and foreward, the dignitee of kyng
> Impressid be in the botme of your mynde,
> Consideryng how chargeable a thyng
> That ofice is;[5]

'Though the king's estate', wrote Fortescue, 'be the highest estate temporall in the erthe, yet it is an office in wich he mynestrith to his reaume defence and justice.'[6]

It was, indeed, the notion of duty attaching to the kingship that made it possible for Fortescue to think of the kingdom as at once private property and public office. Hence it is important to take account of the ways in which the kingly duty was conceived.

Fortescue himself tersely summarises the duty of royalty thus: 'Lo! to fight and to judge are the office of a king.'[7] This represents the common and traditional notion of the regal

[1] *V.* the parliamentary sermon by the bishop of Bath and Wells, in 1436 (*Rot. Parl.* iv, 495): 'Tertio, Reges inuncti, in cujus Signum portant Coronam auro et gemmis ornatam, in cujus Corone figura regimen et politia regni presentantur, nam in auro, regimen Communitatis notatur, et in Floribus Corone erectis et gemmis adornatis, Honor et Officium Regis sive Principis designatur.'
[2] *Political and Other Poems*, ed. Kail, 51. Cf. note on p. 20, *infra*.
[3] Jenny, J., in *Y.B.* 21 *Edward IV*, Mich. pl. 6 (App. no. 63).
[4] Marowe, in his Reading, *De Pace Terre, etc.*, in Putnam, *op. cit.* 301.
[5] Hoccleve, *The Regement of Princes*, stanza 310, 79.
[6] *Governance*, viii.   [7] *De Natura*, ii, viii, Works, 122.

duties.[1] But to fight and to judge were not the whole duty of
kings: 'But every king is not only a judge; he is also a magistrate,
and is distinguished by honour, dignity, and his administration
of the state (*rei publicae*).'[2] That the king is judge, continued
Fortescue, is evident; for he holds the pure authority who has
the power of the sword for the punishment of evil-doers, and he
holds the mixed authority who has the power of putting men
into possession of their goods when equity requires it. The king
also possesses jurisdiction, for he can appoint other judges under
him; and since the office of magistrate is held by him to whom
the administration of the state is committed, clearly the king is
magistrate also.

Fortescue was here expressing a view of the royal duty in
rather wider terms than was usual at this date. However obvious
it was that the king had the duty of administering the state,
it is very rarely that we find a description of his duty in

[1] Cf. the views of Bracton (ed. Woodbine, II, fo. 1), especially his opening statements, adopted by him from the Institutes: 'In rege qui recte regit necessaria sunt
duo haec, arma videlicet et leges, quibus utrumque tempus bellorum et pacis recte
possit gubernari.' For some discussion of the relation between Bracton and
Fortescue, *v.* Chapter IV, Excursus I, *infra.* Wycliffe asserted that the duty of the
king was to defend the estate and rights of his subjects (*De Officio Regis* (1378), ed.
A. W. Pollard and C. Sayles, 55): 'Tercium ad quod oportet principaliter regem,
in quantum talis, attendere est providum regimen regni sui. Stat autem regimen
regni in paucarum et iustarum legum institucione, in illarum sagaci et acuta
execucione, et generaliter in status ac iuris cuiuscumque legii sui defensione.'
(Cf. Chapter III, p. 194, *infra.*)

[2] *De Natura,* II, liii, Works, 170: 'Nam quod ipse judex est patet, cum imperium
habeat merum et mixtum ac jurisdiccionem. Et ista habere officium est judicis ut
ff. *De Jurisdictione Omnium Judicum,* l, j., juncta Glossa ibidem. Ipse namque habet
merum imperium qui gladii habet potestatem animadvertendi in facinorosos, et
mixtum habet imperium qui potestatem habet homines mittendi in bonorum
possessionem, cum equitas id poposcerit. Similiter et jurisdictionem habet, nam
alios judices sub se ipse constituere potest. Et quod ista sunt meri et mixti imperii
atque jurisdictionis, est textus expressus ff. *De Jurisdictione Om. Jud.,* 1, *Imperium,*
Imperator etiam, cui totus olim mundus obtemperaverat, adhunc prout nunc
fungebatur officio judicis, ut ff. *De Constitutionibus Principum,* l, j., et Cod. eod. tit.
1 fin. Et quod omnis rex magistratus sit, et honore resplendeat cum administracione
rei publicae, non expedit legum allegationibus edocere, cum notoria sint et quasi
omnes legum libri inde sint secundi; tamen quia quid sit honore fungi ediximus,
etiam quid sit magistratum gerere convenit ut dicamus. De hoc vero ff. *De
Accusationibus,* 1. *Qui accusare,* et presertim in Glossa sic dicitur, "Cui est commissa
prae ceteris solicitudo sive administracio rei publicae, is magistratum gerit."
Quare regem, cui prae ceteris solicitudo et administracio hujusmodi attinet, magistratum gerere haec descriptio neminem patitur dubitare....'

terms which add to the obligations of defending the realm
and maintaining the laws. Even in this passage, Fortescue was
not pretending to argue from the facts of everyday political
life, but was deducing the duty of administration from the civil-
law texts. The more usual type of view of the royal duty is that
expressed by Arundel in his sermon to the first parliament of the
new Lancastrian régime. The archbishop (with some blas-
phemy) alluded to Henry in these terms: 'iste Vir', he said, 'est
talis quod dicetur, "Regnabit Rex, et sapiens erit, et faciet
judicium et justicium in Terra."'[1] Even if it be admitted that,
in this text, the meaning of the clause 'regnabit rex' is not
exhausted by what follows, still the only explicit emphasis is
upon the judicial duties of monarchy. The prominence in the
Old Testament of the idea that the king's first duty is to do
justice, and the frequency of the use of Old- and New-Testament
texts of a strong royalist flavour in parliamentary sermons, must
have acted as a considerable conservative influence upon the
development of more extended notions of royalty.[2]

The necessity of the king's providence in order to maintain
the laws was urged, as we have seen, in Bagot's case. In the
course of the same case, Billing, J., went further and asserted
that 'it pertains to every king, by reason of his office, to do
justice and grace, justice in executing the laws, and grace in
granting pardon to felons.'[3] Marowe, in his Reading on the
keeping of the peace, thought it necessary to state: 'by reason
of office, the lord king is the principal preserver of the peace.'[4]
The king, the lawyers said, was the chief justice,[5] the conservator of the law, which is the commonweal.[6]

A rather more significant view of kingly duty appears in the

---

[1] *Rot. Parl.* III, 423; *Jeremiah* xxiii, 5.
[2] For a list of texts used in parliamentary sermons during the century, see
Chapter II, Excursus I, *infra*.
[3] *Y.B.* 9 *Edward IV*, Pas. pl. 2 (App. no. 53 (iii)). *V.* p. 4, *supra*.
[4] Putnam, *Early Treatises*, 301.
[5] *Y.B.* 20 *Henry VII*, Mich. pl. 17 (App. no. 108).
[6] *Y.B.* 8 *Henry VII*, Trin. pl. 1 (App. no. 91); and *v.* also *Y.B.* 6 *Henry VII*, Hil.
pl. 9 (App. no. 85).

instructions drawn up for the ambassadors to the conference of Calais, in 1439. The princes of both parties, it was written, 'owe to considere that God made not his people in the said to remes ner in other for the princes, but he made the princes for his service and for the wele and behove of his people, that is to say to reule theim in tranquillite, namly by the mene of deue ministracion of justice'.[1] These may not be original sentiments, but the appearance of them in such a place as this is notable.

It was these moral duties to the performance of which it had been customary, from time immemorial, to bind the king by the terms of his coronation oath. By the taking of this oath, the king committed himself to a formal acceptance of the duties of his estate[2]—and so it was that Richard II's opponents were able to make a free use against him of the charge of perjury:[3]

> A kyng is made to kepen and maynteene
> Iustice, for she makith obéisant
> The mysdoers þat proudë ben and keene;
> And hem þat ben in vertu habundant
> Cherisith; a kyng is, by couenant
> Of ooth maad in his coronacioun,
> Boundë to iustices sauuacioun.[4]

The extraordinary conservatism of the wording of the coronation oath throughout its history, and especially up to 1626, is standing testimony to the extreme slowness with which extra-regal constitutional ideas encroached upon the public formulae of regality.[5] The text of the coronation oath remained unaltered

---

[1] *Procs. and Ords.* v, 357.

[2] 'In diesen Throngelübden', observes Kern ('Recht und Verfassung im Mittelalter', *Hist. Zeit.* (1919), cxx, 47), 'liegt der Anfang zum modernen Verfassungseid. Wenn man die Vorgeschichte der Verfassungen schreiben will, wird man diese Selbstbindung des mittelalterlichen Herrschers zum Ausgangspunkt nehmen müssen; es ist die ausdrückliche Bindung der Staatsgewalt an das über ihr stehende Recht.'

[3] *Rot. Parl.* III, 417b. Variants of the expression 'quare perjuriam incurrebat' occur in the list of thirty-three abuses at least eight times.

[4] Hoccleve, *The Regement of Princes*, stanza 360, 91.

[5] On the whole subject, *v.* L. G. W. Legg, *English Coronation Records* (1901); A. Taylor, *The Glory of Regality* (1890); and *Liber Regalis*, ed. Roxburghe Club (1890). H. G. Richardson and G. O. Sayles, 'Early Coronation Records' (*Bull. I.H.R.*, XIII (Feb. 1936), 129–145, *et seq.*), is indispensable.

from 1307 to 1603, and even then was but translated; and
moreover, the form adopted from 1307 was not very materially
different in substance from that in use since the eighth century.[1]
As it appears in the earliest recension of the coronation service,
that known as the pontifical of Egbert, archbishop of York, the
oath takes the form of a grant or decree;[2] and this form was in
use probably until 1307.[3] At least as early as Edward II's
coronation, the form of oath by question and answer was used;
and this remained unaltered for the following three centuries.

The oath, therefore, that Richard II had taken, and was said
to have broken, was the same as that taken by his successors
during the fifteenth century.[4] The essential terms of it headed
the list of Richard's enormities, and were recorded on the rolls
of parliament in 1399. The threefold question which had been
put to Richard had run thus: 'Seruabis ecclesie dei cleroque et
populo, pacem ex integro et concordiam in deo, secundum
uires tuas? Facies fieri in omnibus iudiciis tuis equam et rectam
iusticiam et discrecionem in misericordia et ueritate, secundum
uires tuas? Concedis iustas leges et consuetudines esse tenendas
et promittis eas per te esse protegendas et ad honorem dei
roborandas quas uulgus elegerit, secundum uires tuas?' The
response by the king to each question was respectively: 'seruabo,
faciam, concedo et promitto.'[5]

---

[1] Legg, *op. cit.* p. xxxi.

[2] For the typical wording, *v.* Stubbs, *Select Charters*, 69.

[3] But Liebermann showed that the form of this text is not earlier than Knut,
though the substance may be of the eighth century.

[4] Material changes in it were slight until 1689. It is perhaps a point to be
recollected that not until that date did the king swear to govern according to 'the
statutes in parliament agreed on'. Henry VIII's revision of the oath in an autocratic sense, by his own hand, was not adopted by any of his successors.

[5] In the actual order of the coronation service, these promises were preceded by
a statement thus: 'Si leges et consuetudines ab antiquis iustis et deo deuotis regibus
plebi anglorum concessas cum sacramenti confirmacione eidem plebi concedere et
seruare uolueris, et presertim leges consuetudines et libertates a glorioso rege
Edwardo clero populoque concessas.' This was followed, after the promises, by a
prayer for, and grant of, pardon and protection to the church and clergy: 'Domine
rex a uobis perdonari petimus ut unicuique de nobis et ecclesiis nobis commissis
canonicum priuelegium ac debitam legem atque iusticiam conseruetis et defensionem exhibeatis; sicut rex in suo regno debet unicuique episcopo abbatibus et

The king, in taking his coronation oath, was thus morally committed to the discharge of precisely those duties which constituted royal office. He swore to keep the peace to clergy and people, to do justice in mercy and in truth, and to maintain the laws.[1] Hence Fortescue was able to say that by his corona-

ecclesiis sibi commissis.' Response: 'Animo libenti et devoto promitto vobis et perdono quia unicuique de uobis et ecclesiis uobis commissis canonicum privelegium et debitam legem atque iusticiam seruabo, et defensionem quantum potuero adiuuante domino exhibebo sicut rex in suo regno unicuique episcopo abbatibus et ecclesiis sibi commissis per rectum exhibere debet.' (*V.* Legg, *op. cit.* 87–88.) Legg says (*ibid.* p. xxx) that before the fifteenth century the oath was taken on the Bible; and thereafter, on the sacrament on the altar. But in the rolls of parliament it was expressly stated (*Rot. Parl.* III, 417) that Richard had taken the oath in the latter way.

[1] The old controversy as to the true meaning of the third promise in the coronation oath—'to keep the laws and righteous customs "quas vulgus elegerit"'—will perhaps never be quite settled on the merits of the texts alone. The French text has in that place: 'les quiels la communaute de vostre roiaume aura esleu.' Stubbs adopted as the translation of this clause (*Const. Hist.* II, 331–332) the words: 'which the community of your realm shall have chosen'; and these, no doubt, are the words necessitated by the requirements of grammar and by the two texts read in conjunction with each other. But the meaning of the clause still stands open. Prynne, as we should expect, insisted (*The Soveragne Power of Parliaments and Kingdomes* (1643), i, 56; ii, 75) that the verb bore a future sense, and that by 'vulgus' was meant 'parliament'. Brady (*True and Exact History of the Succession of the Crown of England*, Glossary, *s.v.* 'Elegerit', 35) took the opposite view, and asserted that the verb had a preterite sense, and that 'vulgus' meant 'the community of higher clergy, earls, barons, and great men'. Stubbs does not state specifically his position with regard to the sense of the verb; but in general he seems to lean towards Prynne's view, and remarks (*loc. cit.* 332) on the coincidence that this clause should first appear immediately after the 'consolidation of the constitution by Edward I'; and he equates the word 'vulgus' with the Edwardian parliaments. Perhaps the most reasonable view to adopt is really a compromise between Prynne's and Brady's opinions. It is hard not to agree with Prynne that the verb 'elegerit' had more than a merely preterite sense. It is hard to believe that the clause did not contemplate future enactments as well as the great series of laws promulgated by Edward I. But it is impossible not to agree with Brady that 'vulgus' or 'communaute' did not mean parliament. We know very well that before and after this date legislation was enacted without any mention of parliamentary sanction. If the clause is considered, not in relation to the controversies of the seventeenth century, but in relation to what is known of fourteenth-century constitutional and legal conditions, there seems little reason to lay great stress on any particular words in it. The whole clause seems to amount to little more than a recognition that there had been, and was likely to be, some law-making in addition to, and equally as binding as, the ancient laws of the confessor and the king's other progenitors. By the new clause, the king was only promising to uphold legislation as legislation, and custom as custom.—It is interesting to notice that this part of the oath as it appears in a fifteenth-century version has apparently a definite future sense in the place equivalent to the disputed word of the 1308 text. The *Vieux Abridgement* of the Statutes (*v. Stat.R.* I, 168) has: 'et que il grauntera a tenur' les leyes et customes du

tion oath the king was bound to the observance of the laws—a circumstance which, he said, was not wholly agreeable to some of our kings.[1] The rebels of Kent, in 1450, declared that the king swore in his coronation oath to keep the law, and that therefore he was not above the law nor the maker of it at pleasure.[2]

But, though the kingdom was property and gave to the king proprietary rights, and though the kingship was office and imposed on the king moral duties, yet the king was more than proprietor and official. He had a divine vocation:

> God geueth his doom to alle kynges that be;
> As a god, in erthe a kyng hath mygt.[3]

royalme et a sa pouvoir lez face garder et affirmer que les gentes de people aver' faitz et eslies.' [Since the above note was written, Dr B. Wilkinson has shown, in his article on 'The Coronation Oath of Edward II' (*Historical Essays in Honour of James Tait* (1933)), that there is good reason to suppose that the French version of the oath was probably the one actually used at Edward II's coronation; and that the clause in question was probably 'the product, not of constitutional growth, but of present discontent' (p. 407)—a mere polemical promise to the barons. This promise, once broken, he says, was not of great constitutional value—at least to the barons; though it was highly rated in the stormy early days of the reign.]

[1] *De Laudibus*, xxxiv, 363: 'Audisti namque superius quomodo inter leges Civiles precipua sententia est, maxima, sive regula, illa que sic canit, "Quod Principi placuit, legis habet vigorem"; qualiter non sancciunt leges Anglie, dum nedum regaliter, sed et politice Rex ejusdem dominatur in populum suum, quo ipse in coronacione sua ad legis sue observanciam astringitur sacramento: quod reges quidam Anglie egre ferentes, putantes proinde se non libere dominari in subditos, ut faciunt reges regaliter tantum principantes....' A comment of Legg's (*op. cit.* p. xx) upon the character of the coronation service is notable: 'From the literary point of view it cannot be said that the coronation service attains great excellence. The prayers are long rambling compositions filled with a wealth of Old Testament illustration that would not have disgraced one of Scott's Covenanters, interspersed with truculent allusions to heretics. And the dread of violence and injustice on the part of the king is very evident. It seems as if the writer of the prayers was not satisfied that the oath was efficacious in preventing either of these misfortunes, and that he was determined, by means of the prayers, to preach to the king the excellence of peace and justice, while at the same time invoking the aid of Heaven to keep the king to these virtues.'

[2] *Magdalen College, Oxford, MSS.* (*Hist. MSS. Comm.* 8th Rep., App. VIII, 266–267). *V.* Chapter IV, *infra*. King Richard was said to have held this condemned doctrine (*Rot. Parl.* III, 419, no. 33).

[3] *Political and Other Poems*, ed. Kail, 53. The poems from which these and other extracts in the present book are taken were written in the first quarter of the 15th century by an author who probably came from the south-western midlands. He shows a strong democratic viewpoint in all the twenty-four poems of his printed by Kail.

Eche a kyng hath goddis power
Of lyf and leme to saue and spille.
He muste make god his partener,
And do not his owen wille.
For god receyueth eche pore mannys bille,
And of here playnt, god hereth the soune.[1]

Al-thogh a kyng hábundance of myght
In his land, at his lust knytte and vnknytte,
Good is þat he his power vse ariȝt,
That fro the way of iustice he ne flitte,
Leste our lord god hym from his gracë schitte,
Of whom al rightwis power is deryued;
ffor if he doo, of blisse he schal be pryued.[2]

'The people at large', wrote Bishop Russell, chancellor of England, 'must stand afar off'; but the lords and commons in parliament were like Moses and Aaron, who ascended into the mount where the law was given: they spoke with the prince— who was 'quasi deus' in the land—as once Moses and Aaron had spoken with God, face to face.[3] 'The Lord has called me from the womb'; 'God hath called me in my tender age to be yowe kynge and sovereigne'—with such texts as these the chancellor proposed to edify the first parliament of Edward V. God, he wrote, had called the king to the occupation of his office.

By a dexterous use of common-law principles of real property, God summoned the king to discharge the duties of his kingly office—so, we may say, the fifteenth century conceived the Great Mystery.

[1] *Ibid.* 54.
[2] Hoccleve, *The Regement of Princes*, stanza 367, 93.
[3] *V.* drafts of Russell's sermons in *Grants of Edward V* (Camden Society, LX (1854)). (*V. infra*, Chapter II, Excursus VI, p. 173.)

§ 2. THE CROWN IN THE CONSTITUTION

Whilst there was probably unanimity upon the matter of the indispensability of the monarchy, the same cannot be said of the question of the lawful mode of accession to the royal estate. At the end of the century, it seemed to the Italian envoys who put into writing a description of their impressions of the English realm, that the kingdom had been governed by one king for six hundred years. The king, they thought, was not elected, but succeeded by hereditary right; if there were no direct heir and the succession were disputed, the issue was often tried by force of arms.[1]

Since it is precisely at times of dispute that a rule of law on the matter should emerge, this view of the Italians amounts to saying that they were unacquainted with any accepted public law on the subject. It does indeed seem that no such public law existed. In the absence of a direct and competent heir, politics, not law, determined the succession. Hence both judges and commons avoided the topic. This lack of a law of succession to the crown was admitted at one time even by Fortescue. In the retractation of his Lancastrian pamphlets, Fortescue excused himself for his former errors by declaring that 'sithen thies maters to whiche ye stere me, concernen the right of succession in kyngedoms, whiche is the grettest matier temporall in all the worlde, they oughten to be treted and declared by the mooste profounde and grettest lerned men that can be gotten tharto, and not by men of my simpleness that haue not moche labored or studyed in any faculte except the lawes of this londe, in whiche the studientes lerne full lytell of the right of succession of kingdomes.'[2]

This may have been an excessively cautious statement; but it only repeats the opinion of the judges in 1460, when they were

[1] *The Italian Relation*, 46.
[2] *The Declaracion upon Certayn Wrytynges*, Works, 532. Nevertheless, in another place (*De Natura*, II, ii) he admitted that the question of the succession was one of law only.

required to give their view of York's claim to the crown: the king's high estate, they said, was above the law and passed their learning, 'Wherfore they durst not enter into eny communication thereof, for it perteyned to the Lordes of the Kyngs blode and th'apparage of this his lond to have communication and medle in such maters.'[1] The judges may have been Yorkist partisans, but it is hardly disputable that such a repudiation of legal capacity to review the claim was unavoidable.

The dubiousness of precisely what constituted a lawful claim to the crown is illustrated by, and helps to account for, the diversity of the titles that were made to serve the purposes of the successive contestants during the century. Henry Bolingbroke's necessities obliged him to pay deference to all the notions which from time immemorial had with varying emphasis been associated with royal succession. Invoking the Holy Trinity, he claimed the realm, the crown, and all the members and appurtenances thereof, by right of descent of the true line, by the right of divine favour as exemplified in his 'recovery' of it, and by a right and/or duty of removing a lawless monarch which he implied by a vague allusion to the misgovernance of his predecessor.[2]

There is no doubt that this was a clever combination of claims on Henry's part; for even though the claim by right line was false, still the claimant paid lip-service to tradition without committing himself to any definition of what constituted a legally complete title to the crown. Moreover, the lords spiritual and temporal, and all the estates present at the time of the challenge, neither committed themselves to such a view nor took it upon themselves formally to elect him king. They merely consented unanimously, without difficulty or delay, that the duke should reign over them.[3]

---

[1] *Rot. Parl.* v, 376. Fortescue himself was chief justice at this time, but it is not clear that he spoke on behalf of the other judges.

[2] *Rot. Parl.* III, 422b. On the whole of this subject, Lapsley, 'The Parliamentary Title of Henry IV' (*loc. cit.*), is indispensable.

[3] *Ibid.* 423: '...iidem Status, cum toto Populo, absque quacumque difficultate vel mora ut Dux prefatus super eos regnaret unanimiter consenserunt.'

An entirely new factor entered into the possible legal claims to the crown when an attempt was made to establish the succession by statute. This, it appears, was first done in the statute 7 Henry IV, c. 2.[1] As early as 1404 there had been recorded in parliament an oath of the lords and commons to observe the right of Henry's sons and the heirs of their bodies to succeed; but this was not a statute—it was only a declaration in affirmance of the estates of Henry and the princes.[2] In the month of June 1406, a more precise measure was agreed upon to exclude females from the succession;[3] but in December this exclusion was abandoned, and a statute was passed entailing the kingdom and crown upon Henry's sons and the heirs of their bodies (male or female).[4] Possibly this act may be regarded as more than simply a statutory declaration of existing law. For it ordained and established that the inheritance of the crowns and realms of England and France, etc., not merely *was* in the person of Henry and his heirs, but *should be settled* and remain so. Still, the wording of the statute, alone, cannot be considered conclusive on such a point, and the probabilities are that it was no more than declaratory. The statute did nothing but determine the line of succession; it recognised but did not create Henry IV's title.

---

[1] The settlement of the succession on Mortimer, in 1397, was recognised by parliament, but was not statutory (*v. Cont. Eulogium*, iii, 361).

[2] *Rot. Parl.* iii, 525. Stubbs (*Const. Hist.* iii, 46, 58) speaks as though it were a statute. Similarly, in 1399, Prince Henry had been created and ordained heir apparent (*Rot. Parl.* iii, 434). As the record-commissioners observed (Introduction, *Statutes of the Realm*, xxxvii), the presence of a petition and answer on the rolls of parliament is no evidence that it was ever put into the form of a statute.

[3] The succession was restricted to heirs male of their bodies (*Rot. Parl.* iii, 576). By the declaration of 1404, Prince Henry's sisters were ignored, but the term 'heirs of his body' would include his daughters, and in the case of his brothers, their daughters. No doubt this exclusion of females was aimed at March's claim through his grandmother. This measure is described in the repealing act of December as 'Statutum et ordinatio' (*Rot. Parl.* iii, 580).

[4] The reason stated in the preamble for the change was: 'quod statutum et ordinatio hujusmodi jus successionis eorundem filiorum nostrorum et liberorum eorum, sexum excludendo femininum, nimium restringebat, quod aliquo modo diminuere non intendebant, sed potius adaugere.' (*Ibid.* 582.)

It is the manner of the enactment, rather than its provision, that is significant.[1] The Speaker, it was said, came before the king and the lords in parliament, and prayed that the commons might have communication with all the lords; and the king granted the prayer. After consultation with the lords and commons, the archbishop, in the name of the lords and commons, put forward a petition touching the inheritance and succession to the crown, and prayed that the king would affirm the petition in parliament, and that it should be enacted and enrolled on the roll of parliament, and held and proclaimed as a statute. Finally, it was accorded and assented to by the king and the lords that the petition should be exemplified under the great seal, and also sealed under the seals of the lords and the seal of arms of John Tiptoft, the common Speaker for the commons, and in their name.[2]

The ordinary legislative form was thus felt to be not quite enough for the settlement of the succession. This was deemed to be a matter rather for the sealing of a legal conveyance than for the passing of a statute;[3] notions of private-property law were active and uppermost in the minds of the parties. But whether we regard it as a statute making new law or as one declaring existing law, it is clear that henceforth there was a title to the throne at least recognised by statute. It remained to be seen whether a title by statute would be strong enough, in the face of political exigencies, to stand against a claim not merely of hereditary, but of indefeasible hereditary, right. It so happened

[1] Cf. E. F. Jacob, 'Sir John Fortescue and the Law of Nature', *Bull. J.R.L.* (July 1934), XVIII, 4.

[2] *Rot. Parl.* III, 580–581; *Stat. R.* II, 151.

[3] The idea that enactments of law should be sealed with the seals of those assenting to them is a very old one. For example, the so-called 'Lex Gundobada', the Burgundian code of the early sixth century, was sealed by thirty-one counts. (*V.* Jenks, *Law and Politics*, 7; and *Select Essays in Anglo-American Legal History*, I, 35.) Sealing as part of the authentication of statutes is occasionally mentioned in the *Year Books* (*v.* Plucknett, *Statutes and their Interpretation*, 11). But the examples there given refer to sealing by one or other of the royal seals; and it would be interesting to know whether there are other instances of the sealing of statutes (as distinct from other enactments such as charters, etc.) by a group of assenters (or should we say 'witnesses'?).

that during the century the tide of political events flowed in the direction of legitimism by hereditary right, and for a time, at least, submerged title by parliamentary enactment. Legitimism speedily became the theoretical solace of Bolingbroke's enemies.[1] Thus in the manifesto issued by Archbishop Scrope and his associates, in the conspiracy of 1405, much was made of the oath taken to Richard: 'that wee so long as we lived should beare true allegeance and fidelity toward him and his heires succeeding him in the kingdome by just title, right, and line, according to the statutes and custome of this realme'.[2] This allusion to the statutes might have been unfortunate after the passage of statute 7 Henry IV, c. 2; and even in the second manifesto, promulgated after the death of Scrope but before the end of 1406, a more discreet programme was proposed—namely, to restore 'coronam regni Angliae suae lineae vel cursui'.[3] It was not, however, until the twenty-third parliament of Henry VI, in 1460, that an explicit claim to the crown was put forward on the grounds of indefeasible hereditary right *alone*. By that date the twenty years' opposition of York and his friends to the court party had reached its climax.

From the dissolution of the Coventry parliament a year before this, events had moved rapidly. In that parliament, York and his associates had been attainted, whilst the remaining lords had sworn solemn oaths of allegiance to Henry as king 'by succession born to reign'. Dispersed and driven into exile by these measures, the Yorkist lords were free to plot and bide their time. York, buoyed up by his popularity in Ireland, and Warwick, sustained by his commanding position at Calais, concerted

---

[1] As Dr Lapsley suggests (*op. cit.*), Henry IV himself flouted the opinions of his own party, in order to obtain a legitimate instead of a parliamentary title for himself. The dynastic controversies of the century thus became, not a struggle between parliamentary and legitimist claimants, but—despite the statute of 1406—a struggle between rival legitimists.

[2] *Petyt MSS., Inner Temple*, 538, 17, fo. 237a. (Cf. Wylie, *Henry IV*, II, 213.) The reference to the statutes can only be considered as part of a common formula. There were no statutes relevant to the succession at the date alluded to.

[3] *Gascoigne*, ed. Rogers, 230–231. (Cf. Wylie, *op. cit.* 217.)

their plans with such success that the latter, accompanied by
the earls of March and Salisbury, invaded the country on the
20th of June. Their attempt was triumphant. London received
them with open arms; Henry's chief officials thought it high
time to resign; and at Northampton on the 10th of July a severe
defeat was inflicted upon a large section of Lancastrian supporters. When, on the 30th of July, writs were issued for a
parliament to meet on the 7th of October, Warwick was master
both of the king's person and of the city of London; and before
long Yorkist nominees were busy in the chief offices of state.
But the parliament had met and had been sitting for three days,
before York himself appeared in London. He had dallied in
Ireland until the beginning of September, and had been
leisurely beating the big drum *en route* from the coast of Lan-
cashire. Perhaps he thought to create a greater impression by
arriving late for the play at Westminster. But the first impression he gave was a bad one. His arrogant and pretentious
bearing met with a frigid reception from the Londoners, and,
more curiously, from the lords who in fact were going to provide
the vote for the partial acceptance of his claim. It almost seems
that even at this eleventh hour in the proceedings, York's own
partisans were not wholly resolved and determined to set him
on the throne. Queen Margaret with her army was, after all,
not very far away. At any rate, they were not going to be
rushed into it; they proceeded with great caution, and carefully
sought all that theoretical justification for their action without
which no revolution could be respectably compassed. Whatever
their political motives or family ties were, the lords insisted, not
only on adhering to legal forms, but also on setting forth their
and York's theoretical position in relation to the situation. Even
if that situation were not really governed by those theories, they
are nevertheless interesting as representing the best case that
could be put forward by either side.

On the 16th of October York submitted in writing a claim
to the crown, citing his pedigree as the sole grounds for it. The

lords,[1] on being asked by the chancellor whether they would have the document read to them, agreed that it should be read, since every person high and low suing to the high court of parliament must of right be heard, though they insisted that it should not be answered without the king's command.

On the next day they consulted the king himself, and were asked by him to state objections to the claim. On the 18th they appealed to the opinion of the judges, who repudiated the responsibility, since they were the king's justices and had to determine such matters as came before them in the law, between party and party, and in such matters between party and party they might not be of counsel.[2] This matter, they said, was between the king and the duke of York, as two parties, and it was not customary to call the justices to counsel in such matters. Moreover, as has been mentioned above, they declared that the matter was so high that it was above the law and passed their learning, and they referred the question to the lords of the blood and to the peerage.[3] The matter was then put to the serjeants-at-law and the king's attorney, and these too excused themselves. The lords, doubtless anxious to procure support, were unwilling to accept excuses, and pressed for an answer, and told them that they were the king's particular counsellors and therefor they received their fees and wages. The lawyers, however, were obdurate, and replied that they were indeed the king's counsellors in the law, in such things as were under his authority or by commission, but this matter was above his authority, and therein they might not meddle.[4]

The lords were thus obliged to deal with York's claim by

---

[1] It is said that the majority of them stayed away from the meeting (William of Worcester, *Annales*, 484). But presumably the Yorkist party attended in force, which makes the diffidence apparent in the proceedings all the more remarkable. The truth appears to be that even York's supporters were reluctant to put him on the throne at this stage. Warwick, apparently, was opposed to such a project. (*V.* Oman, *Warwick the Kingmaker*, 97 *et seq.*)

[2] I cannot agree with Professor Baldwin's interpretation of these words to mean 'political parties' and 'the Council' (*King's Council*, 205).

[3] *V. supra*, p. 23; and *Rot. Parl.* v, 376.

[4] *Ibid.*

themselves. However partisan they were, a great obstacle in their way was the solemn oath of allegiance to Henry, of protection for the queen, of acceptance of Prince Edward as heir, that they had taken at Coventry not twelve months previously. To this difficulty they gave the prime place. They reminded York of his oaths of allegiance, and of the fact that Henry IV had claimed as heir of Henry III, not as conqueror;[1] and they threw some doubts on York's account of his own descent. But above all, they said, statutes barred his claim; it was 'to be called to remembraunce the grete and notable Acts of Parlements made in dyvers Parlements of dyvers of the Kyngs Progenitours, the which Acts be sufficient and resonable to be leyde ageyn the title of the said Duc of York: the which Acts been of moche more auctorite than eny Cronycle and also of auctorite to defete any manere title made to eny persone'.[2]

The precise meaning intended by these words is not very clear. A good deal of the lords' obscurity was no doubt due to the fact that they were not sure of the theoretical position of a statute. Apart altogether from political motives, belief in royalty as conferred by birth was far too strong, far too ancient, for them to have been capable of pressing to the full the notion that a statute could disinherit the true heir—whomsoever that was. It looks as though the lords who put forward this objection were thinking of the acts of parliament mainly as evidence rebutting the evidence of the chronicles, which recorded the descent and therefore the title of 'any person'. Probably this conservative idea of the nature of an act was uppermost in their minds. But the concluding words of the quoted passage seem to show that an interpretation of the view which they were stating which confined itself to that conservative limit, would not quite do justice to the complete idea which was being expressed. They said not merely that the acts were of much *more authority* than any chronicle, but also that they were of authority to *defeat* any

[1] Actually, he had claimed as both heir and conqueror (*v. supra*, p. 23).
[2] *Rot. Parl.* v. 376.

manner of title made to any person. The lords could hardly have added these words if they had aimed at representing the acts only as evidence of title, and had not had in mind at least a suggestion that the acts were final authority, final in the sense of conferring statutory recognition on Henry's title.

The case for a parliamentary title was thus alluded to, and the fact that it was passed over by those who made the allusion cannot be ignored in any estimate of the place of parliamentarism in the ideas of the period.

York answered that the oaths of allegiance were invalid in the face of God's law and commandment,[1] since the virtue and nature of an oath was to confirm truth, and the truth was that the peers and the lords ought to help and assist him in truth and justice, notwithstanding any oath of fealty made by him or them. He denied (rightly) that there had been made any acts of parliament entailing the crown, save one, *i.e.* statute 7 Henry IV, c. 2. 'And', he said, very pointedly, 'yf he [Henry] myght have obteigned and rejoysed the seid Corones, etc., by title of enheritaunce, discent, or succession, he neither neded nor wold have desired or made thaym to bee graunted to hym in suche wise, as they be by the seid Act, the which taketh noo place, neyther is of any force or effect ayenst hym that is right enheriter of the said Corones, as it accordeth with Godds lawe, and all naturall lawes, howe it bee that all other Actes and Ordenaunces made in the said Parliament and sithen, been good and suffisant ayenst all other persones.'[2] Further, his right, he said, being well-grounded, was imperishable, though it had been in abeyance; while Henry's claim had never been more than a pretence.[3] York, that is to say, submitted that parliament had given Henry a title which he would not otherwise have had, and that this was *ultra vires*.

---

[1] Cf. Chapter III (§ 1), *infra*.

[2] *Rot. Parl.* v, 377.

[3] *Ibid.* Fortescue made much of the doctrine of prescription, on behalf of the Lancastrian cause (*v.* Works, 83, 86, 501, 515). (*V.* Excursus II, *infra*.)

In face of this argument, the lords decided in the end that York's claim could not be defeated. This was no doubt the intended result all through; but, in arriving at it, the *theory* of parliamentary right to determine the succession—not to mention title, supposing there were any such theory—to the throne was subordinated to the *theory* of the right of God's law of inheritance to determine it. Such a decision[1]—if it had been logically pursued and applied—must have impeded the expansion of the notion of the 'authority of parliament'—growing though that notion was.[2]

The theories put forward at the time of Edward IV's accession naturally followed the lines of his father's arguments.[3] It was said that he had taken upon him, to the pleasure of God and the joy of his subjects, the reign and governance of the realm whereunto he was righteously and naturally born. Henry, the late earl of Derby—the commons' petition was made to say—had been a usurper; and by God's law, man's law, and law of nature,[4] the right title was, and had been since the death of his father, in the person of Edward; and moreover, since that day he had been in lawful possession. This right and title, by the advice and assent of the lords spiritual and temporal in the parliament, and by the authority of the same, was to be declared, taken, accepted, and reputed true and righteous, and was to abide forever as of record.

The stress on lawful possession, and the appearance of the common-law principle 'of record', are noticeable in this declaration, and hark back to the private-law conception of the succession. But the contention that the Lancastrians had been merely usurpers could not be pressed too far. In Bagot's case,[5]

---

[1] It is significant that, although the statute of 7 Henry IV was repealed (*Rot. Parl.* v, 379), no statute was enacted or enrolled recording the new settlement.

[2] The present writer does not intend to suggest that either side in the dispute regarded parliament as a sovereign legislature.

[3] Henry VI was said to have been 'deposed' by an assembly of Yorkist bishops and barons in London, on 3 March, 1461 (*Gregory's Chronicle*, 215; *Hall's Chronicle*, 253).

[4] Cf. Chapter III (§ 1), *infra*.   [5] *Y.B. 9 Edward* IV, Pas. pl. 2 (App. no. 53 (ii)).

for example—in which the judicial acts and charters of pardon of a king *de facto* were upheld—it was said by Bagot's counsel, in the course of the argument: 'Sir, the said king Henry was not merely a usurper, for the crown was entailed on him by parliament.'[1]

The theoretical force of legitimism having been so magnified by these transactions, it might, as Richard of Gloucester found in 1483, be possible to obtain a title by the simple process of procuring the bastardisation of the alleged heirs. This action was Richard's tribute to the doctrine of legitimism. The tenuity of a right so obtained, however, was tacitly admitted by resort to other forms of sanction.[2] It was declared that he had been elected king by the three estates of the realm out of parliament, but that in as much as the court of parliament was of such authority, and the people of the realm of such nature and disposition, as experience taught, that any declaration of a truth or right made by the three estates in parliament made before all things for safety and certainty and quieted men's minds, and removed the occasion for all doubts and seditious language, this election was ratified by the lords spiritual and temporal and the commons in parliament.[3] Richard was declared king as well by right of consanguinity and inheritance as by lawful election, consecration, and coronation.

The notable point in this proceeding is that notwithstanding the tribute paid to the authority of parliament, there was no allusion to a title by parliamentary act. The election was said to have been made by the three estates out of parliament, and the parliament merely confirmed this extra-parliamentary proceeding.

Two years later, Henry Tudor obtained a settlement as definitive as it was cautious. No fictions were employed, nor were any

---

[1] At Henry VI's restoration, in the parliament of November 1471, the crown was entailed on him and the heirs male of his body, with remainder to George, duke of Clarence, brother of Edward IV (*Rot. Parl.* vi, 194).

[2] He referred also to the attainder of Clarence, which debarred his issue from claiming, and to Edward IV's misgovernance.   [3] *Rot. Parl.* vi, 240.

dubious questions of legitimism or election raised. Simply it was enacted by the authority of parliament that the inheritance of the crown, with all the pre-eminence and dignity royal, was, rested, and remained in the person of Henry VII, 'our now sovereigne lord king', and in the heirs of his body, perpetually so to endure.[1]

[1] *Rot. Parl.* VI, 270. 'Words studiously ambiguous', observes Hallam (*Const. Hist.* I, 8), 'which, while they avoid the assertion of an hereditary right that the public voice repelled, were meant to create a parliamentary title, before which the pretensions of lineal descent were to give way.' Henry's subsequent marriage with the daughter of Edward IV of course merged the hereditary claim in the Tudors. Cf. Pickthorn, *Early Tudor Government*, I, 2–5, 13. Mr Pickthorn's account of Henry VII's succession seems to suffer somewhat from an insufficient distinction between the deed and the theory of it (*ibid.* 10–13). The fact that Henry assumed royal rights immediately after Bosworth has little bearing on the theoretical claim when that came to be stated. Any action of Henry's before his title was formally recognised was of course the action of a king *de facto*. The recognition of his claim would be necessary to make him king *de jure*. Certainly it is misleading to say that Henry 'assumed he was king by divine right' (*ibid.* 13)—unless by 'divine right' is meant 'inheritance and conquest'. The expression savours too much of later ideas to be wholly applicable to Henry, and is perhaps due to an insufficient attention to the implications of the notion of the kingdom as real property. There is undoubtedly a strong strain of real-property ideas present in the theory of succession all along, and we may doubt whether there was much more divine right in Henry VII's theory of his claim than there was in that of any successor to landed property, though, indeed, divine right *was* there. As Bracton said, 'only God can make an heir'. It is also an exaggeration to make up an hypothesis such as 'if the transmission of kingship is altogether to escape human control, the insistence on unction... requires some qualification' (*ibid.* 8). It is quite evident that every claimant during the century considered it a necessary part of the proceedings that his claim should receive some form of recognition or election. No claim was quite complete without it. Such recognition or election can hardly, perhaps, be called 'human control'; but it certainly accords, in theory at least, a share to human choice in the matter. Mr Pickthorn seems rather to over-simplify the traditional ideas and usages which even Henry VII must have found it desirable to propitiate. It will not do to say that 'Henry Tudor, by the mere fact of being Henry Tudor, was king' (*ibid.* 16). Obviously he was Henry Tudor long before the battle of Bosworth, but he was not king. The judges did not say he was free of attaint because he was Henry Tudor, but because he was king. Mr Pickthorn rather overlooks the fact that the coronation service of the English kings is far older than any parliament, and that the coronation service always provided at least the form of appeal to popular acceptance. Moreover, the opinion of lawyers hardly encourages an exclusive stress on the 'divine right' side of Henry's claim. Thus we find counsel arguing, with the approval of the court, in the seventh year of the reign: 'Come si le roy morust cest jour, et mesme le jour un autre est esleu, in cest cas il sera pris le jour de cesty qui est mort' (*Y.B.* 7 *Henry VII*, Mich. p. 6 (App. no. 87)). This observation itself modifies the significance that Mr Pickthorn would have us attach to the fact that Henry and other kings put as early a date as possible for the commencement of their reigns. It was legally necessary that they should do so, irrespective of the nature of their claims or titles.

The absence of any definite principles of public law is manifest throughout these transactions. There was no clear law of succession, and it was thus possible for the various claimants to the crown to make up a plausible case for themselves by magnifying one or other of the traditional modes of access to the estate of king. But it is also noticeable that there was a tendency to utilise, for the purpose of definition, the language and the ideas of the positive law of succession to private property. In lieu of a differentiated public law regulating the succession, men had recourse to the principles and rules of private law.

The lords in 1455, we have noticed, seemed convinced that the attributes of the estate royal were resting and always must rest in the king's person. Was the royal estate, then, inseparable from the royal person?

It is well known that the doctrine of capacities had emerged in legal thought long before the beginning of the fifteenth century.[1] It manifested itself in the distinction drawn between the spiritual and temporal capacities of ecclesiastics at least from the time of Lanfranc, who distinguished the two capacities of Odo of Bayeux; and in the late years of Henry III's reign, a clear differentiation was made by a certain injured party between the public and private capacities of the chancellor.[2] There is even evidence that counsel for Edward I drew a distinction between Edward as king and Edward as prince.[3] The dis-

---

[1] Cf. G. T. Lapsley, *op. cit.* 578–579.

[2] *V.* J. Conway Davies, *The Baronial Opposition to Edward II*, 22–23. Mr Davies omits to mention the material point that the differentiation was emphatically disallowed in court when the case came up for trial before the justices (*v. Coram Rege Rolls, Trin.* 2 *Edward I, W. Salt Society Collections*, VI, i, 63–64).

[3] *V.* Davies, *op. cit.* 23. Perhaps Mr Davies claims a little too much for this case. It is somewhat difficult to see that this distinction 'would lead by implication... to a distinction between king and crown'. The distinction between one status and another enjoyed by the same person at successive times is a different thing from the distinction between person and office (or crown). Moreover, in the case in point (*Placita de Quo Warranto*, 429–430), the franchise which Earl Warenne contested was the return of writs for the vill which Edward as prince had conveyed to him; and such a franchise could hardly have been given him by Edward as prince, since return of writs was a strictly royal prerogative. Edward's counsel must have been on sure ground in arguing that a gift of such a franchise by Edward as prince was invalid.

turbances of Edward II's reign brought into prominence the differentiation between the crown and the royal person, until the doctrine incurred baronial condemnation at the time of the younger Despenser's fall; and though little more seems to have been heard of it during the remainder of the fourteenth century,[1] there are some traces of its existence in the period under review. For example, a plain separation was made between the rights of the king as king and his rights as the duke of Lancaster.[2] It is true also that Fortescue, in his account of arguments among imaginary rival claimants to a throne, differentiated sharply between a king's capacity as public office-holder and his capacity as private proprietor.[3] But this was a piece of purely abstract theorising, and was not applied by him to the actual monarchy of England. The ruling of the judges in the first year of Henry VII's reign, which held that an attainted person by assuming the regality was *ipso facto* relieved of his attainder, perhaps from one point of view implies the distinction; but from another point of view it implies the inability to conceive of the attainder of the king's person apart from his office.[4]

But these points are more than counterbalanced by the evidence which shows the absence of any serious application of the doctrine of capacities to the kingship during the century. Not only was there the emphatic judicial ruling that the royal prerogatives must be intact in the king's person alone,[5] but the events of the century evoked elaborate statements to the effect that the royal authority was indistinguishable from the royal person.

Thus it was clearly a familiar fact, before the century was over, that the royal person could suffer the disabilities of nonage or of infirmity; but on each occasion of one or the other

[1] Cf. Pollock and Maitland, *Hist. Eng. Law*, I, Bk. II, ii, § 13; Tout, *The Place of Edward II in English History*, 150; and Lodge and Thornton, *Constitutional Documents*, 3, 11, 19.

[2] *V. Y.B.* 6 *Henry IV*, Hil. pl. 2 (App. no. 11). Cf. Wylie, *Henry IV*, II, 187.

[3] *V. supra*, p. 11 *et seq.*

[4] *V. infra*, p. 51.

[5] *V. Y.B.* 5 *Edward IV*, Mich. fo. 118–123 (App. no. 48).

of these disabilities, it was admitted that the royal authority was nevertheless unimpaired. So, in 1427, when Protector Bedford was in England, and the whole question of the settlement of the country was reviewed in the council, the lords stated they understood 'howbeit that the Kyng as nowe be of tendre age, neverthelesse the same auctoritee resteth and is atte this day in his persone that shall be in hym at eny tyme hereafter when he shall come, with Goddes Grace, to Yeres of discretion'.[1] Forasmuch as the king was then of such tenderness of age as by the possibility of nature he could not indeed rule or govern in person, and that neither God nor reason would that this land should stand without governance, forsomuch, 'The execution of the Kynges said auctoritee, as toward that that belongeth unto the Politique[2] Reule and Governaille of his Lande and to th' observaunce and kepyng of his Lawes, belongeth unto the Lordes Spirituall and Temporall of his Lande, at suche tyme as thei be assembled in Parlement or in grete Consaille, and ellus hem not being so assembled, unto the Lords chosen and named to be of his continuel Counseill....'[3]

Much the same view of the persistence of the authority of the king was expressed by York when, in 1435, he was appointed protector during Henry VI's illness. He accepted the office, he said, 'but onely of the due and humble obeissaunce that I owe to doo unto the Kyng our most dradde and souveraine lord and to you the Perage of this lande, in whom by th'occasion of th' enfirmite of our said Souveraine Lord restethe th'exercice of his auctoritee'.[4]

The fullest expression of this notion appears in the latter half of the proclamation announcing the appointment of a council

---

[1] *Rot. Parl.* v, 410; and *Procs. and Ords.* III, 231–236.

[2] I am not able to infer, as Ramsay did (*Lancaster and York*, II, 189, n. 2), that the word 'politique' may be deemed equivalent to the modern 'constitutional'. There are certainly many ideas in that modern word which would have been novel to the lords in 1427, and there is really no need to interpret the word 'politique'— in this and the following instances, at least—as meaning anything more than simply 'politic'.

[3] *Rot. Parl.* v, 410.   *Ibid.* 242.

to exercise the royal authority in 1455. As we have noted above,[1] the lords therein insisted that the authority of his majesty, and also the sovereignty of them and all the land, was resting, and always must rest, in the king's person. But, we may say, during minority or illness the indivisible estate of the king is incomplete, since it lacks will and reason, which must therefore be supplied by the council or parliament, in order to exercise the king's authority.

The same notion of the impossibility of a dichotomy of royal person and royal authority—that is, of any alienation or delegation of sovereignty—is well illustrated by the care with which the lords, and even the protectors themselves, avoided giving colour to the suggestion that any partition of the source of authority was involved in the establishment of a protectorate during Henry's minority. At the time of the settlement of the government, in 1422, Gloucester, though dissatisfied with the title of 'defender'—which it was proposed to give him at such periods as Bedford was in France—and though claiming the name of governor under the king, or, as William Marshall had had, the title of 'rector regni', nevertheless did not claim to be 'rector regis', and declared: 'he vil nat desire ne to make his seel of such auctorite as the seid William Mareschall dide.'[2]

Similarly, the lords avoided giving countenance to any usage of the word 'tutela' in discussing the functions to be ascribed

---

[1] *Ibid.* 289–290. The relevant portion runs thus: 'the which Lordes protestyng, that the high prerogative preemynence and auctorite of his Mageste Roiall, and also the soverauntee of thaym and alle this lande, is and alwey mot reste and shall reste in his moost excellent persone, offre thayme of humble obeissaunce to put thaym in as grete diligence and devoir, to doo all that that mowe preferre or avaunce the said high prerogatyve, preemynence and auctorite of his moost Excellence, and also his high regalie and honorable astate and welfare, and the felicitee and suertee of his moost noble persone, and also to the politique reule and governaunce of his lande, and the good publique reste and tranquillite of his subgettes as ever did eny Counsaillers or subgettes to theire moost drad Soverayne Lord; and therunto at all tymes to be redy, not sparyng therfore at eny tyme that it shall nede, to putte theire bodies in jeopardie.' (Cf. *supra*, p. 6, *et infra*, p. 41, n. 1.)

[2] *V.* a note by the present writer, 'The Pretensions of the duke of Gloucester in 1422', *E.H.R.* (1930), XLV, 101–103.

to the 'defender', because, they said, it was such a term of the civil law that they dared not agree to it.[1]

A similar caution appears in the arrangement of York's title in 1453. It is reported that there was devised for him a name different from that of other counsellors, not the name of tutor, lieutenant, governor, or regent, nor any name that would import 'authority of governance of the land', but simply that of 'protector and defender', which imported only the personal duty of attending to the actual defence of the land.

On the whole, then, we can be confident that during the fifteenth century a distinction was not normally drawn between the person of the king and the crown,[2] even though the notion of a corporation sole was growing, and the doctrine of capacities was sometimes applied even to the king. But the possibility of differentiating between person and office was growing, and the *De Facto* Act of 11 Henry VII must be considered as giving it a statutory recognition.[3]

The moral duties attached to the royal office and recognised by the king were, it may be thought, the mainspring of constitutional development. For, given duties, it was always possible to imply certain consequences which were needed to implement their due execution; and even if the duties themselves remained moral only, the implied consequences might in the course of time be reduced to legal obligations. There can be no responsibility without corresponding authority.

First among these consequences, both in time and in importance, must always have been the need for power. The king, in

[1] *Ibid.* 'The essence of "tutela"', writes Sohm (*Institutes*, ed. Ledlie (1901), 395), 'consists in the so-called "auctoritatis interpositio", *i.e.* the assistance of the tutor which is required for the conclusion of juristic acts.' Naturally the lords would not lend any countenance to an idea which would have suggested that Gloucester's compliance was necessary to make the king's acts lawful.
[2] By 1465 the idea was current that demise of the king dissolved parliament. *Y.B. 4 Edward IV*, Pas. pl. 4 (App. no. 45). *V.* the extract printed by Lodge and Thornton, *English Constitutional Documents*, 36.
[3] Cf. Pickthorn, *op. cit.* 26, 45, 140, 161–162.

taking the oath, swore to perform those duties, 'secundum suas vires'. And the prime requisite for power was inevitably economic resources—whether the king's own or those of his supporters. The king must have his patrimony, and he ought to use it honestly in the discharge of his duties without, in peace time, oppressing his people with taxation—even though it were granted in parliament.[1] His realm was bound to provide him with the means of maintaining his estate;[2] and hence it was not very clear that parliament had the right to refuse him a grant.[3] But the king ought not to alienate the endowments of his crown nor remove its property out of the realm, without the assent of the estates in parliament; and the charge of having done so formed two of the main objections to Richard's government.[4]

Next to material resources the king at all times needed counsel —a second requisite for power. A great part of the constitutional history of England in the mediaeval period might be said (if such sayings have any value) to be a commentary, not upon *Magna Carta*, but upon the simple fact of the king's crying need for counsel and ever more counsel. For, as Fortescue said, the

[1] *Rot. Parl.* III, 419, no. 32. Cf. Pickthorn, *op. cit.* 21–22.

[2] Fortescue, *Governance*, viii: 'ffor his reaume is bounde by right to susteyne hym in euery thyng necessarie to his estate.' Cf. Chief Baron Fray, in *Y.B.* 19 *Henry VI*, Pas. pl. 1 (App. no. 25): 'The law which binds the king to defend his people also binds the people to grant of their goods to him in aid of that defence.' Fortescue advocated heavy endowment and slight taxation (*v.* Chapter IV, Excursus II, *infra*).

[3] As Mr Pickthorn points out (*op. cit.* 21–22). But at least one instance is known of the refusal of a grant by the lords, in 1405. (*V.* Walsingham, *Hist. Angl.* II, 268; and cf. Chapter II, p. 152, *infra.*)

[4] *Rot. Parl.* III, 417, no. 18: 'Quod propter malum regimen suum, videlicet, Bona et Possessiones ad Coronam suam spectantia etiam personis indignis donando, et alias indiscrete dissipando, et ob hoc collectas et alia onera gravia et importabilia populo sine causa imponendo, necnon alia mala innumerabilia perpetrando; alias de assensu et mandato suis per totum Parliamentum ad gubernacionem regni certi prelati et alii Domini Temporales erant electi et assignati....' *Ibid.* 420, no. 41: 'Item, Thesaurum, Coronas, Reliquias et alia Jocalia, videlicet, Bona regni, que ab antiquo dimissa fuerant in Archivis Regni, pro Honore regis et conservatione regni sui in omnem eventum, praefatus Rex exiens Regnum suum versus Hiberniam abstulit, et secum deferri fecit, sine consensu statuum regni, etc.' Dr Lapsley considers these clauses show a distinct advance in constitutional theory (*op. cit.* 578).

good sense of any king whomsoever, even if he be a son of
Solomon, is insufficient to govern his realm without the support
of counsellors. He who is taught by the prudence of many is
strong in their wisdom; but he who depends upon his own wit
alone evidently has the wisdom of only one:[1]

> Now purpose I, to trete how to a kyng
> It nedeful is to do by consail ay;
> With-outen whiche, good is he do noþing;
> ffor a kyng is but a man soul, parfay!
> And be his witt neuere so good, he may
> Erre and mistake hym oþer while among,
> Where-as good counsail may exclude a wrong.[2]

Moreover, counsel always enabled the king to manage and to
commit in advance those who gave it. But the necessity of
relying on counsel leads by slow degrees to the conversion of the
giving of advice into the determination of policy. Hence it was
that, in the list of Richard's abuses,[3] there appeared as an
enormity the allegation that he had repudiated the discreet
counsel of justices and of others in great councils. Hence the
explicit, though cautiously vague declaration on behalf of
Henry IV: 'qil est la volunte du Roy d'estre conseillez et
governez par les honorables, sages et discretes persones de son
Roialme, et par lour commune conseil et assent faire le meulx
pur la Governance de luy et de son Roialme; nient veullant
estre governez de sa volunte propre ne de son purpos voluntarie, singulere opinione, mais par commune advis, conseil et
assent.'[4]

Fifty years later, at the settlement of the government during
Henry VI's illness in the winter of 1455, the notion of the royal
need for counsel to help him in his charges was fully stated; for, as
it was said, to the 'politique governance and restfull reule of this

[1] *De Natura*, I, xxiii.
[2] Hoccleve, *The Regement of Princes*, stanza 695.
[3] *Rot. Parl.* III, 420, no. 23.
[4] *Ibid.* 415.

his realme apperteneth grete diligence and actuell laboure'—
more than the king himself could bear.[1]

Counsel, however, was not enough, if the king was to discharge his duties. He must also be able to maintain his office
and to ensure his effectiveness. The reverse of duty is privilege
or rights, and to consider the king's privilege or rights is to consider his prerogative—the third requisite for power. As in the
case of many other words which were in use during the period,
it is difficult to define exactly what was meant by the word
'prerogative' when associated with the kingship. But it seems
possible to distinguish a general and a particular sense in which
the term was being employed. It is not, I think, sufficient to say
that the word usually meant 'either a treatise on feudal law in
respect of the king and his tenants, or the tenurial, procedural,
and pleading rights of the king'.[2] There is little room for doubt
that the word was being used in a sense different from these
throughout the century; and Serjeant Starkey was hardly in-
novating quite so much as Professor Plucknett suggests, when,
in 1482, he contrasted the authority of convocation with the

[1] The wording of the whole proclamation is interesting (*Rot. Parl.* v, 290):
'The xxii.ti. of Novembr, the yere of oure seid Souverayne Lord xxxiiii.ti., the moost
Christen Prince the Kyng our moost drad souverayne Lord at his Paleys of Westm'
remembryng that to the politique governance and restful reule of this his realme,
apperteneth grete diligence and actuell laboure, the which is to his moost noble
person full tedious and grete to suffre and bere. Also that every Prince must of
verray necessitee haue Counsaillers to helpe hym in his charges to whome he muste
trust and leene; for these causes and such other as his high wisedome, consideryng
that God hath endued such as been of his Counsaill with grete wisdom, cunnyng
and experience, and know the direction to be had moost expedient for the sadde and
politique reule of this his lande, whoos trouthes, love and good zele that they
bere to his Roiall persone, been to hym approved and knowen, openyng his
gracious disposition, ordeyned and graunted, that his Counsaill shuld provyde,
commyne, ordeyne, spede and conclude, all such matiers as touche and concerne
the good and politique rule and governaunce of this his land and lawes thereof, and
directe thayme as it shal be thought to theire wisdomes and discretions behovefull
and expedient; soo alwaye that in all such matiers as touchen the honour, wurship
and suertee of his moost noble persone, they shall late his Highness have knowelech
what direction they take in theym, desiryng his seid Counsaill hertely, for the wele
and ease of his said persone and kepyng and beryng up his Roiall astate, to take
this his wille and ordenaunce upon thaym....' (For the remainder of this proclamation, *v. supra*, p. 37.)
[2] T. F. T. Plucknett, *The Lancastrian Constitution*, 175.

authority of the king in his prerogative.[1] Tout was assuredly
right in suggesting that the first definite formulation of the
theory of the royal prerogative appears at least as early as the
declaration of the judges at Nottingham, in August 1387, to the
effect that the baronial commission was illegal because deroga-
tory to this prerogative.[2]

Certainly in that instance[3] the word 'prerogative' does not
mean merely 'feudal rights', but means something very much
akin to 'sovereignty'; and it was so used in subsequent years,
with some frequency. In 1406, for example, Speaker Tiptoft
protested that he had not spoken against 'les Prerogatif ou
Estate roiale mesme nostre seigneur le roy'; and Henry assented
to some articles for administrative reform, always saving to him
his estate and the prerogative of his crown.[4] Much the same
terms were used in similar instances in 1411.[5] Henry V, in 1414,
accepted the commons' petition relating to the engrossment of
statutes, saving always his royal prerogative to grant or deny.[6]
Fortescue, in a passage in the *Governance*, both adopts and
develops this usage. In his discussion of an ordinance for the
king's routine charges, he observes: 'so is the kynges power
more, in that he may not put ffrom him possescions necessaries
for his own sustenance, than yff he myght put ham ffrom hym,
and aliene the same to his owne hurte and harme. Nor this is
ayen the kynges prerogatiffe, be wich he is exaltid above his
subgettes; but rather this is to hym a prerogatiff. Ffor no man
saue he mey haue ayen the lande þat he hath onis aliened.'[7]

There is in this passage a suggestion at least of a distinction
between *the* prerogative and *a* prerogative; and this fact en-

---

[1] *Ibid.* For this case, *v.* Appendix, No. 63.

[2] *Chapters*, III, 423.

[3] *Rot. Parl.* III, 233: 'Inprimis, querebatur ab eis, An illa nova Statutum et
Ordinatio atque Commissio, facta et edita in ultimo Parliamento apud Westm'
celebrato, derogant Regalie et Prerogative dicti domini nostri regis? Ad quam
quidem Questionem unanimiter responderunt, Quod derogant, presertim eo quod
fuerant contra voluntates Regis.'

[4] *Ibid.* 572, 585.   [5] *Ibid.* 648, 658.   [6] *Rot. Parl.* IV, 22.

[7] *Governance*, vi. Cf. Holdsworth, *The Influence of the Legal Profession on the Growth
of the English Constitution*, 27.

courages us to hold to our separation of Prerogative from prerogatives. Prerogative, we may say, meant that reserve of undefined power necessary to any government to enable it to deal with emergencies. Certainly Prerogative, long before the end of the period, implied that vague notion of the amplitude of power wherewith to discharge the moral duties of kingship—that notion of the sovereignty of the king's majesty—which was destined to provide one of the main lines of theoretical development during the next two centuries. It was this development which, among other results, made it possible for the learned Dr Cowell, in his *Law Interpreter* of 1607, to define 'Prerogative' as 'that especiall power, pre-eminence, and privilege that the king hath in any kind, *over and above* the ordinary course of the common law, in the right of his crown', and to conclude therefrom that the 'king of England is an absolute king'.

On the other hand, the notion of 'prerogatives' was the source of that line of ideas which made it possible for Coke to assert that the term 'prerogative' 'legally extends to all powers, pre-eminences, and privileges which the law *giveth* to the crown'.[1] But we can hardly say that this definition would be sufficient for the fifteenth century, for the prerogatives seem to be rather those particular exercises of the Prerogative which have received definition and therefore restriction, by litigation and the process of law.[2] The steady process of such definition and restriction of prerogatives we can see being carried on in numerous cases in the courts during the period; and some of the more interesting and outstanding of these cases are worth individual attention, as illustrating the constitutional significance of the resulting definitions and restrictions.

It is notable, in the first place, that some of the leading judges of the century expressly repudiated the notion that the ancient statement of the king's tenurial and procedural privileges—the

---

[1] *Institutes*, I, lib. 2, v.
[2] Cf. *Rot. Parl.* IV, 201: '...the Kynges Justices, which be lerned both in his prerogatifs and his commune lawe....'

statement known as the *Statuta Prerogativa*—was to be held as a statute. Maitland, in one of his papers,[1] quoted the classic case on this point.[2] In this case (of wardship disputed between the king and the bishop of Ely), it was claimed by the respective counsel that the *Statuta* were, and were not, in affirmance of the common law. Littleton, J., and Choke, J., both gave their judgement on the point, and were in agreement that the *Statuta* could not be held as a true statute, but only as in affirmance of the common law. A statute, said Littleton, was limited to a certain time at which it had been made, and to a reign and a place in which it had been enacted. For *Magna Carta* was not a statute at the beginning, but only after it had been confirmed by the statute of Marlborough (c. 5); and *Quia Emptores* and divers other statutes had a definite time-limit in respect of the specified date of their enactment. The *Statuta* had no such time-limit, and could be no more a statute than the *Dies Communes in Banco*,[3] or the *Dies Communes in Dote*, or the *Expositiones Vocabulorum*, which were written in their books. Moreover, if it had really been held as a statute, it would have been held effectual in all points; but in fact it had not been held thus effectual, for he himself had seen Markham, J. make an exception to it. It could not, therefore, be held as a statute, but only as in affirmance of the common law.

Maitland was unsatisfied as to what precisely was meant by this expression 'in affirmance of the common law'.[4] In law, 'to affirm' is, of course, to make a solemn confirmation or ratification; and Littleton seems to have thought of the *Statuta Prerogativa* as written statements of admitted common law relating to the king as privileged landlord. At least it is clear enough that he abandoned any notion that the king's prerogatives in these respects were dependent on, or derived, or derivable from, a statute.

[1] *Collected Papers*, ii, 182–189.
[2] *Y.B. 15 Edward IV*, Mich. pl. 17 (App. no. 61).
[3] This document figured as a statute in *Y.B. 8 Edward IV*, Pas. pl. 9 (App. no. 51); but Pigot, Sjt. therein denied that it was a statute in affirmance of common law.
[4] *V. infra*, Chapter iii (§ 3).

From time to time, during the century, various points of the *Statuta* were used in judgements in cases between the king and his subjects. The tenurial prerogatives involved have not in themselves much constitutional significance, and they are not in any way discussed here.

Old doctrines—such as that the king cannot be said to commit a wrong[1] and that the goods of felons dying mute under the 'peine forte et dure' were to be adjudged to the king[2]—occasionally appear; and many procedural privileges received further definition or declaration, during the period.[3] Thus, in a certain case of dispute as to a right of wardship which the king had granted away by letters patent, it was ruled—the trial was going badly for the king—that he could not join a second and different issue unless a fresh inquisition on the facts were made.[4] In another case, it was agreed that he could alter a title which had been stated in a writ;[5] and also, it was possible for him to amend his count during a trial.[6]

But sometimes points of more constitutional importance than these emerged in the course of litigation. Thus, in a case of *quare impedit* in the thirty-fifth year of Henry VI, a plea was raised by the defendant's counsel that the statute of Westminster II (c. 5) was general and must be deemed to bind the king as well as any other person. Ashton, J., however, ruled to the contrary. The statute, he asserted, could not be deemed to extend so far; for if a remedy were prescribed by statute, it would not be intended against the king unless it were expressly so stated.[7]

---

[1] *Y.B.* 1 *Edward V*, Trin. pl. 13 (App. no. 65).

[2] *Y.B.* 8 *Henry IV*, Mich. pl. 2 (App. no. 13).

[3] Cases concerning or involving these procedural privileges are very numerous in the *Year Books*, especially for the later years of the century. A detailed study of them would probably repay the intricate labour which it would entail.

[4] *Y.B.* 9 *Henry IV*, Mich. pl. 20 (App. no. 15).

[5] *Y.B.* 11 *Henry IV*, Mich. pl. 20 (App. no. 17 (ii)).

[6] *Y.B.* 11 *Henry IV*, Mich. pl. 67 (App. no. 19 (ii)).

[7] *Y.B.* 35 *Henry VI*, Trin. pl. 1 (App. no. 33 (i)). (Cf. *Y.B.* 12 *Henry VII*, Trin. pl. 1 (App. no. 101 (i) and (ii)).)

That a certain latitude of choice of alternative legal rules was open to the king in some circumstances involving matters of public policy is evident from at least one case which was discussed in the exchequer chamber in the fifth year of Edward IV. The earliest reports of cases in the exchequer chamber come from the reign of Henry IV, and the main development of the procedure took place during the century. From the beginning of the century, it had become the practice to consult the judges in the exchequer chamber, on cases of special difficulty caused by doubts on obscure questions of law, by incompetence of judicial authorities, or by fear of overmighty subjects.[1] The original purpose of the consultations was to deal with difficulties which had arisen in courts outside the sphere of the common law; but by the time of Henry VI's reign, the common-law judges themselves had abandoned the old practice of joint discussions by the two benches for the solution of difficulties, and had adopted the procedure of adjourning doubtful cases to the exchequer chamber. In some cases the king himself intervened, and ordered the submission of questions to all the judges in the chamber. The judgements given in the chamber were advisory only—though of great weight and authority, they were not legally binding; and no regular records of the chamber's proceedings were kept.[2] In the case in point, it was stated before

---

[1] *V.* the summary of Dr Mary Hemmant's thesis, 'The Exchequer Chamber, being the Assembly of All the Judges of England for Matters in Law', in *Bull. I.H.R.* (1929), VII, 116–119. Dr Hemmant's volume on the exchequer chamber (in the Selden Society's Publications) illuminates this neglected subject.

[2] Hemmant, *loc. cit.* 118; and also the Introduction to her volume in the Selden Society Series, No. 51 (1933). By Coke's time, at least, two modes of procedure were in use, according as the matter emerged from the common-law courts or from other courts. In the first case, the adjournment to the chamber occurred on a motion of the court in which a difference of opinion among the judges had arisen on a given point, and the chamber itself was generally constituted by agreement among the judges. In the second case, the given matter was formally committed to the judges in the exchequer chamber, summoned by the lord chancellor. The case in point was there rehearsed; arguments by both judges and counsel followed; and a decision was given by a majority of the judges. Of the hundred-odd cases selected from the *Year Books* for the purpose of the present study, eleven are cases in the exchequer chamber, and are all of a higher grade of constitutional interest than most of the others.

the judges in the exchequer chamber that a certain J. B. of London had been indicted of trespass and convicted. His counsel, however, showed that the indictment had described him as 'servant', and claimed that under the statute this 'addition' was invalid.[1] All the judges agreed that this claim was justified, and they upheld it. This formality of stating the proper 'addition' in writs for actions which might result in a sentence of outlawry was of considerable importance in safe-guarding the liberty of the individual by preventing fictitious and fraudulent indictments.[2] The discussion of the case by some of the judges has, therefore, a more than ordinary interest. Choke, J., argued the case on the basis of the analogy provided by the statute of safe-conducts. He said that that statute ordered the name of the ship's master and the number of his sailors to be specified in the text of all safe-conducts,[3] and authorised the invalidation of any such licences which omitted those particulars. But many safe-conducts, he pointed out, were in fact issued, even at that date, without those particulars, and yet were not held to be invalid. Apparently the statute had origin-

[1] The statute of additions (Stat. 1 Henry V, c. 5) had provided that in every personal action, appeal, or indictment in which the exigent might be awarded, the addition of the defendant's estate, degree, or mystery, of his town, hamlet, or place, and of his country should be made to his name in the given writ, abatement of which should be allowed by exception of the parties.

[2] Cf. the various statutes made to avoid, among other objects, the bringing of indictments of treasons and felonies alleged in non-existent places: *e.g.* Stat. 7 Henry V, c. 1; Stat. 9 Henry V, c. 1; Stat. 18 Henry VI, c. 12. Cf. also Marowe's remarks on additions, in his Reading, *De Pace Terre* (Putnam, *Early Treatises*, 384–385): 'Et vncore', he says, 'al comen leie home couient de auer done addicions al partie en presentementes, mez ceo fut lou lendite auoit vne nome de dignitie come de Duke, Erle, vicount, count, evesque, chiualer ou seriaunt de le leie, quar toutz ceux nomez sount nomez de dignite et fait par creacion. Mez autrement fut de Barons, Banerrettes, esquyers; quar tulx hommez de dignitie ne fueront faitz par creacion et issint al comen leie home ne fut tenuz doner a eux addicion pur cause de loure dignite. Mes si home soit (un homme qui demeure) en Irelande, il ne couient de auer tile addicion par cest nome et vncore bone quar il nest tenuz de vener a notre parlement. Mes si tile presentment soit fait de vne countie en Scot-lande, la il couient de doner a luy tile addicion ou autrement est voide, come de le vicount de Angivis (Angus).'

[3] Stat. 15 Henry VI, c. 3. It provided that in all safe-conducts to be granted henceforth to any person or persons, the names of the ships and of the masters, and the numbers of the mariners, and the portage of the ships, were to be stated in the text of the licences.

ally been made in order to restrain the issue of safe-conducts in general and unspecific terms; but it was not, at the time he was speaking, considered to be a restraint on the king himself. The reason for this view was, according to some people, that the statute itself was in the affirmative, and therefore the king could either observe its requirements or not, as he pleased. On the other hand, if the statute had been in negative terms, the king would have had no option but to enforce it. So in the case then before the court, the indictment had been brought at the suit of the king, and since the statute of additions bound him no more than the statute of safe-conducts, the writ might include the addition or not, at the king's good pleasure.[1]

This important distinction between statutes in the affirmative and in the negative was not questioned by the other judges, but it was not held sufficient ground to decide the case. Illingworth, CB., denied the accuracy of the analogy which Choke had drawn. The two statutes, he held, were not similar; for one of them affected the king only, and this certainly was enforceable at the king's pleasure; since no man was thereby injured, he could apply either his prerogative or the 'especial law' of the statute. But when a law affected one of his subjects—were it common law, or a statute such as the statute of additions—the king had no choice but to enforce it. For such a law was to the advantage of every man, and the king could not defeat a common right.[2] Danby, CJCP., followed up this argument with the further point that an 'addition' was every man's inheritance as much as any other common law, which the king could defeat only with the authority of parliament. All the justices thereupon agreed that the addition must appear in writs at the suit of the king as in those of others, in actions which might lead to outlawry. Nevertheless, Markham, CJKB., was not quite satisfied, and deemed it best to make sure by a 'melius inquirendo par le roy'.

These distinctions between statutes in the affirmative and in the negative, and between laws which concerned the king only

---

[1] *Y.B.* 5 *Edward IV*, Pas. fo. 32–34 (App. no. 46).   [2] *Ibid.*

and those of which every man had the advantage—together
with the assumption that the king was entitled to choose whether
or not the former kind in each of these two classes of statutes was
to be operative—confirm the opinion that the modern doctrine
of the absolute authority of statutes does not appear until the
very end of the fifteenth century.[1] Choke's view that the king
had a discretionary power in applying or not applying statutes
in the affirmative seems to raise a question of very considerable
significance; for even a cursory survey of the statute book shows
that the great majority of the enactments therein were not expressed in the negative. Of that majority, doubtless most could
be construed as conferring advantage upon every liege man;
but the residue, if understood to be operative or not at the king's
choice, must have left a wider scope for the exercise of the royal
discretion than can be readily appreciated. If the king could
choose to use or not to use, to apply or not to apply, statutes
which were in the affirmative and did not affect common right,
or even only if a number of those learned in the law thought he
had such discretionary power, it may be necessary to modify
our view of the relation of the king to statute-law during the
period. We may discern a greater trust in the expediency of
leaving it to the king to determine what was convenient for
public policy to enforce and what not, and a greater reluctance
to conceive of the king's discretion as being curtailed by any
rules other than those of the common law, than the surface of
the statute book would suggest.

The distinction between courts of record and courts not of
record is an ancient one, and was derived from the king's
assertion that his own word was incontestable in all that had
taken place in his presence, and from his communication of
that privilege to his own courts.[2] A fifteenth-century version of

---

[1] Cf. Allen, *Law in the Making*, 263. On the whole subject of statutory law in the
early fourteenth century, *v.* Plucknett, *Statutes and their Interpretation in the Fourteenth
Century.* Cf. also E. F. Jacob, 'Sir John Fortescue and the Law of Nature', *loc. cit.*
(*V.* Chapter III, *infra*, for the whole subject; and for affirmative and negative statutes,
v. especially § 3 (ii).)   [2] Pollock and Maitland, *Hist. Eng. Law*, II, 669.

an aspect of this prerogative can be inferred from a rather obscure case of which a brief and corrupt text is given in the black-letter edition of the *Year Books*. The case was on a writ of trespass by chattels seized, and apparently arose from the king's having granted away a gift the original validity of which was questioned. Choke—then still a serjeant—said in argument that nothing could vest in the king nor anything pass from ('du') the king without matter of record; and he insisted that no feoffment to the king was valid before enrolment of record. Danvers, J., demurred; and the court admitted that if an act of feoffment to the king were made and delivered to him in the exchequer or otherwise 'a son coffre', the right to the land was then in the king, even if the act had not yet been enrolled, and that the same applied to gifts. Furthermore, it was common course that when a man enfeoffed another for a term of life or of years or in tail, with the remainder to the king, the remainder was then in the king; and so if the king gave a man something, and that man took it by the king's command, the act of seizure was good and justifiable. 'Quod nota'—as the reporter very naturally observed.

Choke contradicted this latter admission. Nothing, he said, could pass out of the king except by a written matter of record; for all that the king did was (must be?) of record, just as were the judges' acts. They, for instance, could not command a man to arrest anyone by law for surety of the peace outside of their presence, without matter of record: to wit, a writ or warrant whereby they were of record; and so of the king, because he could not order an officer to arrest anyone outside his presence, without writ or warrant.[1]

The difficulties of understanding this case are increased by the fact that as reported it is left undecided, and the question whether or not enrolment was essential for the validity of feoffments or gifts to the king is left undetermined. But a few

---

[1] *Y.B.* 37 *Henry VI*, Mich. pl. 20 (App. no. 37). Choke's reply is obscured by the corruption of the text printed in the black-letter edition.

years later, Markham ruled that enrolment of record was necessary for the validity of acts of feoffment;[1] and letters patent were themselves of record.[2]

Among the remarkable reports of formal and informal discussions among the judges, during the early months of Henry VII's reign—reports which appear in the *Year Book* for the Michaelmas term of the first year—there occur two doctrines relating to the prerogative which deserve mention here.[3]

Firstly, a point was discussed by the justices in the exchequer chamber—arising out of the larger question of the proper procedure for the annulment of certain attainders—what was to be done about the awkward fact that Henry Tudor himself was an attainted person.[4] The judges escaped the difficulty by agreeing that the king was discharged of any attainder *ipso facto*, on taking upon himself to reign and be king. Townsend, J., recollected that Henry VI, in the time of his restoration, had held his parliaments, although he had been an attainted person whose attainder had not been reversed. But all the other justices said that he never had been attainted—that he had only been disabled of his crown, kingdom, dignity, lands, and tenements; and that when he recovered the crown, all that disablement was *ipso facto* void. The king could relieve himself of his disability, and hence there was no need for an act to reverse the attainder.

So among the king's prerogatives must be reckoned the not inconsiderable one that when he put on his crown with intent to reign, he put off his attainted past.[5]

Secondly, unique in all the *Year Books* is a report of a discussion among the justices and bishops in the parliament chamber—a report which comes from the Hilary term of this same year; and among other matters, illustrates one of the most effective

---

[1] *Y.B.* 7 Edward IV, Mich. pl. 11 (App. no. 49).

[2] *Y.B.* 34 Henry VI, Mich. pl. 16 (App. no. 31).

[3] These reports were briefly used by Vinogradoff in his paper, 'Constitutional History and the *Year Books*', *Collected Papers*, I, 194–196. It is hoped to deal with them more fully elsewhere.

[4] *Y.B.* 1 Henry VII, Mich. pl. 5 (App. no. 74).

[5] Cf. *supra*, p. 35.

of the weapons in the king's armoury of prerogatives. This weapon was the principle that the pope could not act in derogation of the king and his crown.[1]

On the 4th of February, 1486, the chancellor demanded of the justices in the parliament chamber what was to be done about the excommunication of English subjects by order of the pope on the grounds that they had seized alum from Florentines in England. The judges thought that when merchandise came into the country by the king's safe-conduct, the king ought to protect the merchants from spoliation—especially by his own subjects. Hussey, CJKB., however, apparently scented here more of Rome than was to his taste; and he recalled that, in the time of Edward IV, a legate had come to Calais and had asked the king for his protection in order to come into the land, and that in full council, before the lords and the justices, the question of what was to be done about it had been debated. It had been resolved that if the legate would swear that he was carrying with him nothing that would be in derogation of the king and his crown, he should have permission to come; but that otherwise he should not. And besides all this, alum was a very necessary commodity in the cloth-making industry, which could not be carried on without it.

The chief justice pursued the theme of less popery, and affirmed that in the days of Edward I, when the pope wrote to the king and said that Scotland was a fief of his, the king had replied that in the temporality he had no one over him, and that he was immediate of God; and the barons of England had written likewise.

The bishop of London joined in the reminiscences, and recalled that in the time of Henry VI, when papal letters arrived

[1] Cf. *Rot. Parl.* III, 419, no. 27: 'Item, quamvis Corona regni Anglie, et Jura ejusdem Corone, ipsumque Regnum, fuerint ab omni tempore retroacto adeo libera quod Dominus Summus Pontifex, nec aliquis alius extra Regnum ipsum, se intromittere debeat de eisdem', nevertheless Richard had supplicated the pope to confirm statutes, etc. 'Que omnia contra coronam et Dignitatem Regiam, ac contra Statuta et Libertates dicti Regni tendere dinoscuntur.'

in derogation of the king, and the lords spiritual dared not speak of it, he had seen Humphrey, duke of Gloucester, take the letters and throw them in the fire; and they were burnt. This story of Gloucester's audacity apparently heartened the justices; and the conclusion of the discussion, as reported, states that they wished to be advised as to whether the alum should be returned or not. But at least there was agreement that the pope could not lawfully be allowed to act in derogation of the king and his crown.[1]

The definition of prerogatives by judicial process, however, might be double-edged. It might, as in the foregoing cases, serve to determine what the prerogatives were; or it might, as in other cases, serve to declare what they were not. A considerable and probably growing body of cases in the reports have the effect of defining what the king might not lawfully do. His procedural privileges, for example, were restricted; his actions were in some particulars restrained by act of parliament, and his powers of dispensation were curtailed; his officers could not do anything they liked in his name; he was unable to defeat common law and right; he was bound by his predecessor's judicial acts; and above all, he could not grant away his prerogatives to other persons. A selection of the cases which illustrate these important points are worth mentioning in a little more detail.

We have noted above that counsel for the king, unlike others, could alter the original statement of complaint in real actions, but, like others, could not come to another issue in the course of pleading—unless in consequence of fresh findings by an inquisition on the facts.[2] We have seen, too, that all the king

---

[1] The report (*Y.B.* 1 *Henry VII*, Hil. pl. 10) is given in full in Appendix no. 77, *infra*.—In a case of 'quare impedit' between the king and the bishop of St David's (*Y.B.* 11 *Henry IV*, Mich. pl. 67, Pas. pl. 10, Trin. pl. 18 (App. no. 19 (i)), in which the king sought to oust the bishop from a prebend which he held by papal dispensation in the church of Salisbury (*v.* Maitland, *Canon Law*, 69–70), two justices took opposite views of what the pope could do. Thirning, J., said that the grant of the Apostle could not change the law; whereas Hankford, J., declared that the pope could do everything.   [2] *V. supra*, p. 45.

did was as incontrovertible as any record of the high courts; but an escheator who seized lands to the king on the strength of the findings of an inquisition alone was guilty of an unlawful act.[1] However convenient it may have been, the king could not grant to anyone cognizance of all pleas, nor could he create prescriptive rights or ancient demesne.[2] Even if statutes framed in affirmative words were operative at the king's discretion, statutes in the negative were not.[3] The king, moreover, could not defeat statutory provisions by the authority of his letters patent; and a statute could be successfully pleaded against the king himself. Thus, when granting letters of protection, it was held that he must abide by the terms of statute 13 Richard II, c. 16; and the courts would disallow such letters if they failed to observe those terms. No such protection was allowable if its effect were to deprive a man of his due inheritance and common right.[4]

The king's officers could not claim the king's authority for all and sundry of their actions in the king's name. Thus, if a fifteenth were exacted tortiously by a collector, the king derived no title to the money from the exaction.[5] If a commissioner appointed by the king to treat with certain people in fact consulted others, he did so without warrant or authority.[6] But a king's officer alone—bailiff, sheriff, escheator, or the like—was perhaps entitled to plead the authority of the king for an act otherwise unlawful committed by the king's command.[7]

---

[1] *Y.B. 7 Edward IV*, Mich. pl. 11 (App. no. 49).

[2] *Y.B. 37 Henry VI*, Trin. pl. 3 (App. no. 40). (Cf. Vinogradoff, *Collected Papers*, I, 202.)

[3] *V. supra*, pp. 46–49.

[4] *Y.B. 11 Henry IV*, Mich. pl. 17 (App. no. 16). (Cf. Vinogradoff, *Collected Papers*, I, 204; and *Y.B. 39 Henry VI*, Hil. pl. 3 (App. no. 42).) Cf. *infra*, pp. 279–283.

[5] *V.* the interesting case of the abbot of Glastonbury *versus* a purveyor, in *Y.B. 11 Henry IV*, Mich. pl. 66 (App. no. 18 (i)). The abbot alleged that, in the time of Edward III, a certain grant of a fifteenth by the 'commonalty of the county of Somerset' had been improperly assessed; and that this fact had led to the appointment of a commission to ascertain and to re-assess the contributions of the various vills. The abbot of that day had found it convenient to consult this commission with respect to readjusting the assessment of the lands of his abbey, for the purpose of the payment of tenths. But now the abbot had suffered distraint at the hands of the collector of the fifteenth voted in the parliament of 1407.

[6] *Ibid.* (iii).   [7] *Y.B. 39 Henry VI*, Mich. pl. 21 (App. no. 41).

Though it was admitted that the king, in certain cases, had a discretionary power to apply or not to apply statutes, he could not, however, dispense with common right, nor change common law on his own authority. To make such changes, the co-operation of parliament was deemed necessary in law. He could not, for instance, by his charter make tenements devisable where they had not been devisable before, without parliament.[1] A grant by letters patent could not change the common law.[2]

Even if the king had made a county palatine without parliament, nevertheless he could not without parliament deprive his liege man of common right.[3] Statutes which affirmed the inheritance or the advantage of every liege man were not—as we have noted—considered to be at the choice of the king. A confirmation by parliament to the crown of all its ancient inheritance was not to be construed to the prejudice of the rights of individual subjects.[4]

The principle that the king was bound by his predecessor's judicial acts—even if his predecessor's title to the crown were questionable—was admitted by the court in 1470, in Bagot's case.[5] In this case, Henry Bagot and W. Swyrenden (who died during the trial) brought an action of novel disseisin against a certain Thomas Ive, who had disseised them of the offices of clerks to the hanaper. The case turned on the question whether Bagot, who had been born in France, and could show letters of denizenship only in the name of Henry, late usurper of the crown of England, was entitled to bring the action at all. Bagot's counsel urged that these letters were good. For Henry had been

---

[1] 49 *Lib. Assisarum*, pl. 8 (App. no. 10).
[2] *Y.B.* 14 *Henry IV*, Mich. pl. 6. Cf. Brooke's *Abridgement*, sub-tit. 'Prerogative', no. 18 (App. no. 20).
[3] *Y.B.* 32 *Henry VI*, Hil. pl. 13 (App. no. 29): a case in the exchequer chamber, involving the question of the authority of the king's writs in the counties palatine.— The old view of the county palatine of Durham as being of royal creation—herein held by Fortescue—has been abandoned by Dr Lapsley (*The County Palatine of Durham*, 12–30).
[4] *Y.B.* 1 *Henry VII*, Hil. pl. 25 (App. no. 78).
[5] *Y.B.* 9 *Edward IV*, Pas. pl. 2, pl. 20; Trin. pl. 3 (App. no. 53). (Cf. Vinogradoff, *Collected Papers*, I, 199.)

the king in possession; and it was necessary that the realm should
have a king under whom the laws could be upheld and maintained. The judicial act of the king by usurpation must bind
the king *de jure*. The king *de jure* had the advantage of forfeitures, etc., which had been made to the king *de facto*, and of
all the judicial acts made in the interests of the crown. Besides,
Henry had not been merely a usurper, for the crown had been
entailed upon him by parliament.

Some of the serjeants and apprentices opposed these arguments. The letters, they said, were void, because otherwise the
king would be put in a worse position than any common person,
since a regressor was not bound by the acts of his disseisor.[1]
Moreover, the denizenship was to the disadvantage of the king,
because it was unreasonable that an alien should be denizened
against the king's will; and twenty thousand Frenchmen might
have received letters of denizenship. The wording of the letters
was faulty, also; and the evidence of Bagot's seisin of the office
itself was questionable.[2]

But after long debates and adjournments, the judges said that
they had communicated with the justices of the common pleas,
and that it seemed to them none of these objections sufficed to
defeat the plaintiff's case; and hence that they adjudged him the
recovery, etc. They thus vindicated the continuity of legal right
from one reign to another.[3]

Whatever other restrictions there were on the king's prerogatives—and no doubt many others could be illustrated from
the *Year Books*—there is one more (if, indeed, it can properly

---

[1] The real-property analogy to kingship is again apparent.

[2] *Y.B. loc. cit.* An interesting allusion to the manner of appointment to the offices
of the courts occurs in the course of the trial (fo. 5 (App. no. 53 (iv))).

[3] *Ibid.* (App. no. 53 (v)). It is noticeable that Vinogradoff speaks of this case
(*loc. cit.*) as illustrating the principle of the 'continuity of law'. I adopt a suggestion
made to me by Dr Lapsley, to the effect that Vinogradoff was here thinking of the
continuity of 'Recht'; and that in the writing of the passage, this word got turned
into the English word 'law'—whereas the context needs the word 'right' in order
to be relevant to the case. Cf. *Y.B.* 1 *Henry VII*, Hil. pl. 5 (App. no. 76), wherein
all the justices save two are found upholding assignments on collectors of tenths
made by Richard III, notwithstanding the fact that he had died before part of
them fell due.

be called a restriction) which must be mentioned. This one arose from the question whether he could lawfully alienate or delegate the prerogatives themselves.

Bracton, two centuries before the middle of our period, set out the official doctrine on this matter: 'Ea vero,' he said, 'quae iurisdictionis sunt et pacis, et ea quae sunt iusticiae et paci annexa, ad nullum pertinent nisi tantum ad coronam et dignitatem regiam. Nec a corona separari poterunt cum faciant ipsam coronam. Est enim corona facere iusticiam et iudicium et tenere pacem et sine quibus corona consistere non poterit nec tenere.'[1] In brief, it would seem a fair statement of Bracton's view to say that the rights of the crown could not be alienated, although, by the king's especial grace, some of them could be delegated.

Maitland was inclined to think that Bracton was here representing the ideal of the king's court, rather than the actual rule seriously applied;[2] but we have good reason to suppose that at any rate something very like that rule was being acted upon, not only in Bracton's day, but many years previously.[3] It was the theory which lay behind the whole of the famous 'Quo Warranto' proceedings; and whether we hold that the statutes of 1290 'did not represent any departure from Edward's original intentions in those proceedings',[4] or whether we hold that they 'constitute a retreat from his original position',[5] or whether we see in them merely a definition of what had been doubtful in the practical application of the theory, makes very little difference to the fundamental fact that such was the official doctrine of the royal courts.

Without pursuing the topic into all its ramifications, we can see that the principle was being acted upon in the courts during our period. The king could not lawfully grant away his own

---

[1] *De Legibus*, fo. 55, ed. Woodbine, II, 167.

[2] Pollock and Maitland, *Hist. Eng. Law*, I, 528–529, 572.—Holdsworth (*Hist. Eng. Law.* 88–89) adopts the same attitude.

[3] *V.* especially H. M. Cam, 'The "Quo Warranto" Proceedings under Edward I', *History* (July 1926), x, 143–148; and cf. G. T. Lapsley, 'John de Warenne and the "Quo Warranto" Proceedings in 1279', *Cambridge Historical Journal* (1927), 110–132.

[4] Cam, *loc. cit.* 144.   [5] Lapsley, *loc. cit.* 132.

prerogatives to another and common person.[1] 'That which is a prerogative of the king', said Yelverton, J., before all the justices in the exchequer chamber (*nem. con.*), 'he cannot dismember from the king's person.'[2] The royal prerogatives must be deemed intact in the king's person and in the king's person alone.[3] The courts would attack claims to exercise 'regalem potestatem'.[4] The king could not grant away his prerogative.[5] His patents in any grant would be interpreted strictly, and favourably to him;[6] and there were some things he could not grant without the assent of parliament, whilst in all his grants he was bound by previous parliamentary enactments.[7]

---

[1] *Y.B.* 14 *Henry IV*, Mich. pl. 6. Cf. Brooke's *Abridgement*, sub-tit. 'Prerogative', no. 18 (App. no. 20).

[2] *Y.B.* 5 *Edward IV*, Mich. fo. 118–123 (App. no. 48). The case was on a petition of right, sued against the king by the abbot of Leicester, in respect of a corrody in the abbey, which it was contended had not been involved in the forfeiture to the crown of the advowson of the abbey itself, incurred at the time of the forfeiture of Simon de Montfort, 'que fuit en temps le roy Henry le iij et leva guerre enconter le Roy'.

[3] Bishop Stafford declared, in his parliamentary address of 1397 (*Adam of Usk's Chronicon*, 9): 'quod potestas regis esset sibi unica et solida et quod eam tollentes vel insidiantes pena legis essent condigni.'

[4] *V. Y.B.* 16 *Henry VII*, Trin. pl. 17 (App. no. 107): The abbot of Battle claimed cognisance in a certain plea, on the grounds of a charter of William the Conqueror granting 'regalem potestatem'. Counsel objected to the charter on many grounds, but stressed in particular the fact that it had not been allowed before justices in eyre, time out of memory; and it was disallowed. The principles of the treatment of such claims had been stated in general terms by Hussey, C.J., and all the court, in *Y.B.* 10 *Henry VII*, Hil. pl. 6 (App. no. 95). Ancient grants, it was ruled, would be taken according to ancient allowance. If the king had granted to another 'omnia jura sua regalia', or had used in a grant such terms as 'as free as tongue can speak', or 'as heart can think', such grants would not be taken according to the purport of their words, but according to ancient allowance. There was a diversity between the allowance of a grant in 'Quo Warranto' proceedings, and the allowance thereof in some other proceedings of a royal court. If a grant had been allowed in the former, the king was bound; but if a grant had been allowed in the latter, it was at the suit of the king to try the franchise.

[5] *Y.B.* 20 *Henry VII*, Mich. pl. 17 (App. no. 108).

[6] *Y.B.* 21 *Henry VII*, Hil. pl. 6 (App. no. 111).

[7] *Y.B.* 1 *Henry VII*, Trin. pl. 1 (App. no. 79); and *Y.B.* 10 *Henry VII*, Mich. pl. 20 (App. no. 93). *V. infra*, Chapter III § 4 (iv *b*), for further on these points. Grants without a clause *non obstante* might sometimes be void (*v. Y.B.* 2 *Henry VII*, Mich. pl. 20 (App. no. 80); and *infra, loc. cit.*). The king could still grant a leet, but only according to custom; and such a jurisdiction would not include statutory felonies (*v. Y.B.* 6 *Henry VII*, Trin. pl. 4 (App. no. 86)). But he could grant in what he did not yet possess, such as an exemption from a fifteenth to be granted in the next parliament (*v. ibid.*). There was some doubt whether he could change the services by which land was held of him (*v. Y.B.* 10 *Henry VII*, Pas. pl. 26 (App. no. 98)).

But important as was the mass of these negative definitions of the king's prerogatives or rights, they must not obscure the much greater importance of the question whether there was understood to be any limit to or control of the king's Prerogative or authority. If we consult the strictly legal sources of the time, we shall probably be hard put to it to find any serious evidence for the belief that the law knew of any binding restrictions on the king, other than those which could be brought within the list of legally defined prerogatives, or under the rubric of indefeasibility of common law and right.

When, however, we turn to other categories of opinion, we sometimes find expressions of other conceptions of the king's position. We notice Henry IV's own dispatch of a letter to Pope Alexander V, in which he avers that without the assent of the nobles and estates of his realm assembled in his parliament, no statutes or ordinances previously made could be revoked or changed.[1] We can see the lords of the council, in 1427, sternly rebuking Gloucester for his pretentious claims to the regency, and saying finally that 'we fond youre saide desire nought caused nor grounded in precident, nor in ye lawe of ye land; ye whiche ye king yat ded ys, in hys lyf ne migzt by his last will nor otherwyse altre, change nor abroge, with oute yassent of ye thre Estates, nor committe nor graunte to any persone, governaunce or rule of yis lande lenger yanne he lyved....'[2] To Philip de Commynes it seemed that it took the king of England a long time to raise money: for he did not do that without assembling parliament, 'qui vault autant come les trois Etats'.[3]

Above all, in the political writings of Sir John Fortescue we read that 'in the kingdom of England, the kings do not make

---

[1] *B.M. MSS.*, *Harleian* 431, fo. 42—quoted by E. F. Jacob, in *Bull. J.R.L.* xv, 379. (Cf. Chapter II, p. 117, *infra*.) Moreover, probably more ought to be made than has been made of the fact that the royal response to a petition of 1348 specifically stated (*Rot. Parl.* II, 203): 'Qe les Leis eues et usees en temps passeez, ne le Proces d'icelle usez cea en arere, ne se purront changer saunz ent faire novel Estatut.' Cf. Lodge and Thornton, *op. cit.* 141. [2] *Rot. Parl.* IV, 326.
[3] *Mémoires*, I, 266: 'Mais les choses y sont longues, car le roy ne peult entreprendre une telle oeuvre sans assembler son parlement....'

laws nor impose subsidies on their subjects without the consent
of the three estates of their kingdom'.[1] We even read that the
king of England '*cannot* at his pleasure change the laws of his
kingdom'; that 'the statutes of England are established not only
by the prince's will but by the assent of the whole kingdom';
and that 'the laws of England sanction no such maxim as
"Quod principi placuit legis vigorem habet"'. We learn, too,
that 'the king of England does not by himself or his ministers
impose on his subjects any tallage or burden, nor change their
laws nor make new ones, without the express consent or concession of his whole kingdom in his parliament'.[2]

We look in vain, in these texts, for any suggestion that the
king's authority was controlled. But it is clearly asserted that
his authority was limited. It was limited because he did not or
lawfully could not (precisely which is not plain) act in certain
ways, without the assent of some body variously known as his
parliament or as the estates of his realm. No assertion is made,
however, that this body or any other either did or could lawfully
control the king, if in fact he were to act in any of those ways.
Nevertheless, to limit by assent is a great power. Who or what,
then, were these 'estates' or 'parliament', that their assent
should be necessary even to the king himself? The answer to
this question is the subject of the next chapter; but whatever
that answer may be, clearly the thought of the fifteenth century
was in harmony with the ideas of the preceding centuries in one
respect at least. The typical mediaeval theorists found what we
should call sovereignty not in the king but in the law, and the
fifteenth century did not depart from this view. The king was
below the law: he could not at his own pleasure defeat common
law and right. But all his legislation and his taxation must
necessarily prejudice someone's rights; and to do that lawfully,
the assent of those whose rights were to be infringed must be

---

[1] *De Natura*, I, xvi.
[2] *De Laudibus*, ix, xviii, xxxiv, xxxvi.· (For a discussion of Fortescue's political
theory, *v.* Chapter IV, *infra.*)

secured. That assent could conveniently be got in parliament, and it had to be so obtained. No other assent could make lawful that which was unlawful.

The estate of king, in the fifteenth century, was thus conceived to be inseparable from the king's own person. To him belonged lordship and power, rule and empire, and all the honour and highness of that estate; the divine favour on him was displayed by marvellous healing powers; to him were given will, liberty, and grace, that the laws might be upheld and the peace maintained. The king was indispensable; but the rules by which he succeeded to his estate were not precise. In so far as the kingdom was real property, it seemed that he inherited it in much the same way that land was commonly inherited; in as much as the kingship was an office, he was called to occupy it by divine vocation, and God might make His choice known through the voice of 'the nobles and estates'. For the kingship was office, and in accepting it, the king was bound to discharge the duties appertaining to it. He must do justice and defend his people. He should act with the advice of wise counsellors.

He might and did enjoy his privileges, which were great and many. But he could not himself decide where his own privileges ended, and those of others began. He must leave that to his judges to determine in proper form. For the due performance of his duties he wielded great power with unquestioned authority —power so great that no one could say what the king could not do if he tried, so long as he kept within the law; authority coming to him from above, and from below as well; power great enough to maintain the rights and to protect the lives of his people; authority by the will of God, and by the will of his people to be subject to him. But all-powerful he was not; he could neither break nor make the law. To impose upon his people new laws, and to exact from them financial aid for his own activities, he was dependent upon the consent of his very subjects. Before he might make law that which was not law, and before he might fill his exchequer with taxes, it was necessary that he should have the authority of his people, in his own high court of parliament assembled. Otherwise, his law-making and his levying ought to be, might be, and very likely would be, in vain.

EXCURSUS I

FORTESCUE'S ARGUMENTS ON THE RIGHT OF WOMEN TO SUCCEED TO THE CROWN

An account has been given above, in the text, of those portions of Fortescue's works which may be considered illustrative of a general theory of succession. Much of his writing on this theme, however, is special pleading against the right of women to succeed to the crown; and some of his arguments in his minor tracts are interesting, especially as he himself supplied the refutation of most of them. These arguments are of two general types: those which support a theory of the universal ineligibility of women to succeed to the throne, and those which are directed against the specific claims of the house of York.

The succession of women to the throne, he argues, is uncustomary, inconvenient, and unlawful. Women, husbands claiming on pretext of their wives' titles, and children claiming through their mothers, have always been excluded from the succession by the law and custom of England.[1] The inconveniences of a woman's right to or possession of the throne were numerous: co-heiresses would seek to divide the realm; if the woman succeeding were unmarried or a widow, endless trouble would ensue from hopeful suitors; she might marry a man vile in race and of the lowest degree of virtue, or a foreigner; her

---

[1] *De Titulo Edwardi Marchiae*, 78; *Defensio Juris Domus Lancastriae*, 511. The statement has been true only when no heir in the direct male line has been available. Succession through females was contemplated when Mortimer was recognised as heir, and when Edward III laid claim to the throne of France. For the whole subject, *v.* Lapsley, 'The Parliamentary Title of Henry IV', Part II, *loc. cit.* 594–595.

daughters' husbands would be rivals; female caprice would rule the realm. No woman could be anointed in the hands, and therefore she could not expect to exercise the thaumaturgical powers of a king; nor could she bear the sword, nor be fitted to act as a judge in criminal causes.[1] Besides, it was unlawful for women to rule over men; God had made a law that women should not have power directly from Him over man, and so be without a sovereign on earth. God's word to females was: 'Eris sub potestate viri et ipse dominabitur tui.'[2]

But when he came to refute these contentions, Fortescue discovered doubts on this doctrine of the submission of all women to men. The topic ought, he said, to be treated by learned men, and not by those of his simpleness;[3] moreover, in any case the woman was always in fact subject to one man: the pope; so even the female ruler always did have an earthly sovereign.[4]

His second type of argument disparaged the precedents and claims put forward by the Yorkists. He asserted that Philippa, daughter of Lionel, duke of Clarence, through whom the Yorkists claimed, was illegitimate. The chronicles, it was pointed out, made no mention of Lionel's issue; Philippa had not borne his arms; he would not have allowed a legitimate daughter of his to marry the attainted Mortimer; indeed she had been begotten by Sir James of Audeley, during Lionel's absence.[5] But, in the refutation of this part of the case against York, the

[1] *De Titulo*, 80–81; *Defensio*, 513; *Of the Title of the House of York*, 498. It is generally held that no king after Henry IV sat in the king's bench as a judge (*v.* Potter, *Introduction to English Legal History*, 57). But according to Stow (*Annals*, 416), Edward IV sat in the king's bench for three days together, in open court, to understand how the laws were executed. Perhaps he was influenced by Fortescue's advice to the prince, in the *De Laudibus*. Moreover, there is good reason to suppose that he actually sat in person for several days at least in the parliament of 1461 (*v. Fane Fragment*, ed. Dunham).

[2] *Ibid.*   [3] *Declaracion*, 532.

[4] *Ibid.* 531–535: 'And therfor Christe is Kinge of all kinges and lord of all the worlde, havynge in the handes of the Pope his Vicare, both swerdes, for which he is called Rex et Sacerdos, and compellith all princes as well spirituell as temporell to come to his gret councilles. By whiche matiers and by many moo...it may undoubtedly appere that ther is now noo kingdome in the erthe of Cristen men of which the Kynge is not subjecte also welle in temporaltes as spirituelles' (p. 535).

[5] *De Titulo*, 82; *Defensio*, 499, 517.

The Estate of King

discovery of a convenient exchequer account sufficed to defeat this assertion.[1]

The precedents cited by Yorkists were, he contended, unsatisfactory. Edward the Confessor, and not Margaret of Scotland, wife of King Malcolm, succeeded Edmund Ironside; Stephen, not Matilda, succeeded Henry I;[2] Henry II succeeded, not because of his mother's title, but by consent of the whole realm.[3] But, for the purposes of refutation, it was discovered that Margaret's claim had been invalid, not because she was a woman, but because Edgar Atheling was still alive, and Edmund was a bastard. New chronicles had been searched, and had shown that Stephen had not been elected, and that Henry II had claimed the crown before election, and that the settlement then made had not been by authority of parliament but had been a private treaty. Furthermore, he denied ever having cited the Edmund Crouchback legend, and denied its truth; and when now he examined Henry V's claim to the throne of France, he understood why that king's council had needed to repudiate the right of women to succeed.[4]

EXCURSUS II

THE DOCTRINE OF PRESCRIPTION AND THE SUCCESSION

The most devastating argument Fortescue made against the Yorkist claim was surely that drawn from Lancastrian prescription. His retractation provided no answer to it, although the argument appears to be not invulnerable.

It was indubitable, he wrote, that a king reigns duly by God, if he is duly anointed, crowned, and sceptred according to the law and custom of the realm, in conformity with the law of God and of the Church. Neither the inhabitants of England nor of any

---

[1] *Declaracion*, 536.   [2] *De Titulo*, 79–80.
[3] *Defensio*, 511.   [4] *Declaracion*, 523–530, 536.

other kingdom were allowed to transfer the realm from a duly constituted king reigning according to law and custom, to another.[1] Every dynasty, affirmed St Augustine, was just, if it enjoyed divine and ecclesiastical approval, the consent of the people, and possession through a long period. The house of Lancaster had enjoyed all these advantages.[2] Any right that the Yorkists may have had was defeated by sixty years' prescription, had been renounced and abjured, and was barred by matters of record. Henry IV had been anointed and crowned king of England by the whole assent and will of all the land, no man objecting, 'after the common law used in all the world'.[3]

The prescriptive right of the house of Lancaster was indeed undeniable. But was prescription a valid title to the throne? Fortescue seems never to have refuted the argument; but York himself denied its validity,[4] and certainly it can hardly be reconciled with the common law principle that 'nullum tempus occurrit regi'.[5] It must, therefore, have been open to grave objection.

---

[1] *De Titulo*, 86.   [2] *Ibid.* 84; *Defensio*, 501–502.
[3] *Ibid.* 500.   [4] *Rot. Parl.* v, 376. (Cf. *supra*, p. 30.)
[5] Cf. Bracton, *De Legibus*, fo. 103 ed. Woodbine, II, 293. 'Item de rebus et libertatibus et dignitatibus, quae pertinent ad dignitatem domini regis et coronam, et in quibus casibus nullum tempus currit contra ipsum.'...

Chapter II

THE NATURE OF PARLIAMENT

The history of parliament is essentially paradoxical. In origin it was of royal creation; in time it came to limit and at last to control the king himself. Born by the expression of the irresistible will of the king, it grew to express the irresistible will of the people. The king's own court it always was, yet it became also a politically representative assembly. The great problem in parliamentary history is to trace and explain these paradoxes. Little or nothing which goes very far towards the solution of that problem will be said in this second of the present studies. In some sense our main purpose is the humbler one of illustrating these paradoxes themselves, during one phase of their growth. We shall not be very much concerned with what parliament in fact *did* during the fifteenth century, nor to any great extent with its relations to other parts of the governmental system. What we shall try to discuss, in some detail, is how parliament was in fact being *thought of*, as an institution, by the men of the century. We shall be discussing, not so much parliament itself, as parliament's image in men's minds.

Unless some major discoveries remain to be made, we cannot suppose that the fifteenth century witnessed any prominent attempt to examine very closely into the nature of the assembly[1] which by that time had almost, if not quite, come to monopolise the name of 'parliament'.[2] Even Fortescue, the most dis-

---

[1] Cf. Tout, 'Parliament and Public Opinion, 1376–1388', *Collected Papers*, II, 173. He says that only late in the fourteenth century did chroniclers mention parliament; public opinion was as yet uninterested in parliament. But cf. the attention called by John of London to Edward I's parliaments, cited by H. Johnstone in *Camb. Med. Hist.* VII, 407.

[2] An assembly of the lords only on May 3rd, 1429, is called a full parliament in the minutes of the council (*Procs. and Ords.* III, 324); and the same thing occurs again in 1436 (*ibid.* IV, pp. cxvi, 352).

tinguished publicist of the century, was at no pains, so far as we know, to pursue very far such an examination. Indeed the term 'parliament' does not appear in the whole bulk of his writings more than about half a dozen or so times; and in one place he disclaims the possession of any minute knowledge of its structure and composition.[1] Nevertheless, it is obvious enough that at the date when Henry Bolingbroke was led to the throne, parliament had in one sense or another figured prominently in the national life for more than a hundred years. Whatever view is taken of the origins and early history of parliament, no one can doubt that by 1400 the activities in parliaments of successive generations of lords, and knights of the shires, of citizens, burgesses, and officials, had sufficed to diffuse far and wide the notion of parliament as a factor in the government of the country. For long, no doubt, the response of men to the new royal command to come or to send to the parliament was merely acquiescence; for at first there did not seem to be anything very peculiar about it. It was but a parley, a conference; and it did not involve any fresh ideas, and therefore aroused no controversy and no opposition. It was only as the accumulation of practice began, slowly and obscurely, to transform a conference into an institution, that the stock of constitutional ideas required some expansion if they were to cover the manifest facts of governmental life. Men began to be provoked into formulating explicit ideas about the parliamentary phenomenon; and since not all expressed the same ideas, conscious discussion and re-examination of the facts ensued. The general state of ideas about parliament in the fifteenth century may be said to attain this level. They have become conscious. Certain men reveal—usually as *obiter dicta*—ways in which they are thinking of parliament; other individuals express divergent views; and the seeds of future speculation and controversy are sown—to

---

[1] *De Laudibus*, xviii: '...sed plusquam trecentorum electorum hominum quali numero olim Senatus Romanorum regebatur, ipsa edita sunt, ut hii qui parliamenti Anglie formam, convocationis quoque ejus ordinem et modum noverunt, hec distinctius referre norunt.'

ripen in a later century, no doubt; but sowing the seed is an act only antecedent in time, not inferior in value, to that of gathering the fruits.

Interesting in their significance, if not in their substance, are the curious descriptions of parliament by more or less grotesque analogies which were occasionally advanced early in the century. It is good evidence of the existence of speculation as to the nature of parliament, to find people suggesting what parliament seemed to resemble—even if the resemblances themselves were extremely far-fetched. That the permanent ends of social and political institutions have often been served by the wildest superstitions is a commonplace of critical historical investigation. 'From false premises man often arrives at sound conclusions, from a chimerical theory he deduces a salutary practice.'[1] The prevalence of anthropomorphic analogies of the state must be recorded in the fourth of the present studies; and it is unsafe to suppose that the institution of parliament was necessarily built up by wholly rational concepts. Perhaps the so-called myth of the three estates had an influence no less fundamental on the evolution of parliamentarism than have innumerable other myths on other developments in other spheres.[2]

Analogical speculations on the nature of parliament were especially prominent during the Speakership of Sir Arnold Savage in 1401. Probably they were symptoms of Savage's own well-known verbal energy; and doubtless they were inspired by the parliament's hostility to heresy. It is recorded that the commons, in parliament, showed to the king how it seemed to them that 'le fait de parlement' could well be likened to a Mass.[3] The commencement of the parliament, when the archbishop read the epistle and expounded the Bible, was like the commencement of the office. The king's repeated declaration that it was his will that the faith of Holy Church should be sustained and governed as it had been by his progenitors, and

---

[1] Sir James Frazer, *Psyche's Task*, p. vii.
[2] On this subject, *v. infra*, p. 81 *et seq.*   [3] *Rot. Parl.* III, 456.

that the laws should be held and kept in all points, as well by rich as by poor, to the great pleasure of God and comfort of his subjects, seemed like the sacrifice in the Mass to be offered to God by all Christians. Then, at the end of the Mass, it was necessary to say: 'Ite, missa est', and 'Deo gratias'; and at that time it seemed to the commons that they had come to the point when 'Ite, missa est' was the appropriate form of words, and for three reasons all the people ought to say 'Deo gratias'. For God had given them a gracious king, who wished to do justice and was endowed with humanity; moreover, he had destroyed the 'malvoise doctrine' and the sect which was threatening the church; and finally, the lords and commons of the realm and the king were possessed of good and whole hearts towards each other.

Savage sometimes indulged in what to-day sounds like sheer waggery. For on another occasion in the same parliament, he came before the king, and told him that the grandest treasure and wealth of every king was to have the heart of his people—'qar par consequence sil ait le coer, il est verraisemble qil avera ceo qe luy besoigne de leur bons.'[1]

Parliament was said to be not only like the Mass, but also like the Trinity. The circumstances of the violent quarrel between the earl of Rutland and Lord Fitzwalter were probably the reason for the little homily which the commons offered to the king before the 'Ite, missa est' stage had been reached. The estates of the realm (*i.e.* parliament, in this context) could, it was said, well be likened to a Trinity, wherein the members were the person of the king, the lords spiritual and temporal, and the commons. If there were any division among these estates, it would be in great desolation of all the realm—'que dieu defende'.[2]

Occasionally analogies of a lesser degree of piety, but of more intelligibility, appear. As has been mentioned, Fortescue compared parliament with the Roman senate; and this analogy was carried further by Bishop Russell, in the drafts of his parlia-

---

[1] *Ro'. Parl.* III, 456.   [2] *Ibid.* 459.

mentary sermons: 'I see the policie of thys Reme', he wrote, 'in the tyme of holdynge of parliamentes grettly correspondente to the same maner of the Romanes. Thys ys the howse of the senate. The commons have ther apart. And lyke as yn thys house one *tamquam consul* makithe the questions, soo yn the lower house in lyke wyse alle ys directed by the speker *quasi per tribunum*.'[1] But Russell could at times make more pregnant observations than this: 'Notwithstandyng', he said, 'by cause we stonde at thys tyme yn *the place of wor[l]dely policie*, to be persuaded....'[2] Here a more modern note is struck; the idea of parliamentary debate could not be put more succinctly: parliament is the place of worldly policy.[3]

But if we leave the topic of analogies, and attempt to make a survey of notions that were held as to what parliament actually was, account must first be taken of the notion of parliament as a (or the) high court of law. This notion was throughout the century prominent, explicit, and reiterated.

We hardly need remark here that parliament was, in fact, from the first the king's court, and has always remained so. It began as an enforcement of the king's council. 'Habet enim rex', wrote Fleta in the early fourteenth century, 'curiam suam in consilio suo in parliamentis suis.'[4] That parliamentary forms were from the outset those of a court, of a tribunal, is obvious enough. It is no part of our concern here to discuss the judicial functions or curial forms of parliament. But, however familiar the fact must have been, we have to note the comparatively late emergence of a distinct and explicitly formulated *theory* of parliament as the king's high court. As we should indeed expect, the theory followed after—and a good while after—the facts. Even the passage in Fleta was written a little too early to allow

---

[1] *Grants of Edward V*, p. xlv; and *infra*, Excursus VI, p. 174.

[2] *Ibid*. p. liv and *infra* p. 183.

[3] Cf. the verse quoted *infra*, Excursus I. Parliament, the poet says, is ordained to amend that which is amiss.

[4] Cf. the expression in 1425: 'in ejus consilio in parliamento' (*Rot. Parl.* IV, 299); and in 1434: 'in domo consilii parliamenti' (*Procs. and Ords.* IV, 213).

of the expression of a theoretically differentiated notion of parliament as a court. Parliament itself is not called a court: the king's court is said to be held in his parliament. Indeed, it is hard to find any evidence that the word 'court' was actually and explicitly applied to parliament until after 1380.[1] For example, the bill which the lords appellant put forward in the year 1388 was declared by the judges to be inadmissible, whether tested by the common law of the realm or by the course of the law civil. The lords of parliament thereupon asserted that the high crimes in the appeal, perpetrated by peers of the realm, could be dealt with only in parliament and by the law of parliament. It appertained to the lords of parliament, they insisted, to be judges in such cases, with the king's assent; for the realm of England had never been, nor ought to be, governed in such a matter by the civil laws nor according to the law of any inferior court, since such inferior courts were but executors of the laws of the realm and of the ordinances of parliament.[2]

From time to time this expression of the idea of parliament as the high court reappears, both in the rolls of parliament itself and in the reports of arguments in the law-courts. Thus, in the commons' petition of privilege[3] for William Larke, in 1429, the aggrieved person was described as 'servant to William Milrede', 'venant al vostre Court de icest parlement pur le citee de Londrez...'.[4] In Thorpe's case, in 1454, the judges themselves carried the notion forward, by admitting that it was not the usage that they should in any wise determine the privileges

---

[1] Professor H. L. Gray points out (*The Influence of the Commons on Early Legislation*, 417) that in 1384 the chancellor used the expression: 'Parlement, q'est la pluis haute courte del Roialme' (*Rot. Parl.* III, 169).

[2] Cf. Stubbs, *Const. Hist.* II, § 266; and Tout, *Chapters*, II, 432. *Rot. Parl.* III, 236: '...et auxint lour entent n'est pas de reuler ou governer si haute Cause come cest Appell est, que ne serra aillours trie ne termine q'en Parlement come dit est, par cours, processe et ordre use en ascune Court ou Place plus bas deinz mesme le Roialme, queux Courtes et Places ne sont que Executours d'aunciens Leys et Custumes du Roialme et Ordinances et Establisementz de parlement.'

[3] The essential connection of the notion of parliamentary privilege with the notion of parliament as a court is manifest.

[4] *Rot. Parl.* IV, 357-358.

of that high court of parliament; for it was so high and so
mighty in its nature that it might make law and unmake that
which was law. The determination and knowledge of that
privilege, they said, belonged not to them, but to the lords of
parliament. Yet, though there were many and diverse writs
brought in the lower courts which stayed proceedings therein
on the grounds of parliamentary privilege, still there was no
such writ having a general effect; and if there were, it would
seem that that high court of parliament, which ministered all
justice and equity, would hinder the due process of common
law.[1] The duke of York's claim, it will be remembered, was
received by the lords with the words: 'in asmuche as every
persone high and lowe suying to this high court of parlement
of right must be heard.'[2]

Occasionally the commons used the same expression in other
connections. In the same year as Thorpe's case, for example,
they requested that they should not be asked to make another
grant, considering the great poverty and penury that there was
among them; and that their excuse should be enrolled in the
high court of parliament.[3] An important aspect of the curial
theory was touched on by certain commissioners who discussed
with the king the appointment of various officers and requested
likewise that their report should be enrolled *of record* in that
high court of parliament.[4] In the first parliament of Edward IV,
the commons prayed that it might be enacted in his high court
of parliament, by the advice and assent of the lords spiritual and
temporal in the same assembled, and by the authority of the
same, that the acts judicial in the reigns of the three Henries
(late in deed but not in right successively kings of England) be
held as lawful as though they had been done under a king ruling
rightly and by just title.[5]

The expression 'the comens that been comen to this your high
court of parliament' is a not infrequent one. It occurs at the

---

[1] *Rot. Parl.* v, 239–240. (For further on this case, *v. infra*, pp. 131, 152, 253.)
[2] *Ibid.* 375.   [3] *Ibid.* 240.   [4] *Ibid.* 242.   [5] *Ibid.* 489.

parliament of 1453, in the petition for relief from further taxation (above mentioned).[1] Again, in 1455, it was 'thought by them that be come to this high courte of parliament for the communes of this lande' that a protector should be appointed.[2] To Edward IV, in 1461, the commons that were come by his high commandment to his high court of parliament returned their hearty thanks;[3] and six years later, the king himself began an address to the commons in these words: 'John Say, and ye sirs, comyn to this my court of Parlement for the comon of this my lond....'[4] In the parliament of 1472, the commons expressed their disapproval of certain riotous conduct in Southwark, and deplored that those culpable 'no consideration take to that that youre high presence is had here at youre Paleis of Westminster, ne to that that youre high Court of Parlement is here sittyng...and [it] is in a manere a contumelious contempt of youre Highness and youre Courtes here hold and kept....'[5]

Bishop Russell, in his drafted speeches, also used the curial terminology. 'The power and auctorite of my lord protector', he proposed to say at Edward V's parliament, 'is so behoffulle and of reason to be assented and established by the auctorite of thys hyghe courte, that amonges alle the causes of the assemblynge of the parliamente yn thys tyme of the yere thys ys the grettest and most necessarye furst to be affermed.'[6] 'The due and beauteous proporcion of mannys both ies', he said in the first draft of his sermon for Richard III's parliament, 'ys that the oone be lyke the other both yn colour and quantite. Hyt ys a monstruose syght oo man to have ij ies of diverse colours lyke as they have that techythe oone and doethe another.' Wherefore he hoped that provision 'be made by autorite of thys high court by the clere syght of the ryghte ie, that ys to say, of the undrestondynge'.[7] In the sermon which he actually did deliver at that parliament, he said: 'In thys grete body of Englonde we

[1] *Ibid.* 240.   [2] *Ibid.* 285.   [3] *Ibid.* 462.
[4] *Ibid.* 572.   [5] *Rot. Parl.* VI, 8.
[6] *Grants of Edward V*, p. xlix; and *infra*, Excursus VI, p. 178.
[7] *Ibid.* p. lv; and *infra*, *ibid.* p. 183.

have many diuerse membres vndre oone head. Howe be hyt they mey alle be reduced to iij chyef and princypalle, whyche make thys hyghe and grete courte at thys tyme, that is to seye the lordes spiritualle, the lordes temporalle, and the commens....'[1] Fortescue also at least once made use of the expression 'court of parliament'. Speaking of the French kings, he said: 'yet Seynt Lowes some tyme kynge ther, nor eny of his progenitors sette neuer tayles or oþer imposicion vppon the peple of þat lande withowt the assent of þe iij estates, wich whan thai bith assembled bith like to the courte of the parlement in Ingelonde.'[2]

But the fullest expression of the conception of parliament as a court comes from the lawyers themselves. Chief Baron Fray's exposition of it in detail has already been referred to.[3] 'The parliament is the king's court,' said Fray in 1441, 'and the highest court that he has; and the law is the highest inheritance that the king has, for by the law he himself and all his subjects are ruled. And if the law were not, there would be no king and no inheritance; therefore, by his law he is to have all amercements and revenues of his courts, in the king's bench, common pleas, and elsewhere. By his authority and his writ, parties are to be called into his court to respond; so are the lords by his writ called to come to his parliament, and likewise knights and burgesses, to be elected by his writ. And attainders and forfeitures which are adjudged in the same parliament are revenues of this court, and so are the fifteenths by this grant of revenues.'[4] Other judges, at other times, were prepared to observe that an act of parliament was only a judgement.[5]

Similarly, Markham, J., in Pilkington's case—in which parliamentary procedure was discussed—said to the clerk of

---

[1] *Grants of Edward V*, p. lix; and *infra*, Excursus VI, p. 187.   [2] *Governance*, iii.

[3] Cf. *supra*, p. 13; and *Y.B.* 19 *Henry VI*, Pas. pl. 1 (App. no. 25). The case is exhaustively analysed by Mr T. F. T. Plucknett, in his essay, 'The Lancastrian Constitution' (*loc. cit.*).

[4] *Ibid.* (App. no. 25).

[5] *Y.B.* 8 *Henry IV*, Mich. pl. 13 (App. no. 14); *Y.B.* 7 *Henry VII*, Trin. pl. 1 (App. no. 90).

parliament, who had admitted that no enrolment was made of the date when the bills were received by him: 'truly this is dangerous, for the court of parliament is the highest court the king has,...'.[1] In another very important case[2] (which will have to be considered in discussing the nature of an act of parliament), Vavasour, J., discussing the validity of a certain doubtful act, urged that 'every court will be held according to the manner in which it has been accustomed to be as a court, whether it be the exchequer, king's bench, chancery, or the court of parliament, which is the highest and most solemn court that the king has...'. An act of parliament, it was said in the course of the same case, is only a judgement. Parliament was the bounteous source of remedies unobtainable elsewhere. The judges advised aggrieved parties to sue to parliament for redress.[3]

Whatever the full facts of the parliamentary practice may have been, there can thus be no doubt that the *theory* of parliament as a court was flourishing throughout the century; and the acceptability of this theory ensured its continued vogue for several centuries. The theory went far to explain in familiar phraseology a great deal of the outer semblance and many of the manifestations of parliamentary activity. It offered an explanation of the relation of parliament to the king and of parliament to the law courts, and avoided any noticeable innovation of ideas in respect of royal or legal theory. It was not necessary, on the basis of such a theory, to assume or suggest that any modification had occurred in the relations of king and subject by the emergence of parliament, nor to invoke the aid of radical political ideas. Ordinary notions of royal inheritance and command, and the due process of familiar law, sufficed to

[1] *Y.B.* 33 *Henry VI*, Pas. pl. 8 (App. no. 30). (*V.* Chapter III (§ 2), Excursus I, *infra*.)
[2] *Y.B.* 7 *Henry VII*, Trin. pl. 1 (App. no. 90). Cf. *Y.B.* 8 *Henry IV*, Mich. pl. 13 (App. no. 14), wherein Tirwhit, J. speaks of an ordinance as a judgement in parliament. Cf. also Holdsworth, *Hist. Eng. Law*, II, 434.
[3] 37 *Lib. Assisarum*, pl. 7 (App. no. 9); *Y.B.* 4 *Edward IV*, Hil. pl. 3 (App. no. 44); *Y.B.* 8 *Edward IV*, Trin. pl. 1 (App. no. 52); *Y.B.* 2 *Richard III*, Mich. pl. 49 (App. no. 69).

explain the parliamentary phenomenon. Moreover, they were
not only plausible in face of the facts—they were also obviously
true historically. But only a shade less obviously were they not
the whole truth. It was impossible to describe the entire parliamentary phenomenon solely in terms of a court, however high
and mighty. Hence there emerged, almost simultaneously
with the notion of parliament as a court, a set of notions which
conceived it in terms of a representative assembly, over and
above any characteristics it was supposed to possess as a court.
It was observed to have extraordinary features of which no
simple court, however high, could possibly boast. It had a
unique capacity for binding all and sundry, essentially because
it represented all and sundry, which no ordinary law-court
could be supposed to have or to do.

At least as early as the thirty-ninth year of Edward III, this
aspect of the parliamentary phenomenon was acknowledged in
the courts. In a case of that year—in which the bishop of
Chichester was sued on a writ authorised by the statute of
Provisors—an objection was raised that the statute had not been
proclaimed in the counties.[1] Thorpe, CJ., however, brushed
this demurrer aside, and said: 'Though proclamation has not
been made in the county, everyone is held to know a statute
from the time it was made in parliament, for as soon as parliament has decided anything, the law holds that everyone has
knowledge of it, for parliament represents the body of all the
realm, and therefore proclamation is not necessary unless the
statute itself requires it.'

This doctrine of representation clearly goes beyond the strict
court theory; but so far as explicit statement is concerned, it
appears to be unique for many years. It is unsafe to be positive on
such a point; but it looks as though a great many years elapsed
before the same notion was generally stated in the courts.
It was, perhaps, in the case of the abbot of Glastonbury *v.*
A Purveyor, in 1410, implicit in Hill, J.'s disapproval of the

---

[1] *Y.B.* 39 *Edward III*, Pas. pl. 3, fo. 7 (App. no. 8).

notion that the fifteenth was an inheritance of the king: 'For', he said, 'he cannot have it without the grant of his people.' This contention was doubted by Norton, Sjt., but it was not pursued.[1]

Yet it is true that Chief Baron Fray's theory of parliament as 'the court and inheritance of the king' was not wholly acquiesced in by members of the court. Newton, CJCP., for instance— in the same case—denied that the fifteenth was to be deemed in the category of profits of his court of parliament. It was, he said, 'a grant by the spontaneous will of his people'.[2]

Hody, CJKB., was able to meet this contention only by asserting that the law which bound the king to defend his people also bound the people to grant their goods to him in aid of that defence—a fact which proved the inheritance; and that even after a grant had been made by the people, it was necessary for the lords of the realm to approve it, and for the king to accept it. But still, he did contradict it. No positive conception of parliament emerged from the debate which could rival Fray's clear-cut theory; and Markham, the counsel for the rector of Eddington, whose charter of exemption from taxation was the subject in dispute, even denied that the grant of parliament would bind every one. It is true that he hinted at a somewhat novel idea of parliament as a kind of commonalty or corporation, as Professor Plucknett has shown. But, for our present point, the conspicuous feature of the case is the absence of any notions which might be deemed in a line of descent from Thorpe's assertion in the late Edwardian days—notions of parliament as representing the body of all the realm, and therefore of everyone's having cognisance of its doings.

Nevertheless, as the century passes, there does re-emerge in the courts this notion, so essential, it would seem—as an offset to the limitations of the conception of parliament as a mere

---

[1] *Y.B.* 11 *Henry IV*, Mich. pl. 66 (App. no. 18 (ii)).

[2] *Y.B.* 19 *Henry VI*, Pas. pl. 1, fo. 64 (App. no. 25). (Cf. Mr T. F. T. Plucknett's analysis of the case, in 'The Lancastrian Constitution', *op. cit.* 164.)

court—in the development of the more modern theory of parliament. Thus, in an otherwise not specially important case of trespass, between the provost of King's College, Cambridge, and the warden of Merton, in 1464, Laicon, Sjt., said in argument that the plea of a certain act of parliament, made by the defendant in bar to the plaintiff, was a good plea, because an act of parliament was the highest record in the law, for by such record every man was bound, since every man was party to it; wherefore the plaintiff was party and privy to that record, which would bind him.[1] It is true that Littleton, J., had some words to say about it which reduced it to a status analogous to a record or fine in any of the king's courts;[2] still, the act was admitted to be the highest record because any (every) man was party and privy to it.

This important notion received further expression in the abbot of Waltham's case in 1482.[3] The case was one in which the Abbot found himself obliged to convince the whole bench in the exchequer chamber that a royal patent of exemption from the duty of collecting a clerical subsidy was valid, although convocation had made a grant with a proviso that no privileged person was to have the benefit of any exemptions whatever. The most significant feature of the case was, as Professor Plucknett has shown, the note struck by Serjeant Starkey in contrasting the authority of convocation with the authority of the king in his prerogative. We may, as has been suggested above,[4] doubt whether Starkey was using the notion of prerogative in any specially new way, though his direct contrast of the king in his prerogative to convocation does seem a substantially novel position. But for our immediate purpose of tracing the development of a notion of parliament which implied more than the notion of it as an ordinary court would imply, it is Catesby, Sjt., for the crown, who contributed most. In the course of his argu-

---

[1] *Y.B.* 3 *Edward IV*, Trin. pl. 1, fo. 2 (App. no. 43).
[2] *Ibid.* fo. 7.
[3] *Y.B.* 21 *Edward IV*, Mich. pl. 6 (App. no. 63). (*V.* Plucknett, *op. cit.* 172–178.)
[4] *V. supra*, p. 41.

ment against the Abbot, Catesby urged that convocation was as powerful among the clergy as the parliament was among the laity, and that by any act of parliament everyone to whom the act extended would be bound, for everyone was party and privy to the parliament, since the commons had one or two for every 'commonalty' to bind or unbind all the 'commonalty'. Catesby, with his notion of everyone's being party and privy to parliament, was thus carrying forward that notion of parliament as a representative assembly which was destined to qualify very substantially any theory of it as merely one among other courts.

The same notion appears, slightly enlarged, in a case of the twenty-first year of Henry VII. In an action on a writ of annuity—which is reported at almost overwhelming length in the books, and which has to be considered again in another context[1]—a certain act of parliament was pleaded, on behalf of the defendant, which gave rise to an observation by Butler, Sjt., as to the nature of parliament. An act, he said, was one of the highest records that there was in the law, and was such a record as everyone in England was privy to, and would be bound by.[2] Vavasour, Sjt., adopted the same expression later on in the case.

Thus we may say that by the end of the century there appears to have been current among the lawyers a theory of parliament as indeed a court, but a peculiar, a unique court. Its great peculiarity lay in the fact that in some sense it represented all men, and therefore to it every man was party and privy. Its acts were very much like the records and the fines in any other king's court; but whereas in the latter only those specific persons were bound who were party and therefore privy to those rulings, the acts of parliament bound all persons because all were represented therein, and for that reason party and privy thereto. From these ideas it is but a step to the idea of an act of parliament as deriving its force less from the fact

[1] *V. infra*, pp. 286, 292.   [2] *Y.B.* 21 *Henry VII*, Hil. pl. 1 (App. no. 110).

that it had the sanction of the king in his court and more from
the fact that every man in England was party and therefore
privy to it. Because parliament was representative, its acts were
binding; its authority existed *per se*, and not merely in the
sanction of the king's court: that is the logical development of
the expression of these ideas. As, with extreme slowness, that
development went on, Chief Baron Fray's ideas of parliament
necessarily became old-fashioned and inadequate.

It has been very justly said[1] that the real problem in the
history of parliament is not to explain the occasional association
of popular representation with a session of parliament in England or elsewhere, but to explain why popular representation
became an essential and inseparable feature of English parliaments. The explanation is not to be found, Mr Richardson
believes, through any examination of the origins of parliament
—however far-reaching and ingenious—but must rest in some
kind of grafting of new ideas on old institutions.[2]

This problem may perhaps be stated in a different and rather
broader way, by asking what possible development of ideas
engendered that slow, fundamental conversion of the institution
of parliament. It began as an institution called into being as a
matter of administrative convenience by the force of royal
behest, and it acted and looked like yet another royal court

[1] By Mr H. G. Richardson, in a paper, 'The Origins of Parliament', *T.R.H.S.*
(1928), 4th ser. XI, 137.

[2] Cf. the valuable essay by Mr J. G. Edwards, 'The "Plena Potestas" of the
English Parliamentary Representatives', *Oxford Essays presented to H. E. Salter*
(1934). Mr Edwards says that the evidence he adduces (154) 'suggests that historically the legal sovereignty of parliament sprang, not from a single, but from a
double, root. One root was the character of Parliament as a high court. The
second root was the "plena potestas" of the representatives of the commons.' This
suggestion is an important one; but it has to be remembered that the legal 'plena
potestas' could not be more than local in its range, and that legally an area which
failed to send up representatives with 'plena potestas' would not, on such a purely
legal theory, be bound by the deeds of other representatives. The 'plena potestas'
accounts for much, but not for everything, in the development of the representative
assembly. It leaves unexplained the fact that parliament came to be regarded as
binding all the king's subjects, whether they had legal representatives therein or
not. For the commons described as the procurators and attorneys of all the people
of the kingdom, v. the Act of Succession of 1407, and cf. *infra*, p. 131. For the
question of the binding of minorities, v. *infra*, pp. 133–137.

constituted by obedience to yet another series of king's writs. It changed into an institution which eventually functioned in ways not consonant with such an origin, but rather in the manner of a popular representative assembly acting politically with the sense of a sanction and an authority emanating, not only from the king and his writ, but also from its own or the 'people's' will. Granted that this conversion was very slow and reached its fullness only by almost microscopic and mainly unconscious steps, still the problem of the dichotomy of ideas is there and has to be faced.

Now it is submitted that this divergence in ideas of court and of assembly is a little eased by some reconsideration and examination of that notion which has recently been designated the 'myth' of the three estates of the realm.[1] If a detailed and critical examination of the place which the notion of the three estates of the realm apparently occupied in men's minds in the fourteenth and the fifteenth centuries is attempted, it seems that the 'missing link', as it were, in the evolution of the parliamentary notion lies precisely in this so-called myth. The dichotomy of *ideas*, it is suggested, was bridged by this notion which we may call 'the estate theory'.

The conception of estates has, as is well known, suffered various vicissitudes in modern historical literature.[2] Hallam certainly regarded parliament, if not as a system of estates, at least as in some sense reflecting the estates of the realm. The name 'estate', he contended, referred to representatives in assemblies only in an elliptical sense. The lower house of parliament was not, in proper language, an estate of the realm, but rather the image and representative of the commons of England, who, being the third estate, with the nobility and clergy made up and constituted the people of the kingdom and liege subjects

---

[1] A. F. Pollard, *The Evolution of Parliament*, IV.
[2] For a very valuable study of the idea of estates in the history of literature, *v.* Ruth Mohl, *The Three Estates in Mediaeval and Renaissance Literature* (Columbia University Press, 1933).

of the crown.[1] The king, he pointed out, was not properly an estate of the realm, as had sometimes been thought; for the primary sense of the word was an order or class in society. The 'movement from *Lehnstaat* to *Ständestaat*' was for long, and to a great extent still is, the common formula used by continental historians to describe the political history of mediaeval Europe.[2] Both Stubbs and Gneist seem to have had this formula in mind when writing their histories of the English constitution.

Stubbs, writing some fifty years after Hallam, attributed a more concrete constitutional significance to the estates than did the latter. In Stubbs's view, parliament was consciously founded upon a system of estates; and he credited Edward I with a design which 'as interpreted by the result was the creation of a national parliament composed of the three estates, organised on the principle of concentrating local agency and machinery in such a manner as to produce unity of national action, and thus to strengthen the hand of the king, who personified the nation'; and the design, he thought, was perfected in 1295.[3]

In Gneist's Hegelian interpretation of English constitutional development, the estates and their significance loomed larger still. He professed to observe in the Norman period the formation of the estates which afterwards evolved into the two houses of parliament.[4] He believed that the reign of Henry III witnessed the first attempt at government by the estates of the realm. To him, by the time of Edward I, the prelates and temporal magnates, who by reason of their services to the state constituted a ruling nobility, the middle classes of knights, freeholders, and burgesses, who, according to the ideas of rank in those times, formed a regular third estate, were the three then

---

[1] *View of the State of Europe*, 2nd ed. 105.

[2] As recently as 1913 the formula was fully applied to English history by J. Hatschek, in his *Englische Verfassungsgeschichte*; *v.* for example, 169: 'Wie auf dem Kontinent, so waren auch in England zunächst verschiedene Gründe massgebend, das Ständewesen zu entwickeln, die vertikale Schichtung der Feudalgesellschaft in eine horizontale Schichtung der Stände zu verwandeln.' In some measure the formula is applied to England also by Professor Powicke (*Mediaeval England* (1931), 47).

[3] *Const. Hist.* 3rd ed. II, 305.

[4] *History of the English Parliament,* trans. Keane (1889), 60.

legally recognised 'status civiles' of the English parliamentary constitution; and on their account he described the fourteenth and fifteenth centuries as the period of the estates of the realm.[1]

Maitland did not deal specifically with these doctrines; but his insistence that English mediaeval law had little to say about estates or ranks of men, that tenure was far more prominent than status in the middle ages, and that the land law was vastly more important than the law of ranks, contained the germs of scepticism as to the validity of Stubbs's and Gneist's doctrine.[2] Still, he himself employed much the same phrases when speaking of parliament in the thirteenth and fourteenth centuries. 'We cannot,' he wrote, 'in dealing with Henry [III]'s day, insist that a statute must be enacted with the consent of the three estates of the realm'; and in a later place: 'but under Edward I it became apparent that to invent new remedies was to make new laws, and events were deciding that only in a parliament of the three estates could new laws be made.'[3] 'Before the end of the thirteenth century', he asserted—following Stubbs's view— 'the national assembly was ceasing to be a feudal court and was becoming an assembly of the estates of the realm. The three estates were clergy, barons, and commons, those who pray, those who fight, those who work; this seems to have been an exhaustive classification of the divers conditions of men.'[4] And elsewhere he observed that 'The parliament of 1305 was a full parliament, for the three estates of the realm met the king and the council.'[5]

---

[1] *History of the English Constitution*, trans. Ashworth (1889), II, 80–81.

[2] *Hist. Eng. Law*, I, 408: 'But very soon after his [Bracton's] death, we hear of a man having a *status* in fee simple or a *status* for life, and though such a phrase as "the three estates of the realm" may endure, and our church bid us pray "for all estates of men"' (Maitland apparently made a slip here. There is no such prayer in the Book of Common Prayer. Probably he was thinking of the prayer for 'all those afflicted in mind, body, or estate'; but that is a quite different usage of the word 'estate'), 'still the English lawyer, when he hears of estates, will think first of rights in land, while the English layman will, like enough, think of land itself, of fields and houses. This means that our land law has been vastly more important than our law of ranks.'

[3] *Ibid.* 181, 196.   [4] *Constitutional History* (1888), 75.

[5] *Memoranda de Parliamento* (1893), p. xxxv.

Tout, publishing in 1920 the first volume of his *Chapters in Administrative History*, introduced a note of caution in the use of the expression 'estate of the realm'. In an early page of that volume he had occasion to remark: 'It is rather in the fourteenth than in the thirteenth century that the true differentiation of French and English institutions began to be worked out. It is then that aristocratic control, entrenched within the most stable *system of estates* known to the middle ages, permanently restricted the scope of the English monarchy, without depriving it of its national and representative character....'[1] And to the italicised words he appended the following note: 'I use the word "estate" with hesitation, because it was not even in France employed earlier than the second half of the fourteenth century to designate the estates of the realm. I cannot find a use of the term "trois états" in France earlier than 1357. In England, Wyclif speaks[2] of the three estates of priests, knights, and commons. It remained, however, a very unusual word in England, especially in the middle ages.'

Alongside, however, of Tout's very salutary caution on this point, must be noted that throughout his writings before and after this first volume of the *Chapters*, and with reference to many different dates within the fourteenth century, he employed the expression 'estates' in a way which makes it a synonym for the expression 'full parliament'.

In 1920 appeared Professor Pollard's *Evolution of Parliament*, in which a chapter was devoted to the discussion of what was there described as the 'myth of the three estates'. By this phrase was meant the theory, most fully expounded by Stubbs, and said to be accepted almost universally, that parliament was founded upon some system of estates. No one, presumably, would wish to withhold that theory from the limbo of mythology; but it is important to bear in mind that what Professor Pollard banished to that limbo was, after all, only an historian's myth. It is no myth that the idea of estates was being made use of in a

[1] *Chapters*, i, 8. Cf. *England and France*, 101, 103, 135. [2] *English Works*, 184.

variety of ways in the later middle ages in England. It is no myth that the term 'estates of the realm' was applied to parliament during the fifteenth century with such effect that the name adhered for four centuries thereafter.

Even in instances where it is possible to show that notions entertained with regard to a given institution were erroneous and invalid, it is still often necessary to consider whether such notions have not had a moulding influence upon that institution, and have worked themselves into the history of the very thing which they at first misrepresented.

But in the problem which is before us, nothing is to be gained by criticism which bases itself upon the assertion that the theory of estates did not fit the facts of the parliamentary phenomenon. For at no time were there objective criteria of exactly what constituted estates of the realm. Where no objective test could or can be applied, it is beside the mark to allege that the attribution to parliament of the character of estates of the realm was erroneous. All that can legitimately be done is to trace the actual course of the play of ideas, and to estimate its probable effect.

Whatever effect upon parliamentary history the estate theory may have had can be suggested only after a detailed survey of the available evidence for the use of the term 'estates' in the numerous contexts which the sources afford.

If such a survey is attempted, it is first necessary to distinguish carefully the several meanings of the word 'estate'; and few other English words have a greater mass of accumulated senses. The *New English Dictionary* gives us thirteen major interpretations of it, together with a quantity of subdistinctions. But a varied usage is not the same thing as a vague usage; and it is difficult to follow Professor Pollard's suggestion that its use in the fourteenth century was necessarily 'almost as vague as its use to-day—when we can speak of a man's "estate" meaning either his "property" or his "manhood"'.[1] For neither of these

---

[1] *Evolution of Parliament*, 63.

meanings is at all vague; the need for making distinctions is exactly contrary to the vagueness which results from failure to distinguish. All of the usages of the word 'estate' admitted by the *New English Dictionary* are perfectly definite in sense; and they are, in brief, as follows: (i) state or condition in general; (ii) condition with respect to worldly position; (iii) status or degree of rank; (iv) outward display of that status—pomp; (v) a class, order, rank, in a community or nation; (vi) an order or class regarded as part of the body politic, and as such participating in the government either directly or through its representatives; (vii) the three estates of the realm (as an institution); (viii) political constitution, or form of government; (ix) administration or government; (x) a body politic, kingdom, commonwealth (state); and in legal phraseology—(xi) the interest in land; (xii) property, possessions, fortune, capital; (xiii) a landed property.

Now no doubt it would be too much to say that in every case in which the word 'estate' occurs in the texts of the fourteenth and fifteenth centuries, it is possible to determine conclusively in which of these known senses it was being used. But with a judicious attention to the dates at which these senses are believed, respectively, to have emerged, and with an open-minded appreciation of the context in point, it is, I think, possible to interpret the word, in the great majority of instances, with a high degree of probability that we have determined very nearly the exact meaning. Certainly some such attempt must be made, if any clear conception of the place of the estate theory in the history of ideas is to be gained.

Illustrations of all the above-listed usages of the word can be adduced from definitely pre-Tudor sources—with the exception (to all seeming) of nos. (viii),[1] (ix), and (x). In some sense this exception is in itself a commentary on the general level of constitutional ideas in the fifteenth century—but that is not the point here. Neither need we here be minutely concerned with

---

[1] But on this point, *v. infra*, p. 90.

the legal usages of the word, though we may recall Maitland's observations thereon. In Bracton, he pointed out, the word 'status' referred only to personal condition, not to proprietary rights; but as the art of conveyancing developed, the word and its French and English equivalents acquired further meaning; instead of speaking simply of the land their ancestors held, people began to talk of estates in the land, and more and more the word got involved in those complexities of the land law which the estates of the realm suffered to exist.[1]

Neither is it necessary to multiply illustrations of the use of the word to mean 'state' or 'condition in general'—though it will be pointed out that the interpretation of at least one rather celebrated text, in this simple and most ancient meaning of the word, makes sense where no other does.

Professor Pollard states that 'neither Edward nor anyone else in England of the thirteenth and fourteenth centuries seems to have had any clear conception of what was meant by an "estate". The word has not been traced back beyond 1307, when the famous letter of the barons to the pope speaks of "L'estat du roialme" and "tous [sic] ces estats du prelacie."'[2] It is not at all clear from this which sense of the word is being employed; but as it stands, the statement is inadmissible. Even no more recondite an authority than the *New English Dictionary* shows the use of the word—and that, of course, in English—as early as 1225. It appears then—with the meaning 'degree of rank'—in the following sentence: 'And te eadie Johan in onliche stude þer ase he was þeos þreo astatz of earnede him one.'[3] The word was also used at that date to mean a special state or condition, and at least from 1230—and occasionally thenceforward, in Middle English—to mean state or condition in general.

The passage quoted by Professor Pollard must, however, be admitted to present some difficulties; though it seems, indeed,

---

[1] *Collected Papers*, II, 180–181.   [2] *Op. cit.* 63.

[3] *I.e.* 'And the blessed John, when he was in solitude, earned for himself alone these three estates' (*Ancren Riwle*).

that the whole context has little or nothing to do with the 'myth of the three estates of the realm'. The text of the baronial petition runs as follows:

A nostre Seigneur le Roy prient Contes, Barons, et tote la Communaute de la terre aide et remedie des oppressions southescrites, qe L'apostoille fait faire en ceste Roialme, en abbessement de la foi Dieu, et anyntissement de *l'estat de seinte Eglise* en Roialme, et a desheritezon et prejudice du Roi et de sa Coronne, et des autres bones gentz du dite Roialme, et en offens et destruction de la lei de la terre, et a graunt damage et enpoverissement du poeple, et en subversion *de tut l'estat* du Roialme, et encountre la volunte et l'ordenement des primes foundours....[1]

Up to this point in the petition, the word offers no special difficulty. Here, clearly enough, it signifies simply the state or condition—particularly the healthy condition[2]—of the church and realm respectively. But the interpretation is less easy when the petition continues—

La primer, des Provisions; come seinte Eglise *en toutz ces estats* de Prelacie en ceste Roialme soit funde par le Roi et par ses ancestres, et par les ditz Contes, Barons, et lour auncestres, pur eux et le Poeple aprendre de la foi Dieu, et faire oreisons et aumeynes, et hospitalites, en les lieus ou les Eglises sont foundeez, pur les almes des foundurs et de lour heyres, et certeynes possessions qe amontent a les deux parties du Roialme, soient per les ditz foundurs assignetz as Prelatz pur sustenir les charges susditz....

It is far from obvious what was meant, in this part of the petition, by the peculiar expression 'en toutz ces estats de Prelacie'. If we interpret it to mean 'in all these estates or orders of prelacy', we are faced with the difficulties of explaining the reason for the plural form, and of explaining away the implication that the order of prelacy itself was founded by the king and the barons. The first of these difficulties might be met by understanding

---

[1] *Rot. Parl.* i, 219. (The italics are mine.)

[2] Kelham's *Dictionary of Old French* (1779) gives 'statute, condition, health' as the meanings of 'estate'.

the allusion to be to the degrees of prelacy—archbishops, bishops, abbots, etc. But the second difficulty would remain. There is a possible alternative interpretation, to the effect that the phrase 'toutz ces estats' refers to the estates or properties of the prelates; and at first sight, this is an attractive solution of the problem. For it avoids the two difficulties arising from the other interpretation, and fits in with the fact that it was the endowment of the prelates, not the order of bishops, which was founded by the king and barons. But such a solution has its own grave difficulties. In the first place, there is no known instance, in any other context, of the use of the word 'estate' to mean 'land' or 'interest in land', 'endowments', 'property', until more than a century later than 1307. Secondly, the whole question of endowments is fully covered in the petition, in the passage which follows immediately after the paragraph in point, and which begins with the words 'et certeynes possessions qe amontent...'. The form and content of this passage make it unlikely, to say the least, that the expression 'toutz ces estats de Prelacie' was intended to allude to property.

On the merits of the text as it stands, there are probably no means of arriving at a satisfactory interpretation. But it is possible to derive some aid from a consideration of a later version of the same petition. When, in 1351, the statute of Provisors was drawn up, a liberal use of this baronial petition of 1307 was made. A large part of the petition was quoted, to form the preamble to the statute.[1] It is plain that the preamble closely paraphrases the petition, but equally plain that the loose expressions occurring in the baronial composition have been avoided or converted into sharper and more exact language. For instance, where the petition reads: 'a graunt damage et enpoverissement du poeple, et en subversion de tut l'estat du Roialme', the statutory preamble runs: 'et grant damage de son poeple et subversion de l'estat de tut son Roialme susdit'. The expression 'estate of all the realm' is more intelligible than

[1] *Stat. R.* 1, 316.

the words—in the baronial petition—'all the estate of the realm'. Several verbal emendations of this kind appear in the preamble. But the one of chief interest for our present point is that which modifies the baronial phrase 'en toutz ces estats de Prelacie'. This phrase has been reduced to 'en estat de pre-lacie'. The relevant passage from the preamble is worth quoting, in order to show the recasting of the phrases:

Come jadis, en le parlement de bone memoire Sire Edward Roi Dengleterre, Ael nostre seigneur le Roi qore est, lan de son regne trentisme quint a Kardoil tenuz, oie la peticion mise devant le dit Ael et son conseil en le dit parlement par la communalte de son Roialme, contenant qe come seinte eglise Dengleterre *estoit founde en estat de prelacie*, deins le Roialme Dengleterre, par le dit Ael et ses progenitours, et Countes, Barons, et Nobles de son Roialme et lour ancestres, pur eux et le poeple enfourmer de la lei Dieu, et pur faire hospitalites aumoignes et autres oeuvres de charite es lieux ou les eglises feurant foundes par les almes de foundours et de lour heirs et de touz Cristiens; et certeins possessions, tant en feez terres et rentes come en avowesons qe se extendent a grande value, par les ditz foundours feurant assignez as prelatz et autres gentz de seinte eglise du dit Roialme, pur cele charge sustenir....[1]

There is little doubt that in the minds of those who drew up this preamble, there was no idea that the expression 'en toutz ces estats de Prelacie' alluded to the endowments of the bishops. They drafted the preamble in accordance with their inter-pretation of the words of the petition, and wrote: 'the church was founded in estate of prelacy'. There can be no possibility of supposing that in this instance there was any allusion to episcopal endowments: the reference was to the order of prelacy as the form of church government. The interpretation of the word 'estate' in this context seems to be divisible between nos. (vi) and (viii) of the above-listed meanings, viz. 'order or class' of persons, and 'form of government'. It is true that there is no other known illustration of the latter usage in the English language, until a hundred years later; but it may well

[1] Italics mine.

have been anticipated in French,[1] and it is difficult not to see some idea of governmental form present in the terms of the preamble. Granted this, we may safely argue that much the same meaning was intended by the more slipshod language of the baronial letter of 1307. But there is no reason at all to suppose that in either case there was any allusion to the prelacy as an estate in the sense in which the clergy came normally to be described.

It is unnecessary, for our purposes, to accumulate illustrations of the use of the word to mean simply 'condition with respect to worldly position'. This is a common sense, and is of course the one in which it is used in the Anglican prayer for all sorts and conditions of men, in any ways afflicted in mind, body, or estate; and its earliest appearance, according to the *New English Dictionary*, was in 1300. This sense is also the one in which the word is used in sumptuary provisions, as, *e.g.* 'Chescun persone mesnez en son estat et degree'.[2] Similarly, in 1433, the duke of Bedford, when challenging critics of his conduct in France, invited any such defamer to come forward, 'cujuscunque status, gradus vel conditionis fuerit'.[3] But one highly specialised use of the word in this sense must again be stressed —namely, its use in the expression 'estate of king'. We have already defined this expression[4] as a collective term meaning 'the mass of rights, attributes, and powers centring in the king'. It will be recollected how the Lancastrians, in 1399, said to Richard that they deprived him 'of the Astate of Kyng';[5] and how the Speaker, in 1406, affirmed that 'combien qu'il avoit riens parlez de les prerogatif ou estate roiale';[6] and how Henry IV accepted certain articles, 'sauvant toutesfoitz a luy son estat et prerogatif de son corone'.[7]

Other examples of the same usage of the word were quoted above;[8] and if we cannot say that 'estate' was ever employed

---

[1] I do not, however, find authority for it in the Dictionaries by Littré, Godefroy, or Cotgrave.

[2] *Rot. Parl.* III, 415 (1399).   [3] *Rot. Parl.* IV, 420.   [4] *Supra*, p. 3.
   Rot. Parl. III, 424.   [6] *Ibid.* 572.   [7] *Ibid.* 585.   [8] *Supra*, pp. 3–4.

as a synonym for 'prerogative', certainly prerogative was one element in royal estate. Thus, when in the statute of York of 1322 it was provided that 'Les choses que serount a establir pur l'estat de nostre Seigneur le Roi et de ses Heirs et pur l'estat du roialme et du poeple soient tretes accordees establies en parlementz...',[1] we cannot say definitely that by the term 'estate of king' was meant the 'king's prerogative'. But in the light of the evidence of the subsequent usage of that term, we can certainly believe the statute to refer to that mass of rights, duties, and attributes which constituted the kingship; and this belief would agree with the interpretation of the statute—as relating to fundamental constitutional changes—which was convincingly advanced by Dr G. T. Lapsley in 1913.[2] It is not, however, quite so easy to be sure what was really meant by the second clause in the statute—the clause which speaks of the 'estate of the realm and of the people'. It is difficult to see what could have been in mind in this instance of the use of the word, if it were not 'state or good condition in general' of the realm and of the people; and if it were—and if that second clause were intended to be taken at its face value—then it can hardly be said that the statute necessarily contemplated constitutional changes only. But on the other hand, even on such a general interpretation, it would not follow that all legislation—constitutional or otherwise—was in view; for all legislation did not necessarily affect the estate or condition of the realm and of the people as a whole. Many chapters in the statute book, for long after this, can hardly be said to touch the estate of the realm and of the people. One might almost say that 'estate of the realm' is the fourteenth-century equivalent—and therefore minus its *social* content—of the nineteenth-century 'condition of England'.

To argue back a century, especially in regard to the use of words and ideas, is of course a method subject to large reservations; but to some extent it assists in an interpretation of the word in the statute, to notice the terms used in the episode

[1] *Stat. R.* i, 189.   [2] *E.H.R.* xxviii, 118.

about the money grants in 1407. On that occasion it was said
that there had been a discussion among the lords, in the presence
of the king, about the estate of the realm and the defence of the
same; and after the protest which the commons made against
the lords' fixing of the taxation, it was agreed by the king that
it was lawful for the lords to discuss among themselves the
estate of the realm and the remedy needful for it, and equally
lawful for the commons to discuss the estate of the realm and
the remedy aforesaid. 'Estate of the realm' in this context
clearly means that state of the realm which called for remedy
by the vote (and expenditure) of taxation; and in that state, the
need for defence loomed as the largest element. It may be that
to the framers of the statute of York, in 1322, the clause 'matters
to be established for the estate of the realm and people' meant
'taxes to be granted for the defence of the people'; and if the
clause were intended to have (it may not have been) any concrete and specific significance, it would be hard to suggest any
other than this one. Indeed, when we turn to the ordinances
which the statute itself revoked, and note that one of them forbade the king to enter into war without the consent of the
baronage in parliament, and that some of the others were concerned with regulating the raising of taxation, it looks even
more probable that such was the connotation. We should then
interpret the words 'estate of the realm', in that context, to
mean 'that state of the realm which required extraordinary
expenditure and therefore involved taxation'.[1] Such an interpretation would give more than a shadowy significance to a
clause which otherwise seems very obscure, and would still
further strengthen that view of the statute—as not contemplating general legislation—argued by Dr Lapsley and widely
accepted as the most probable view of it.[2]

---

[1] Clearly the word bore a financial connotation in 1433, when Ralph Cromwell, as treasurer, 'exhibuit...dictos Libros de Statu Regni, per officiarios et Ministros Regis Scaccarii predicti ut premittitur editos...' (*Rot. Parl.* IV, 432).

[2] But cf. Richardson and Sayles, 'Early Records of the English Parliaments', *Bull. I.H.R.* VI, 76—and references given in n. 6 therein.

It is convenient to note, at this point, that in a less specialised connotation, the word 'estate' was often employed elliptically, to designate not simply exalted position, but *persons of* exalted position: that 'estates' may mean 'persons of estate'. This use of the word[1]—especially the immense outcrop of it in the documents of the deposition of Richard II, and particularly with close reference to its relation to the concept of the three estates of the realm—will have to be minutely examined a little later in this study. First, however, by way of introduction, something may be said as to the general theory of the threefold division of society, which underlies the notion of the three estates of the realm in its constitutional bearings.

'That there was something natural, if not also divine,' remarks Professor Pollard, 'in the separation of mankind into three classes seemed as clear to mediaeval philosophers as it did to nineteenth-century railway companies'[2] (and does—he might have added—to some university examining boards). The idea, he reminds us, is as old as Plato; and no doubt it is much older. But we need not investigate the mysterious attraction which the number 'three' has always had for the human mind, nor attempt to trace the course of the idea in the Christian Fathers and in the mediaeval philosophers. The immediate point is precisely the feeling of the naturalness or even divinity of the threefold division of society—a division in no respect thought to be a result of royal will.

Nevertheless, it is pertinent to recall that this notion had had, by the fifteenth century, a very long history in England— dating at least from the time of Alfred's translation of Boethius. Perhaps even Alfred himself is the father of the idea in England;

[1] For example, the *Somnium Vigilantis* says: 'It is ayenste the curtasye of re-thorique namely before eny prynce or high astat, to whom all honoure and dred-fulness be du with lauly subjeccioun, to entremedle eny wordis that ben sounynge to menasses offeringe...' (*E.H.R.* (1911), XXVI, 514). The use of the word to mean 'pomp', as well as 'persons of rank', occurs in *The Brut*, ed. Brie, II, 445; 'Off þe statis at þe Coronacion of Keteryne, þe Quene of England. Fyrst þe Quene sate in hyr estate,...the King of Scotland in hys estate....'
[2] *Op. cit.* 64.

for the following passage—a notably royal interpretation of it—does not occur in Boethius's own text, but only in Alfred's translation:

> Moreover thou knowest that no man can show any craft, or exercise or steer any power, without tools and materials. That is, of every craft, the materials, without which man cannot exercise the craft. This, then, is a king's materials and his tools to reign with: that he have his land well peopled. He must have prayer-men and soldiers and workmen. Thou knowest that without these tools no king can show his craft.[1]

In a tenth-century source—in sermons attributed to the prolific Aelfric—the same notion was elaborated:

> Every just throne stands on three props, that stands perfectly right. One is Oratores, and the other is Laboratores, and the third is Bellatores. The Oratores are the men of prayer, who shall serve God, and by day and night intercede for the whole nation. The Laboratores are the workmen, who shall labour in order that all the nation shall live thereby. The Bellatores are the men of war [*i.e.*, knights], who shall defend the land valiantly with weapons. On these three props shall every throne stand with justice among Christian people.[2]

By the fourteenth century, the same threefold division could be attributed, in more familiar terms, to the church or *respublica christiana* itself—thus:

> But þis spekiþ of one hede and alagatis of one hede of soule. þre partis ben in þe chirche prestis, lordes, and commyns. And god haþ ordeyned alle þes þre to helpen eche oþer to gendre love, and noon of hem to be superflu but do þer office þat god haþ ordeyned. . . .[3]

---

[1] Alfred's *Boethius*, ed. Cardale (1829), lib. ii, prosa 7, xvii, 91.

[2] *Political Songs*, ed. T. Wright, Camden Society, vi, 365. (A further sermon on this theme occurs in a MS. tract, also attributed to Aelfric, contained in *Camb. Univ. Libr. MS.* Ii, 1, 33, fo. 193–194. For this and for the following reference, I am indebted to Dr H. H. Glunz, of Trinity College, and Professor in the University of Frankfurt a. M.)

[3] *Pembroke College MS.* 237, fo. 3 r, *Fourteenth-Century Homilies*.

And a similar passage—though more important, because still later and because written by Wyclif—is this one:

> Ideo necesse est esse tres Ierarchias in regno que omnes unam personam unicordem constituant, scilicet sacerdotes vel oratores, seculares dominos vel defensores, et plebeos vel laboratores.[1]

Wyclif also uses the word 'estate' in describing these orders:

> It is knowun bi Goddis lawe þat þer ben in þe Chirche þre statis þat God haþe ordeyned: state of prestis, and state of knyʒtis, and þe þridd is staat of comunys.[2]

It seems reasonable, then, to hold that by the fifteenth century the notion of a natural threefold division of society into the order of clerks, secular magnates, and commons, was accepted without question. It is important to pursue the use of the word 'estate', during the century, in this sense of a social order in the community. The main stress, in the illustrative texts which follow, seems to be on this social sense of the word; but in some of them it may have been employed elliptically to mean persons of estate, or may have possessed a certain political significance. And perhaps all three of these senses of the word are present at once.

A statute was passed, in 1382, against heretical preaching, which was said to be causing 'discord and dissension betwixt divers estates of the realm, as well spiritual as temporal'.[3] In this use of the word, it is hard to allocate the stress of meaning as between persons and orders; but there is less doubt about the emphasis on the social sense in the king's letter to the sheriff of Derby, in 1393–94,[4] wherein it was said that the late insurrection

---

[1] *De Officio Regis*, 58.
[2] *English Works*, ed. Arnold, III, 184 (*c.* 1380). The *N.E.D.* is surely wrong in placing this example of the use of the word 'estate' under its *sixth* meaning of that word, viz. 'a class or order participating in the government'. Surely the proper place for this example is under its *fifth* meaning of that word, *i.e.* simply 'a class or order in a community'.
[3] *Stat. R.* II, 23.
[4] *Rot. Parl.* III, 316.

of Sir Thomas Talbot, in Chester, was 'en anyntisment de les Estatz et de Loys' of the realm. There is also a more social than personal significance in a sumptuary law of 1402, in which 'le roy voet commander a toutz Estatz de son Roialme q'ils se governent en leurs arraies chescun selonc son degre en lessant les superfluitees'.[1] And in such a sermon before parliament as Cardinal Beaufort's in 1433, we can see the social sense of the word with a political connotation in an explicit form. This sermon is given with unusual fullness in the rolls, and deserves to be quoted here in its entirety. The text taken for it was: 'Suscipiunt montes pacem populo et colles justiciam';[2] and it runs as follows:

> In quibus verbis asseruit, quod *triplex regni status* potuit ut sibi videbatur rationabiliter annotari; videlicet, per Montes, Prelati, Proceres, et Magnates, per Colles, Milites, Armigeri, et Mercatores, et in Populo, Cultores, Artifices, et Vulgares. Quos quidem status enucliacius exponendo asseruit, et per nonnulla Auctoritates, Historias, et Exempla summarie demonstravit; quod triplex deberet virtus politica, eisdem tribus statibus specialiter pertinere; Videlicet, Prelatis et Magnatibus, Pax, Unitas, et vera Concordia, absque fictura vel dissimulatione; Militibus et Mediocribus, equitas et mera justicia, absque manutenentia et pauperum oppressione; Vulgaribus vero et Inferioribus, voluntaria Regi et ejus Legibus Obedientia, absque perjurio et murmuratione. Ex quibus si in Regno Anglie taliter se haberent, maxima Deo complacentia ac Regi et Regno Commoda quamplurima sine dubio provenirent. Ad providendum igitur qualiter in dicto Regno, Montes predicti Pacem suscipiant, Collesque Justiciam vulgari populo administrent, ipsi etiam populi vulgares, eorum antiquis relictis perjuriis divinis legibus et humanis plus solito fideliter obediant et intendant.[3]

With this sermon—remarkable for its strictly social distinction of the three estates as 'magnates spiritual and temporal', 'the middle classes', and 'the inferior'; and equally remarkable for its strong royalist doctrine—we may leave the use of the word

---

[1] *Rot. Parl.* III, 506.
[2] *Psalms* lxxi, 3.
[3] *Rot. Parl.* IV, 419. (Italics mine).

'estate' to mean 'social orders in the nation'. We may note finally, however, that in the parliament of 1461, in the commons' address to Edward IV—when it was recalled how Henry VI had declared that Richard of York was rightful heir to the crown, and that he was to be accepted as such 'in worship and reverence by all the estates and persons of the realm'[1]— the word was probably being employed in this social sense only. It is significant, too, that the Italian envoys who wrote an account of their impressions of England about 1500 thought it worth remarking that 'Sono in Inghilterra 3 stati, popolare, militare, et ecclesiastico'.[2]

We are now able to discuss the question of the relation of the notion of estates to the notion of parliament. To begin with, we must single out the use of the word 'estate' to mean the degrees, grades, ranks, or orders of persons present in a parliamentary session. This is apparently the earliest formal use of the word in a parliamentary context. No particular political or constitutional significance is to be ascribed to this use, so far as can be judged from the texts—unless, indeed, it contributed, as it may have done, to the slightly later assimilation of the notion of estates of the realm to the parliamentary notion. But dating from 1381 at the latest, it is notably early.

It will be remembered that as far back as 1332, in the two parliaments held respectively at Westminster and York, the prelates, the lords, and the commons deliberated separately; and of that arrangement Tout observes: 'there we have the three estates, in fact though not in name'.[3] But many years were to elapse before the estates of parliament were understood to be three only. Witness the following petition from the year 1381:

Et priast outre la dite Commune que les Prelatz par eux mesmes, les grantz Seignours Temporelx par eux mesmes, les Chivalers par eux, les Justices par eux et *touz autres Estatz* singulerement fussent

---

[1] *Rot. Parl.* v, 465.
[2] *Italian Relation*, 34.
[3] *Chapters*, iii, 61, n. 1. Cf. *Rot. Parl.* ii, 66–67.

chargez de treter et communer sur ceste lour Charge et que lour advis fust reportez a la Commune, afyn que bon remede fust ordenez. A quoy fust dit et responduz, Qe le Roi ad fait charger les Seignours et autres Sages de communer, et treter diligeaument sur les dites matires, mais l'anciene custume et forme de Parlement a este toutdys qe la commune reporteroit leur advis sur les matires a eux donez au Roi notre Seignour et as Seignours du Parlement primerement et noun pas e contra. Et ce fait adonques l'advis des Seignours sur ce lour serroit monstrez. Et purce le Roi voet, qe les ancienes et bones custumes et forme de Parlement soient tenuz et bien gardez.[1]

The expression 'estates of parliament', of which this petition apparently contains an early form, was in fairly common use for a period of about thirty years thenceforward. In 1393, for instance, the matters in the bill charging Sir Thomas Talbot with treason were said to be

si notorie et overtement conuz au Roi et as Seignours et as touz les Estatz du Parlement et par tout le Roialme.[2]

Then in 1397 the chancellor in his parliamentary sermon explained that

Par quoy le Roy ad fait assembler l'Estatz de Parlement, a cest foitz pur estre enformez si ascuns Droitz de sa Corone soient suistretz ou amenuz;

and that

Dont le Roy vourra savoir, si aucun de ses liges soient oppresez ou distourbez qils ne purront suir et avoir remede par la commune Ley et sur ce estre conseillez par toutz les Estatz du Parlement et ent faire bone et due remede en cest present Parlement.[3]

Subsequently, the same parliament was adjourned by the king

ovek toutz l'estates et degrees de Parlement come ils sont en cest lieu de Westm' a present.[4]

Similarly, in the parliament of 1398, eighteen commissioners were named to discuss the complaints put forward by the duke

---

[1] *Rot. Parl.* III, 100. Cf. Stubbs, *Const. Hist.* II, 200, n. 1.
[2] *Rot. Parl.* III, 316.   [3] *Ibid.* 347.   [4] *Ibid.* 355.

of Hereford, and were empowered to act with the assent of all the estates of parliament.[1] Later, the king himself announced Hereford's pardon, 'reherceant la matire avant dit a toutz l'estatz du parlement'.[2]

As late as 1420 the expression was still in use; and it occurs in those candid words addressed by the king himself to Speaker Thomas Chaucer, which may be regarded as providing a fair insight into Henry V's notion of the commons' place and function in parliament. To Chaucer—who added to the usual protestation a request to have resort to his 'companions', in order to be corrected if he reported otherwise than they had agreed—the king replied:

Q'ils aueroient lour Protestations en manere come il ad estee acustumez devant ces heures. Et outre ceo lour dist, qe toutz les Estates du Parlement feurent venuz pur commune bien et profit du Roy et de Roialme et pur unite et union faire d'un assent et d'un acorde. Et partant il feust bien certein, qe les ditz Communes ne voudroient riens attempter ou parler autrement qe ne serroit de honestee, et pur norrer bon amour et concorde des toutz parties. Et por ce lour feust comandez d'aler ensemble et d'entrecommuner des matires besoignables et profitables pur le Roy et le Roialme et pur bon esploit de Parlement.[3]

In the stormy parliament of the next year, in which Henry refused to have any 'novellerie', the commons, in the end, thought it as well to pray the king:

Qe vous tenuz avez et reputez touts les Estats et chescun de eulx de mesmes voz Parlementz pour vox foialx et loialx liges et humbles soubgis.[4]

This is the latest instance, so far as has been noted, of the use of the expression 'estates of parliament'.

The distinction between the terms 'estates of parliament' and 'estates of the realm' having been established, the ground is cleared for a survey of the notion of estate in its wider and more

---

[1] *Rot. Parl.* iii, 360.   [2] *Ibid.* 367.   [3] *Ibid.* 623.   [4] *Ibid.* 658.

significant constitutional bearings. Yet even now it is desirable —before proceeding to this survey itself—to make another investigation in order to appreciate better the several aspects of the gradual consolidation of the ultimately permanent trinity of estates—*i.e.* of the lords spiritual, the lords temporal, and the commons—during the period. For this purpose there is no better material than the sanctioning clauses of the statutes from 1377 to 1485; and if the following table of these sanctions is carefully perused, it will then be possible to draw some conclusions which require to be borne in mind as a preliminary to the next stage of our enquiry.

SANCTIONS TO STATUTES, 1377–1485

Statute	Sanctioning Clauses (abbreviated)
1 R. II, 1377	by the whole assent of the prelates, dukes, earls, barons of this our realm, at instance and request of the commons....
2 R. II, 1378	the king at this parliament amongst other things assented and accorded hath made certain statutes and ordinances....
3 R. II, 1379	of the assent of the lords and other in the said parliament.
4 R. II, 1380	by the assent of the prelates and lords....
5 R. II, s. 1, 1381	of the assent of the prelates, lords, and commons....
s. 2, 1381	made by the lord king, the prelates, lords, and commons....
6 R. II, s. 1, 1382	by assent of prelates, dukes, earls, barons, and commons....
s. 2, 1382	with assent of prelates, nobles, and great men....
7 R. II, 1383	of the assent of the prelates, lords, and commons....
8 R. II, 1384	of the assent of the prelates, great men, and commons....
9 R. II, 1385	of the assent of prelates, dukes, marquesses, earls, barons, and commons.
10 R. II, 1386	of the assent of lords and commons.
11 R. II, 1387	of the assent of lords and commons.
12 R. II, 1388	of the assent of lords and commons.
13 R. II, s. 1, 1389	of the assent of the prelates and *lords temporal* and commons.
s. 2, 1389	of the assent of great men and nobles.

Statute	Sanctioning Clauses (abbreviated)
13 R. II, s. 3, 1389	complaint made to us as well by *lords spiritual* and *temporal* as by commons,...we have ordained... by advice of our great council.
14 R. II, 1390	by assent of the said parliament.
15 R. II, 1391	by assent of the said parliament.
16 R. II, 1392	by assent of the said parliament.
17 R. II, 1393	by assent of the said parliament.
20 R. II, 1396	by assent of the prelates, lords, and commons.
21 R. II, 1397	of the assent and accord of the prelates, dukes, earls, barons, and commons....
1 H. IV, 1399	of assent of the prelates, dukes, earls, barons, at instance and request of the commons....
2 H. IV, 1400	of assent of the prelates, dukes, earls, barons, at instance and request of the commons....
4 H. IV, 1402	by assent of the lords spiritual and temporal at instance and request of the commons.
5 H. IV, 1403	by advice and assent of the lords spiritual and temporal at request of the commons.
6 H. IV, 1404	by advice and assent of the great men of the realm in parliament.
7 H. IV, 1405	by advice and assent of the lords spiritual and temporal at instance and/or request of the commons.
9 H. IV, 1407	by advice and assent of the lords spiritual and temporal at instance and/or request of the commons.
11 H. IV, 1409	by advice and assent of the lords spiritual and temporal at instance and/or request of the commons.
13 H. IV, 1411	by advice and assent of the lords spiritual and temporal at instance and/or request of the commons.
1 H. V, 1413	by advice and assent of the lords spiritual and temporal at instance and/or request of the commons.
2 H. V, s. 1, 1414	by advice and assent of the lords spiritual and temporal at instance and/or request of the commons.
s. 2, 1414	by advice and assent of the lords spiritual and temporal at instance and/or request of the commons.
3 H. V, 1415	with assent of the lords spiritual and temporal at instance and/or request of the commons.
4 H. V, s. 1, 1416	with advice and assent of the lords spiritual and temporal at instance and/or request of the commons.
s. 2, 1416	with assent of the prelates, dukes, earls, barons at instance and/or request of the commons.
7 H. V, 1419	by assent of prelates and great men at instance and/or request of the commons.
8 H. V, 1420	by assent of lords spiritual and temporal at instance and/or request of the commons.
9 H. V, s. 1, 1421	by assent of lords spiritual and temporal at instance and/or request of the commons.

Statute	Sanctioning Clauses (abbreviated)
9 H. V, s. 2, 1421	by assent of lords spiritual and temporal at instance and/or request of the commons.
1 H. VI, 1422	by advice and assent of the lords spiritual and temporal at instance and/or request of the commons.
2 H. VI, 1423	by advice and assent of the lords spiritual and temporal at instance and/or request of the commons.
3 H. VI, 1425	by advice and assent of the lords spiritual and temporal at instance and/or request of the commons.
4 H. VI, 1425	by advice and assent of the lords spiritual and temporal at instance and/or request of the commons.
6 H. VI, 1427	by advice and assent of the lords spiritual and temporal at instance and/or request of the commons.
8 H. VI, 1429	by advice and assent of prelates and great men and by assent of the commons.
9 H. VI, 1430	by advice and assent of lords spiritual and temporal and at request of the commons.
10 H. VI, 1432	by advice and assent of lords spiritual and temporal and at request of the commons.
11 H. VI, 1433	by assent of lords spiritual and temporal and at request of the commons, and *by authority of parliament.*
14 H. VI, 1435	by advice and assent of lords spiritual and temporal and at request of the commons.
15 H. VI, 1436	by advice and assent of lords spiritual and temporal and at request of the commons.
18 H. VI, 1439	by advice and assent of lords spiritual and temporal and at request of the commons.
20 H. VI, 1441	by advice and assent of lords spiritual and temporal and at request of the commons.
23 H. VI, 1444–45	by advice and assent of the lords spiritual and temporal and of the commons, *by authority of parliament.*
25 H. VI, 1446	by advice and assent of the lords spiritual and temporal and of the commons, *by authority of parliament.*
27 H. VI, 1448	by advice and assent of the lords spiritual and temporal and of the commons.
28 H. VI, 1449	by advice and assent of the lords spiritual and temporal and at instance and request of the commons, and *by authority of parliament.*
29 H. VI, 1450	by advice and assent of the lords spiritual and temporal and at instance and request of the commons, and by authority of parliament.
31 H. VI, 1452	by advice and assent of the lords spiritual and temporal and of the commons, and by authority of parliament.

Statute	Sanctioning Clauses (abbreviated)
33 H. VI, 1455	by advice and assent of the lords spiritual and temporal and of the commons, and by authority of parliament.
39 H. VI, 1460	by advice and assent of the lords spiritual and temporal and at the request of the commons, and by authority of parliament.
1 Ed. IV, 1461	by advice and assent of the lords spiritual and temporal and at the request of the commons, and by authority of parliament.
3 Ed. IV, 1463	by advice and assent of the lords spiritual and temporal and of the commons, and by authority of parliament.
4 Ed. IV, 1464	by advice and assent of the lords spiritual and temporal and request of the commons, and by authority of parliament.
7 Ed. IV, 1467	by advice and assent of the lords spiritual and temporal and request of the commons and by authority of parliament.
8 Ed. IV, c. 1, 1468	by advice and assent of the lords spiritual and temporal and request of the commons.
c. 2, 1468	by advice and assent of the lords spiritual and temporal and request of the commons, and by authority of parliament.
12 Ed. IV, 1472	by advice and assent of the lords spiritual and temporal and request of the commons, and by authority of parliament.
14 Ed. IV, 1474	by advice and assent of the lords spiritual and temporal and of the commons, and by authority of parliament.
17 Ed. IV, 1477	by advice and assent of the lords spiritual and temporal and at request of the commons, and by authority of parliament.
22 Ed. IV, 1482	by advice and assent of the lords spiritual and temporal and at request of the commons, and by authority of parliament.
1 R. III, 1483	by advice and assent of the lords spiritual and temporal and of the commons, and by authority of parliament.
1 H. VII, c. 1, 1485	by advice and assent of the lords spiritual and temporal and at the request of the commons, and by authority of parliament.
c. 2, 1485	by advice and assent of the lords spiritual and temporal and of the commons, and by authority of parliament.

[Henceforth unvaried.]

The facts in this table which seem to call for emphasis may be summarised thus:

(i) From 1377 to 1400, the parliamentary estates are named with a good deal of at least formal diversity, and with no definite tripartite distinction.[1] Variations such as 'prelates, dukes, earls, barons, commons', 'lords and other', 'prelates, nobles, and great men', 'great men and nobles', etc. all occur, amongst others, up to 1402. The instance and request of the commons do not always appear, until after 1405. From 1390 to 1393, the only assent mentioned is 'the assent of the said parliament'.

(ii) The term 'lords temporal' occurs first in 1389.

(iii) The term 'lords spiritual and temporal and commons' occurs first in the third statute of the same year, 1389, which was enacted at their complaint, by advice of the great council. A statute by assent of the lords spiritual and lords temporal, and at instance of the commons, occurs first in 1402; and thenceforward, with four exceptions (1404, 1416, 1419, 1429), these three estates appear in the sanctioning clause of every statute.

(iv) Although the four statutes of the years 1390–93 were said to be assented to by 'the said parliament', the phrase 'and by authority of parliament' does not occur until 1433, and not again until 1444; but from then on, with the exception of 1448 and of the first chapter of the eighth statute of Edward IV (1468), it is invariably present.

With these facts of parliamentary usage in mind, we can now survey the history of that expression 'estate of the realm', wherein the word 'estate' must have meant (in the words of the *New English Dictionary*) 'an order or class regarded as part of the body politic, and as such participating in the government

---

[1] The word 'estate' is never used in the assenting clauses; but since at least from 1381 it was employed to designate the orders in parliament, we may use it to mean those orders in parliament which are explicitly stated to assent to the statutes. It must, however, be borne in mind that, though for a time after 1377 justices and others were alluded to as estates of parliament, nevertheless justices were never after that date explicitly mentioned in statutes as assentors.

either directly or through its representatives'. Our starting-place for this purpose is the record of the parliament of 1399, and the documents appertaining to the deposition of Richard II contained therein.

The meaning of the whole transactions at Henry IV's accession in 1399 has recently been subjected to a searching analysis and restatement.[1] It is no longer possible to assume, as hitherto it usually has assumed, that Henry IV succeeded on the strength of a parliamentary title, or even that parliament as such participated in his elevation. There may be, as Dr Lapsley shows, strong reason to believe that the Lancastrian party as a whole intended that Henry should have a parliamentary title;[2] but there is almost equally strong reason to believe that Henry refused to have any such title, and manœuvred himself into a position in which he could make himself 'what parliament could never make him, nor revolution either —a legitimate king having no less a measure of power than, and no sanction inferior to, those that Richard had enjoyed'.[3] 'I suggest', says Dr Lapsley, at the end of his penetrating examination, 'that our evidence is best interpreted by supposing that Henry could have had a complete and technically correct parliamentary title, that his supporters intended that the revolution should be accomplished in that way, and that Henry by a *coup de main* at the last moment was able to obtain the

[1] G. T. Lapsley, 'The Parliamentary Title of Henry IV', *E.H.R.* (1934), XLIX, 423–449, 578–606.
[2] This seems a reasonable inference from a statement in Adam of Usk's *Chronicon*, 24. The text runs thus: 'Item, per certos doctores, episcopos, et alios, quorum presencium notator unus extiterat, deponendi regem Ricardum et Henricum, Lancastriae ducem, subrogandi in regem materia, et qualiter et ex quibus causis, juridice committebatur disputanda. Per quos determinatum fuit quod perjuria, sacrilegia, sodomica, subditorum exinnanicio, populi in servitutem reduccio, vecordia, et ad regendum imbecilitas, quibus rex Ricardus notorie fuit infectus, per capitulum "Ad Apostolice" (extractus De re judicata in Sexto) cum ibi notatis, deponendi Ricardum cause fuerant sufficientes; et, licet cedere paratus fuerat, tamen ob causas premissas ipsum fore deponendum cleri et populi autoritate, ob quam causam tunc vocabantur, pro majori securritate fuit determinatum.' (The reference to the canon law is to *Sext. Decret.* II, tit. XIV, § ii.)
[3] Lapsley, *op. cit.* 596.

Crown on the grounds of conquest, inheritance, and some loose form of acceptance.'[1]

It is pertinent to our present purpose to notice what, in the complete absence of any parliamentary sanction, exactly was this 'loose form of acceptance'. If the acceptance was not by parliament, then by whom was it? In so far as any definite answer is possible to this question, it must be: 'by the estates of the realm'. In lieu of parliament, it was the estates which were invoked by that name to discharge the formalities involved in the revolution. This fact becomes evident when the documents[2] are examined, and usages therein of the term 'estates', in one form or another, are noted. The name 'parliament', indeed, was not once mentioned as the sanctioning body in the course of the proceedings—the only collective name applied to that body was 'the estates'.

It has never been in dispute that Richard, in his own name and in the usual form, even if not of his own free will, issued, on the 19th of August, 1399, writs of summons to a parliament to meet on Tuesday, the 30th of September.[3] So far as we know, these writs were obeyed in a perfectly normal way. The great abnormality did not occur until the day before the parliament was due to meet. On that day—Monday, the 29th of September—Richard (according to the official Lancastrian account, with which alone we are concerned here) abdicated, and absolved all his subjects from their allegiance.[4] He then, it was said, immediately stated that if it were in his power, Henry of Lancaster should succeed him. He appointed the archbishop of York and the bishop of Hereford to be his proctors, and to read

---

[1] *Ibid.* 606.

[2] For a most important discussion of the documents, *v.* M. V. Clarke and V. Galbraith, 'The Deposition of Richard II', *Bull. J.R.L.* (1930), XIV, 125–155. The partisan character of the account of the transactions on the parliament roll is here exposed; but this character, of course, adds to the value of the documents as evidence of Henry's views and intentions.

[3] Cf. *Annales Henrici Quarti,* 251: 'Post haec, missa sunt brevia, sub nomine Regis Ricardi, ad omnes status regni qui Parliamento interesse debebant.'

[4] *Rot. Parl.* III, 416.

his renunciation to all 'the estates of the kingdom' (*not* to
parliament, be it noted). This the bishops did on the next day,
Tuesday, the 30th of September. In the great hall of Westminster, in the place prepared for holding parliament, they
announced Richard's renunciation in Latin and in English,
before the lords and people there gathered 'propter factum
Parliamenti'.[1] By these 'estates and people' the renunciation
was admitted, a list of Richard's crimes drawn up, and his
deposition authorised; to them Henry submitted his claim, by
them it was accepted, and by them were appointed commissioners to read the sentence to Richard; to them it was proclaimed that parliament would be held *on the following Monday*,
summoned by writs issued on that day by the new king.[2]
Finally, when that parliament met and was addressed by the
archbishop, it was suggested by him that until that moment in
the proceedings no lawful parliament had met. He mentioned
the fact of Richard's summons, and expressly stated that that
summons had been made of no force or effect, because of the
acceptance of Richard's abdication and his deposition.[3] Moreover, though the 'record and process' of the renunciation and
deposition were enrolled on the roll of this parliament, no suggestion whatever was made that the proceedings were being ratified
in any way by the parliament; they were merely recorded, and
in that record the authority of parliament was not once invoked.

It is clear enough who most of the people at Westminster
were, during the crucial scenes. The crowd in the hall were

---

[1] Cf. *Chronicles of London*, 23: 'And in the morowe, that is fforto say on the
Tewesday in the ffeste off Seinte Jerome, in the grete halle at Westm. in the place
ther the parlement shulde be holde, worshypfully arayed, beyng ther present the
Erchebisshopes off Canterbury and offe Yorke, the Duk off Lancastre, and other
Dukes, and lordes both Temporell and Spirituell, whos names ben wretyn her
affter, and also other peple off the same Rewme, thanne beyng ther ffor nedys off
the parlement with grete multytude.'

[2] *Rot. Parl.* III, 417–422.

[3] *Ibid.* 415: 'Quelle summons ne feust du null force n'effect a cause de l'accep-
tation de la Renunciation fait par le dit Roy et de la deposition de mesme le roy
Richard que feust fait le Maresdy suis dit....' Dr Lapsley considers (*op. cit.*
602–603) that this doctrine of the invalidation of the writs by the cession of the
crown was first formulated during these transactions.

those lords spiritual and temporal, and at least many of the commons, who had come there in response to Richard's writ of summons, together with a mob of indefinite status. All these were, throughout the proceedings, described and referred to, in some sense or other, as the 'estates of the realm', and the usage of this term we must examine in detail.

Richard, as already noted, on the Monday read out his renunciation to certain lords and other notable persons in the council chamber, and was reported to have declared that if it were in his power, the duke of Lancaster should succeed him in the kingdom, 'set quia hoc in potestate sua minime defendebat'; he appointed the archbishop of York and the bishop of Hereford to be his proctors to declare his cession and renunciation, 'omnibus statibus dicti regni';[1] and he asked them to announce 'in ea parte populo' his wish and intention to that effect. On the next day these proctors, in Westminster Hall, before the lords spiritual and temporal and a great multitude of people there gathered on account of the parliament, discharged this duty. And then

Statim ut fuerat interrogatum a Statibus et Populo tunc ibidem presentibus, primo videlicet ab Archiepiscopo Cantuarien' predicto ...si pro eorum interesse et utilitate Regni vellent Renunciationem et Cessionem eandem admittere. Status iidem et Populus... unanimiter et concorditer admiserunt.[2]

So far it might possibly be said that the word 'estate' was being used only to mean 'persons of estate'; and no doubt that may be true. But it was a different matter when, in the list of 'objections' to Richard, it was alleged that in the last parliament he had subtly procured 'quod Potestas Parliamenti de consensu *omnium Statuum Regni* sui remaneret apud quasdam certas Personas',[3] etc., and had alienated the property of the crown and the crown jewels and regalia, without permission of the estates of the kingdom.[4]

---

[1] *Rot. Parl.* III, 417, no. 14.   [2] *Ibid.* nos. 15, 16.   [3] *Ibid.* 418, no. 25.
[4] *Ibid.* 420, no. 41. The term also appears in no. 50.

When the list of enormities was exhausted,

quoniam videbatur omnibus Statibus illis, superinde singillatim ac etiam communiter interrogatis, quod ille Cause Criminum et Defectuum erant satis sufficientes et notorie ad deponendum eundem Regem, attenta etiam sua Confessione super ipsius Insufficientia et aliis in dicta Renunciatione et Cessione contentis patenter emissa, omnes Status predicti unanimiter consenserunt, ut ex habundanti ad depositionem dicti Regis procederetur, pro majori securitate et tranquillitate populi, ac Regni comodo faciendam. Unde Status et Communitates...

appointed commissioners to draft the sentence of deposition, and to depose him from all the dignity, majesty, and honour of king,

Vice, nomine et auctoritate omnium Statuum predictorum prout in consimilibus casibus de antiqua consuetudine dicti Regni fuerat observatum.[1]

The form of this sentence was then drawn up, and these words therein call for careful notice:

'In dei nomine Amen. Nos Johannes Episcopus Assaven'', etc., etc., 'per Pares et Proceres Regni Anglie Spirituales et Temporales et ejusdem Regni Communitates *omnes Status ejusdem Regni representantes*, Commissarii ad infra scripta specialiter deputati...'

in view of Richard's crimes—'coram dictis Statibus palam et publice propositis'—and in view of his renunciation,

ac de voluntate et mandato suis coram dictis Statibus publicata, eisque notificata et exposita in vulgari, prehabita super hiis et omnibus in ipso negotio actitatis coram Statibus antedictis et nobis deliberatione diligenti, vice, nomine et auctoritate nobis in hac parte commissa, etc.,

they deposed him.[2] The record then goes on to report that,

volentes autem preterea dicti Status ut nichil defit quod valeat aut debeat circa premissa requiri,

---

[1] *Rot. Parl.* III, 422, no. 51.   [2] *Ibid.* no. 52.

they appointed these commissioners to be proctors to withdraw the homage and fealty that they all owed to Richard, and to intimate to him his deposition.[1]

At this point Henry intervened with his claim to the crown, upon which

tam Domini Spirituales quam Temporales et omnes Status ibidem presentes singillatim et comuniter interrogati, Quid de illa vendicatione et clameo sentiebant? Iidem Status, cum toto populo absque quacumque difficultate vel mora ut Dux prefatus super eos regnaret unanimiter consenserunt. Et statim ut idem Rex ostendit Statibus Regni Signetum Ricardi Regis, sibi pro intersigno traditum sue voluntatis ut premittitur expressum. . . ;

and he was led to the throne by the archbishop, who thereupon delivered his extraordinary sermon, concluding with the words

et iste vir est talis quod dicetur, regnabit rex et sapiens erit et faciet judicium et justiciam in terra.[2]

Henry then returned thanks, beginning with the words

Sires, I thank God and yowe Spirituel and Temporel and all the Astates of the lond. . . .

After this, the justices and principal officers took the oath to the new king; and it was proclaimed that parliament would be held on the following Monday, and the coronation a week thereafter. A declaration was then made to the effect that this shortening of the time fixed for the parliament was not going to be to the prejudice of the estates of the kingdom:

Quantum autem ad Abbreviationem assignationis diei Parliamenti predicti, fuerat pro parte dicti Regis Protestatio talis facta, videlicet, Quod non erat intentionis sue ut Statibus Regni sui prejudicium afferatur exinde, nec quod hoc trahatur de cetero in exemplum; quin-ymmo quod Abbreviatio illa fiebat tantummodo pro commodo et utilitate Regni; et specialiter, ut quorumcumque ligeorum suorum parcatur laboribus et expensis, quodque super Gravaminibus Populi celere possit remedium adhiberi.[3]

---

[1] *Ibid.* no. 53.   [2] *Ibid.* 423, nos. 54, 55.   [3] *Ibid.* no. 57.

On the next day the last step in the whole transaction took place. That was the announcement to Richard himself of the sentence of the estates and people. William Thirning, J.,[1] for himself, his co-proctors, and as spokesman for all the estates and people, addressed to Richard, in his chamber in the Tower, these words:

> Sire, it is wele knowe to yowe, that ther was a Parlement somond of all the States of the Reaume for to be at Westmynstre and to begynne on the Teusday in the morne of the fest of Seint Michell the Archaungell that was yesterday, by cause of the whiche summons all the States of this Londe were ther gadyrd, the whiche States hole made these same persones that ben comen here to yowe nowe her Procuratours, and gafen hem full auctorite and power, and charged hem, for to say the wordes that we shall say to yowe in her name and on thair behalve; that is to wytten, the Bysshop of Seint Assa' for Ersbischoppes and Bysshoppes; the Abbot of Glastenbury for Abbotes and Priours and all other men of Holy Chirche Seculers and Rewelers; the Erle of Gloucestre for Dukes and Erles; the Lord of Berkeley for Barones and Banerettes; Sir Thomas Irpyngham, Chaumberleyn, for all the Bachilers and Commons of this Lond be southe; Sire Thomas Grey for all the Bachilers and Commons by north; and my felawe John Markham and me, for to come wyth hem for all these States. And so, Sire, thes wordes and the doyng that we shall say to yowe is not onlych our wordes bot the wordes and the doynges of all the States of this lond and our charge and in her name.

At this point Richard answered, and said 'that he wyst wele that we wold noght say bot os we were charged'; and Thirning continued:

> Sire, ye remember yowe wele that on Moneday in the fest of Seint Michell the Archaungell, ryght here in this Chaumbre and in what presence, ye renounsed and cessed of the State of Kyng, and of Lordeship and of all the Dignite and Wirshipp that longed therto and assoiled all your lieges of her ligeance and obeisance that longed to yowe, uppe the fourme that is contened in the same Renunciation and Cession which ye redde your self by your mouth, and affermed

---

[1] It is noticeable that a justice and not a peer was chosen spokesman.

it by your othe and by your owne writyng. Opon whiche ye made and ordeyned your Procuratours the Ersbysshopp of York, and the Bysshopp of Hereford, for to notifie and declare in your name thes Renunciation and Cession at Westmynstre to all the States and all the People that was ther gadyrd by cause of the sommons forsayd; the whiche thus don yesterday by thes Lordes your Procuratours, and wele herde and understonden, thes Renunciation and Cession ware pleinelich and frelich accepted and fullich agreed by all the States and People forsayd. And over this, Sire, at the instance of all thes States and People ther ware certein articles of Defautes in your Governance redde there; and tho wele herd and pleinelich understonden to all the States forsaide, hem thought hem so trewe and so notorie and knowen that by thes Causes and by no other, os thei sayd, and havyng consideration to your owne Wordes in your owne Renunciation and Cession that ye were not worthy no sufficeant, ne able, for to governe for your owne Demerites, os it is more pleinerlych contened therin, hem thoght that was resonable and Cause for to depose yowe, and her Commissaries that thei made and ordeined, os it is of record ther, declared and decreed, and adjugged yowe for to be deposed and pryved, and in dede deposed yowe and pryved yowe of the Astate of Kyng, and of the Lordeshipe contened in the Renunciation and Cession forsayd, and of all the Dignite and Wyrshipp and of all the Administration that longed ther to. And we, Procuratours to all these States and People forsayd, os we be charged by hem and by hir autorite gyffen us, and in her name yeld yowe uppe, for all the States and People forsayd, Homage liege and Feaute, and all Ligeance, and all other bondes, charges, and services that long therto. And that non of all thes States and People fro this tyme forward ne bere yowe feyth, ne do yowe obesiance os to thar Kyng.

And Richard replied, and said 'that he loked not ther after; Bot that after all this he hoped that his Cosyn wolde be goode Lord to hym'.[1]

Up to the beginning of this final scene in the deposition drama, as we have noted, there has been little indication of what was meant by the expression 'these estates', except the implied

---

[1] *Rot. Parl.* III, 424, no. 59. The *Annales* relate how Richard was reluctant to renounce his spiritual honour. *V. supra*, Chapter I, p. 7.

meaning of 'the persons of estate here present', etc. Not even
in the passage[1] in which the bishop of St Asaph and his fellow-
commissioners speak of themselves as representing all the
estates of the land can it be said that the word 'estate' necessarily extended to include others than the particular persons
of estate who had appointed them. But here, in Thirning's
delivery of the sentence to Richard, we have the estates on
whose behalf and in whose name Richard was deposed set out
not merely as particular persons, but as orders or ranks in the
nation at large. These were the prelates, other clerics, the
greater magnates, the barons and bannerets, and the bachelors
and commons. These five groups, then—in no respect to be
confused with estates *of* parliament, but distinctive mainly on
social grounds—were, for the moment at least, conceived to be
the estates of the realm, and were, throughout the whole
episode, again and again said to be responsible for the momentous constitutional function of authorising the substitution of
one monarch for another. The sanction of the estates was the
only sanction invoked throughout the entire proceedings.

It would, I think, be rash to suppose that Henry was exercising
any deliberate ingenuity in thus employing the sanction of the
estates, however ingeniously he avoided a parliamentary one.
It is, indeed, not wholly impossible that such was the case. It is
possible that Henry was, in lieu of the parliamentary sanction,
craftily using the idea of the estates for his own purposes. But
more probably the reiterated use of the term 'estate' throughout
the episode was not due to any very deliberate forethought. It
was the natural word to spring to mind in describing the groups
of persons there gathered. No great subtlety was needed for such
a use; but the usage certainly had its consequences. It clearly
made current a notion that the estates of the realm, though not
assembled and operating in the ordinary legal form of parliament, could nevertheless perform the important constitutional
functions involved in the occasion. There could be no doubt

[1] *Rot. Parl.* III, 422, no. 52. Cf. *supra*, p. 110.

henceforth that the estates of the realm authorised the substitution of one monarch for another. There also could be no doubt that the name, and therefore the associated ideas, of the estates of the realm had been very prominently applied to Richard's last and still-born parliament. This application might have encouraged the currency of the idea that the high court of parliament was itself the estates of the realm, and thus have closely identified the notion of the popular sanction of the estates with the curial authority of parliament.

It does, in fact, look as though something of this kind actually happened. We would not, of course, suggest that the national-assembly idea of parliament had not gone far before 1399. But it is not without significance that before 1399 there is no evidence that parliament was ever actually called 'the estates of the realm', whereas soon after that date it frequently was so called. Henry, perhaps, was increasing the popularity of ideas which had a greater future before them than he could have imagined.

The background of ideas—the ideas of the natural orders of society, of the spiritual, noble, and plebeian estates, the usages of the word 'estate', and the distinctions of various estates of parliament, which would seem to have made the employment of the word natural in 1399, we have already endeavoured to trace. It now remains to note how to all appearances, during the course of the century, any constitutional significance that the estates of the land might have enjoyed became identified with parliament itself; how the old idea of the threefold division of society facilitated the definition of the estates as the three orders of lords spiritual, lords temporal, and commons; how these three estates were conceived to constitute parliament—so that Fortescue, in the sixties, could say that the 'king did not impose subsidies or make laws without the consent of the three estates';[1] and how, moreover, parliament itself was conceived to be the three estates of the realm. To attempt this task, we

[1] *De Natura*, 77.

must trace the history of the expression 'estates of the realm' in constitutional contexts during the century.

A passage which has already been quoted earlier in the present study has an added force here. It will be remembered that in 1401 the commons were reported to have come before the king, and to have indicated how it seemed to them that the estates of the realm might be likened to a Trinity—that was to say, the person of the king, the lords spiritual and temporal, and the commons—and how it would be to the general desolation if there were any dissension among these estates.[1] This appearance of the 'estate of king' in the guise of an estate of the realm is, I think, repeated only once again,[2] and is obviously anomalous.

More significantly, we find that in the rebellious manifesto put forward by the Percies in 1406, it was alleged that Henry had promised not to impose taxes 'nisi per considerationem trium statuum regni in parliamento'.[3] Then, in the parliament of 1404, Bishop Beaufort, the chancellor, in his sermon, 'resembla chescun Roialme a un Corps de Homme, per ont la partie dextre il resemble a seinte Eglise, et la partie sinistre a la Temporaltee, et les autres membres a la Communaltee du Roialme, per ont mesme nostre Seignour le Roi veullant avoir advis, conseil, et assent generalment des toutz les Estates de son Roialme, ad fait sommoner son Parlement au present'.[4] Two years later, Thomas Langley, pro-chancellor, said much the same thing—that the king wished 'en si grand bosoigne avoir l'advis et conseil de plusours et pluis notables persones de son Roialme, come sont les Estatz d'icel en cest present Parlement'.[5] The famous articles of reform of 1406 included a request that the fixing of two special days in the week for the hearing of petitions by the king should be intimated 'as toutes les Estates du Roialme en cest present Parlement'.[6]

[1] *Rot. Parl.* III, 459. Cf. *supra*, p. 69.
[2] By Bishop Russell, in 1483 (*v. infra*, p. 168).
[3] *Hardyng's Chronicle*, 351–354, n.   [4] *Rot. Parl.* III, 522.
[5] *Ibid.* 567.   [6] *Ibid.* 586.

Of great interest for our purpose is the famous incident of 1407, when the commons took exception to the fact that the lords, after discussing the estate of the realm, informed the king —without consulting the commons—how much taxation they thought was necessary. The representations that the commons made to the king led to a statement which shows explicitly how far the estate notion had gone by this date. 'Et depuis qe nostre dit Seigneur le Roy', it was said, 'ce avoit entenduz, nient veullant qe riens soit fait a present, n'en temps advener, que tournir purroit ascunement encontre la Libertee de l'Estate pur quelle ils sont venuz au Parlement,' etc., etc.; and it was agreed that nothing should be done 'a prejudice ou derogation de la Libertee de l'Estate pur quell mesmes les Communes sont presentement venuz, ne en cest present Parlement, ne en null autre en temps advenir. Mais voet, que luy mesmes, et toutz les autres Estates soient auxi franks come ils feurent par devaunt.'[1]

Then quite exceptionally significant is the assertion by Henry IV himself, in the letter he dispatched in 1409 to Alexander V, after the council of Pisa had come to an end.[2] He expressed the hope that the work of the council would be continued, and said that 'in this event we propose to send ambassadors to give clear answers upon the matters expounded to us discretely and elegantly by the envoys of your holiness, after first taking mature counsel, as is right and fitting, with the nobles and estates of our realm in parliament to be summoned especially on that account, without the calling of which or the assent of the estates aforesaid, since it touches their interest, no statutes or ordinances previously made can be revoked or changed'.[3]

---

[1] *Ibid.* 611. This text illustrates the idea that an estate could be in the country and also by its representatives be in parliament at the same time.

[2] Cf. *supra*, p. 59.

[3] *Harleian MSS.* 431, fo. 42. This passage was brought to light by Professor E. F. Jacob, in 'Some English Documents of the Conciliar Movement', *Bull. J.R.L.* (1931), xv, 379. The text runs: 'Habito primitus ut est opus et congruit

We can detect, henceforward,[1] an apparent facility with which the kings invoked the necessity of consulting the estates of the realm in the course of their foreign diplomacy—especially at moments when it seemed desirable to show reluctance or make difficulties in granting unpalatable concessions to other rulers. But before we pass to that phase of our survey, we may well note a curious reference unearthed by Wylie, which suggests that in some sense even Richard's supporters shared a notion of the right of the estates to set up a king.[2] This seems to be the meaning of the words which got Philip FitzEustace, prior of St Botolph's, into trouble at Colchester, in 1404. It was alleged that he had spoken derisively of the king 'as not elected by the magnates and *state* of England, but by the London rabble'.

Just as Henry IV probably had done, so Henry V, in 1419, informed the pope that the statute of Provisors could not be repealed without the consent of the three estates.[3] Then in the treaty of Troyes, as is well known, the three estates of each realm were invoked to ratify and confirm the agreement between the monarchs. In the preamble to the English ratification of the treaty, it was stated that 'in cujus Pacis tractatu inter cetera continetur, quod dicta Pax nedum per dictos Duos Reges jurari, set etiam per tres status utriusque Regni debeat laudari,

---

superinde cum proceribus et statibus regni nostri deliberacione matura, praesertim in parliamento nostro propterea celebrando, sine cuius vocatione et statuum predictorum assensu, cum illorum in premissis interesse versetur, nulla statuta vel ordinaciones in eo parte prius edita reuocari poterunt aut mutari.' Professor Jacob suspects that the particular reference to statutes was meant to allude to the question of provisors.

[1] Cf. a letter of Richard II to Pedro IV of Aragon, in 1386, relating to giving satisfaction for injuries committed by Englishmen to Barcelonese ships (*Diplomatic Correspondence of Richard II*, ed. E. Perroy, Camden Society, 3rd ser. (1933), XLVIII, no. 65): '...Super quo vestre elutescat nobilitati quod circa tanta et tam ardua negocia nos et regnum nostrum tangencia iam existimus occupati, quominus super hiis que ut predicitur nobis scripsistis in aliquo deliberare poterimus pro presenti, volumus nichilomini et disposuimus tam pro debito nostro quam pro vestre magestatis complacencia ad nostrum proximum parliamentum vel magnum consilium in complementum iusticie super huiusmodi....'

[2] Wylie, *Henry IV*, I, 420; *P.R.O. Exch. Treas. Recpt.*, 21 a/8(6).

[3] *Rymer*, ix, 808; Wylie and Waugh, *Henry V*, III, 171.

acceptari et approbari'.[1] The treaty, it was said, had already
received the approval of the French estates, viz. 'Prelatorum et
Cleri, necnon Procerum et Nobilium, ac etiam Civium Burgen-
sium Civitatum, Villarum ac Communitatum dicti Regni'. It
then remained for the same to be done by the three estates of
this realm, viz. 'Prelatis et Clero, Nobilibus et Magnatibus
necnon Communitatibus dicti Regni'; and for this and other
purposes the king had summoned these estates. Before these
three estates the peace was explained by the chancellor, who
by the king's command required 'quod dicti Tres Status
tenorem dicte Pacis inspicerent et visitarent; quibus sic diligenter et mature peractis, ipsi Tres Status considerantes, cen-
sentes, et reputantes, dictam Pacem laudabilem', etc., 'utrisque
Regnis et subditis eorumdem, ymmo et toti Christianitati,
ipsam Pacem, et omnia et singula contenta in eadem, ipsius
Domini nostri Regis ut prefertur, mandato, velud Tres Status
dicti Regni sui approbarunt', etc.

The clear distinction here of precisely what was held to
constitute the three estates in the two countries would in itself
make improbable Professor Pollard's contention that 'the
advantages of uniformity at the confirmation of this treaty
suggested the employment of identical phraseology'.[2] But it is
unnecessary, after all the evidence which has been adduced, to
labour the point that there was nothing novel at this date in
speaking of the 'three estates' as performing constitutional
functions. We need only continue with our survey of the usage
of the expression which Professor Pollard tells us 'from this time
comes slowly and doubtingly into English official and popular
use'.[3]

On the receipt of the news of Henry V's death, it will be
remembered, certain lords spiritual and temporal assembled to
make provision for the necessities of governance, and arranged
for the summons of a parliament, 'a l'entente que par le com-

[1] *Rot. Parl.* IV, 135.
[2] *The Evolution of Parliament*, 70.　　[3] *Ibid.*

mune assemble de toutz estates du Roialme et lour sages con-
seilles et discretions', to do the better for the estate both of the
king and of all the realm.[1] Thenceforward, from time to time,
the phrase 'the three estates in parliament' was used. For example, the articles for council procedure in 1429 were said to
be read 'coram Domino Rege in eodem Parliamento, in pre-
sentia trium regni Statuum'.[2] Again, in 1433, Bedford chal-
lenged his critics 'coram Domino Rege et tribus regni Statibus
in presenti Parliamento'.[3] Furthermore, the expression became
common form in prorogations, and was so used in 1433, 1449,
1450, 1459, 1473, 1488, 1489, 1491,[4] when the announcement
was made 'domino rege et tribus regni Statibus in presenti
Parliamento existentibus'.

When the negotiations at the congress of Arras, in 1435,
went against the English hopes, John Stafford, bishop of Bath
and chancellor, could refer in his parliamentary sermon to
'Constitutio et Assignatio Diete illius absque ipsius Domini
nostri Regis, aut Statuum utriusque Regnorum suorum predictorum consilio vel assensu, contra formam et effectum dicte
magne Pacis' (of Troyes), which had been approved 'per
utriusque Regnorum predictorum Trinos Status'.[5] In his
sermon at the parliament of 1439, the same bishop went further,
and asserted that in the three estates of parliament resided
'Principatus, potestas, et prudentia ad ipsius Regni direc-
tionem'.[6] In 1447 it was said by the chancellor, apropos of the
business in hand: 'cujus quidem Provisionis Ordinatio, Trac-
tatum et maturam deliberationem cum sano et salubri Consilio
Trium Statuum dicti Regni necessario exigit et requirit'.[7]
Even in private letters the same terminology was by this time in
vogue. Thus Sir John Fastolf, one of the duke of Bedford's
executors, writing in 1456 to John Paston—about getting

---

[1] *Rot. Parl.* iv, 170.   [2] *Ibid.* 343.
[3] *Ibid.* 420.
[4] *V.* respectively *Rot. Parl.* iv, 420; v, 67, 172, 213, 370; vi, 39, 424, 426,
444.
[5] *Rot. Parl.* iv, 481.   [6] *Ibid.*   [7] *Ibid.* 128.

counsel's opinion on the drafting of a bill for the recovery of certain of Bedford's goods—proposed that the said bill 'be put up to the Kyng whiche is chief supervisor of my said lordis testament, and to the Lordes Spirituelle and Temporelle, as to the Comyns, of this present Parlement, so as the iii astates may graunte and passe hem cleerly'.[1] It was soon after this—between 1461 and 1463—that Fortescue wrote his *De Natura Legis Naturae*, in which he asserted that 'in regno namque Angliae reges sine trium statuum regni illius consensu leges non condunt nec subsidia imponunt subditis suis'.[2]

Then we are indebted to another bishop of Bath, Robert Stillington, for an exceptionally clear statement of the estate theory. His sermon in 1467 deserves nearly full transcription here:

It was shewed [runs the report] by the Kynges commaundement and in his name by the mouth of the Ryght Reverent Fader in God, the Bysshop of Bathe and Welles, Chaunceller of Englond, unto the seid Lordes and Commons, that Justice was grounde well and rote of all prosperite, peas and pollityke rule of every Reame, wheruppon all the Lawes of the world been grounde and sette, which resteth in thre; that is to say, the Lawe of God, Law of Nature, and posityfe Lawe; and by seying of all Philosofers, felicite or peas in every Reame is evermore caused of Justice, as it appereth by probabill persuacions of Philosofers. Wherfore first be asked, what is Justice? Justice is, every persone to doo his Office that he is put yn accordyng to his astate or degre, and as for this Lond, it is understoud that it stondeth by iij estates and above that oon principall; that is to witte, Lordes Spirituell, Lordes Temporell, and Commons, and over that, State Riall above, as oure Soverayn Lorde the Kyng, which had yeven unto hym in commaundement to sey unto theym, that his entent fynall was to ministre Lawe and Justice and to plante, fixe, and sette peas thorough all this his Reame, by th' advis of his Lordes Spirituell and Temporell [note the omission of the commons] and also entended to provide an outward pease for the defence and suerte of this Reame....

[1] *Paston Letters*, ed. Gairdner, 1, no. 272.
[2] *De Natura*, 77.

At this point he made some reference to foreign policy and to the possibility of a French War, and then concluded:

> ...These causes and thinges, and meny other moeved the Kynges Highnes, so that he might have thi assistens of the iij estates of this Lond, and that every of theym wold do his office and duete, to procede and folowe the recovere of his Reame of Fraunce and Lordshipes be yonde the See for the wele, suerte, peas and defence of this Lond, with the grace of God.[1]

The grafting of the idea of estates on to the idea of parliament as a court had by this time, it is clear, gone very far. But there still remain some further illustrations of that process which are of outstanding interest; and even at the cost of still further lengthening our survey, we must bring them to notice.

The views of such a man as Bishop Russell, chancellor in 1483, must carry great weight as evidence of the political and constitutional ideas current in his own day; and his drafted speeches deserve a much closer consideration than—buried in an obscure volume of the Camden Society's publications, printed eighty years ago—they have ever received.[2] Here we are concerned only with certain abstracts from them. The first of these—from the speech drafted for the parliament of Edward V, which of course never met—shows a view of the identity of the three estates that depended on a confusion of the nature of the estate

---

[1] *Rot. Parl.* v, 622–623. With the views in this sermon cf. the similar attitude in *Somnium Vigilantis*, attributed by some, but doubtfully, to Fortescue (*E.H.R.* (1911), xxvi, 518): 'I remember that amonge many thinges by the whiche the commone welth of a royame stondyth the most principall is this, a due subjeccion with fayithful and voluntarie honoure and thair appertenaunce to be yolden to þe soverain in the sayd royame and that none incompatible astat be usurped by ony personne; also that thay that have undre the kynge a governance of his peple that they be dylygent to þe kepynge of the kynges lawes and that no wronge be done in ony wyse, but that alle controversies and debates civile or criminalle, realle or personale, ben decided by the kynges lawes withoute mayntenance or wylfull interrupcion of the cours of justice, and in cas that ony thinge falle of the which the determinacion is not expressed in the common lawe, than the prince moste be asked and inquired and by his excedynge auctorite and prudens of his conseyle an expikan shalbe made tharopon, and so that no thinge be done by singular wille and senceall affeccion.' Perhaps Bishop Stillington was the author of this tract.

[2] They are reproduced in Excursus VI, *infra*, pp. 167–191.

royal with that of an estate of the realm proper: 'The policie in christian Remes schewethe,' he proposed to argue, 'over alle yn the dayes that we be yn, how theyr public body is compowned of iij notable partes, of the prince, the nobles, and the peuple. And ther fore havynge to speke at thys tyme of alle iij as they be nowe here assembled for the wele of thys most nobylle and famous Reme of Englond, I have taken a trimembrid text suche as I fownd yn the divine servise of yestirdayes fest, the whyche to my purpose implyethe the present astate of owre nobles, owre commons, and of owre glorious prince and kynge Edward the Vth here present.'[1]

But in the first draft of a revised speech designed for Richard III's parliament, this statement was modified: 'In thys politike body of Englonde', he now wrote: 'there be iij estates as principalle membres vndir oone hede—thestate of the lordys spiritualle, thestate of the lordes temperalle, and thestate of the cominallete. The hede ys owre souuerayne lord the kynge here presente.'[2] Then in the speech which actually was delivered at that parliament, we find an explicit statement which may well form a climax to the whole line of development of ideas which we have been attempting to trace: 'In thys grete body of Englonde we have many diuerse membres vndre oone hede. Howe be hyt they may alle be reduced to iij chyef and princypalle, whyche make thys hyghe and grete courte at thys tyme, that ys to seye, the lordes spiritualle, the lordes temporalle, and the commens.'[3]

But it is the straits to which Richard III was reduced in order to make his title to the throne legally and constitutionally acceptable that provide us with the best and fullest commentary upon, and the conclusion to, this line of development. When Richard's *coup d'état* had been accomplished, and his first parliament had assembled, the following explanation of how he

---

[1] *Grants of Edward V*, p. xxxix; and Excursus VI, *infra*, p. 168.
[2] *Ibid*. p. li, and *infra*, p. 180.
[3] *Ibid*. p. lix, and *infra*, p. 187.

had taken upon himself the crown and governance was enrolled
on its rolls:

> Where late heretofore, that is to say before the Consecracion,
> Coronacion and Inthronization of our Soveraign Lord the King
> Richard the Thirde, a Rolle of Perchement conteyning in writeing
> certaine Articles of the tenour undre writen, on the behalve and in the
> name of the thre Estates of this Realme of Englond, that is to wite,
> of the Lords Spirituals and Temporalls, and of the Commons, by
> many and diverse Lords Spirituells and Temporalls and other
> Nobles and notable persones of the Commons in grete multitude...

was presented to and accepted by the king; and the statement
continues:

> Nowe forasmuch as neither the said three Estates, neither the
> said personnes, which in thair name presented and delivered as is
> abovesaid, the said Rolle unto our said Souverain Lord the Kyng
> were assembled in fourme of Parliament, by occasion whereof,
> diverse doubts, and questions and ambiguities, been moved and
> engendred in the myndes of diverse personnes, as it is said; There-
> fore, to the perpetuall memorie of the trouth, and declaration of thi
> same, bee it ordeyned, provided and established in this present
> Parliament, that the tenour of the said Rolle, with all the contynue
> of the same presented... in the name and on the behalve of the said
> three Estates out of Parliament, now by the same three Estates
> assembled in this present Parliament and by auctorite of the same,
> bee ratifyed, enrolled, recorded, approved and auctorised, etc. etc.[1]

This roll of parchment itself reviewed the 'title' of Richard,
affirmed the illegitimacy of Edward V's sons, and went on to
say that

> we humbly desire, pray, and require youre seid Noble Grace, that
> accordyng to this Eleccion of us the Thre Estates of this Lande, as
> by youre true Enherritaunce, ye will accepte and take upon You the
> said Crown and Royall Dignite, with all thyngs therunto annexed
> and apperteynyng, as to You of Right bilongyng, as wele by En-
> herritaunce as by lawful Eleccion.

[1] *Rot. Parl.* vi, 240.

Finally, the roll stated

howe that the Courte of Parliament is of suche auctorite, and the people of this Lande of suche nature and disposicion, as experience teacheth that manifestacion and declaration of any trueth or right, made by the Thre Estates of this Reame assembled in Parliament, and by auctorite of the same, maketh, before all other thyngs, moost feith and certaynte, and, quietyng mens myndes, remoeveth the occasion of all doubts and seditious language. Therfore, at the request, and by assent of the Thre Estates of this Reame, that is to say, the Lordes Spirituelx and Temporelx, and Commoens of this Lande, assembled in this present Parliament, by auctorite of the same, bee it pronounced, decreed, and declared that oure said Soverayne Lord the Kyng, was, and is, veray and undoubted Kyng of this Reame of Englond, with all thyngs therunto...as well by right of Consanguinite and Enheritaunce, as by lawefull Elleccion, Consecration and Coronacion....[1]

The development that had taken place in constitutional ideas since the events of 1399 is thus manifest. As in the case of Henry IV, the estates are invoked as the sanction for Richard III's accession, apart from the alleged hereditary claims; but the estates have, by this time, been clearly defined as the three orders of lords spiritual, lords temporal, and commons. And moreover, though these orders are conceived as acting out of parliament, still it is admitted that in form of parliament their authority is much greater; and their action is now ratified and approved in parliament, and, above all, by the authority of parliament. Parliament is all it was in 1398; but it is now more than that—it is now also a meeting of the three estates of the realm. The older royalist and legal idea of parliament as the king's court, summoned by the force of his writ, has seemingly had grafted on to it the extraneous political and social idea[2] of the national sanction of the estates of the realm, acting—whether for themselves or through representatives—in their own name and with an authority of their own. It was, surely,

---

[1] *Ibid.* 241–242.
[2] Cf. *Livio da Forli* (5, relating to 1413): '...per Concionem publicam totius regni, quam parliamentum vocant....'

this very idea, with the ultimate implications involved, which gradually worked that transformation in parliamentary theory which appeared during the three centuries from 1399 to 1688; and the fifteenth century, we may say, witnessed the completion of the grafting of this idea on to the older idea of parliament as a court. Henceforth nothing was thought of as being enacted by the king in his parliament, save by *assent* of the three estates of lords spiritual, lords temporal, and commons, and by the *authority* of parliament. But of course the evolution of ideas is one thing, and the working out of the practical results thereof is another. It is no part of our business here to discuss the results; but it is hoped that the present study has made a little clearer the actual development of the *notion* of parliament during the period under review, and has also made a little more intelligible that process of constitutional evolution which rendered possible Coke's definition of the high and most honourable court of parliament as consisting 'of the King's Majesty sitting there as in his royal politick capacity, and of the three estates of the realm, to wit, the Lords spiritual, the Lords temporal, and the Commons representing the Commons of all the land'[1]—a definition admitted by the royalist lawyer Cowell, in his legal dictionary of 1607; acceptable to Jacob, in his dictionary of 1744; and adhered to by Blackstone.

It has generally been supposed that the division of parliament into two houses, in the modern sense, was not a mediaeval development. We do not, to be sure, find the term 'houses of parliament' used during the fifteenth century, though 'house of parliament' and 'parliament house' occasionally appear in the documents.[2] Nevertheless, there can be no doubt that the

---

[1] *IV Institutes*, i.

[2] *E.g. v. Anonimalle Chron.* ed. Galbraith, 83: '...et vendrent al huse de parlement'; *Scrope's Articles* (1404), *Inner Temple, Petyt MSS.* 538, 17, fo. 240: '...the said Lord Henry standing upp in the Parliament house stoutly and proudly before them all said and affirmed that the kingdome of England...did pertain to him'; C. Welch, *History of the Pewterers*, 27–28 (1461), 'Item, paid for making of a bill to Cobbe for to put in parliament house...iij s.' (cited Dunham, *Fane Fragment*, 65);

existence of two distinct houses was recognised clearly before the century was over. We can trace the term 'house of commons' from the very beginning of the century; and though for long it is not possible to say that this term was used in any but a locative sense, yet by the end of the century it had, it seems, acquired its definite institutional sense.

The earliest use of the term 'common house' apparently occurs in a piece of reminiscence written by John Hardyng, who was for many years a member of Henry Percy's household, and whose account, therefore, of the manifesto which he said Hotspur had issued before the battle of Shrewsbury is of great value. Among the recollections appended to his chronicle, he includes—apropos of Lancastrian pretensions—the following: 'Also I herde the seide erle of Northumberlonde saie divers tymes, that he herde duke John of Lancastre, amonge the lordes in counsels and in parlements, and in the common house amonge the knyghtes chosyn for the comons', ask to be admitted heir-apparent to Richard. 'To the which the lordes spirituell and temporell and the commons, in the common house, be hoole aduyse' replied that Roger, earl of Mortimer, was the true heir-apparent.[1] The term 'common house' is in this anecdote probably, though not certainly, merely locative in sense.

In the year 1404, the Speaker in parliament found it desirable to ask the king to command all the knights, citizens, and burgesses to be in the house assigned them at Westminster every day by eight o'clock;[2] and a similar command was given to the lords by the chancellor.

A slightly more developed sense of the term appears in 1433, when an oath to abstain from wrong-doing was taken by Protector Bedford and the lords, and applied by Bedford to the commons: 'In eorum domo communi', the commons, it was

and *Paston Letters*, III, no. 720 (John Paston to Sir John Paston, March 26th, 1473): '...no more, but I prey God send yow the Holy Gost amonge yow in the Parlement Howse, and rather the Devyll, we say, then ye shold grante eny more taskys.'

[1] *Hardyng's Chronicle*, 353.
[2] *Rot. Parl.* III, 523 a.

said, were sworn as the lords had been.[1] Sixteen years later, in the parliament which saw the ruin of Suffolk, the Speaker 'opened, and declared in the Common Hous' the events leading to the duke's committal to the Tower.[2] Again, in Gloucester's protest against the release of the duke of Orléans, in 1440, we read that 'Item, as in your tendre age the saide cardinal [Beaufort], thanne being bisshop of Winchestre and chauncellier of Englande, delivered the king of Scottes upon certaine appointements, as may be shewed, and is presumed to be doen by auctorite of parlement, where in dede I have herd full notable men of the Lower Hous saye that they never hard of it amonges them.'[3] Here it seems that an institutional sense is being given to the word 'house'. This institutional sense of the word is also to be found in the Latin phrase of Abbot Whethamstede, who wrote that a number of bills were put 'in Domum Inferiorem, inter Communes', during the parliament at Reading in 1453;[4] and who alluded to Thomas Charletone's appointment to the Speakership (in the room of the unfortunate Thomas Thorpe), with the words 'regimen Domus Inferioris in se suscipiens'.[5]

But it is in the somewhat unlikely context of private letters which emerged from the prison of the Fleet in 1454, that the earliest definitely institutional use of the term 'house of commons' appears to occur. A certain Thomas Denyes, at one time a dependant of the earl of Oxford (whose enmity, however, he subsequently incurred), wrote to John Paston, on the 20th of March, setting forth his woes. He laid chief emphasis upon the point that 'how be a full straunge acte is passid agayn me in the Higher House before the Lords, whereof I send you a copie. Neverthelesse I hope to God that it shal not passe in the Comon

---

[1] *Rot. Parl.* iv, 422 b.   [2] *Rot. Parl.* v, 177 a.
[3] *Letters and Papers of Henry VI*, ii, ii, 444.
[4] *Whethamstede Johannis Registrum*, ed. H. T. Riley, i, 92: 'Cujus tractatus in temporibus, inferebant quamplures billas suas in Domum Inferiorem, inter Communes, petebantque ab ipsis pacificam audientiam, bonamque gratiam expeditionis.'
[5] *Ibid.* 136.

House....'[1] Here, no doubt, the sense of the latter term is mainly, if not purely, locative—though the application of the adjective 'higher' to the house of lords suggests a distinct institutional sense in that instance. But in the next letter by the same writer on the same theme, dated May 3rd, the institutional idea is plain. In this letter Denyes wrote: 'for sith myn enmyes coude not avail to send me to the castel of Bristow (which was their purpose, whan thei undirstood the disposicion of the Comons House agayn their billes), ever sith they make a privy labor to haf me remevid.'[2] The same idea is clearly present in the Lords Journal of 1461. 'Item', it reads, 'this day there come up from the lower house a notable nomber of the substans of the same house.'[3]

For many years, nevertheless, the merely locative sense remained in use. Thus, in 1455, Young's petition referred to the freedom of the commons to speak 'in the Hous of their assemble', and to the house 'accustomed for the Commons';[4] and in 1460, Clerk's petition likewise referred to 'the house for the Commens accustumed'.[5] Again, in 1483, the chancellor strictly charged the commons to assemble in their common and accustomed house.[6] But the institutional sense seems to be present when Friar Brackley writes to John Paston—apropos of a county election—that 'we sey in this cuntre that Heydon is for Barkschir in the Comon Hows';[7] and also when, in 1467, the commons petitioned that various lords and certain 'persones of the Comen House' be appointed to a committee on coinage problems.[8] Bishop Russell, in one of his parliamentary addresses, used the word in both its senses: 'Thys', he wrote, 'ys the howse of the senate. The Commons have ther apart. And lyke as yn thys house one *tanquam consul* makithe the questions, soo yn the

[1] *Paston Letters*, I, no. 199. [2] *Ibid.* no. 204.
[3] *Fane Fragment*, 19. [4] *Rot. Parl.* v, 337 a.
[5] *Ibid.* 374 b. Cf. *The Brut*, I, 530: 'At which parlement [of 1460] þe commones of þe reame being assembled in þe common house....'
[6] *Rot. Parl.* VI, 196. [7] *Paston Letters*, I, no. 355.
[8] *Rot. Parl.* v, 634 b.

lower house in lyke wyse alle ys directed by the speker *quasi per tribunum.*'[1]

The burgesses for Colchester, in their diary of the parliament of 1485, leave us in no doubt of the institutional sense in which they employed the word. They reported that 'it pleased the Kyng and all his lords for to sende for Maister Speker and all the howse in to the parliament chambir. And we cam theder and wayted upon his grace. So it pleased his grace for to commaunde my lord Chaunseler to proloye his high Co't of parliament....'[2] The *Year-Book* report of case 1 *Henry VII*, Hil. pl. 25 —to the effect that 'an important question was put by the chancellor of England to all the justices, concerning a bill sent into the common house by the Lords in parliament, praying for their assent', etc.[3]—gives another instance of the same sense. Again, when Marowe, in his Reading of 1503 on the keeping of the peace, instructed the apprentices that 'Item, the common house of parliament can grant surety of the peace on petition made to them by any person, and without the assent of the Lords',[4] he was plainly thinking and speaking of the house of commons in the institutional or modern sense.

But though we are thus, seemingly, bound to recognise that by the end of the century the commons had developed sufficient corporate unity and consciousness to be justly conceived as a House, we need to remember that this corporative organisation was still rudimentary and hardly independent. The idea of institutional capacity was there, but only slightly worked out.[5]

When we turn our attention to the ideas current about the place in parliament of the commons, we are at once struck by

[1] *Grants of Edward V*, p. xlv; and Excursus VI, *infra*, p. 174.
[2] *The Red Paper Book of Colchester*, ed. W. G. Benham (1902), 64.
[3] '...un grande question fuit demande per le chancelier de Angleterre de touts les justices, de ceo que ou bill fait mis en le common hous a les seigniours en le parlement eux priant d'assenter....' (App. no. 78.)
[4] Putnam, *Early Treatises*, 303: 'Item, le comen howse del parliement poient graunter surete de peas al peticion fait a eux par ascun person et ceo saunz lassent dez seignurz de mesme le parlement.'
[5] Cf. Pickthorn, *Early Tudor Government*, I, 91, 96, 107.

the fact that the century is pre-eminently the one during which it was becoming usual to conceive of the commons as coming to parliament, not merely for the strictly legal purposes, not merely as parochial representatives, but as delegates of all the commons of the land: in short, representation was passing in idea from local to national implications. This fact is well shown by the commons' use—for a time very rarely, but with increasing frequency—of the expression 'we that be comen for al the common of the land'. The employment of this expression or of varieties of it proves that the house of commons clearly recognised its own character as representative of the whole nation, and not merely of separate localities. As early as the act of Succession of 1407, the commons were described as the 'procurators and attorneys of all the counties, cities, and boroughs and of all the people of the realm'.[1] Then, again, the same idea was expressed in the petition put forward in 1414, asking for recognition of the right of assent and of the right to obtain for their petitions either acceptance or rejection without alteration. In that petition it was said: '...youre humble and trewe lieges that ben come for the Commune of youre lond bysechyn on to youre rigt rigtwesnesse....'[2] But nearly forty years seem to have passed before the expression again appears in the rolls,[3] this time as used by the lords in their reply to Thorpe's petition on privilege, in 1454: 'The seid Lordes Spirituel and Temporel,' it was stated, 'not entendying to empeche or hurt the Libertees and Privelegges of theym that were commen for the Commune of this lande to this present

---

[1] *Rot. Parl.* III, 581.

[2] *Rot. Parl.* IV, 22.

[3] In 1423, however, the commons were expressly instructed to expound to their neighbours 'en sa paiis' the great needs of the country, as declared to them by the lords, so that those needs might be known to the whole commonalty of the realm (*v. Rot. Parl.* IV, 200 b). On occasion, rebels might represent themselves as aiming at the realisation of the wishes of the house of commons. Thus the captain of Kent, in the rebellion of 1450, is said (*Six Town Chronicles*, Bale's Chron. 130) to have 'demeaned him to the lordes in such wyse and called him self and his peple peticioners, answeryng to theym þat his comyng to the heth was not to doo any harme but to have the desires of the comones in the parliament fulfilled'.

Parlement',[1] dealt with the petition. In the same parliament, the commons requested that they should not be asked for another grant, in view of 'the grete poverti and penurie that be among the Communes of this land, for whom they be comen at this tyme'.[2]

In the parliament of 1455, the commons represented themselves as having in consideration the requirements of their constituencies. They desired to know who was going to be Protector during the king's illness, to the 'entent that they myght sende to theym for whom they were commen to this present Parliament knowelege who should be Protectour and Defensour'.[3] And in the same parliament, it was thought 'by theym that be comen to this high Court of Parliament for the Communes of this lond' that—considering the grave riots of the earl of Devon in the west, and the nearness of Christmas —it might please the Protector and the lords to adjourn parliament.[4]

By Edward IV the idea of national representation in parliament was given royal countenance. He began his speech in his first parliament by saying: 'James Strangways, and ye that be commyn for the Common of this my Lond,. . .';[5] and the speech he made in his third parliament by saying: 'John Say and ye Sirs,[6] comyn to this my Court of Parlement for the Comon of this my Lond,. . . .'[7] Moreover, in the latter parliament, the chancellor's sermon was said to have been delivered in the presence of the king, lords, and 'also the Comons commen for the Communalte of this Londe'.[8] And in 1472, the king's humble subjects 'comyn for Comons of the land' described themselves as comforted by the king's victories; and the same prayed for the suppression of certain offensive riots in Southwark.[9]

---

[1] *Rot. Parl.* v, 239 b.   [2] *Ibid.* 240 b.   [3] *Ibid.* 284–285.
[4] *Ibid.* 285 b.   [5] *Ibid.* 487 a.
[6] During Edward IV's reign members of parliament were for the first time called 'esquires' in the sheriff's returns (*v.* Hallam, *View of the State of Europe*, VIII, part 3, § 17).
[7] *Rot. Parl.* v, 572 a.   [8] *Ibid.* 622 a.   [9] *Rot. Parl.* VI, 8 a.

For our concluding illustration of the development of this notion of parliament as a nationally representative assembly, we may well quote, again, from Bishop Russell's intended speech to the parliament of Edward V: 'Wherefor,' he wrote in his first draft of that speech, 'it ys not to doulte but that the rule and governaile of the Reame appereth then in most temperaunce and moderacion when the kynges juges and commisses be obeyd at large in every parte of the londe, so that hys hyghenes and hys nobylle counselle be not letted, where the kynge lystythe best to be, to entend the politik establysshynge of the Reme. *Attendite igitur populi de longe*, Gyff then your attendaunce, ye peuple that stonde ferre of, to the lordes and nobille men whyche be in auctorite: they come from the wele hedd, ye stonde *a longe*. I speke not to yowe that nowe represent the hele, but to them that ye come fro, whome for ther gret and confuse nombre and multitude nature can not wele suffre to assemble in oo place apt to the makynge of a lawe....'[1]

The principle of majority rule is one of great importance in the history of parliament; but its origins are still very obscure. The history of the principle itself is complicated and curious; and a thorough investigation of it would probably throw light on some dark corners of politico-legal thought. In England the principle seems to have been adopted early in political assemblies, but also rejected early in juries.

The English conception of the principle, Redlich tells us,[2] was founded on the Teutonic theory that the formation of a corporate will must always be unanimous, because the minority gives way and conforms its will to that of the majority. This principle can be called the majority principle only because the minority acquiesce in the vote of the majority; should the

---

[1] *Grants of Edward V*, p. xliv; and Excursus VI, *infra*, p. 174. Cf. the diary of the Colchester burgesses (*Red Paper Book of Colchester*, 63): 'The XXVIII day of Novembre there was a comonyng for the comen well of all the lond for to se a remedy for this fals money....'

[2] *The Procedure of the House of Commons* (1907), II, 261: 'The Majority Principle.' He refers to G. Jellinek, *Das Recht der Minoritäten* (Vienna, 1898).

minority refuse to acquiesce, presumably a state of stalemate arose, and no decision either way, unless, indeed, a purely negative one, was arrived at. The development of this unanimity principle into a majority principle proper was due, it seems, mainly to the inventive power of the canon law.[1] The majority principle as a basis of corporate decision in Roman law rested only on a political foundation, *i.e.* on the power of the majority to coerce the minority; but canon law introduced the idea that *sanioritas* was necessary for corporate decisions, and—as Gierke says—linked it to the Roman doctrine by contending that the act of the majority raised a presumption of *sanioritas*.[2]

This developed principle was not entirely without its influence in the English courts. For instance, the *Leges Henrici Primi* laid down that if the judges in the county disagreed, the opinion of the majority was to prevail.[3] 'The general opinion of the time' [*i.e.* of the twelfth century], Maitland observes, 'demands that the prevailing opinion shall be that of the "maior et sanior pars".'[4] Nevertheless, while various ideas on the subject are traceable in the history of the jury, unanimity became the requisite for all verdicts of juries, even though not invariably so until the late fourteenth century.[5] The reasons for the ultimate establishment of this rule were several. 'From the moment when our records begin', Maitland says, 'we seem to see a strong desire for unanimity.' The jury's verdict was regarded as the voice of the country; and just as a corporation can have but one will, so a country can have but one voice. Besides, the unanimous voice of the jury always tended to relieve the judges

---

[1] Gierke, *Das Deutsche Genossenschaftsrecht*, III, 323: 'Although we can find in the older canon law traces of the notion that the majority principle was taken in the sense of Teutonic law (*i.e.* only as a means by which to arrive at the requisite unanimity, through the duty of submission incumbent on the minority), the developed theory of the canonists makes the validity of the majority principle depend upon a legal fiction' (cited by Redlich, *loc. cit.*).

[2] *Ibid.* 152–157, 323–330.

[3] *Leges Henrici Primi*, c. 5, § 6; but cf. c. 31, § 2: 'Vincat sententia meliorum et cui iustitia magis acquieverit.' Cf. Pollock and Maitland, *Hist. Eng. Law*, I, 509, 552.   [4] *Hist. Eng. Law*, I, 552, n. 3.

[5] *V.* Holdsworth, *Hist. Eng. Law*, II, 431, n. 4; and Thayer, *Evidence*, 87, n. 4.

of responsibilities and difficulties that would otherwise have ensued.[1] Moreover, the jury system was settling down into its usages before the majority principle as developed by the canon law was widely accepted.[2]

This majority rule, however, was adopted quite early in political bodies and assemblies. The barons in 1215 proposed that the twenty-five of their number who were to enforce their articles on the king should proceed when necessary by the vote of the majority;[3] and this proposal was incorporated in the first issue of *Magna Carta* itself.[4] The principle must, therefore, have enjoyed considerable publicity thenceforward; and it appeared again, as a rule for the king's council, in the *Provisions of Oxford*.[5]

Redlich considers that this evidence makes it clear that decisions of the *magnum concilium* were arrived at by a majority long before representatives were regularly called to a parliament in union with the *magnum concilium*. He thinks it natural to conclude that the fundamental rule was carried into the business of the commons at an early date.[6] But it would seem that one must be careful not to attribute the rule to the commons at too early a date.[7] Redlich himself produces no evidence at all to

[1] *Hist. Eng. Law*, II, 626.
[2] Redlich, *op. cit.* II, 262. Mr Pickthorn notes (*op. cit.* I, 116) that the verdict of the jury in the court of the steward was by majority, but omits to mention that this rule was based only on the forged precedent dated 1400 but composed probably not before 1499 (*v.* L. W. V. Harcourt, *His Grace the Steward and Trial of Peers*, 438). Harcourt suggests that this majority rule would never have been tolerated if the public had not been familiar with procedure on attainder in parliament, and that the latter was the source of the forger's principle. Mr Pickthorn says that judgement in impeachment was given by the majority of the lords.
[3] *Forma Securitas* (Stubbs, *Select Charters*, 291): 'In omnibus autem quae istis XXV baronibus committuntur exsequenda, si forte ipsi XXV praesentes fuerint et inter se super re aliqua discordaverint, vel aliqui ex eis vocati nolint vel nequeant interesse, ratum habebitur et firmum quod major pars ex eis providerit vel praeceperit, ac si omnes XXV in hoc consensissent.'
[4] *Ibid.* (Stubbs, *ibid.* 302): '...quod major pars eorum qui praesentes fuerint providerit, vel praeceperit, ac si omnes viginti quinque in hoc consensissent.'
[5] Stubbs, *ibid.* 381: 'E ces quatre unt poer a eslire le cunseil le rei, et quant il unt eslu, il les mustrunt as vint et quatre; et la u la greinure partie de ces assente, seit tenu.'
[6] *Op. cit.* II, 263.
[7] Professor McIlwain shows (*Growth of Political Thought in the West*, 303), following Dr Previté-Orton's new edition of the work, that the majority principle is not advocated in Marsiglio of Padua's *Defensor Pacis*, as has sometimes been thought.

show how early such a rule was adopted by the commons, but merely assumes it must have been early because the majority principle was old-established and uncontested by the time Hooker and Sir Thomas Smith wrote about parliament. Yet it has to be remembered that all the instances above quoted concern political expedients at times of crisis, and therefore suggest that the principle was not regularly in use. Moreover, it is curious that the writs of summons have never referred to such a principle; and since we know that the house of commons was slow to evolve for itself the ideas and habits of a corporation, we may well hesitate before assuming too readily that the majority principle was one acted upon by it in the earliest stages of its existence. Indeed, what evidence we have from the fifteenth century suggests that the acceptance of the rule in both council and commons was neither very old-established nor entirely uncontested. And apparently the principle that parliamentary elections should be by the majority was not definitely established until the franchise act of 1429.[1]

Even in the council, the rule was the subject of special provision as late as 1423. Among the provisions for which the lords of the council obtained a parliamentary sanction in that year was one which reads as follows: 'Item, if so be that eny matere suyd in the Counsail falle in to diverse opinions, that oo lesse than the more partye of the Consaill beyng present, in the tyme of discord, falle to that oo part, that it be naught enacted as assented. And the names of the both parties enact by the Clerk of the Counsaill, wyth here assent or disent.'[2] In 1429, it was specifically provided that the punishment or removal of any counsellor or great officer should proceed by the assent and advice of the majority of all those appointed to the council.[3]

In 1432, a special memorandum was drawn up and enrolled, recording that Gloucester, notwithstanding his royal birth, agreed to accept, in deliberations upon business touching the

---

[1] Pickthorn, *op. cit.* I, 99; *Interim Report*, 35–36.
[2] *Rot. Parl.* IV, 201 b.   [3] *Ibid.* 343 b.

king and kingdom—whether in parliaments or in councils—
the advice and assent of the other lords, or at least of the greater
number of them.[1] Still, even as late as 1441, Serjeant Markham
—in the rector of Eddington's case—denied that a grant of a
fifteenth in parliament would necessarily bind everybody;[2]
though, indeed, he based this view not upon opposition to the
simple majority rule, but upon his notion of parliament as a
kind of corporation, the vote of which in its corporate capacity
would not override prior arrangements between some of its
members in their individual capacity and the king. Views of
this kind must have impeded the general acceptance of the
majority rule; but by 1476 it had apparently become established.
So, at any rate, it seemed to Littleton, J., who, during the course of
a case in that year, stated from the bench: 'Sir, si en le parliament
si le greindre party des Chivallers des Counties assentent al feasans
dun act du parliament et le meindre part ne voil' my agreer a cel
act, uncore ce sera bon statute a durer en perpetuity....'[3]

If the majority rule was late in being accepted, so likewise was
the notion of the 'authority of parliament'. Clearly it was a very
considerable advance in constitutional ideas when parliament
as an entity came to be thought of as possessing an authority
distinguishable from the king's authority, and also from the
authority of the lords or other of its constituent members; and
to note the lateness of the emergence of that idea is to receive
yet another reminder of the extreme slowness of the approach
to modern notions of parliament.[4] There is not, apparently, any

---

[1] *Ibid.* 389a.

[2] *Y.B.* 19 *Henry VI*, Pas. pl. 1 (App. no. 25). In this connection it is interesting
to notice that in 1404 Colchester was exempted from sending burgesses to parliament, *provided* that the town kept and supported all statutes and ordinances and
charges made and granted in the parliament (*v. Cal. Pat. R.* 11, 355).

[3] *Y.B.* 15 *Edward IV*, Mich. pl. 2 (App. no. 60).

[4] Sir Courtenay Ilbert considered (*Legislative Methods and Forms*, 5) that the
'significant addition to the legislative formula' made by the phrase 'by authority
of parliament' was due to 'the comparative decline of royal power under the
Lancastrians', which enabled parliament 'to assert its right of dictating the terms
on which the laws for which it asked should be made'. But the idea that parliament
dictated terms for laws which it itself asked for seems to be as illusory as it is self-
contradictory.

evidence of the use of the phrase 'authority of parliament' until the very end of the fourteenth century. No use was made of it in the statute of York in 1322, nor in the various transactions in the crisis of 1341. It occurs earliest in the most unlikely of places—namely, in the record of the delegation of powers to a small committee to deal with petitions, by the Shrewsbury parliament in 1398. This committee was stated to have been appointed 'by the authority and assent of the parliament'.[1] And when in the following year this act was repealed, the king —by the advice and assent of the lords spiritual and temporal and all the commonalty—adjudged the Shrewsbury parliament and *the authority thereof given* to be of no force or value.[2] Thus it looks as though the idea of 'authority of parliament', like so much else in our constitutional heritage, first saw the light under royal patronage.[3] But the idea was one that could cut two ways; and, in the charges against Richard II, the point was made that statutes were always binding until they were specially revoked by the authority of another parliament.[4]

Further mention of parliament's authority occurs occasionally, but not very conspicuously until the first parliament of Henry VI, wherein it was ordained and assented to by the authority of parliament that the commissions of officers, and its own writs of summons, which had been issued by the lords of the council, should be held good and effectual.[5] Then, in 1429, the forty-shilling-freeholder franchise act was ordained by authority of parliament; and in 1433, for the first time, the statute of the year was sanctioned by the assent of the lords spiritual and temporal, at the instance and request of the commons, and *by authority of parliament*.[6] This 'authorising' clause was used regularly in such sanctions from 1444–45,

---

[1] *Rot. Parl.* III, 368b.   [2] *Stat. R.* II, 111.

[3] On the whole subject of the committee of 1398, *v.* Mr J. G. Edwards's article, *E.H.R.* XL, 321–333.

[4] *Rot. Parl.* III, 419: 'Item, quod postquam in Parliamento suo certa Statuta erant edita, que semper ligarent donec auctoritate alicuius alterius Parliamenti fuerint specialiter revocata....'

[5] *Rot. Parl.* IV, 170b.   [6] 11 *Henry VI.*

except for one lapse in 1468. In 1461, the commons prayed that the judicial acts of the late *de facto* king should be declared lawful, by authority of parliament.[1] A striking distinction between the authority of parliament and the king's grace was drawn by the king himself, and also by the lords, in the same parliament.[2] Bishop Russell, in 1483, proposed to exhort the lords and commons to renew by authority of parliament the grants that had been made to the young king's predecessors.[3] Also, in the same year, when—as we have seen—Richard III's title was being put on record, it was emphasised that the court of parliament was of such authority, and the people of such nature and disposition, that declaration of any truth or right by the three estates assembled in parliament, and by authority of the same, made above all things for the quieting of men's minds and the removal of all doubts and seditious language.[4] Some ten years before this, Fortescue had written that if a general resumption of alienated royal lands were to be made, it should be done by authority of parliament;[5] and a chronicler of London had noted that in 1460 'it was condescended and aggreed by all thauctoritie of the parliament' that Henry should be king for life.[6]

Even as early as 1410, Hankford, J., had admitted that the power of the court was restrained by authority of parliament;[7] and by 1441, Hody, CJKB., could assert on the bench that a statute was made by authority of parliament, and was general as well within franchises as without, and that when by authority of parliament a writ could issue to a franchise, that act of parlia-

---

[1] *Rot. Parl.* v, 489a.

[2] *V. Fane Fragment*, 12: 'Dyvers Lords should Declare unto the Commons, that the kinges pleasure is that he wull not auctorise their said ffraunchises and liberties by auctoritie of parliament, no more then his progenitors have don, but that they shall have it of the kynges liberalitie and free disposicion as farforthe as it may accorde with reason and the Kinges consideracion. Item as to the iiiith for Signement of paying of Judges. It is thought necessary that they be truly paid but not to be signed by Auctoritie of parliament but at the Kinges pleasure, as it is entered on the names of Lords hereunder written.' Cf. *ibid.* 9–11, 70.

[3] *Grants of Edward V*, p. xlvii; and Excursus VI, *infra*, p. 176.

[4] *Rot. Parl.* vi, 241 b.   [5] *Governance*, xiv.

[6] *Chronicles of London*, 172. *The Brut*, I, 530, has the same phrase.

[7] *Y.B.* 11 *Henry IV*, Mich. pl. 20 (App. no. 17 (i)).

ment was general, notwithstanding the franchise, and would
be held as such—and that to that the court agreed.[1]

From the beginning of the fifteenth century, then, we have
evidence that persons engaged in parliamentary and legal
activities had begun to formulate some working theories of the
nature of the parliamentary phenomenon. All such formulations
of theory, however, were occasioned by immediate purposes,
political or litigious, and were not the result of scientific analysis
or disciplined speculation, and therefore need to be accepted
with caution. Still, early in the century, the commons—more
particularly, the Speaker—from time to time described parliament by analogical conceits; and these suggest that interest had
been by then in some measure awakened in the nature of
parliament as an institution. By the middle of the century, some
section of the legal profession had developed logically the theory
of parliament as the king's high court; but concurrently with
that development there progressed ideas of parliament as a
representative political assembly possessing attributes in excess
of those accorded to any ordinary court of law. Conspicuous
among the idea-forces—to say nothing of the influences of
political events—which probably tended to fuse together these
two sets of notions were the political and constitutional reper-
cussions of the old estate theory of society. The circumstances of
the revolution of 1399 gave unprecedented currency to the term
'estates of the realm'; for by their sanction were carried
through both the deposition of Richard II and the accession of
Henry IV. It became more and more common, as the century
passed, to regard parliament—both in official and in popular
contexts—as composed of the three estates of the realm, and
therefore as an assembly possessing an authority innate in the
natural social orders as well as an authority inherent in the
king's court. Before the end of the century, the three estates
of the realm were invariably conceived to be the spiritual lords,
temporal lords, and commons; and these three, together with

[1] *Y.B.* 19 *Henry VI*, Mich. pl. 2 (App. no. 23 (ii)).

the king, were thought to constitute a parliament, and all statutes were enacted by the king with the assent of these three estates, and by the authority of parliament. Until this assimilation of ideas had gone far, there was no suggestion that parliament possessed any authority distinguishable from the ordinary authority of the king in his court; but in the second half of the century some such distinction had developed enough to effect an explicit mention of parliamentary authority for legislative enactments. Before the century was over, it was clearly understood that parliament was the place of worldly policy, the place where laws were made and where that which was amiss was amended.

During the century the phrases and ideas of houses of parliament emerged, at first only in a locative sense—*i.e.* with reference to the places of meeting—but before very long, in a distinctly institutional sense. Among the commons, the most significant development in general ideas—as distinct from various claims which they made respecting their share in the functions of parliament, and of which some were admitted—was their grasp of the notion that they were come to parliament to represent not merely a number of local communities, but an estate: the commons of all the realm.

The authority of the high court of parliament, by the end of the century, was thus a compound of the king's own assent with the assent of at least a majority of the lords spiritual and temporal, and of at least a majority of the members of the house of commons, representing all the commons of the realm. Upon the votes of such an assembly as this the sovereign lord king depended for his law-making and tax-levying. By the advice and assent of his lords spiritual and temporal and his commons in parliament assembled, and by the authority of the same, he ordained, established, and enacted. Statutes thus made were certainly the law of the land. But they were not the only law, not the most ancient, not necessarily the most lucid, not always the most acceptable, and often not the best obeyed. How, then, was statutory law to be understood and applied?

EXCURSUS I

SOME MOTIVES FOR THE SUMMONS OF PARLIAMENTS

The chancellors' speeches at the opening of parliament generally alluded to the objects for which the parliament had been called. Though there was some tendency for these allusions to become commonplace and conventional, a few of them are specific enough to provide some real insight into the motives of the crown in issuing the summons; and others express in general words the constitutional proprieties of the occasion. Thus, in 1402, Bishop Stafford stated to the parliament[1] which met soon after the battle of Homildon Hill, that the king, wishing to be *informed* by the lords and commons upon various matters, and wishing to have the aid, counsel, and advice of every party, had summoned that present parliament. Furthermore, inasmuch as before that time some of the lords and commons had attended more to their own separate interests[2] than to the common profit, the chancellor charged them, by the king's command, to attend entirely to the requirements of the parliament, and to come in good time every day to the place assigned to them.

In the following year, Westmorland sent a memorandum to the king suggesting measures to be taken in order to deal with the rebellion of the Percies, and recommended the summons of a parliament to advise the king and his council.[3] Thomas Langley, the chancellor in 1406, gave a gloomy account of the perils that were ensuing in Wales, Guienne, Calais, Ireland, and Scotland, and declared that the king, 'en si grand bosoigne', wanted to have the advice and counsel of some of the more

---

[1] *Rot. Parl.* III, 485.

[2] 'Et pur ceo que devaunt ces heures plusours des Seigneurs et Communes venuz par Sommons au Parlement ont estee pluis entendentz pur lour singulers bosoignes que pur les Commune profit et aide du Roialme.'

[3] *Procs. and Ords.* I, 210: 'Item quant un parlement ce soit al avys de nostre tressouverain seigneur et de soun counseil.' This memorandum was sent in July, but no parliament met until the following January.

notable persons of the realm, such as the estates thereof assembled at the parliament.[1]

At the opening of the parliament of 1410, the lords and commons were treated to a learned discourse by Bishop Beaufort, upon the subjects, 'De jure regiminis' and 'De jure subjectionis'. He began with some vague allusions to the perils threatening the land, particularly Burgundy's menace to Calais, and then proceeded to distinguish 'most discreetly' these two manners of governance. He reminded his listeners how Alexander the Great, having captured a great city, asked of Aristotle whether he could fortify it best by a wall or by other means. To this query Aristotle replied that the sovereign surety and guard of every realm and city was to have the entire and cordial love of the people, and to keep them in their laws and rights; and that the people ought of right to render to the king honour and obedience, reverence and benevolence, and cordial assistance. Since, he continued, the business to be mentioned required loyal co-operation and speedy execution, the king had sent for the lords and commons to attend before him to have their advice 'et choses necessaires a lui et son roialme'.[2]

Three years later Beaufort set forth Henry V's three objects in calling his first parliament. These were, firstly, due and competent provision for his high and royal estate; secondly, the good governance and maintenance of the laws within the realm; and thirdly, furtherance of good relations with foreigners who were his friends, and resistance to those who were his enemies.[3]

At the parliament of 1428, Archbishop Kemp of York discoursed on the mutual duties of rulers and subjects. Rulers, he observed, have three special duties to perform on behalf of their subjects. They ought to protect and defend them from the insults of their enemies abroad, to conserve the peace among them at home and to administer justice equally. Subjects, on the other hand, ought to submit effectually to their rulers' protection

---

[1] *Rot. Parl.* III, 567.
[2] *Ibid.* 622. [3] *Rot. Parl.* IV, 3.

and defence, to obey them in the preservation of peace, and to redress their grievances not by their own will but by process of law. Because these duties, concluded Kemp, are, by the royal providence, to be observed in England as well by rulers as by subjects, the king had caused his present parliament to be convoked.[1]

This academic kind of edification is fairly characteristic of the common run of opening speeches.[2] Sometimes, however, in the midst of such homilies, we find a statement of objective which is refreshingly practical. Thus the bishop of Bath, in 1442, after much vague talk about 'sex virtutes morales', came down to business by saying that the object of parliament was 'novas leges condere ac veteres leges ubi necessitas exigit et requirit renovare'.[3]

Occasionally the discursive part of the address was omitted altogether. Archbishop Stafford, facing parliament in 1449, when things in France were going very badly, curtly alluded to the war, and said that the king, because of certain difficult and urgent business concerning the government of the country, which could not be expedited out of parliament, had summoned the present parliament, in order to confer thereon with lords and commons.[4]

It was seldom that the chancellor entered into such a wealth of detail as did Archbishop Bourchier, after the defeat of the Lancastrians at the first battle of St Albans, in 1455. Parliament had been summoned, he said, to establish and ordain a substantial rule for the king's household, to provide the payment of wages to the garrison of Calais, to guard against the enemy both at Calais and at Berwick, to arrange the employment of the archers which had been voted in the previous parliament, to prevent the export of gold and silver, to provide for Wales and for the keeping of the sea, and above all, 'to sette a parfaite love

---

[1] *Rot. Parl.* IV, 316.

[2] *V.*, for similar examples, *Rot. Parl.* IV, 261, 295, 419 (by Beaufort), 367 (by William Lyndwood); IV, 495; V, 3 (by Stillington).

[3] *Rot. Parl.* V, 35 b.   [4] *Ibid.* 171.

and rest among the lordes to. . . the politique and restful rule and governance of this his land and people'.[1]

Bishop Russell intended to declare to the parliament of Edward V that 'the power and auctorite of my lord protector is so behoffulle and of reason to be assented and established by the auctorite of thys hyhe courte, that amonges alle the causes of the assemblynge of the parliamente yn thys tyme of the yere, thys ys the grettest and most necessarye furst to be affermed'.[2]

In short, we may say with the poor poet that

> Whanne alle a kyngdom gadrid ysse
> In goddis lawe, by on assent,
> For to amende þat was mysse,
> Þerfore is ordayned a parlement.[3]

EXCURSUS II

NOTES ON THE PLACE OF THE LORDS IN PARLIAMENT AND IN COUNCIL

The expression 'peers of the realm' first cropped up in a constitutional sense in the manifestos launched by the baronial opposition to Edward II. It appeared again when the barons combined to overthrow the rule of Mortimer, and occurs first in official records in those of the parliament of 1330, when Mortimer was judged by his peers. The king himself gave sanction to the term when in 1340 he appointed his brother-in-law, William of Jülich, to be earl of Cambridge, and a peer of the realm. Then at the crisis of 1341, as Tout said, 'In imposing the doctrine of peerage on the constitution the parliament of 1341 made its most prominent mark on history. A strictly hereditary peerage was in baronial eyes the best safeguard against the household system, and the rule of the upstart courtier'.[4]

---

[1] *Ibid.* 279.
[2] *Grants of Edward V*, p. xlix, and *v. infra*, Excursus VI, p. 178.
[3] *Political and other Poems*, I, 55. Cf. *supra*, p. 20, n. 3.
[4] *Chapters*, III, 138.

Edward III's repeal of the statutes which had been imposed upon him, however, was no doubt the chief among other causes which contributed to the notable slowness with which the doctrine of peerage, especially the hereditary principle, gained acceptance. Thus, as Tout also pointed out, 'the persistent description of some of the magnates summoned to parliament as bannerets shows how, even up to Richard II's reign, it was unsafe to describe "peers of parliament" as necessarily "barons" or "sitting by hereditary right". Apart from higher and clearly marked out categories such as those of the bishops and abbots and the dukes and the earls it is misleading to assume that the average "lord of parliament" was necessarily described as a "baron".'[1] Even in 1399, the proctors appointed by the estates to announce to Richard his deposition, included the lord Berkeley for the barons and bannerets.[2] Moreover, as Pike showed, as late as the reign of Henry VI a legal doctrine of strict hereditary peerage had not yet become established.[3]

But, admitting these facts, there can be little doubt that the fifteenth century witnessed the climax in the history of the peerage (or, more cautiously, of the lords of parliament) at least so far as the idea of their importance in the constitution was concerned. The circumstances of the long minority of Henry VI provided the lords with their golden opportunity for taking over the reins of government, and for establishing their place in constitutional theory. To the peers, whether in parliament or in the continual council, fell the task of making some kind of provision for the carrying on of the government. We are not in this place in any way concerned with their achievements or lack of achievements in that respect, but the constitutional ideas which they acted upon or advanced, call for review.

---

[1] *Ibid.* 296, n. 1. These words of Tout are quoted without prejudice to the grave doubts cast by Miss H. M. Chew on the current view that the bishops were summoned as barons. Miss Chew's arguments reduce still further the classes of persons in parliament who can be described as barons. *V.* 'The Ecclesiastical Tenants-in-Chief and Writs of Military Summons' in *E.H.R.* xli, 161–169, and *The Ecclesiastical Tenants-in-Chief and Knight Service* (1932).

[2] *Rot. Parl.* iii, 424.   [3] *Const. Hist. of House of Lords*, vi.

The prime care of the lords, on receipt of the news of Henry V's death, was, to all seeming, to ensure as far as possible a lease of aristocratic government. It is likely to remain a matter of conjecture what were the motives of Bedford in sending from Rouen on the 28th of October the curious letter which survives among the archives of the city of London.[1] In this letter, presumably addressed to the city itself, Bedford claimed that, inasmuch as the king had been called from this world, the governance of the realm according to the laws and ancient usage and custom thereof, belonged, during the tender age of the new sovereign, to him the elder surviving brother of the late king, being next unto the crown and having chief interest in it. He prayed and required the city, by the faith and allegiance that it owed to God and the crown, that it would not in any wise assent to, or counsel, or support any proposition to be made in derogation of those laws and custom, or in prejudice of himself. He gave assurance that his request proceeded not of ambition nor of desire for worldly worship, but only of intent that the laws and customs of the realm should not be blemished nor hurt by his own negligence or default. He did not desire that any prejudice should be engendered towards any sufficient and able person to whom the governance of the realm might likely belong in time coming.

What effect, if any, on the actual settlement of the government this cautious letter had, it is difficult to suggest. The general theory that the governance belonged of right to the elder surviving brother of the king cannot, however, be deemed the theory upon which the lords of England acted. Government by the aristocracy collectively was undoubtedly the aim which the lords put before themselves during the minority. This is shown clearly enough by the following facts. On the 5th of November in a council meeting at which the only names recorded are those of twenty-two magnates—the archbishop, seven of the greater bishops, two dukes, three earls, and nine lords—it was insisted

---

[1] *London and the Kingdom*, III, App. A, 367.

that the commission to be issued to Gloucester (who had been lieutenant of England at Henry V's death) should include the words: 'Ad parliamentum illud finiendum et dissolvendum de assensu consilii nostri plenam commisimus potestatem.' Gloucester protested against the words 'de assensu consilii nostri', but the lords obstinately refused to yield the least rein to Gloucester's personal pretensions.[1] Then, on the roll of the parliament which met on the 9th of November,[2] it was recorded that on the news of the king's death, certain honourable lords spiritual and temporal had assembled to provide for the imminent necessities of governance, the conservation of peace, the confirmation of offices, and for the summons of the parliament itself. During parliament, it was decided by the king, with the assent of the lords and commons, that the duke of Bedford should be Protector and Defender of the kingdom and of the English church, and be the king's Principal Counsellor, provided that such power and position were to appertain to him only whilst he was in England, and in his absence to his brother the duke of Gloucester. But the actual powers attached to these offices were of the most trivial character, and amounted to no more than rather paltry rights of patronage over minor offices.[3] All the important powers were reserved for the council as a whole; to the council were appointed 'by advice of lords and commons', sixteen great lords—five greater prelates, a duke, five earls, and five barons. The sole restriction proposed on the executive power of these was the vague one that 'in business wherein it was usual to consult the king', the council was not to proceed without the advice of either Bedford or Gloucester.[4] Moreover, it was agreed that petitions remaining unanswered after the end of the parliament were to be left to the determination of the council at its discretion.[5]

Furthermore, the constitutional theory upon which the lords were acting was explicitly formulated five years later, during a spectacular incident which occurred whilst Bedford was in

[1] *Procs. and Ords.* III, 6–8.   [2] *Rot. Parl.* IV, 172 b.   [3] *Ibid.* 175.
[4] *Ibid.* 174.   [5] *Ibid.* 174.

England in 1427. The turbulence and restless ambition of Gloucester caused Beaufort, the protagonist of government by the aristocratic council as a whole, to send over to France in 1425 for Bedford to return in haste to England,[1] and oil was poured on the stormy seas of domestic politics by Bedford's return and the proceedings in the parliament of Bats in February 1426. After all these events, at the time when he was preparing to resume his activities in France, Bedford was invited by the lords of the council to declare his allegiance to the principle of government by the council as a whole, *i.e.* by a select committee of magnates. On the 28th of January, 1427, Bedford was addressed in the star chamber by the chancellor (John Kemp, bishop of London), in the name of the council.[2] He stated that he was commanded by all the lords of the council there present to declare to Bedford that it was in no wise their intent to diminish or in any part to withdraw any worship or estate belonging to his high person or birth, but to increase it and the king's estate and the good governance of the realm, over which they did not doubt no creature was more tender than he. The lords had still in mind the notable exhortations which, at divers times of his great zeal and tenderness for the weal and good governance of the king and his realm, he had made to them, to the effect that they should apply themselves diligently, without fear of any person, to the administration and government of right and justice. They remembered especially how he had pointed out the great perils and inconveniences that would arise to the king when he came to years of discretion, or to himself, if God should do His will with the king, or to his brother Gloucester if he himself died without issue, should the lords of the council fail

---

[1] In the present writer's opinion the view of these happenings made current by Mr Vickers—in his *Humphrey, Duke of Gloucester* and *England in the later Middle Ages*—in which Beaufort, instead of Gloucester, appears as the rebellious culprit, is quite untenable. Cf. 'John, duke of Bedford; his work and policy in England, 1389–1435', *Bull. I.H.R.* VII (1929), 110–113.

[2] Two slightly different versions of this episode (*Cott. M.S. Cleop.*, fo. iv, and *Titus*, E iv.) are printed respectively in *Procs. and Ords.* III, 237, and in *Rot. Parl.* V, 409.

to acquit themselves indifferently, without partiality or favour, to the good governance and weal of the realm and the laws.

The chancellor went on to say that it was understood that though the king was then of tender age, nevertheless there was the same authority resting in his person, and was at that day, as would be in him at any time thereafter when he should come, with God's grace, to years of discretion. The king's government must be carried on, and the lords were responsible for that task during that period. 'Forasmuche as the Kyng is nowe of such tendrenesses of age', the chancellor explained, 'that by possibilitee of nature he may not in dede Reule ne Governe in his owne persone, and that God ne reson wol that this Lande stande withouten Governaunce; for soemuch the execution of the Kynges said auctoritee, as toward that that belongeth unto the Politique Reule and Governaille of his Lande, and to th' observaunce and kepyng of his Lawes, belongeth unto the Lordes Spirituall and Temporell of his Lande, at suche tyme as thei be assembled in Parlement or in grete Consaille; and ellus, hem not being so assembled, unto the Lordes chosen and named to be of his continuel Conseill...,[1] the whiche Counsaille, the Kyng beying in such tendrenesse of age, represent his persone as toward execution of the same Politique Reule and Governaille of his Lande, and observaunce and kepying of his said Lawes, withouten that eny oo persone may or owe ascribe unto hymselfe the seid Reule and Governaille; savynge alway unto my said Lord of Bedforde and of Gloucestre, that is especiall reserved and applied unto hem by Act of Parlement....' The lords therefore were anxious to be assured, which they did not doubt, that Bedford would be ever, as at all times thitherto he had been, ruled and demeaned as the lords would advertise and advise him, and not otherwise, as truth and reason and the king's laws required.

To this address Bedford replied, without hesitation, that he thanked the lords for having sent for him, and promised forth-

---

[1] The first and generally fuller version omits the word 'continuel'.

with that in all matters touching the profit and weal of the king
and his realms he would be ruled and governed as the lords would
counsel and advise him, and prayed they would let him know
if they thought he erred in any matter, and he promised to
relinquish his own opinion in that event, unless indeed they
thought it better than their own. He then of his own free will
swore on the Gospels open before him, to observe these promises.[1]
Finally, he commanded that his words should be enacted, and
declared that he would not, in time to come, vary from all or
any of them.

In this transaction we have the fullest and most explicit
statement of the idea of the paramount importance of the lords'
place in the constitution. If the king himself were unable to
execute his authority, then to them alone and as a whole belonged the function of doing it for him. This principle, after
some thirty years, crystallised into a rather more specifically
'peerage' doctrine. When, in 1454, York was called upon to
assume the Protectorate, he did so, he said, only of the due and
humble obedience that he owed to the king and to the peerage
of the land, to whom by the occasion of the infirmity of the king
rested the exercise of his authority.[2] Even the judges, in 1460,
admitted that the discussion of York's claim to the crown pertained, not to them, but to the lords of the king's blood and the
peerage of the land,[3] whilst York urged that the peers and lords
of the realm ought to help him in truth and justice, notwithstanding any oath of fealty made by them, in the furtherance of
his claim.[4]

Similarly, it is significant to note the importance of the place
given to the theory of aristocracy by Bishop Russell in his
speeches of 1483.[5] No more vivid exposition of the aristocratic

---

[1] The picture of the lords shedding tears at these agreeable words is too good not
to be quoted once again. The memorandum continues: 'Those words and many
other gentle words my seid lord of Bedford there said so benignly and goodly that
for very hearty affection and truth the tears sprang as well out of his eyes as out of
the eyes of all my seid lords that were there present' (*Procs. and Ords.* III, 240).
[2] *Rot. Parl.* v, 242a.   [3] *Ibid.* 376a, and *supra*, pp. 6, 22, 28.
[4] *Ibid.* 377a.   [5] *V. infra*, Excursus VI, esp. pp. 169–170.

theory of the constitution in the fifteenth century could be desired than these unique sermons.

Occasionally less purely theoretical statements about the position of the lords in parliament occur. First in importance among these is the solemn declaration of the judges in Thorpe's case in 1454 to the effect that 'the determination and knowledge of that Privelegge (of the high court of parliament) belongeth to the lordes of the parlement, and not to the justices'.[1] The judges were not, of course, delivering a legally binding judgement in this statement; they were giving their advice and opinion after being consulted by the lords, but we may take this declaration as representing the accepted view of the matter. It belonged to the lords of parliament to determine the privileges of the members of the whole parliament, and this no doubt was the natural outcome of the judicial history of the upper house.

Some points connected with the question of money grants by the lords emerge during the century. It is memorable that as late as 1400 it was possible for the lords spiritual and temporal to grant an aid to the king on their own account in order to avoid summoning a parliament.[2] In 1405 they refused a grant altogether.[3] The famous episode of 1407, when the commons protested against the lords' settling the amount of the grant without consulting the commons, led to the explicit recognition, not only of the right of the commons to deliberate on the estate of the realm and the needful remedies,[4] and to report thereon to the king by the speaker, but also of the right of the

---

[1] *Rot. Parl.* v, 240.

[2] *Procs. and Ords.* I, 104: 'Et sur ce les ditz seigneurs espirituelx et temporelx considerants la necessite bien grande et pur eschuire aucuns parlement estre sommonez par celle cause parmy la quele le comun poeple deveroit estre chargez par imposicion taxe ou taillage ou briefment par autre voie quecunque les ditz seigneurs espirituelx et temporelx fuerent assentuz de graunter aide a notre dit seigneur le roi en la manere qensuit.'

[3] Walsingham, *Hist. Anglicana*, II, 268.

[4] *Rot. Parl.* III, 611: '...de l'estate du Roialme et de le remedie a ce busoignable.' When what the speaker is to report to the king is mentioned, the word 'grant' is used. The use of such a heading as 'Commons to originate money bills' to describe this episode, as *e.g.* in Adams and Stephens, *Constitutional Documents*, 175, is inaccurate and misleading.

lórds to deliberate upon the same subject in the absence of the king.

There is at least one instance, however, of the lords' acting with the advice of the justices, and overruling the terms upon which the commons had made a grant. In the parliament of 1425 the commons introduced a number of conditions, mostly aimed at increasing the tax-liability of alien merchants as compared with that of others, on the non-observance of which the grant of tonnage and poundage was to be void.[1] But in the ensuing parliament (of Bats) at Leicester, in 1426, it was enacted that the king, with the counsel of the justices and other lawyers, had declared, through the duke of Bedford and other lords spiritual and temporal, that the subsidy in question was in all respects to be paid and levied, notwithstanding any conditions whatsoever attached to the original concession.[2]

By the time of Henry VI's reign, it would seem that there was at least some recognition that money grants actually were voted by the commons and assented to by the lords. That would seem the inference to be drawn from Hody, CJ.'s admission in the rector of Eddington's case in 1441. It will be remembered that when Newton, CJ., in that case[3] insisted that a fifteenth was not an inheritance of the king but a grant by the spontaneous will of the people, Hody contradicted this by urging that the law which obliged the king to defend his people, obliged also the people to grant him of their goods in aid of that defence, which proved the inheritance. Then he went on to say, 'Et ou est dit que tiel grant prend son effect de son people; jeo dit que non, mes

---

[1] *Rot. Parl.* IV, 276.
[2] *Ibid.* 301–2: 'Item pro eo quod inter Communes Parliamenti predicti diverse oppiniones, de et super concessione et levatione Subsidii Tonagii et Pondagii, Domino Regi in Parliamento suo apud Westm' ultimo tento concessi, mote fuerunt, ut dicebatur, et suborte; visa tandem et diligenter examinata forma concessionis Subsidii predicti, in dicto presenti Parliamento, habita quoque inde Justiciorum et aliorum legis peritorum deliberatione matura; consideratum fuit et plenius declaratum per magnificum Principem Ducem Bed' Commissarium Domini Regis, omni esset solvend' et levand' aliquibus conditionibus in concessione ejusdem Subsidii contentis in aliquo non obstantibus.'
[3] *Y.B.* 19 *Henry VI*, Pas. pl. 1 (App. no. 25).

covient apres tiel grant eu par son people, que les seigniors du Royaulme approuvent ceo, et auxy que le roy accept.' So that even Hody, the protagonist of a conservative view of the parliamentary phenomenon, implied that the function of the lords in regard to money grants was only to approve that which was made by the 'people'.

But in Pilkington's case of 1454, of first-rate importance as evidence of parliamentary procedure at that date and as such to be treated later,[1] we find Kirkby, clerk of chancery[2], in his testimony before the judges in the exchequer chamber, contemplating grants of tonnage and poundage by the lords and commons separately, and postulating the necessity of further conference between the two, only if the lords made a grant for a longer period than the commons.

Then in the Abbot of Waltham's case in 1482, it was still possible, as has several times been pointed out,[3] for counsel to argue that a fifteenth was a grant by the commons, and that such a grant in parliament without the assent of the lords would be good. Professor Holdsworth is doubtless quite right in pointing out that this argument cannot be said to be in any way authoritative. It is only counsel's argument, and there is no report that the judges made any ruling on the point. But then surely Professor Pollard is equally justified in calling attention to the opinion held by the counsel; for after all, counsel do not make arguments in court unless they expect at any rate some one to believe them—or at least to be unable to refute them—and Pigot when he argued thus had been a serjeant for twenty years. We are therefore at least bound to suppose that in 1481 an opinion was still current that a grant of a fifteenth by the *communitas* would be binding without the assent of the lords. But it is more difficult to follow Professor Pollard when he says

[1] *Y.B.* 33 *Henry VI*, Pas. pl. 8 (App. no. 30). *V. infra*, Chap. III, § 2, and Excursus I thereto.

[2] His precise designation is doubtful. *V.* Dunham, *Fane Fragment*, 46.

[3] *Y.B.* 21 *Edward IV*, Mich. pl. 6 (App. no. 63). Cf. Plucknett, *Lancastrian Constitution* (*op. cit.* 172); Holdsworth, *Hist. Eng. Law*, II, 440; Pollard, *Evolution of Parliament*, 2nd ed. 328 and App. III, note (*n*).

that by *communitas* in this passage was meant the knights of the shire only. That seems to be a gratuitous assumption, for there is abundant reason to suppose that by 1482 *communitas* meant the house of commons. We may, then, say that the idea of the possibility of a grant by the commons without the assent of the 'upper house' was current in 1482, but whether such a grant would in fact be held legally binding remains an open question.[1]

Some points relating to the share of the lords in legislation may be conveniently touched on in this place. Firstly, we may well emphasise an interesting case[2] from the twenty-second year of Edward III, which presumably should be read as a sequel to the crisis of 1341.[3] It is reported that a writ came to Sir William Thorpe, CJKB., to cause to be produced in parliament the record and process of a judgement which was rendered for the king at the suit of a certain Edmund Hadelow and his wife. It was noted that a petition was sued to the king before this writ had been granted. Therefore the roll which contained the process and the judgement was carried by the said Sir William Thorpe into the parliament. Whereupon the king assigned certain earls and barons and with them the justices, etc., to determine these matters. But before anything was done therein, the parliament was ended, and though the 'deputies' stayed, the king himself departed. Before these deputies (assignees) it was alleged that the judgement could not be reversed, unless in parliament, and since it was ended, nothing could be done in the matter. But then it was said that the king made the laws by the assent of the peers and of the commune, not through the peers and the commune; that he had no peer in his own land, and ought not by them to be judged. In the time of King Henry and previously, he had been impleaded as had any man of the

[1] For the liability of the lords to contribute to the expenses of the knights of the shire see article by Miss L. C. Latham in *E.H.R.* XLVIII, 455–464, and note by the present writer in *ibid.* XLIX, 306–308.

[2] *Y.B.* 22 *Edward III*, Hil. pl. 25, fo. 3 (App. no. 7).

[3] But cf. Holdsworth, *Hist. Eng. Law*, II, 435; Pollock and Maitland, *Hist. Eng. Law*, I, 516.

people.[1] But King Edward, his son, had ordained that a man should sue against the king by petition. Still, kings would not be judged unless by themselves and their justices.

This very notable episode, obscure in its details as it is, must be held to have administered a severe snub to the peers' legislative pretensions, and to the theory of peerage in general. The peers (and commons) were stated to be mere assentors to the laws made by the king, who is peerless in the realm.

Still, assertions of such a kind have to be taken with caution, for seventeen years later than this we find Thorpe himself asserting in court a view hardly compatible in idea with this high royalist doctrine. In that action,[2] of the King *v.* the Bishop of Chichester, on the statute of Provisors in 1366, wherein we have already noted[3] Thorpe's expression of the view of parliament as representing the whole body of the realm and so forth, it was argued by the bishop's counsel that no ordinance would be held as a restraint in certain instances, 'sil ne agree en plein parlement par tout les communes'.

But to this, Thorpe replied with the rather startling judicial opinion, that when all the lords were assembled they could make an ordinance, and it would be held as a statute, and indeed 'pur cel cause' the king had commanded them 'to hold that (the statute of Provisors) for a statute'.[4]

If a justice on the bench in 1366 held an opinion such as this, it is clear enough that the modern doctrines of statutory law were still far off, and we may well have to modify our view of the place that the lords were thought to have in legislation.

---

[1] On this point, cf. Pollock and Maitland's comment (*loc. cit.*): 'In the middle of the fourteenth century the common belief was that down to the time of Edward I the king could be sued like a private person, and a judge said that he had seen a writ beginning with "Praecipe Henrico Regi Angliae". If he had seen anything of the kind, it was some joke, some forgery, or possibly some relic of the Barons' War.'

[2] *Y.B.* 39 *Edward III*, Pas. pl. 3 (App. no. 8).

[3] *V. supra*, p. 76.   [4] *V. infra*, p. 235.

EXCURSUS III

NOTES ON THE PLACE OF THE COMMONS IN PARLIAMENT

The various claims and disclaims explicitly put forward by the commons during the century provide us with evidence as to how they themselves viewed their actual functions in parliament. We have already noted[1] one of the most conspicuous disavowals made by the commons, namely, their repudiation in the parliaments of 1406 and 1411 of any intention to speak in derogation of the prerogative and estate royal. Equally instructive is the disclaimer put in by the commons in the parliament of 1399 to the effect that they were not parties to judgements in parliament. They showed to the king, 'ce come les Juggementz du Parlement appertiegnent soulement au Roy et as Seigneurs et nient as Communes sinoun en cas qe s'il plest au Roy de sa grace especiale lour monstrer les ditz Juggementz, pur ease de eux, qe nul Record soit fait en Parlement encontre les ditz Communes q'ils sont ou seront parties as ascunes Juggementz donez ou a doners en apres en Parlement'.[2]

To this declaration, doubtless inspired by the fact that just a week earlier the king in parliament, and with the assent of the lords spiritual and temporal, had adjudged Richard 'nadgairs Roy' to perpetual imprisonment,[3] it was replied by the chancellor at the king's command that, 'Comment mesmes les Communes sont petitioners et demandours, et que le Roy et les Seigneurs de tout temps ont eues et aueront de droit, les Jugementz en Parlement, en manere come mesmes les Communes ount monstrez. Sauve q'en Estatutz a faires, ou en Grantes et Subsides, ou tiels choses a faires pur commune profit du Roialme, le Roy voet avoir especialment leur advis et assent. Et qe cel ordre de fait soit tenuz et gardez en tout temps advenir.'

[1] *Supra*, p. 42.
[2] *Rot. Parl.* III, 427–479.
[3] *Ibid.* Cf. Lapsley, 'The Parliamentary Title of Henry IV', *op. cit.* 427.

It may be that both these disclaimers deserve more attention than they have generally received, but it is true enough that through the century, claims by the commons, rather than the reverse, were in prominence. Of these some call for review here. The sealing of the statute of Succession to the throne by the Speaker's seal for all the commons in 1406 has already been mentioned, and need not be re-examined here. More celebrated is the petition of 1414, and a careful inspection of it is demanded.[1]

Some other claims by the commons met with a definitely favourable reception. Thus in 1401, Speaker Savage requested ample time for the commons to deliberate upon the business in hand before the session was brought to an end, and it was replied that the king 'imagined no such subtlety' as suddenly demanding answers on the business from the commons at the end of the sessions, which the commons alleged had been done before.[2] From time to time, the commons desired to consult with some or all of the lords, and at first the allowance of this was admitted to be a matter of grace on the king's part. In 1402 such a consultation was consented to, but the king expressly stated that he did so, not by duty or custom, but of special grace. He required the clerk of parliament to record that fact, and sent the seneschal of his household and Master John Prophet, his secretary, to announce it to the commons, who replied that they knew well, 'qils ne pourroient avoir ascuns tielx Seigneurs pur entrecommuner ovesque eux d'ascuns bosoignes du Parlement sanz especiale grace et mandement de mesme nostre Seigneur le Roi'.[3]

In 1406 a committee of both lords and commons was appointed to supervise the enactment and engrossment of acts;[4] the statute of Succession in that year was sealed after communication by the commons with all the lords,[5] and in the next parliament the request for a consultation was renewed.[6] But

---

[1] For this *v. infra*, Excursus IV.   [2] *Rot. Parl.* III, 455.
[3] *Ibid.* 486.
[4] *Ibid.* 585; cf. Maxwell-Lyte, *The Great Seal*, 197.
[5] *Ibid.* 580.   [6] *Ibid.* 610.

the claim to receive replies to petitions before making a money grant, advanced in the parliament of 1401, was rejected by the king and the lords, on the grounds that such a practice had not been in use before, and that the king did not wish to change the good customs in any way.[1]

EXCURSUS IV

THE COMMONS' PETITION OF 1414

Until recently, the famous commons' petition praying that their bills should not be altered when enacted save with their assent, presented in Henry V's second parliament (at Leicester) in 1414, has been regarded as a substantial landmark in the development of the commons' share in legislation, and therefore as a constitutional document of outstanding importance. Stubbs described the commons' gain resulting from this petition as 'a great constitutional boon' for which the parliaments of Edward III and Richard II had striven in vain,[2] and Stubbs's view of it has found its way into numerous works, textbooks and others.[3]

But to Stubbs the petition and its response conferred upon the commons 'a great constitutional boon' because he believed both that the commons had long been seeking security for the enactment of their petitions in the same form as that in which they were presented, and that this desired security was obtained

---

[1] *Ibid.* 458. An interesting small point relating to the opinion held as to the place of the commons in authorising royal grants is unearthed by Maxwell-Lyte in *The Great Seal*, 196. In 1402, Sir John Ikelyngton petitioned Henry IV to release him from possible claims by the crown, and forwarded a draft of letters patent which he desired to be issued 'de assensu prelatorum, procerum et magnatum ac communitatis regni'. The commons were deliberately struck out, and the letters issued were stated to be 'ex mero motu et certa scientia nostri de assensu prelatorum, procerum et magnatum regni nostri Anglie in presenti parliamento nostro', and the chancery enrolment was 'per ipsum regem in parliamento'.

[2] *Constitutional History*, § 325.

[3] *E.g.* Maitland, *Constitutional History*, 189; Ramsay, *Lancaster and York*, I, 183; Wakeman and Hassall, *Essays Introductory to English Constitutional History*, 243; F. C. Montague, *Elements of English Constitutional History*, 84; Adams and Stephens in their *Select Documents of English Constitutional History* print the document under the caption (p. 181) 'King agrees not to alter the petitions of the Commons'.

on this occasion in 1414, when the king 'undertook that the acts when finally drawn up should correspond exactly with the petitions'.[1] Now, no doubt, if Stubbs's beliefs in these two respects are justified, the commons must indeed be held to have gained a great boon in 1414, and the document must be ranked high in the constitutional scale. But the progress of research challenges both of those beliefs, and tends to reduce the document from the position of a landmark to that of a signpost on the constitutional highway.[2]

The first of Stubbs's suppositions, that the commons had for long been seeking the security which he thought was actually provided by Henry V's response in 1414, must be abandoned in the light of Professor H. L. Gray's researches upon the original parliamentary petitions of the period.[3] Professor Gray investigated specifically the question whether petitions as enacted differed materially from petitions as presented during certain selected parliaments of Edward III, Richard II, and Henry IV. He found that such differences, though occasionally occurring, were both too rare and too insignificant to be likely to give rise to any prolonged struggle for the 'security' asked for in 1414. But he did discover differences of a fundamental sort between several of the petitions presented in Henry V's first parliament and the enactments made therein; and he consequently argues convincingly that the petition of 1414, so far from being a climax to a long antecedent striving, was elicited by unusual occurrences which had taken place in the preceding parliament of 1413.[4] If, as Professor Gray's researches go far to prove, the

[1] *Constitutional History*, § 369.
[2] For similar modifications of view of such landmarks as (1) Edward II's coronation oath, *v.* B. Wilkinson in *Historical Essays presented to James Tait* (1933), 405–416; (2) The Statute of York of 1322, G. T. Lapsley in *E.H.R.* (1913), XXVIII, 118–124; (3) Parliamentary supremacy in 1388, M. V. Clarke in *Trans. R.H.S.* (1931), 4th ser. XIV, 65–95; (4) Henry IV's parliamentary title, G. T. Lapsley in *E.H.R.* (1934), XLIX, 423–449, 576–606; (5) *Petitio formam actus in se continens*, H. L. Gray, *The Influence of the Commons on Early Legislation* (1932), 42 *et seq.* The cataclysmic element in constitutional history is much lessened as a result of these and other researches.
[3] *Op. cit.*   [4] *Ibid.* 261 *et seq.*

commons had not been confronted, before Henry V's reign, with substantial discrepancies between the terms of their petitions as presented and the terms of them as enacted, no problem of obtaining the 'full security' envisaged by Stubbs could have arisen. The petition of 1414—or the relevant part of it—must, therefore, have aimed at no more than formally establishing as a right what had long been the usual practice. No doubt the establishment of such a right would have been a distinct advantage to the commons, who would thereby have been enabled to hinder, if not to prevent, a recurrence of such drastic unassented revisions of their petitions before enactment as had been imposed in 1413. No doubt such an advantage would have been a boon to the commons—if the king had granted it. But apparently he did not do so, and recognition of this fact casts doubt on the second of Stubbs's beliefs—that the commons actually did obtain in 1414 the 'full security' he supposed they had long been seeking.

Stubbs and all other commentators, until very recently, assumed, rather gratuitously, that this commons' petition—whatever precisely it embraced—really was granted by the king. No scepticism as to the king's intentions in the matter appeared in print until Mr K. M. Pickthorn pointed out, in his *Early Tudor Government* (1934),[1] that the king's reply to the petition granted 'a good deal less than was asked'. Yet a very marked divergence between the terms of the petition and those of the royal response to it—both apparently the earliest known in the English language—seems clear enough. Careful examination of the actual words of the document suggests that Stubbs was deceived as to the nature of the king's concession, and that even Mr Pickthorn's conclusion on the matter is, if anything, too conservative.

Analysis of the commons' petition reveals that they made therein three, or more strictly, only two, claims; one request; and

---

[1] I, 125. D. J. Medley, however, in his *Manual of English Constitutional History*, 2nd ed. (1898), described the king's response as 'an empty formula' (245).

one admission.[1] They claimed, firstly, that no statute (and even
no law) had ever been made without their assent; secondly,
that the commons had ever been a part of parliament, and
thirdly—and this claim is implied in the first—that the commons in parliament had always been assenters as well as
petitioners. They requested that thenceforth no statute (or law)
should be made upon their verbal or written petitions which by
additions, reductions, or any change of terms, would change the
meaning or intention thereof, without their assent. They admitted that, whether they put forward few or many petitions,
the king had the right to grant whichever he pleased, and to
refuse the remainder.

Analysis of the king's reply, however, reveals not only that he
totally ignored the claims embodied in the petition, but also that
he conceded not merely a good deal less than, but something
different from, their request. He granted, of his especial grace,
that thenceforth nothing should be enacted to the commons'
petitions which was *contrary* thereto, whereby they would be
bound without their assent. This concession was followed by a
reservation—usually ominous—to the king of his royal prerogative, in terms which substantially repeated those of the petition
itself. Thus, the king, so far from agreeing to the commons'
request that their petitions should not in any way be changed
before enactment without their assent, appears merely to have
undertaken that statutes should not be enacted to the opposite
effect of their petitions. The royal response, therefore, seems not
only evasive and irrelevant, but perhaps even nugatory, since
the amendment of petitions to the extreme of contradiction was
scarcely a likely contingency.

Whatever degree of subtlety is to be found in this royal
response, there is little doubt that it left the king as free as ever
to *amend* commons' petitions before enactment without obtain-

[1] *Rot. Parl.* iv, 22. *V.* Lodge and Thornton, *English Constitutional Documents,*
1307–1485 (1935), 165, no. 53, where the document is printed under the non-
committal caption of 'Assent of the Commons to Legislation, 1414'.

ing their assent, so long as such amendments did not amount to contradiction. Once this fact is recognised, the otherwise insuperable difficulty of reconciling the older interpretation of the royal promise with the practice of amending commons' bills without assent, recently revealed as very common not merely during the reign of Henry V himself, but throughout the fifteenth century,[1] disappears.

Such unassented amendments can no longer be disregarded, even though their chief discoverer is equivocal in his view of their importance.[2] Amendments which limited the duration of a proposed statute, reconciled it with existing law and commitments, or exempted persons or groups from its operation, and the like—though not radical in character—cannot be dismissed as insignificant. Any such amendment without assent must have violated the promise made in 1414, if that promise had really conceded what the commons had asked for, and the frequent occurrence of them must have made such a promise a dead letter. The dilemma therefore arises that either the promise of 1414 was frequently violated as soon as it was made—and apparently without arousing protest on the part of the commons —or the nature of the promise has been misunderstood. Since the plain meaning of the words of the petition and answer themselves suggest the necessity for a fresh interpretation of the transaction, the second alternative is clearly indicated. The amendments imposed upon commons' petitions without their assent were not violations of the royal promise of 1414, because its terms left the king as free to amend them, short of contradiction, as he had ever been.

The constitutional importance of the transaction of 1414 is thus greatly reduced. No longer can it be regarded as establishing the commons' right to have their bills enacted without unagreed amendments, and the slenderness of the royal concession

---

[1] H. L. Gray, *op. cit.* 168–169, 334; Dunham, *Fane Fragment*, 74–84.
[2] He calls them 'insignificant' (*op. cit.* 199), but elsewhere (p. 266) he admits that changes of exactly the same sort were 'serious'.

in it shifts the main interest of the matter from the sphere of constitutional practice to that of theory. It is to the claims rather than to the request which the commons put forward that attention is to be drawn.[1] Their claims that no statute had ever been made without their assent, that they had always been a part of parliament, and that they had always been assenters as well as petitioners, even though unjustified historically, registered clearly the notion that the commons were entertaining as to the importance of their place in the constitutional scheme. And even though the king ignored these claims in his reply, the claim none the less marked an important advance upon anything that the commons had said before about themselves. So that the petition of 1414, if it be a landmark at all, is a landmark, not in the history of parliamentary procedure, but in that of constitutional ideas.

[1] Thus Lodge and Thornton, *op. cit.*, in their Introduction to the section on Parliament, make no allusion whatever to the whole transaction except to cite it as an illustration (p. 124) of their statement that 'at least the co-operation (of the commons) came to be indispensable for legislation'. Though this statement be true, the value of the transaction as an illustration thereof is modified by the fact that the Crown did not specifically admit the commons' claims. The editors of this useful collection of documents unfortunately seem to imply that Stubbs's 'great constitutional boon' was sought and obtained by a petition of 1348 (*ibid.* 141, no. 19 and 124), but such manifestly was not the case. The 'boon' never was obtained by formal grant, but ultimately by the gradual fixation of the practice of presenting *petitiones formam actus in se continentes*, even though common bills were not, during the fifteenth century, drafted in that form (H. L. Gray, *op. cit.* 181). Professor Gray believes that closer correspondence between petition or bill (the terms were synonymous) was obtained in the second half of the century by the increasing tendency to draft amendments in the form of provisos (*ibid.* 183) but there is slender evidence that commons' assent was got for even those provisos. In the mediaeval period, at any rate, the commons never established a right to assent to amendments made by the Crown to their petitions.

EXCURSUS V

TEXTS OF PARLIAMENTARY SERMONS, 1399–1485

1399	1 Henry IV	Incumbit nobis ordinare pro regno	1 *Maccabees* vi, 57
1400–1	2 ,,	(Address by Thirning J., pro-chancellor)	
1402	4 ,,	Pax multa diligentibus legem	*Psalms* cxviii, 165
1403	5 ,,	Multitudo sapientum	*Wisdom* vi, 26
1404	6 ,,	Rex vocavit seniores terre	3 *Kings* xx, 7
1405–6	7–8 ,,	Multorum consilia requiruntur in magnis	(?)
1407	9 ,,	Regem honorificate	1 *Peter* ii, 7
1409–10	11 ,,	Decet nos implere omnem justiciam	*Matthew* iii, 15
1411*			
1413	1 Henry V	Ante omnem actum consilium stabile	*Ecclesiasticus* xxxvii, 20
1414 (i)	2 ,,	Posuit cor suum ad investigandas leges	1 *Esdras* vii, 10
1414 (ii)	2 ,,	Dum tempus habemus operemur bonum	*Galatians* vi, 10
1415 (i)	3 ,,	Sicut et ipse fecit nobis ita et nos ei faciamus	(?)
1415 (ii)	3 ,,	Iniciavit vobis viam	*Hebrews* x, 20 (?)
1416	4 ,,	Operam detis ut quieti sitis	1 *Thessalonians* iv, 11
1417	5 ,,	Confortamini, viriliter agite et gloriosi eritis	1 *Maccabees* ii, 64
1419	7 ,,	Bonum facientes non deficiamus	*Galatians* vi, 9
1420	8 ,,	Inivit David consilium	1 *Paralipomenon* xiii, 1
1421 (i)	9 ,,	Laudans invocabo Dominum	*Psalms* xvii, 4
1421 (ii)	9 ,,	Lex Domini immaculata convertens animas	*Psalms* xviii, 8
1422	1 Henry VI	Principes populorum congregati sunt cum Deo	*Psalms* xlvi, 10
1423	2 ,,	Deum timete, regem honorificate	1 *Peter* ii, 17

* No texts are mentioned in the Rolls of Parliament in this year.

TEXTS OF PARLIAMENTARY SERMONS, 1399–1485 (continued)

Year		Reign	Text	Reference
1425 (i)	3	Henry VI	Gloria et honor et pax omni operanti bonum	Romans ii, 10
1425 (ii)	4	„	Sic facite ut salvi sitis	Ecclesiasticus iii, 2
1427	6	„	Sine providentia regali impossibile est pacem rebus dari	2 Maccabees iv, 6
1429	8	„	Quomodo stabit regnum	Matthew xii, 26
1430–1	9	„	Firmabiliter solium regni ejus	1 Paralipomenon xxii, 10
1432	10	„	Deum timete, regem honorificate	1 Peter ii, 17
1433	11	„	Suscipiant montes pacem populo et colles justiciam	Psalms lxxi, 3
1435	14	„	Soliciti sitis servare unitatem spiritus in vinculo pacis	Ephesians iv, 3
1436	15	„	Corona regni in manu dei	Isaiah lxii, 3
1439	18	„	Adaperiat Dominus cor vestrum in lege sua et in preceptis suis	2 Maccabees i, 4
1441–2	20	„	Rex et thronus ejus sit innocens	2 Kings xiv, 9
1444	23	„	Justicia et pax osculate sunt	Psalms lxxxiv, 11
1447	25	„	Qui autem ineunt pacis consilia sequitur illos gaudium	Proverbs xii, 20
1449, 1451, 1453, 1455*		„		
1459	38	„	Gratia vobis et pax multiplicetur	1 Peter i, 2
1460	39	„	Congregate populum sanctificate ecclesiam	Joel ii, 16
1461	1	Edward IV	Bonas facite vias vestras et studia vestra	Jeremiah vii, 3
1463–64	3	„	Qui judicatis terram diligite justiciam	Wisdom i, 2
1467–68, 1472–73–74*				
1477	17	Edward IV	Dominus regit me et nichil michi deerit	Psalms xxii, 1
1483	22	„	Dominus illuminatio mea et salus mea	Psalms xxvi, 1
1483	1	[Edward V]	Dominus ab utero vocavit me	Isaiah xlix, 1
1483	1	Richard III	In corpore multa quidem sunt membra, non autem omnia eundem actum habent	1 Corinthians xii, 12

* No texts are mentioned in the Rolls of Parliament in these years.

EXCURSUS VI

BISHOP RUSSELL'S PARLIAMENTARY
SERMONS IN 1483

When Bishop Russell composed the sermon he proposed to
deliver before the first parliament of Edward V, he was chancellor of the University of Oxford, and had been chancellor of
England since the 31st of May of the same year, and had for
many years before pursued a distinguished career in state and in
church—more particularly in state. As a boy he passed through
the foundations of Wykeham at Winchester and Oxford, and he
eventually became a doctor of laws (1459). The subsequent
phase of his career is very dark in the accounts of his life at
present available; but in 1467 he became archdeacon of Berk-
shire, and soon served on a number of royal diplomatic missions
in the name of Edward IV, and also of Henry VI during his
brief restoration. His services received the rewards of high
office when he was appointed keeper of the Privy Seal in 1474,
bishop of Rochester in 1476, and was transferred to the see of
Lincoln in 1480. His diplomatic speciality was apparently the
negotiation of matrimonial alliances; and he was employed for
this purpose in the negotiations between Charles the Bold,
James of Scotland, and daughters of Edward IV, and between
Earl Rivers and Margaret of Scotland. Despite his antecedents,
he was, at least for a time, trusted by Richard III, who kept him
in the chancellorship until the 29th of July, 1485, and employed
his diplomatic abilities in negotiations with Scotland and
Brittany. But Russell, with his usual facility or indifference,
favoured Henry Tudor, by whom his services were also utilised
for diplomatic purposes and for minor offices such as the trying
of petitions. Until his death in 1494/5 he retained the chancellorship of Oxford, and was reckoned as the first of the life-
chancellors. Trimmer though Russell may have been, Sir Thomas
More wrote of him, some twenty years after his death, that 'he

was a wise manne and good, of much experience and one of the best learned men, undoubtedly, that England had in hys time'. The drafts of his parliamentary sermons in 1483 have been printed in full before, by J. G. Nichols in the preface to his work entitled *Grants of Edward V* (Camden Society (1854), LX). In view, however, of their unique interest, their very great value as evidence of fifteenth-century outlook on the topics to which they allude, and the consequent frequency of their citation in the present work, it has been thought worth while to reprint them here. Nichols's text has been collated with the MS. (*Cottonian Vitellius E.X*), but very few corrections have been requisite. Some of Nichols's footnotes have been retained, and are indicated by his initials, and some additional notes and references have been inserted.

(1) Draft prepared for the intended parliament of Edward V

(fo.170 r) [*Audite insule, Et attendite populi de longe, Dominus ab vtero vocauit me.*][1] The[a] policie in christen Remes schewethe, ouer alle yn the dayes that we be yn, how theyr public body is compowned of iij notable partes, of the prince, the nobles, and the peuple. And ther fore hauinge to speke at thys tyme of alle iij as they be nowe here assembled for the wele of thys most nobylle and famous Reme of Englond, I have taken a trimembrid text suche as I fownd yn the diuine seruise of yestirdayes fest,[2] the whyche to my purpose implyethe the present astate of owre nobles, owre commons, and of owre glorious prince and kynge Edward the Vth here present. My mynd ys that thys schuld be the wordes of the kynge, and by me to be spoken at thys tyme in hys name. First to yowe ryghte nobille lordys spiritualle and temporalle, *Audite insule*. Secondly to yowe worshepfulle syrres representynge the commons, *Et attendite populi de longe*. Hyt folowethe, *Dominus ab vtero vocauit me*, Godd hath called me in my

---

[1] *Isaiah* xlix, 1.   [a] The MS. is defective in several places.
[2] 24th June, 1483 (*v.* J.G.N. pp. xx–xxi).

tendire age to be yowre kynge and souerayne. The cosma-
graphers whyche have left to vs in ther wrytynges the descrip-
cion of the rounde worlde descendynge from aboue downeword
principally to the habitable regions and nauigable sees and flodes
here benethe, haue had grete respecte vnto the emergence and
swellynge vp of londes compassed abowt with waters, whose
propre denominacion is to be called Isles. *Papa pius*[1] yn the
begynnyng of hys tretie *De Asia minori* (fo. 170 v) Saith that by
th' opinion of diuers Auctors the occ[ean...] and gothe abowte
iiij princypalle costes of the erthe, that thereby alle the hote
apperynge londe arysethe as yt were vnto .iiij. grete Isle londes.
He rerserseth ferther, aftir the sentence of Omer,[2] that by reson
of the circuit of the ocean rownd abowte thys lower worlde alle
the hole erthe ys redacte into the forme of one Isle. Soo that hyt
be vndoubted that alle the habitacion and occupacion of man ys
eyther in lond or in water. Then yf there be any suerte or
fermenesse here yn thys worlde, such as may be fownde oute of
heuyn, hyt ys rathyr in the Isles and londes enuirounde with
water then in the see or in eny grete Ryvers,[3] *Nam qui mare
nauigant pericula narrant.* And therefor the noble persons of the
worlde, whych some for the merites of ther auncesturs, some for
ther owne vertues, bene endued whyth grete hauours, possessions
and Richesses, may more conueniently be resembled vn to the
ferme grounde that men see in Isle londes then the lower peuple,
whyche for lacke of suche endumentes, not possible to be departed amonges so many, and therefor liuynge by ther casuelle
labours, be not withowte cause likkened vn to the vnstabille and
wauerynge rennynge water. *Aque multe populus multus.* Hyt was

[1] Pius II (Aeneas Sylvius Piccolomini), 'De Asia Minore', printed in his *Opera Geographica et Historica*, 1770.
[2] There is no direct assertion of this kind in Homer, but such an inference can be based on various passages in the poem. (*V.* Merry and Riddell, *Odyssey*, note, x, 508.)
[3] Whether the bishop here intended a reflection upon the 'great Ryvers' to whom the duke of Gloucester was mortally opposed, I leave to the determination of the reader: but I think it highly probable that he intended to lay a particular stress upon these words, so that they should readily catch the ears of his audience, and bear a covert meaning somewhat more intelligible to the majority of his hearers than the rest of his discourse. (J.G.N.)

seyd to synt John in the Apocalipsis *Aque quas vidisti populi sunt
et gentes.*[1] To ley the grownde of noblesse vpon vertu joyned to
possessions and Rychesses, thowe hit be a mater disputabille and
disputed at large by diuerse auctors and (fo. 171r)...peraven-
ture some other opinion ther taken theryn then the commyn vse
of every region requirythe, yet bycause that as for reputacion of
nobelesse ther ys recited the custume of thys land and many
other adioygnaunt sownynge to the same, and that it is not of
eny scole dynyed but that rychesse ys a propre instrumente of
execucion of vertu, addyng there vnto the defunicion that
Aristotle maketh 4° Politicorum *quod Ingenuitas est virtus et diuitie
antique,*[2] Nobelesse is vertu and auncienne Richesse, hit semethe
that conueniently syche fermenesse of ground as may be best
found in thys world, oughte to be appropred vn to the lordes
and nobylle men, and soo they to be sygnifyed and vnderstonded
by that soo ys fownd most stabille, that ys to sey by the Islelondes
and not by the water ne floodes. But who can make eny in-
fallibille or certene suerte amonges gret waters and tempestuous
Rivers,[3] but that by brechys and inundacions the ferme londe
and isles may be oft tymes lost and aneintised, or at the leste
gretly diminisshed. When Plinius in hys second boke *De Naturalibus historiis*[4] writethe of many Isles, som vtterly ouer flowen and
perisshed, some fluctuante and changynge fro place to place,
whether *Insula Vecta* was euer at eny tyme yn that case y can
not sey, the name ys propre to hyt thowe yn owre dayes the
effecte be not there (fo. 171 v) after[5], Soothe hit is that that who
so [searcheth the history of] other nacions, namely the booke of
Boccase *De casibus,*[6] ye, who so goeth no ferther then to owre
owen home, remembryng what fluctuacion and changynge

---

[1] *Revelation* xvii 15.   [2] *Politics* vii, i (?).
[3] In my opinion, another reflection intended to tell against the unfortunate
relatives of the Queen. (J.G.N.)
[4] Pliny, *op. cit.*
[5] This whimsical conjecture regarding the Isle of Wight, which the bishop
inserts by way of parenthesis, had also probably some covert allusion beyond mere
etymological speculation. Among the titles of earl Ryvers was that of lord of the
Isle of Wight. (J.G.N.)
[6] Presumably *De Casibus Virorum Illustrium,* 1350–70.

amonges the nobles hathe fallen in thys Reme, he may lyghtly see that alle owre grownd ys sett with yn the see, alle subiecte to Ebbe and flowe, to wyndes, blastes and stormes. The defense of grownd assayled with rage of waters is wont to be made by dryuynge of pyles or stakys and fastenynge of sure pale to the banke, or the wharfe where the water rebowndethe. Who so herkenethe not vppon the commyn voyce grownded in a resonable presydent, but bydythe hys affayres and doynges in ymagination of hys owne plesaunce, leuing the prouision of thynges that ought to be dradd and doubted, ensuethe not th' entente of Dauid the prophyte seyng *Confige timore tuo carnes meas .i. carnales cupiditates.*[1] Drede is the pale and muralle that closithe and restrayneth mannys brotelle affections, and helpithe myche that by forgetefullnesse he falle not yn to surcuidance. Hyt ys comenly seyd, The best wolle sauf hyt self. But yn thynges of jupertie and doubtfulle aventure the exercise of mannys wyt takythe a gret rome. *Initium sapientie timor.*[2] Drede ys the begynnynge of wyse demenynge. Wysedame can not be atteyned but by herynge, for as the phylosopher seythe, amonges all owr .v. wytts heryng ys the most disciplinable wytt, In so myche that as he (fo. 172r)...they heryng can men be tawghte ne lerned. Man that ys callyd *Animal ciuile*, namely for that he ys endued whythe speche, whyche no best hathe but onely man, and whereby thynges ellys vnknowen may be broughte to knowleche from one to a nother, takithe hys lernynge by herynge. *Sermo, inquit, audibilis causa est discipline*, Speche that ys audible and wele herd ys the cause of lernynge. *Audite ergo insule.* Then the lordes and nobille men, ye that have grete substaunce to lese or sauf, in whoos sure and concord demenynge restithe the wele of alle the commen, open your eeres, send vnto your feythfulle espie3, and here turue and unfayned reportes. Be not lyke them that Jerime speketh of, *qui dicunt videntibus nolite videre sed loquimini nobis placentia,*[3] for the same prophete crieth, Woe be to them that forsakene good counselle, sayng

---

[1] *Psalms* cxviii, 120.   [2] *Psalms* cx, 10.   [3] *Isaiah* xxx, 10.

Ve filii desertores, dicit Dominus, vt feceretis consilium et non ex me[1] &c.
Hyt were a longe occupacion of tyme to reherse the manyfold
hystories bothe oute of scriptoure and of the actes of Romanes,
shewynge the falle of mony noble men for that they despised
syche counselle and aduertisementes as to them were geuyn;
late hyt suffice that vn to us alle it is vndoubted, yf some folkes
hadd followed the commyn opinion that was thoughte allewey
most lykly to falle, moche of ther daunger had been auoyded.
But now trowthe [hit] ys *quod sicut audiuimus sic vidimus*. There for
to diligent herynge (fo. 172 v) Isaie exhorteth bothe princes,
whych may be compared...seynge[2] *Audite celi*, and other
hauyng gret honours and possessions, in thes words, *et auribus
percipe terra*. Hyt ys the same prophete that seythe *Audite insule*,
as whoo wolld sey the most proper meyne to kepe the grette
estates of the public body in ther welthe and prosperite ys
everyche to herken apon other, soo that neyther for supplanta-
cion, dissimulacion, ne enuye, the due proporcion and armonie
of thys body be not disturbed. By concord, as Salustius seythe,[3]
smalle thyngs growe on the gret, and by discord fulle grete
thynges falle to ruine and desolacion. The cause why lordys and
nobille men oughte more to be persuadid to accord, and eche
amyabilly to herken apon other, then the hole generallte of
alle the peuple, is playne and euident inowe, consyderynge how
the polityk rule of every region wele ordeigned stondithe in the
nobles; for after that Rome was peupleed, the fyrst institucion of
the thynge public there made by Romulus was *in centum
senatoribus*; lyke wyse Moises, the leder of the chelderne of
Israel, by th' advise and counselle of Jetro his cosen, chose oute
of the whole multitude a certen nombre of wyse and nobille men
to have power vndre hym in alle causes reserved the grettest;[4]
lyke as in theys dayes in every region where is a monarchie and
one (fo. 173r) prince [the semblable] policie is observyd. To
yow then my lordys perteynethe principally the offyce of herynge

---

[1] *Isaiah* xxx, 1.   [2] *Isaiah* i, 2.
[3] Sallust, *De Bello Iugurthino*, 10, § 6.   [4] *Exodus* xviii, 25.

of the state of every case fallynge a mong your self, or the peuple vndre yowe, yowrself to be reduced by louynge tretie, the peuple be true justice. Ye be lyke to Moyses and Aaron, whych escend vnto the mownt where the lawe ys geuen. The peuple must stond a forr, and not passe the lymittes; ye speke with the prince, whyche is *quasi deus noster in terris*, as they did with God mouthe to mouthe; but hyt suffisith the peuple to receyue with due obeissaunce the prince's commandementes by the direccion of hys wise ministers and offycers, that saynge to everyche of yow, as they of Israel dyd to Moises, *loquere tu nobis et audiemus, non loquatur nobis Dominus.*[1] When the grett prince Allemighty God, lord of alle lordes, gaf the lawe yn the hylle to Moises and Aaron, the peuple stondynge by nethe, nat ferre thens, but att the foote of the mownte, grett thundre clappys were herde, muche lyghtnynge and other terrible impressions were seyn, whyche sore agasted the people, for the whyche they seyd to Moises, as to a mortalle man such as they were them self, how be yt he was yn hye estate and had vndre God the ledyng and governaunce of them, Moises, quod they, our duke and maister, speke thow to us and we shall here and obeye thee, lete not owr Lord speke vn to vs. Hyt ys not vnknowen but that when so euer the kynge in hys person, for the multitude of mysdoers, (fo. 173v) takythe vpon hym to visite hys Reame...yn hys hyghe presence, the criminalle causes of felonyes, murders, and other haynouse and incredible oultrages, the ministracion of justice is wont to be so terrible and precise in processe that alle the pertees and persones adioignaunt quake and tremble for fere. *Dicunt ergo, Non loquatur nobis dominus.* Wherefor it ys not to doulte but that the rule and governaile of the Reame appereth then in most temperaunce and moderacion when the kynges juges and commisses be obeyd at large in every parte of the londe, so that hys hyghenes and hys nobylle counselle be not letted, where the kynge lystythe beste to be, to entend the politik establysshynge of the Reme. *Attendite igitur populi de longe*, Gyff then your

[1] *Exodus* xx, 19.

attendaunce, ye peuple that stonde ferre of, to the lordes and nobille men whyche be in auctorite; they come from the wele hedd, ye stonde *a longe.* I speke not to yowe that nowe represent the hele, but to them that ye come fro, whome for ther gret and confuse nombre and multitude nature can not wele suffre to assemble in oo place apt to the makynge of a lawe. When Romulus lakked peuple and made hys newe cite to be and called *azilum*, that ys to sey a franchese or sanctuary for every person that wollde come and dwelle there, the law was made by the assente of alle the peuple togedyr; they were not in suche nombre but that they mighte welle be assembled in oo place. But after they were so ferre encreased that hyt was hard and in maner impossible (fo. 174r) [for them to meet all together, the] power of the lawe was geuen to the [senate] to the nombre of a.C.noble and wyse men; yet after that chalenged the peuple to haue ther enterlacyng yn gret causes with the nobles, and obteigned a specyalle magistrate called *tribunus plebis* to be ther president in ther consultacions, lyke as yn the senate the one of the consuls proposed and diffined alle that was amonges them. I see the policie of thys Reme in the tyme of holdynge of parliamentes grettly correspondente to the same maner of the Romanes. Thys ys the howse of the senate. The commons have ther apart. And lyke as yn thys house one *tanquam consul* makithe the questions, soo yn the lower howse in lyke wyse alle ys directed by the speker *quasi per tribunum.* Valerie in the seconde boke of the memorable dictes and dedys of Rome rehersythe that,[1] thowe the Tribunes of the peuple might not presume to entre withyn the courte of the Senatours, yet schulde they have setes withoute to examine what were decried by the nobles, suche decrees to be not auayleable unto the tyme they were ratified by the peuple. See the passynge of every act made in a parliament, and alle is oo thynge, that that the Romaynes did in ther tyme, and that that we do nowe in thys the kynges most hyghe and souerayne courte. *Audiunt insule, attendunt populi de longe.* The

---

[1] Valerius Maximus, *Liber Dictorum ac Factorum Memorabilium.*

princes and lordes have the fyrst and principalle vndrestondynge
and knowlege of every gret thynge necessarye to be redressed,
the lower peuple and commens herkene and attende uppon
(fo. 174v) them. And when they agre eche to other...thynge
can be better. That bodye ys hole and stronge whois stomake
and bowels is ministered by the vtward membres that that
suffiseth to be wele degested; for if the fete and the hondes,
whyche seme to doo most paynefulle labour for mannys lyvyng,
wollde complayne ageynste the wombe as ageynste an idelle and
slowthfulle parte of the bodye, and denye the prouysyon of syche
necessarye foode as the stomake calleth for, hyt might sone
happe, that faylynge the belye for lake, the guttes and intestines
compressed and shut by drynesse, alle the other membres sholld
nedes peryshe togedyr. And therefor hyt ys vndoubted in
nature that thys middelle membres of the body, that ys to sey,
the stomake, the bely and partes adjoignante be not unoccupied,
but hafe ryght a besy office; for when they be fedd they fede
agayne, yeldynge vn to every parte of the bodye that withoute
the whyche no man may leve, that ys to wyt, in to all the vaynes
blode, degested out of the best of mannys foode and repast. What
ys the bely or where ys the wombe of thys grete publick body of
Englonde but that and there where the kyng ys hym self, hys
court and hys counselle? for there must be digested alle maner
metes, not onely servyng to commyn foode but alleso to dent...
and some tyme to medicines, such as be appropred to remedye
the excesses and surfettes committed at large. Thidir be brought
alle maters of weight, peax and were with outwarde londes,
confederacions, (fo. 175r) [ligues and alliances, receivynge] and
sendynge of embassades and messages, brekynge of treux, perises
in the see, routes and riotts, and vnlawfulle assemblees, oppressions, extorsions, contemptes and abusions of the lawe, and many
moo surfettes then can be welle nombred. Thys wombe wexed
grete anemst the departure of the prince of blessed memorie the
kynges fader, whome Godd absoyle, consyderynge the inextric-
able curis, pensifenesseȝ, thowghtes and charges wharewith ys

wyse and fercastinge mynd was hugely occupied and encom-
breed, a fore hys decesse, seeyng the crafty and fraudulente
delynge of the outward princes with whome he was allyed, and
howe vntruely they varied bothe for mariages, paymentes,
suretees and other grete and noble appoyntmentes passed fro
them by theor othys and selys. In the myddys of thys moste
chargeable besinesses, the kynge owre souuerayne lord ys callyd
of Godd to reigne vppon hys peuple and therefor hys hyghenesse,
remembrynge how alle hys louynge subiettes in what degree he
fyndythe the state of hys londe at thys hys newe entree, and how
grete and weightye maters most nedes be digested dayly in hys
counselle, as yn the stomak and bely of thys grete body of
Englonde, sayth vnto yowe, *Dominus ab vtero vocauit me*,[1] *Audite
insule*, ye lordes of my counselle here, and yn alle maters gyfe
good and redy audience. *Et attendite populi*, [ye] louinge peuple
and commens denye not yowr deligent attendaunce, (fo. 175 v)
quia Dominus ab vtero vocauit me, for Godd hath called me (vnto
the occupation of mine) office, as a yonge creature comynge out
of the wombe, and middes of ryghte weightye and besy cha[r]ges.
What roten membre is that yn thys gret body of Englonde, how
insensible and mortified ys that membre, that can not have
compassion of the ache of hys hede. Synt Paule seyth, *Si quid
patitur vnum membrum, compatiuntur etiam omnia membra*.[2] Yf ever
the nobles and peuple of this londe were kynde to any of ther
princes, if[a] they hadd at eny tyme a good truste of justice, and
to be delyuered from newe and exactiff inuencions, Iff therefor
hit greued them not to renewe by auctoryte of parliamente syche
grauntes as were thought yn the tyme of other kynges cowde not
welle be spared, whoo can suppose but that they that see the
most towarde and vertuous disposicion of our souueraynge lorde
that now is, hys gentylle wytte and rype vnderstondynge, ferre
passynge the nature of hys youthe, who can thynke but that the
lordes and commens of thys londe wylle as agreabilly pouruey
for the sure maynetenaunce of hys hyghe estate as eny of their

---

[1] *Isaiah* xlix, 1.   [2] 1 *Corinthians* xii, 26.   [a] of in *MS*.

predecessours have done to eny other of the kynges of Englonde afore, namely considered the necessarye charges whych yn the tyme of the kynges tendre age must nedely be borne and supported by the ryght noble and famous prince the duke of Gloucestir hys vncle, protector of thys Reme. In whos gret puis[sance], wysdome and fortunes[a] restethe at thys rason[b] thexecucion of the defence of thys Reme, as wele ageynste the open ennemies as ageynste the subtylle and faynte fryndes of the same. And over that yt ys (fo. 176r)...of the tutele and ouersyghte of the kynges most roialle personne durynge hys the yeres of tendirnesse my sayd lorde protector wylle acquite hym self lyke to Marcus Emilius Lepidus twyes consul of Rome,[1] of whom Valere yn the vjth boke of the dictes and dedys be for remembred spekethe,[2] how vppon the dethe of Tholomee kynge of Egipt, whyche left for hys heyre be hynde hym a yonge son *in pupillari etate*, hauyng grete confidence that the peuple of Rome wolde prouide for the goode and honerabille guydyng of that chylde vn to the tyme he were of rype age. The nobylle synate agreed and ordeigned that the seyd Marcus Emilius Lepidus schuld take thys offyce of tutele defense and protection vppon hym. Whereuppon he adressed hym self to the gret cite of Alexandre where the yonge kynge was resyaunt, and toke such ordres as welle in thedicacion and conduite of the persone of that yonge prince as in administracion of alle grete thynges concernynge hys Reme, so and in suche wyse that the same kynge whan he was come to perfection of hys yeres and toke the rule vppon hym self was in such nobelesse and prosperite that yt was doubted to whois merites that excellente fortune ought to be ascribed, either of hys fadre or hys tutor. Wele ys thys yonge prince our souerayne lord here presente set bitwene ij brethern, that one hys fadir, that othir hys vncle; the rule of the furst is determined by the ouer hastely course of nature. The seconde ys ordeigned as next yn perfyt age of the (fo. 176v) blod Ryalle, to

---

[a] 'fortumes' in MS.   [b] *Sic* MS. 'Seson'?
[1] Consul in 187 and 175 B.C.   [2] *Op. cit.*

be hys tutor and protector. To take example of [the...] marcialle kunnyng, felecite and experience of the oone or the other of thes ij princes[a] can be none error. And what so ever ys shapen by God for eny speciallte of grace expropred to thys our yonge kynge and souerayne lorde a boue hys auncestures, lett yt be taken to aduauntege. The churche singeth of every confessore *Non est inuentus similis illi.* In the meane tyme, tylle rypenesse of yeres and personelle rule be, as by Godys grace they must onys be, concurrente togedyr, The power and auctorite of my lord protector is so behoffulle and of reason to be assented and establisshed by the auctorite of thys hyghe courte, that amonges alle the causes of the assemblynge of the parliamente yn thys tyme of the yere, thys ys the grettest and most necessarye furst to be affermed. God graunte that thys mater and syche othir as of necessite owithe to be furst moved for the we[le] of the kynge and the defense of thys londe, maye have such goode and breff expedicion yn thys hyghe courte of parliament as the ease of the peuple and the condicion and the tyme requireth, Soe that at the departynge of the lordys and of suche as bene here for the commens eueriche to ther propre home where they be as[b] hyt were the shulders, armes, hondes and fete of thys gret body of Englonde yn regarde of thys place where ys the middes and wombe of the same, the kynge oure souerayne lord may have cause largely to reioyse hym selfe and congruently say wyth the prophete, to my sayde lord protector, hys vncle here present, *In te confirmatus sum ex vtero de ventre matris me, tu es protector meus,*[1] Vncle, I am gladde to have yow...conformed yn thys place yow to be my protector in alle my...and besenesse3. *Ita fiat,* amen.

---

[a] This word was perhaps not 'princes'. It is imperfect. (J.G.N.)
[b] 'at' in MS.   [1] *Psalms* xxii, 9.

(2) FIRST DRAFT FOR PARLIAMENT OF RICHARD III

(fo. 177r) [Whatever study that] mortalle men be sett to yn thys worlde, be hyt the study of diuinite, of eny maner of lawe, or of eny of the phylosophies, thende or practike of the same restythe alle wey yn the cure of somme maner kynde of a body, that God,[a] nature, or craft hath ordeigned and ordered here benethe. As Pomponius reherseth, *De vsucapionibus*,[1] there be iij. maner kyndes of bodyes. Oon ys vndre oo spirit and vndir oon elementacion, as a man, a beste, a tre, a stone. An other aggregate of diuers thynges coherent to gedir, as a house, a shippe, and other lyke compowned thynges. The iijd, that ys more most to owr purpose, oo body resultynge of dyuers bodies to gedir associat, and yet eche beyng distaunt from other, as a flokke, a peuple, an oste, a cite, a region. As touchynge the first kynde of bodies, eche hathe hys diuerse ouerseer. The body of man hathe the phisician, the brutalle best hys herde, the tre and herbe hys graffer or gardener, the stone the quarreour, and soo of every thynge that ys simpille yn hys kynde there ys a mayster that knoweth the state and nature of the thynge, what yt ys and howe hyt stondethe. The aggregat bodye made of diuerse thynges joigned to gedyr by nayle or sement, can not be suffred in cites welle gouerned to [peris]che. There be alle wey ordeigned officers to ouersee, and not to permit any owner to abuse the possession of hys own thynge, *Ne ciuitas defloretur ruinis*,[2] lest that by the severalle slouthe and neglygence (fo. 177v) of the land lordes, citees and townes schuld [fall to extreme decay] and ruine. Iff thys lawe be not so well accepted yn thys londe as lybertee, yt ys lyghte to se what ys growen thereof, by the decay of well nyghe alle the citees and borghows of the same. The iijd, whyche ys a bodye politike, whereof we have to speke at thys tyme as fer as hyt concerneth the Reame of Englonde, ys syche

[a] 'good' in MS.
[1] I do not find this passage in the fragments of Pomponius's *De Usucapionibus* that survive. See O. Lenel, *Palingenesia Juris Civilis*.
[2] I cannot identify this saying.

as may not be left withowt cure and goode creatours, *Nam res publica fungitur iure minoris.*[1] The thynge[a] public of a Region or citee ys allewey as hyt were a chyld withyn age, vndir ward, and in tutele tuicion of syche as have the gouuernaunce of the londe. In thys politike body of Englonde there be iij. estates as principalle membres vndir oone hede,—thestate of the lordys spiritualle, thestate of the lordes temperalle, and thestate of the cominallete. The hede ys owre souuerayne lord the kynge here presente. What due proporcion and armonye ought to be yn thys body, amonges alle the membres, grett and smalle, Synt Paule, takynge hys similitude from the naturalle body of man, declareth at large j. Cor. contendynge that, lyke as yn that body naturalle there ys no membre, be he never so nobille, that may sey to the leste[b] or to the vileest of them alle, I have no nede of the, but that eche hathe hys necessarie appropred operacion a parte, So ys hyt yn the mistik or politike body of the congregacion of the peuple, that every estate ys ordeigned (fo. 178r) [to support other, *Vt non sit*] *scisma in corpore,*[2] to thentent, as the apostill seyth, that all maner scisme and division schuld be eschewed. The wyse man seythe, Eccl. vij. *Filie tibi sunt, serva corpus illarum,* ther be many cheldern, many menne of diuerse condicions and estates, yn the Realme of Englonde, whoys body must be preservyd. Hyt ys to be noted that when he speketh of many persons, yet he gevith them all but oo body, *ibi, Serva corpus illarum,* accordyng to synt Paule ys seyng,[3] *Multa membra, vnum autem corpus.* Wolde God that owre peuple of Englond, where every manne nowe severally studethe to hys owen singular advayle, and to thaccomplysshynge of hys own perticuler affeccion, wold thenke vppon hys owne body, the comon and public body of the Realme, where of ryght a gret personne ys ofte tymes but a smalle membre. And yet, be he never so gret,[4] yff by hys doynge thys body fallethe yn decaye, as we see dayly

---

[a] 'kynge' in MS.   [b] 'beste' in MS.
[1] I cannot identify this saying.   [2] 1 *Corinthians* xii, 25.   [3] 1 *Corinthians* xii, 12.
[4] These reflections are evidently levelled against the late duke of Buckingham. (J.G.N.)

hyt doothe by closures and emparkynge, by dryuynge a wey of tenauntes and lattyng downe of tenauntries; and yet, that ys most to be sorrowed, by vnlaufulle assembleus and insurrections, puttyng not only the peuple but allso the nobles to extreme jupertu and peril of lyff and londes, where by thys...ᵃ is gretly dispeupled, suche oone, what so euer he be, is but as yt were a roten membre of the bodye, not abille ne of myghte to sauf yt from fallynge. We see by experience that the vsualle brusere of bodyes [com]ythe by fallyng, and that that person ys yn most danger to falle, (fo. 178v) whych ys blynd, or walkethe yn derkenesse, namel[y when any likely] thinge to stomble at is layd yn hisᵇ wey. Allemyghty God, geuyng to the childerne of Israel the maundementes of the old lawe, forbeded, amonges other thynges, that eny suche offendicle schuld be leyd where the blynd man schulde have hys walke. *Ibi Non ponas offendiculum ceco.*¹ Schalle we thynke ony blyndenesse yn thys bodye of Englonde, and that owre aduersaries be, or haue been, a bowte to ley eny offendicle or stomblyng mater yn owre wey, to give us a falle? y dare welle say, that howe be hyt thys bodye ys not blynd, but endwed as welle with the lyghte of reason and vndrestondynge as eny other, yet myght hyt some tyme be ledde yn derkenesse by mene of the longe and subtille forecaste of owre olde newe-reconciled ennemyes. Be hold what ys fallen of their fayre tretyes, othes, and promyses of peax, treax, and abstinence of werre, of affinitees and alliaunces, of paynge of annualle cesses,ᶜ tributes, or pensions. Was not alle thys withdrawen afore the decesse of the kynge of blessed memorie, Edward the iiijth, brother to owre souerayne lorde at now ys? was not hys pensifous sikenesse encreced by dayly remembruance of the derke weys, that hys subtille feythe fr(endes) had lede hym yn? what have we goten by that blynd bargeyne where by owre frendes were fayne to submytt hemself to the com... (fo. 179r)...and surcuydaunce of hym² was soo exalted that

ᵃ [Blank] in MS.   ᵇ 'my' in MS.   ᶜ 'causes' in MS.
¹ *Leviticus* xix, 14.   ª Louis XI.

[he tru]sted not eny tyme after that to see the state that he stode yn, when he made vs hys fayre promysses. I trowe that haue we welle rekened we haue loste oo dragme at the lest of the x. dragmes whyche makethe the perfeccione of owre commyn wele. The nombre of x. ys that that endethe and perfitethe every nombre, soo that as long as hyt ys hoole yn dragmes, besauntes, or eny other precious thynge limited and ascendyng to that nombre where by perfeccion ys signified, whych as y sayd be foore ys the nombre of x., or ellys yf^a that part that was lost there of perauenture be fownd ageyne, the fyrst owner of hyt makethe grete reioysynge with alle the neyborhede, saynge, I pray you frendes rejoyse ye with mee that have alle my beysauntes and dragmes fownde a geyne. Thys ys towched^b yn the gospelle of Luc, by way of a parable, spekynge of a woman that had x. dragmes, and oone of them was lost. *Ibi, Que mulier habens dragmas decem, et si perdiderit vnam,* &c.[1] Owre womanne that hathe lost oone of her x. dragmas ys *nostra respublica,* whyche ys ferre fallen from her perfeccion, and gretly astoned of the falle and decaye, of the gret hurt and brusere that she nowe seethe yn the membres of the public body of Englonde. A dragme in phisic is called the [we]ytght of iij. scruples, betokenynge to my purpose the forseyd iij. [esta]tes of thys Realme. A scrupule by transsumpcion ys nowghte elles (fo. 179v) but a subtill hard question, and so hyt ys...sayd, *Injeci homini scrupulum.*[2] Hyt ys to suppose that every man [should have] at thys day gret scrupulosite, grete anxiete, grete businesse, and doubte of mynde ho^r pray and vnite ho^c the jeous and prosperos estate whych some tyme was with yn the lond myght be recouered.[3] Then moyen of thys recoueree ys tawht forthe with yn the seyd parable, by takynge emsample of the dede of the womanne that there sekethe out the dragme that she had lost, *ibi, Nouam*

---

^{a} 'yt' in MS. ^{b} 'towchynge' in MS.
[1] *Luke* xv, 8.
[2] I have not been able to trace this quotation.
[3] The scribe has in this passage evidently miscopied some of the bishop's expressions, and it is difficult to guess what they were. (J.G.N.)

accendit lucernam et euerrit domum et querit diligenter donec inueniat.[1]
The woman that had lost the perfeccion of her nombre, oone of
her x. dragmes, what doeth she but fast geteth a lyght and
turnethe up the house, sekynge every cornere with alle dilygence,
tyll she hathe fownde that that she seketh for.

(Here a blank of a page and a half occurs, as if some insertion
was intended.)

(fo. 180v) Welle dryuen at the laste assemble here[2] yn thys...
virtue and grace commynge from a boue castethe a wey all
outward scr[uples?] in theys wordes, *Dominus illuminatio mea et
salus mea, quem timebo?*[3] Not withstandynge, by cause we stonde
at thys tyme yn the place of wordely policie to be persuaded,
moore than directly for the depe serche of mannys conscience,
whych requireth a nother figure and circumstaunce of tyme,
place, and mater to be ministred for that entente, Seynge that
by the forseyd ensample of the woman be fore remembred,
lyghte ys the most necessarye thynge to recouere the bonechief
that we seke fore, hyt ys next to aske, what ys thys lyght? There
to answere the wordys that y speke fyrst, taken out of the gospelle
of thys day, *lucerna corporis tui est oculus tuus.*[4] The lyghte of thyen
body ys thyne ie. The diffinicion of a mannys ie must nedes yn a
perfyt body presuppose the diuision of ij. ies, the ryght ie and the
left ie; and therefore Dauid prayeth for bothe, sayng, *Illumina
oculos meos.*[5] *Oculus igitur est geminus*, there be allewey ij. ies,
seyth Lincoln, yn hys tretie *de oculo morali, quorum dexter est
intellectus, sinister affectus.* The ryghte ie ys vndrestondynge, the
left ye ys affeccion. The due and beauteous proporcion of mannys
bothe ies ys that the oone be lyke the other both yn colour and
quantite. Hyt ys a monstruose syght oo man to have ij. ies of
diuerse colours, lyke as they have that techythe oone and

---

[1] *Luke* xv, 8.
[2] This is an allusion to the Speech which had been addressed to the preceding
parliament, which met on the 20th of January, 1483, when archbishop Rotherham, then chancellor, 'causas summonitionis parliamenti praedicti notabiliter pro-
nunciavit et declaravit, assumens pro suo themate, "Dominus illuminatio mea et
salus mea"', etc. (*Rot. Parl.* vi, 196.)
[3] *Psalms* xxvi, 1.   [4] *Matthew* vi, 22.   [5] *Psalms* xiii, 3.

doethe a[nother]...(fo. 181 r)...be made by autorite of thys [high court] by the clere syght of the ryghte ie, that ys to say of the vndrestondynge, of suche myschefes as schode be remedyed by the same statutes. And yet the left ye of affeccion when they schulde be duly executyd, hathe of tymes pervertyd the true menyng. The quantite alleso of bothe ies wolde be lyke, where yn they offende that spekethe moche and dothe but lytylle, and alleso they that have vnderstondynge, and puttithe no thynge yn[a] execucion. The fyguracion of the ie ys sperik and rownde. The rownde figure ys lauded for simplicite, for that fygure that ys rownde ys conteigned with yn oo lyne, and with oo line yt ys content. Where the trianguler hathe iij. the quadrate hath iiij. and so forthe of all other fygures, everyche of them hath lynes moo then oone, some moo some fewer. Yn presyng of the rownde fygure that hathe but oo lyne, as hyt apperyth yn a mannys ye, hyt folowithe thes day yn the gospelle, *Si oculus tuus fuerit simplex, totum corpus tuum lucidum erit,*[1] yff thyne ye be sengle and not turned to doublenesse, alle thy body schalle be fayre and bryght; and of the contrary, *Si nequam fuerit, totum corpus tuum tenebrosum erit,*[2] yff thyne ye be wikked, [thy whole] bodye schalbe derke. Of thys artificialle diuision spoken by Cryste, (fo. 181 v) yn hys gospell, eny man seeth...ys alle oone thynge, whan *simplex* and *nequam* be set for contrarie, [the] oone to brynge forthe *lucidum*, and that other *tenebrosum*. It were no longe a digression, and yet perauenture hyt were to the purpose, to shew by alle the fetes of them that hathe most guydynge of thys grete body of Englonde, howe their ie, be hyt the ie of vndirstondynge or elles of affeccion, ys wykked and double. Lat yt suffice, besyd the causes that be yn honde, where of at thys tyme noo man ys ygnoraunte, that vndir colour of administracion of justice, by fauour of syche offycers as make the panell, ofte tymes there ys more vengeable wronge committed thorowe fals informacion sene acceptoed,[b] then yff the swerde were drawen.

[a] 'ye' in MS. [b] *Sic* MS.
[1] *Luke* xi, 34. [2] *Ibid.*

Thys ie may wele be called a double ie, pursuyng openly yn apparence for justice, and vndir that conuertly of purpensed entent doynge that ys most vnjustice. And so hyt ys, *Oculus duplex seu oculus nequam, bonum foret quod esset oculus nequaquam*,[1] juxta illum alium locum euangelii, *Si oculus tuus scandaliȝat te, erue eum et projice abs te*.[2] Beholde, then, the rownde figuracion of yowre bodely ie, and shape there after the ie of yowr ynward vndirstondynge. So that lyke as yn the compasse of the bodely ie there ys but oo lyne where of ys not perceued neither the begynnynge nor the ende, soo the ie of yowr vndirstondynge or affeccion, ordeygned to lede thys comyn [wele] fro parell yn tymes of derkeness, may be fyxed vppon oo ry (fo. 182r)...yn malyce, or endynge yn corrupcion. The...of a mannys ryght intencion may be taken not only of the figure of the ie, as yt ys afore towched, but alleso of the maner of seynge, for alle that a man seeythe hyt ys as hyt were vndre forme of a triangle, the vpper poynte remaynynge yn the self ie, and the ij. poyntes abase representyng the thyngys that ben sayn, geuyng vs clerely to vndirstond that alle the termes and lymitees of owre thoughtes and affeccions we oughte to referre to oo singular poynt, that ys to sey, to the auauncynge of the comen wele. We be yn the place where thys schuld be tretyd. Thys tyme ys prefixed for the same entente.

(3) SECOND DRAFT FOR PARLIAMENT OF RICHARD III

(fo. 141r) [*In vno corpore*] *multa membra habemus, omnia autem membra non eundem actum habent*.[3] Seynt Poule, whoos be these wordes *ad Romanos*, taken out for thys tyme of the dominical epistel of thys weke, as wele yn othir hys wrytynge as yn thys namely j. ad Corinthianos xij, lykkenythe the mistyk[a] or the politike body of congregacione of peuple to the naturalle body of man, concludynge that, like as yn the body naturalle every membre hath compassion of other, yn so moche that the moste

a 'Mistys' in MS.
[1] I do not find these words in the Vulgate.
[2] *Matthew* xviii, 9.   [3] 1 *Corinthians* xii, 12?

noble membre may not sey to the leste or vileste of them alle, I
have no nede of the, for eche hathe hys necessarye appropred
office and operacion a part, So is hyt in the politike body
resultynge of moche peuple hauynge oo prince or souuerayne
for ther hede, that every estate, be he hye be he lowe, ys ordeyned to support othyr, *Vt non sit scisma in corpore*,[1] to thentent
as thapostil seythe that alle maner stryfe and diuisyon, where by
thys public body ys oftyme distrased, shuld be eschewed. Ecc°
vij. *Filie tibi sunt, serua corpus illarum.* There be many chyldren,
many menne of diuers condicions and estates, yn thys Reame
of England whoyse body muste be preseruyd. Hyt ys to be
noted that when the wyse manne spekethe of many persons, yet
he geueth them alle but oo body. *Ibi, Serua corpus illarum.*

We see welle by experyence that there ys no maner kynde of
body whyche that God, nature, or crafte hathe sett here be
nethe, but that ther ys...by mannys studye to conserue yt,
and kepe hyt yn good estate. (fo. 141 v) *Pomponius juris consultus*[a]
de vsucapionibus,[2] Rehersethe iij. maner kyndys of bodyes. Oon
vndir oo spirit, as a manne, a beste, a tree, a stone. An othir
aggregate of dyuers thynges ioyned to gedir by nayle, cement, or
other wise, as a house, a schyppe. The iijd oon body resultynge
of dyuerse bodyes to gedyr assecrate, and yet eche distaunte
from othyr, as a flokke, a peuple, a College, a cite, a Reaulme.
In the fyrste kynde the body of manne hathe the physycyan for
hys guyde and ouerseere, the brutalle beste hys herde, the tree
or herbe hys graffer or gardinar, the stone the quarreour. The
aggregate bodye compowned of diuerse matters, *Ad decorem
vniuersi*, to the strenghte and beaute of the cite, towne, or
fortresse that hyt perteynythe vn to, can not be suffered in
territories and iurisdictions well gouerned to perische. Such
wyse officers be there alle wey institute and ordeygned to
ouersee that none owner abuse the possessione of hys owne
thynge. *Expedit enim reipublice ne quis re sua male vtatur.*[3] And the

---

[a] 'consuetus' in MS.
[1] 1 *Corinthians* xii, 25.   [2] Cf. *supra*, p. 179, n. 1.
[3] I cannot identify this saying.

cause ys *ne ciuitas defloretur ruinis*,[1] leste that by the seuerelle slouthe and negligence of the land lordes, citees and townes schollde falle to extreme decaye and ruine. Whethyre thys maner of cure and goode ouersyghte be accepted in thys lande, as well as liberte, hyt ys lyghte to knowe, who soo wylle behold the desolacion of welle nyghe all the citees and borows of the same. If than thies ij. maner bodyes oughte not of reson to be lefte vnattended, moche rathir the iij[d] whyche ys a bodye p[olitike,] whereof we have to speke at thys tyme as ferre as yt concerneth [thys] Reame of Englond, ys suche as may not be lefte without cure a[nd good (fo. 142 r) curators.] *Nam res publica fungitur jure minoris.*[1] The thynge public of a Realme or citee ys alle wey as hyt were a chylde with yn age, vndir warde tutele or cure and tuicion of suche as haue the gouuernaunce of the comine. And therefor the cause of thys noble assemble at thys tyme, ys to prouide howe thys owre politike bodye may be eyther kept in estate, or releued and susteygned from the bruseis and distrasies that hyt ys yn. Whereunto ther ys no thynge soo benificyalle and helpynge to brynge hyt aboughte, as euery particular estate and membre of thys body to do hys dute. *In vno corpore habemus multa membra,*[2] In thys grete body of Englonde we have many diuerse membres vndre oone hede. Howe be hyt they may alle be reduced to iij. chyef and princypalle, whyche make thys hyghe and grete courte at thys tyme, that ys to seye, the lordes spiritualle, the lordes temporalle, and the commens. *Sed omnia membra non eundem actum habent,* but by cause that every particular membre hathe a singulare yeft a part from othyr, therefor hyt ys moste expedyent that every estate perteynynge to thys hyghe courte remember hys own offyce. The prince to geue equalle iustuce with pytie and mercy, and to defende hys londe from vtwarde hostilite, the subgettes to do ther trewe labour and occupacions whereby hys roialle and necessarye charges may be supported. Thys ys the mene to kepe thys body yn goode helthe and estate, for that body ys hole and

[1] Cf. *supra*, pp. 179, 180.   [2] 1 *Corinthians* xii, 12.

stronge whoos stomoke and ynwardes ys ministered by the vtward membres (fo. 142 v) with that suffiseth to be welle diegested; for yf the fete and hondes, whych seme to do moste busy and paynfulle labour for mannys lyuynge, wolde compleyne agaynste the wombe as agaynste an idille and slowthfulle part of the bodye, and denie the prouisyon of suche necessarye foode as the stomoke callethe for, hyt myght sone happe that, faylynge the bely for lakke, the guttes and intestines compressed and shott by drynesse, they and alle the othir membres schulde nedes perishe to gedyr. And therfor hyt ys well assured in nature, that theys myddelle membres of the body, that ys to seye, the stomake, the bely, and the partes adioignaunte, be not unoccupied, but have a ryghte busy office, for whan they be fedde they fede agayne, yeldynge vnto every parte of the bodye that with ought the whyche no manne may leue, that ys to wite, ynto alle the vaynes blode, digested out of the beste of mannys fode and repaste. What ys the belye or where ys the wombe of thys grete publike bodye of Englonde, but that and there where the kynge ys hymselfe, hys courte, and hys counselle? for there must be digested all maner of metes, not only seruyng to commen foode, but alleso to dentithe, and some tyme to medicines, suche as be appropred to remedie the excesses and surfettes committed at large. Thydyr be broughte all maters of wei[ght,] peax and warre with outward londes, confederacions, ligues, and alliances, receyuynge and sendynge of embassades and messages, brekynge of [treux], (fo. 143 r) pryses yn the see, routtes and riottes, and vnlaufulle assemblies, oppressions, extorsions, con-temptes and abusions of the lawe, many moo surfettes then can welle be nombred. Thys wombe of busy thoughte, cure, and pensifinese ys waxed fulle gret yn the dayes that we be yn, not onely by the soubdayne departynge of our olde newe-reconciled ennemyes from suche treties, othes, and promyses as they made yn to thys lande, but allesoo by maruelous abusion with yn, furthe of suche as oughte to haue remayned the kynges trewe and feythefull subgettes. Hyt ys to heuy to thynke and see what case and daungier, by some oo person late ryghte and gret membir of thys bodye,[1] many othyre nobylle membres of the same haue be broughte vn to. Thexample of thys falle and ryghtwous punicion wollde not be forgotten. Whoo soo taketh vpon hym, beynge a membre vndir the hede, that that to hys office and fidelite apperteynethe not, settynge the peuple in rebellion or commocion agaynste the prince, be he neuer so grette or noble yn hys estate, he ys as hyt were a roten membre of the bodye, not able ne of myghte to sauf hyt from fallynge. We see by experyence that the usualle brusere of bodyes comythe moste[a] by fallynge, and howe that person ys yn moste daunger to falle whych ys blynde, or walkethe in derknesse, namely, when eny offendicle or thynge to stomble at ys layde yn hys wey. Allemyghty God, geuyng to the chyldrene of Israelle the maundementes (fo. 143v) of the olde lawe, for beded a monge other thynges that eny suche offendicle scholde be layde where the blynde manne schulde haue hys walke, seynge, *non ponas offendiculum ceco.*[2] Schalle we thynke ony blyndnesse yn thys body of Englonde, and that there hathe be layde any offendycle or stombelynge mater yn owre way to gyff us a falle? Thys dare y saye, that howe be hyt thys body ys not blynde, but endued as welle with the lyghte of Reason and vndirstondynge as many othyr, yet myghte hyt somtyme be ledde yn derkenesse, as I suppose euery manne seethe that so hyt hathe bene nowe of late. Is hyt not a derke way a manne to take vppon hym the moste priuilegied and secrete office of hys maker Allemyghty God? Is hyt not a blynde jugement to deme a certente before, vppon thynges that may happen other wyse, to determe the sentence of God aftyr the pleasir or myscontentyng of mannys mynde, when Seynt Poule assurith us *quod Incomprehensibilia sunt iudicia Dei et inuestigabiles vie ejus.*[3] The cause of hys dede that meueth alle meuabille thynges, whych is[b] onely God, *qui trans-*

---

[a] 'muste' in MS.   [b] 'as' in MS.
[1] The duke of Buckingham, as before. (J.G.N.)
Leviticus xix, 14.   [3] *Romans* xi, 33.

fert reges et regna, cowde neuer yet be comprehendid in mannys wytte, and the wey to comme there to ys soo derke and clowdy that the foorthyr a man serchythe there yn the ferther he ys there fro. *Videmus enim hic per speculum in enigmate.*[1] Leue then, leue thys derke wey, whych ys Goddes secrete and onely vnto hym selfe; vse the lyghte of thyne reson and vndrestondynge whych ys appropred to mortalle m(an). (fo. 144r) *Reddite que sunt Cesaris Cesari*[a] *et que sunt Dei Deo.*[2] Cryste, that payd hys tribute to themperour ys officers, neither stryued ne disputed agaynst that prince in whois name yt was asked, schewyng vnto alle subgettes, by thexample of hys owne dede, that obeissaunce of the peuple to the prince that reygnethe ys that that euery subget schuld content hym with, and therefor thapostille ensuyng the same sentence, wrote longe aftyr that, and seyd, *Obedite prepositis vestris*[3]. The lakke of clere vndyrstondynge of thys wey whyche had be mooste sure to haue be folowed, added theyre vnto suche offendicles as diuerse men ledde by blynde affections stombled at, hathe caused thys grete brusere and febyllenesse that thys public body of Englonde sufferythe at thys day. But nowe a remedie. The remedie agaynste derkenesse ys no thynge ellys but prouision of lyghte, be hyt that abody wollde passe surely yn hys journey, or ellys bye goode and diligent serche attende to fynde that that he hathe loste. Whe who haue somwhat touched the derke wey that menne haue walked yn; late vs see whethyr we haue ony thyng loste that wollde be soughte and fownde agayne. I trowe that haue welle rykened we haue lost oo beisaunte at the leste of the x. whych make the perfeccion of owre comen wele. The nombre [of] x. ys that that endythe and perfitethe euery nombyr, soo that as longe (fo. 144v) as hyt hys hole in dragmes, besauntes, or eny othyr precyous thynge limited and ascendyng to that nombre where by perfeccion ys signified, whyche as y seyd be fore ys the nombre of x. or ellys yf that parte that was loste there of be fownde agayne, the furste

---

[a] 'cesare' in MS.   [1] 1 *Corinthians* xiii, 12.
[2] *Matthew* xxii, 21.   [3] *Hebrews* xiii, 24.

owner of hyt maketh grete rejoysyng with alle the neigborhede, seyng, y pray yow frendes rejoyse yow with me that haue alle my besauntes or dragmes hole to gedyr. Thys ys towched yn the gospelle of Luc by way of a parable spekynge of a woman that had x. besauntes or dragmes, and oone of them was loste. *Ibi, Que*[a] *mulier habens dragmas .x. et si perdiderit vnam.*[1] Owre woman that hathe loste oon of here x. besauntes ys *nostra res publica,* whyche ys ferre fallen from her perfeccion, and gretely astoned of the falle and decaye of the hurt and brusere that she nowe seethe in the membres of thys public bodye of Englond. I fere me that ere we can fynde agayne the auncenne prosperyte whyche semethe now loste, whyle we be sekyng for the besaunte we schalle be occupied for a tyme with a physical dragme. A dragme in physick ys called the weyghte of iij. scrupules.

(Here this copy breaks off, but the immediate continuation will have been as already printed on p. 182.)

---

[a] 'Leo' in MS.   [1] *Luke* xv, 8.

Chapter III

STATUTORY LAW AND JUDICIAL DISCRETION

INTRODUCTORY

The conscious and deliberate making of new law by a legislative authority—obviously the most momentous act in political life—is a phenomenon which has appeared comparatively late in most, if not in all, civilisations. It seems true to say that in every civilisation the source of the earliest law has always been custom, and that the law promulgated in the course of time by law-givers has been at first no more than the declaration or codification of traditional usages. Deliberate creation of law has everywhere been a mark only of the more advanced stages of civilised life.[1]

In the history of Western Europe, however, the normal development of legal ideas has been exceptionally complicated. This complexity has been due to the fact that the typical customary law of the Germanic peoples has never, since the invasions, and indeed even earlier, been wholly free from the influence of the highly advanced theory and science of the law of the Roman empire. The idea of law-creating was alien to the purely Germanic concept of law; to the Teutons law was older than the state—it was the good old custom, unenacted, and unwritten.[2] But the changing and making of law by the state

[1] See especially Holdsworth, *Hist. Eng. Law*, II, Book II, Part I; Pollock and Maitland, *Hist. Eng. Law*, 2nd ed. i. Cf. Anson, *Law and Custom of the Constitution*, 3rd ed. 6: 'For legislation, in so far as it means the breaking up of customs and the introduction of new rules of conduct, is a thing almost inconceivable to an early state of society....But the step is a long one from the time when the state first enforces custom vigorously and constantly, to the time when it takes upon itself without fear or hesitation to recast and alter custom.'

[2] See especially F. Kern, 'Recht und Verfassung im Mittelalter', *Hist. Zeit.* (1919), cxx, 1–80. E.g. (8–9): 'Für das Mittelalter ist deshalb das Recht das Erste, der Staat erst das Zweite. Der Staat ist hier nur das Mittel zur Verwicklung des Rechts; sein Dasein leitet sich ab aus dem Dasein des über ihm stehenden Rechts. Das Recht ist vor dem Staat, der Staat für das Recht und durch das Recht, nicht

was a commonplace in Roman law; and just as this notion was early adopted and exemplified by the Church, so in due time the barbarian peoples began to imitate the activities of law-givers. The Germanic kings, accustomed to declaring the law in their assemblies of wise men, began to codify it and to cause it to be written, and sometimes this action would involve—not always very consciously—the making of actually new law.

But, of the Western peoples, the English were the least affected by the ideas of Roman jurisprudence; the great bulk of English mediaeval law was customary, uncodified, and un-enacted. Hence it was that, though from time to time the kings enacted law and in doing so sometimes created new law, the admission that such creation occurred was far less common than the fact of it. The extreme tenacity and toughness of the common law has always hindered the frank recognition of the making of new law by enactment. King Alfred, indeed, may have realised that he was truly creating law,[1] but the general tendency during the mediaeval period, on the part of both legislators and lawyers, was to regard royal dooms or laws as no more than declarations of the good old customs.[2] To confirm and to main-

das Recht durch den Staat.' But it should be remembered that the majority of Kern's valuable conclusions are applicable without modification only to the earlier middle ages, for most of the materials he cites come from that period.

[1] He said, in the preamble to his laws, that 'I, then, Alfred, king, gathered these (laws) together, and commanded many of those to be written which our forefathers held, those which to me seemed good; and many of those which seemed to me not good I rejected them, by the counsel of my witan, and ordained otherwise. For I dared not write much of my own; for it was unknown to me how that would please those that should come after us.' (See Stubbs, *Select Charters*, 9th ed. 70.)

[2] Cf. McIlwain, *The Growth of Political Thought in the West*, 188: '"Law", the only law in the highest sense, is something that none can "make", not even a king. He should approve it, and men may find, and preserve or maintain it, but it comes solely from ancient custom.' This, McIlwain points out, remained the normal view long after the great advances of monarchy in the eleventh and twelfth centuries: 'These consuetudines or ancient customs are maintained or preserved by usage of the people (more utentium) and the king approves them either tacitly or by making provisions to ensure their enforcement. The latter may be *assisae*, *provisiones*, *ordinationes*, *ordonnances*, *stabilimenta*, or *établissements*, even *statuta*; they are *leges*, but they are not yet "law".' Cf. Kern, *op. cit.* 24: 'Änderung und Erneuerung des Rechts ist möglich, ja geboten, so bald sie Wiederherstellung ist, bzw. als solche sich gibt; kein Umsturz, keine Entwicklung, aber fortwährende Enthüllung, Klärung, Reinigung des wahren guten Rechts, das ewig im Kampf liegt mit Unrecht, Trübung, Missverstand und Vergessen.'

tain the law were the paramount objectives of legislator and
lawyer,[1] and to this very day a *presumption* that the common law
has not been changed by statute is characteristic of the courts.
Hence, although legislation in the sense of promulgation was
a common event in England from the time of Ethelbert,[2] and
although that process sometimes involved the making of new
law, examples of law-making are far commoner than examples
of its recognition as such. Indeed, until quite late in the mediaeval period,[3] it is not easy to point to texts which freely admit that
the king was invested with a legislative power in excess of the
power of mere promulgation. Much new law was made and
enacted, usually, though not always, in formal consultation with
counsellors of some kind, before the theorists had fully revised
their theories of law to reflect the fact. Even in the fifteenth
century, though undoubtedly theory had been brought into line
with the facts,[4] explicit admissions that new law had been made
remain curiously infrequent. The common law has ever been
reluctant to welcome its rival.

[1] Wycliffe declared (*De Officio Regis*, 56) that laws should be few, for several
reasons; and he thought the English laws satisfactory in this respect: 'Oportet
igitur regem statuere leges iustas et per consequens lege domini regulatas ut
secundum illas tam ipse quam sui subditi serviant in iusticia deo suo. Et patet
prudencia quod leges ille sint pauce. Primo quia sunt principales excedentes
statum innocenciae, de talibus autem oportet servos dei solum necessariis conten-
tari, quia superhabundancia distraheret multipliciter a lege dei. Secundo quia
multitudo legum talium generaret confusionem et intricacionem ad ipsas cogno-
scendum et exequendum et per consequens necessitaret ad multiplicandum populum
pro ipsis discendis et subtraheret occupacionem sapientum regni pro ipsis inter-
pretandis. Et hinc leges regni Anglie excellunt leges imperiales, cum sint pauce
respectu earum, quia supra pauca principia relinquunt residuum *epikerie* sapientum.' Cf. *infra*, p. 249. Cf. Maitland, 'Wyclif on English and Roman Law,'
L.Q.R. (1896), XII, 76–78.

[2] Cf. Pollock and Maitland, *Hist. Eng. Law*, I, 11–12: 'They (the laws of Ethelbert) are also, unless discoveries have yet to be made, the first Germanic laws that
were written in a Germanic tongue. In many instances the desire to have written
laws appears as soon as a barbarous race is brought into contact with Rome. The
acceptance of the new religion must have revolutionary consequences in the world
of law, for it is likely that heretofore the traditional customs, even if they have not
been conceived as instituted by gods who are now becoming devils, have been
conceived as essentially unalterable. Law has been old; new law has been a
contradiction in terms. And now about certain matters there must be new law.'

[3] For some discussion of this matter for the fifteenth century see § 3, 'The
classification of statutes', *infra*, p. 249.   [4] *V. infra*, p. 249.

There is much in the history of the earliest legislative activity that still awaits investigation, but we are not, for our present purpose, concerned with the remoter history of enacted law (whether written or unwritten), nor with early examples of legislation by adjudication. We have seen that by the end at least of the fifteenth century, there could, in the theory of the royal courts, be only one kind of legislation.[1] This only proper kind of legislation was written law enacted and promulgated by the king with the assent of his parliament; it was, in short, parliamentary statute-law.[2] Nor are we concerned with the antecedent historical process which reduced the originally diverse kinds of enacted law to this statutory form. But it is necessary, in pursuance of our scheme, to attempt to reach some conclusions as to the nature and position of statute-law during the century; how it figured in legal thought, the procedure by which in fact it was made, its varieties, the range of its binding force, its general relation to other law, and the extent of judicial discretion (if any) in enforcing it. On each of these themes a monograph could probably be written, but for the present we aim at no more than the formulation of some definite and significant conclusions which will make possible an estimate of the position of statute-law in its constitutional bearings.

[1] The question of law-making by proclamation had hardly as yet arisen. In later times it was ruled that the king could not make new offences by proclamation, but an offence against proclamation was an aggravation (*Case of Proclamations* (1611), 12 Co. Rep. 74). This idea of the addition to the penalties of the law by proclamation is closely paralleled by Fortescue's idea that the declaration of law by statute made an offence against it not only law-breaking but disobedience of the command of the prince. (*V. infra*, p. 201, n. 3.)

[2] The Italian envoys observed, in *c.* 1500, that the English generally hate their present and extol their dead sovereigns. Nevertheless, they rejected the Caesarean code of laws, and adopted those given them by their kings. But, they also noted, if the king proposed to change any old established rule, it seemed to every Englishman as if his life were taken from him. (*Italian Relation*, 32, 37.)

§ 1. STATUTES IN LEGAL THEORY

It would be a mistake to assume too readily that *a priori* notions of law had entirely lost their vitality and their practical import in the fifteenth century. The law of God was still a concept to conjure with in practical politics; and Fortescue resorted to the law of nature to prove his views on the succession question. This law of nature, or of reason, as the English wisely preferred to call it, which had loomed so large in the speculations of mediaeval jurists, was still sometimes figuring in the rough-and-tumble of the courts, and could still be a last resort in unprecedented cases.

These notions of law naturally would not entirely lose their practical importance whilst they continued to find a place in the chancellor's sermons before the parliaments—the only formal political discourse likely to reach the average member of parliament. For example, that very unacademic man of affairs, Bishop Beaufort, told the parliament of 1414 that the king 'ought to be and to live under the most commendable disposition and governance of the holy law of God, as the other kings of England his progenitors had done'.[1] A more learned pro-chancellor could turn the idea to highly practical and beneficent effect; for example, the famous canonist, Dr Lyndwood, officiating at the parliament of 1431, invoked the concept of the law of God to urge the ending of the French war and the making of peace: 'As every man', he said, 'endowed with reason may well considere, it nys nought convenable ne sutyng, ne lyke to be to the plesire of God, ne of ye world, a Cristen Prince to refuse Pees offred with menes resonable, ne ye tretee therof, yf it be desired of him, ye which, by ye lawe of God, him owed to pursue and folowe.'[2]

Similar ideas came to the aid of York in his claim to the crown. A grave obstacle to the speedy admission of this claim was the solemn oath in support of King Henry taken by the

---

[1] *Rot. Parl.* IV, 15.   [2] *Ibid.* 371.

lords in 1459. But York sought to overcome this difficulty by asserting that such an oath was invalid in the face of God's law and commandment.[1] Later, his son's title was declared to be true, not only by God's law, but also by the law of nature, as well as by man's law.[2]

Theoretical justice formed the theme of a chancellor's discourse to parliament in 1468, and Bishop Stillington's words on this occasion possess a more than ordinary interest. He showed, it is reported, 'unto the seid Lordes and Commons, that Justice was ground well and rote of all prosperite, peas, and pollityke rule of every Reame, whereuppon all the Lawes of the world been grounde and sette, which resteth in Thre, that is to say, the Lawe of God, Lawe of Nature and posityfe Lawe,[3] and by seying of all Philosofers, felicitee or peas in every reame is euermore caused of Justice, as it appeareth by probabill persuacions of Philosofers....'[4]

If this was still the sort of legal concept then current, it was by no means superfluous for Richard of Gloucester, when setting out his title to the crown, to make capital for himself by declaring that 'the ordre of all politique rule (had been) perverted, the Lawes of God and of God's Church, and also the lawes of Nature and of England, and also the laudable Customes and Liberties of the same, wherein every Englishman is Inheritor, subverted and condemned, against all reason and justice, soo that this Land was ruled by selfewill and pleasure, feare and

---

[1] *Rot. Parl.* v, 377.   [2] *Ibid.* 464.

[3] The use of the term 'positive law' is older than is sometimes supposed. The example of it here quoted is not the oldest, for it occurs as early as 1300, and is found in Wycliffe's writings (*Works* (1880), 392). *V. N.E.D.* Cf. *Somnium Vigilantis*, 520: 'And that they did oponly whan they toke upon thaim th' office of auctour and accusator and th' office of wytnesse and of þe juge ayenst all maner lawes divine or positive.' The difference, it would seem, between the mediaeval notion of positive law and that idea of it propounded by Austin is that the one regards it as any law made by humans, and the other as law established by the sovereign state only. Any law whatever made by man is a positive law to the mediaeval jurists who use the term, but to Austin every positive law is the command of the state. (Cf. Austin, *Jurisprudence*, 221.) Reginald Pecock, however, seems to have used the term as opposed to 'moral law' or 'doom of natural reason'. *V. Repressor*, ii, 455, 'in ech posityf law mad bi the pope, or eny other bischop or bi eny worldli prince'.

[4] *Rot. Parl.* v, 622.

drede, all manner of Equite and Lawes layd apart and despised'.[1] The remarkable modernity—if such it be—of this appeal to the liberties of the Englishman must not blind us to the essential mediaevalism of its juristic assumptions.

The law of nature or reason, however, was more than an academic theory or a weapon in political controversy; it served its turn in the law courts themselves. In the middle of the fourteenth century we find counsel arguing that 'law ought to accord with reason, and to avoid mischief'.[2] In 1468 Yelverton, J., on behalf of the judges in the exchequer chamber, declared that they must act in the case before them as did the civilians and the canonists when they lacked a law. They resorted to the law of nature, which was the ground of all laws. They acted in accordance with whatever the law of nature pronounced to be the most beneficial for the commonweal, and so they, the judges, must make a positive law in the same way.[3] This highly significant declaration clearly indicates that in a case where there was room for the exercise of discretion, the judges considered themselves bound to make a ruling in accordance with the law of nature, *i.e.* in accordance with the welfare of the community, and so frank an admission of judicial legislation is very striking.[4] Equally candid was the statement by the chancellor, five years later, that a certain case would be judged by the law of nature in chancery. The law of nature, he said, was called by some the law merchant, which was law universal throughout the world.[5]

[1] *Rot. Parl.* VI, 240.
[2] *Y.B.* 15 *Edward III*, Pas. pl. 45 (App. no. 3); and *v.* Excursus, *infra*.
[3] *Y.B.* 8 *Edward IV*, Mich. pl. 9 (App. no. 50); *v.* Excursus, *infra*.
[4] This remarkably frank recognition of judicial discretion seems to be unparalleled in the mediaeval Year Books. It is interesting to compare with it a rule of the modern Swiss Code. In § 1 thereof it is laid down that the law 'must be applied in all cases which come within the letter or the spirit of any of its provisions. Where no provision is applicable, the judge shall decide according to the existing customary law, and in default thereof, according to the rules which he would lay down if he had himself to act as legislator. Herein he must be guided by approved legal doctrine and case law.' (See Ivy Williams, *The Sources of Law in the Swiss Civil Code*, 22.) A comparison is also suggested with the recent theories of M. Duguit. For judicial discretion in interpretation, *v.* § 5 *infra*, p. 289.
[5] *Y.B.* 13 *Edward IV*, Pas. pl. 5 (App. no. 58). This is the well-known case of 'breaking bulk'. See Excursus, *infra*. The equivalence here stated by the chancellor

We may, then, conclude that the old notions of God's law and the law of nature still had their appeal, were still a part of accepted jurisprudence, and still had their force in practical politics and legal practice.

Fortescue's jurisprudence is mostly a hotch-potch of Roman law and canon law principles. Both systems were made to serve his turn, and the majority of his definitions were borrowed from the one or the other. Thus, following Gratian,[1] he declared that Jus is to Lex as genus to species. All law is Jus, but it is not convenient to call all Jus Lex; for every man who seeks to have back what is his own possesses the Jus, but not the Lex, to claim it. The law resides in the judge, whereby he decrees the restitution to the plaintiff, and in so doing renders him both Jus and Lex. Law, Fortescue repeats, is the bond of right by which a man is constrained to do or suffer what is just. But, though law be a species of right, it is itself a genus in relation to the law of nature, law of custom, and of statute, and to all special and private laws, 'the number of which is like that of the stones in the heap or the trees in the forest'.[2]

The law of nature is not only the law Fortescue invoked in arguing the succession question, but is also the keystone of his jurisprudence;[3] and he adopts for the most part the doctrines of the canon law for his exposition of it, even though not very consistently. In his theory all human laws are classifiable as law of nature, or as customs, or as statutes.[4] The law of nature

between law of nature and law merchant seems to be unique, though the distinction drawn between *ius naturale* and *ius gentium* was often very vague. For some general observations on natural justice in the common law, see Sir Frederick Pollock, *Essays in the Law* (1922), 68–73.

[1] *Decretum*, Dist. I, c. ii.

[2] *De Natura*, I, xxx, 92–93: 'Et licet lex, ut predicitur, sit species juris, ipsa tamen sic descripta est genus ad legem naturae, consuetudinum, et statutorum; ac ad cunctas leges speciales et privatas, quarum, ut superius memoratur, numerus est ad instar acervorum lapidum arborum ve silvarum.'

[3] For a special treatment of this subject, see E. F. Jacob, 'Sir John Fortescue and the Law of Nature'. *Bull. J.R.L.*, xviii (1934). For the history of the law of nature generally, see Sir Frederick Pollock, *Essays in the Law* (1922), 31–79.

[4] *De Laudibus*, xv. The present writer is preparing a fresh edition of this work, forthcoming in the Cambridge Studies in Legal History Series.

was the law by which the human race had been governed from the time of Paradise to the time of Moses—a period which Fortescue calculated (following Josephus and St Augustine) had exceeded 3644 years. Its governance was continued in the times of the law and of grace; the Lord Himself confirmed it, and enjoined it by the commandment, 'All things whatsoever ye would that men should do to you, do ye even so to them, for this is the law and prophets.' The law expressly declared this Golden Rule (and the prohibition of its opposite) to be the law of nature.[1]

But it is none too clear whether this law in Fortescue's version is human or divine law. In one place he affirms that it excels all *other* human laws,[2] but he also says elsewhere that 'of a truth it is divine'. He quotes, and apparently adopts, the definition proffered by St Thomas Aquinas,[3] to the effect that the law of nature is the participation of eternal law in us (or, as he says, in a rational creature).[4] At any rate, Fortescue was convinced that the natural law had sprung from God alone, was subject to His law alone, and under Him and with Him governed the whole world, so that all other laws were its servants, and there was not a law on earth put forth by man which obeyed not the commands of nature's law. The law of God rules the law of nature for ever.[5] The divine law is whatever divine Providence is,[6] whilst the law of nature is the truth of justice, which is capable of being revealed by right reason.[7] The ends of both divine and human law are the same, namely, to dispose man to virtue.

All human laws are, according to Fortescue, either established by the law of nature or by its authority, as supplementary to it.

[1] *De Natura*, I, iv. This doctrine first appeared in canon law at the head of the *Decretum* of Gratian, and represents the identification by the canonists of the law of nature of Roman jurisprudence with the law of God of canonist theory. Cf. Pollock, *Essays in the Law*, 40.

[2] *De Natura*, I, v.

[3] *Prima Sec. Summae*, quaest. xcvi, De potestate Legis Humanae, Art. 2: 'Ad tertium dicendum, quod lex naturalis est quaedam participatio legis aeternae in nobis; lex autem humana deficit a lege aeterna.' This notion is clearly related to the Pauline doctrine of the 'law written in the heart'.

[4] *De Natura*, ibid.   [5] *Ibid*. xxix.   [6] *Ibid*. xlii.

[7] *Ibid*. xxvi. Christopher St Germain specifically states that the English preferred to call the law of nature by the name of reason. *V. infra*, p. 208.

The laws are all divisible into two classes. Either they are customs or they are statutes; and these, the canons taught, were null and void if contrary to natural law. The rights of kings, if they comprehend anything beyond statute and custom, have derived it not from the prince's authority, but solely from the law of nature, which is common to all the powers of the world.[1] Thus, according to Fortescue, an unjust statute could be disregarded, and a statute could not enact any rule other than natural law or custom.[2]

Lex, as some thought, was so called from *a legendo*, and it is a sacred sanction commanding things honest and forbidding the contrary. Precisely this, in Fortescue's account, is statute-law; for statute-law was usually written when enacted, but customary law is not enacted nor always written. Custom and the law of nature are called law, he thought, not *a legendo* but *a ligando* because they bind without necessarily being read. If custom by the prince's order be committed to writing, it acquires the name of statute, and is thereby enabled to punish offenders more sharply, for they offend in contempt of the command of the prince.[3] This character is, to Fortescue, the essential difference between statute and custom. The *sententiae* of the law of nature or custom, if committed to writing, promulgated by the sufficient authority of the prince, and commanded to be observed, become statutes. In virtue of such promulgation and command, statutes oblige the subjects to their observance under greater penalty than attends breaches of other law.[4] Statutes are thus purely declaratory of law which exists already either as customary or

---

[1] *De Natura*, v.

[2] But whether Fortescue would repeat in his capacity as chief justice what he wrote in his capacity as a theorist may of course be questioned.

[3] *Ibid.* xxx, and as in next note. This statement is a striking antecedent to Coke's view that to commit an offence against proclamation aggravates the offence, though proclamation did not make new law. (*Case of Proclamations* (1611), 12 Co. Rep., 74.) Cf. *supra*, p. 195, n. 1.

[4] *De Laudibus*, xv, 348: 'Scire te igitur volo, quod omnia jura humana, aut sunt lex nature, consuetudines, vel statuta, que et constitutiones appellantur. Sed consuetudines, et legis nature sententie, postquam in scripturam redacte, et sufficienti auctoritate principis promulgate fuerint, ac custoderi jubeantur, in constitutionem sive statutorum naturam mutantur, et deinde penalius quam antea subditos principis ad earum custodiam constringunt, severitate mandati illius.'

as natural law; they therefore do not create new law,[1] even though they may convert natural into positive law. Apart from instances of this conversion, we can say that in Fortescue's view statutes are selected customs promulgated and confirmed by the prince's command, and on that account carrying heavier penalties than they do as custom.

With this somewhat conservative notion of statutes,[2] Fortescue combined a vast ignorance of legal history. The customs of England he rightly asserted to be of great antiquity, but he displayed a little too much credulity in declaring that, though England had endured successive régimes of Britons, Romans, Britons again, Saxons, Danes, and Normans, during which several nations and kings had prevailed, the country, nevertheless, had been continuously governed by the same customs as it was at the time of his writing.[3] They must, he concludes, be the best customs, since there were no others so venerable.

He was equally confident of the excellence of statute-law as it was enacted in England. Statutes here did not come from the mere will of one man, as the laws did in despotic countries. They were not enacted by the sole will of the prince, but with the assent of the whole kingdom, so that they must be considered to be for the good of the whole people. They must be wise and prudent, for they were the result, not of one man's wisdom only, nor of a hundred, but of more than three hundred selected men. Moreover, if any statutes thus made should not answer the intentions of those who made them, they could be speedily reformed, though not without the assent of the community and the nobles, from whom they had previously emanated.[4]

[1] Cf. the definition of a 'rule of law' formulated in *De Natura*, II, xxx: 'Nam juris regula non est nova legis edicio, sed juris quod prius fuit brevis enarracio.'

[2] But Fortescue may have asserted, as chief justice in the parliament of 1454 and on behalf of the other judges in Thorpe's case, that parliament could make new law, even though he omitted the adjective 'new' from his statement. *V. infra*, p. 253.

[3] *De Laudibus*, xvii. Some thought common law dated back to the creation. See Catesby, in *Y.B.* 10 *Edward IV*, Pas. pl. 9 (App. no. 54). Cf. the assertion in *Somnium Vigilantis* that (*loc. cit.* 521) 'it is incredible to any reasonable man that an inveterate *consuetude* might be changed withoute the destruccion of þe subjecte'.

[4] *De Laudibus*, xviii. Cf. *ibid.* lix.

No doubt this notion of the possibility of reforming the law already made by parliamentary action is a significant indication of the transition from characteristically mediaeval ideas to modern ones. We see here, it has been well said, the idea of the supremacy of the law differentiated from the idea of its immutability, and this differentiation forms an important step in the direction of the notion of the sovereignty (or rather supremacy) of parliament.[1] But it is hard to find in Fortescue's theoretical writings any clear admission that parliament in its statutes can make absolutely new (positive) law, and where this admission is lacking, there cannot be the notion of parliamentary supremacy in the modern sense.

Some fifty years after Fortescue wrote his last work, another learned student in the law, Christopher St Germain, issued the first edition of his *Dialogue between a Doctor of Divinity and a Student of the Laws of England*. This was published about the year 1523, and it speedily became a popular and well-approved work in legal circles; Fitzherbert and Coke used it freely, and it was reissued by the author several times, and has since been frequently reprinted. A work published in the third decade of the sixteenth century cannot, of course, be treated too rigidly as a source for the legal ideas of the previous century; but St Germain lived forty years of his life before the end of the fifteenth century; his mind was cast in the mediaeval mould; his chief source of philosophical ideas was the works of the schoolmen, and of John Gerson; and we need not hesitate to accept St Germain's work as representative, in a general way, of the legal

---

[1] See especially A. P. D'Entrèves, 'San Tommaso d'Aquino e la Costituzione Inglese nell' opera di Sir John Fortescue', *Atti della Reale Accad. d. Scienze di Torino*, LXIII (1927), 283: 'La supremazia della legge è, abbiamo visto, una delle concezioni fondamentali della sua dottrina. Ma qui appunto, accanto alla ripetizione di questa idea schiettamente medievale, sembra di scorgere i segni di quella trasformazione, di quell' adattamento di essa alla teoria dello stato moderno che elaboreranno i giuristi e i teorici dell' epoca dei Tudor. Insensibilmente, l' idea della supremazia della legge si dissocia dall' idea della sua immutabilità: la supremazia di una legge che il Parlamento ha stabilito ed il Parlamento può mutare, significa in realtà un gran passo verso l' idea della sovranità del Parlamento e di una forza intrinseca alla legge derivata dall' autorità del legislatore.'

thought which was current at the end of the fifteenth century. We may accept it as such all the more readily because a good deal of his theorising reads much like an elaboration of points in Fortescue's jurisprudence, and it has considerable value as a means of illuminating the latter's ideas.[1]

The first dialogue begins with an exposition by the Doctor of four kinds of law. The first of these was law eternal, the second the law of nature of reasonable creatures ('the which, as I have heard say, is called by them that be learned in the law of England the law of reason'[2]), the third the law of God, and the fourth the law of man.

The law eternal the Doctor defined as the reason of the wisdom of God, moving all things by wisdom made to a good end.[3] This was called the first law, for it existed before all other laws, and all other laws are derived from it. The Student was

---

[1] Christopher St Germain was born in *c.* 1460 and died in 1540. He was at Oxford, and of the Inner Temple. He was in legal practice for a time, and was in government service during a number of years, but was primarily occupied in legal studies and literary work of a theological and legal sort. His work *Doctor and Student* consists of two dialogues between a theologian and a law student (with some additions at the end). The first dialogue is divided between an exposition of law from the theological standpoint by the Doctor of Divinity and an account of the grounds of the laws of England by the Student. It is this first dialogue, together with one or two passages in the second, that is of value for our present purpose. The second, and much longer, dialogue consists in a detailed discussion upon various, not to say miscellaneous, doctrines of Common Law in relation to conscience. With the great historical importance of the work in connection with the development of Equity we are not here concerned. The first dialogue was originally published in Latin: of this first edition no copy is known to exist to-day, but several of the subsequent editions were also printed in Latin. At an early date (1530), however, the author himself printed both dialogues in English. As Vinogradoff pointed out in 'Reason and Conscience in the 16th Century' (*Collected Papers*, II, 190), it is often useful to refer to the Latin text for fuller allusions to St Germain's sources, particularly to Gerson. But as a whole it seems clear that the English edition of the first dialogue is something in the nature of a revised and longer version, and there is nothing to be gained by giving preference to the Latin text, except for the references to sources. Where, in the passages that are of interest for our purposes, the Latin version differs from the English one in a striking way, the difference will be indicated in the notes. The Latin text alluded to will be the earliest one extant, dated 1528. The English version used here is that contained in the reprint by William Muchall in 1815, called the 18th edition. On the whole subject Vinogradoff's paper (*loc. cit.*) is indispensable; and see also Holdsworth, *Hist. Eng. Law*, V, 266–269; Winfield, *Chief Sources*, 321; A. F. Pollard, *D.N.B.* (*sub tit.* St Germain).

[2] *Dialogue*, 3.   [3] *Ibid.*

puzzled as to how this law eternal was to be known, and the Doctor confessed that the only persons who knew it were blessed souls who see God face-to-face. But since God could not be supposed to have bound His people to the impossible, He was understood to reveal to His creatures as much of the law as was necessary to them. This, of His goodness, He did in three ways; first, by the light of natural reason; secondly, by heavenly revelation; and thirdly, by order of a prince or any other secondary governor who has power to bind his subjects to law.[1] The law which came by the first of these means was called the law of reason, that coming by the second the law of God, and that by the third the law of man (though originally it was made by God).

The law of reason, which by some doctors was called the law of nature of reasonable creatures, was a term possessing two senses, the one general and the other special. The general sense was that which referred to all creatures as well reasonable as unreasonable—'for all unreasonable live under a certain rule to them given by nature necessary to them for the conservation of their being'. The content of this law of nature must, presumably, have been those laws which we to-day should think of as discoverable by the natural sciences rather than those which are the subject-matter of legal science.[2] But in its special sense,

---

[1] *Ibid.* 4.

[2] The phrase extending the law of nature to all living creatures was adopted by the compilers of Justinian's *Institutes* from Ulpian (D., 1, 1, *De Just. et Iure*, 1, 3). The passage in the *Institutes* runs thus: 'Ius naturale est, quod natura omnia animalia docuit, nam ius istud non humani generis proprium est, sed omnium animalium, quae in caelo, quae in terra, quae in mari nascuntur, hinc descendit maris atque feminae coniugatio, quam nos matrimonium appellamus, hinc liberorum procreatio et educatio: videmus etenim cetera quoque animalia istius iuris peritia censeri' (*Lib.* 1, *Tit.* 11). As Sir Frederick Pollock has justly said: 'This would seem to be merely a piece of over-ambitious generalisation taken from some forgotten Greek writer, perhaps a rhetorician and not a philosopher' (*Essays in the Law*, 36). Vinogradoff suggested that Ulpian may have taken the idea from the Pythagoreans, for whom there was no gulf between animals and man (*Common Sense in Law*, 236). Savigny, however, attempted to justify Ulpian's attribution of a juristic character to natural instincts by drawing a distinction between the matter and the form of every legal relation. Thus the form of the laws of sexual, parental, and filial relation would be given to mankind by positive law, but the matter thereof would

the Doctor continued, the law of nature pertained only to reasonable beings, whom he identified with man created in the image of God. This law is written in the heart of every man, teaching him what is to be done and what is to be avoided.[1] Because it is written in the heart, it cannot be put away, nor changed by any difference in place or time, nor can prescription, statute, or custom prevail against it. If any prescriptions, statutes, or customs conflict with this law, then they are null and void. All other laws, whether of God or of man, were grounded upon this law. What this law taught was that good is to be loved and evil to be shunned; that one should do to another as one would be done unto; that truth is to be respected, and justice done to every man. This law, in modern terms, was the source of moral notions, and 'it ordereth a man to the felicity of this life'.[2] The Doctor's account of the law of nature applicable to rational creatures is thus the same as Fortescue's, and, like it, clearly implies that statute or custom against conscience is to be disregarded.

The law of God, on the other hand, according to the Doctor, was a certain law given by revelation to rational creatures, showing them the will of God, for the sake of 'the felicity eternal'.[3] This law of God was always just and righteous, for it was made and given by His will, and all the actions of man conformable to it were just and righteous. The Doctor was convinced of the necessity of this law, but left its precise practical

be given to animals also, by nature (*System*, I, 415). But if this is the best defence Savigny could make for the notion, other apologists have no enviable task. The canon law was on much sounder ground when it identified *ius naturale* with natural instincts (*Decretum*, I, vii). Cf. H. F. Jolowicz, *Historical Introduction to Roman Law*, 105. The idea was more or less perfunctorily taken over by mediaeval jurists and later commentators, but no satisfactory explanation has ever been given of what the juristic content of such a law of nature, applicable to all creatures, could be. A natural law obeyed by all living creatures could not be juristic at all, but a law only in the sense of biological and physical law. There seems to be no reason for supposing that the trials and punishment of beasts which were at one time not uncommon were due to ideas derived from this extension of the law of nature. The root of such proceedings is to be found rather in the doctrine of the primitive law of liability.

[1] *Dialogue*, 5.   [2] *Ibid.* 6.   [3] *Ibid.* 7.

scope a little vague. Indeed, the law of God in his exposition seems in practice to mean no more than the laws against heresy and those canons which were concerned with strictly spiritual matters.

The law of man (or positive law) was derived from reason, as a thing of necessity, and probably also from the law of nature and of God—at any rate, so far as the appearance of truth to many, and especially to wise men (who made the law), was in fact justified by reason. Every positive law, therefore, contained something of the laws of nature and of God, though to perceive either of these in the positive law was admittedly sometimes very hard. In order to ensure the justice and righteousness of a positive law, both wisdom and authority were needed at its making. It was necessary that every good law should have these qualities—'that it be honest, right-wise, possible in itself, and after the custom of the country, convenient for the place and time, necessary, profitable, and also manifest, that it be not captious by dark sentences, ne mixt with any private wealth, but all made for the commonwealth'.[1] Every positive law must be consonant with the law of God. If, therefore, the laws of princes, the commandments of prelates, the statutes of commonalties, and even the ordinances of churches were not so consonant, they were not binding. But, on the other hand, if the laws of man were not contrary to the laws of God and of nature they must be observed.[2] For, as the Philosopher said, the intent of a maker of a law is to make the people good and to bring them to virtue.[3]

The Doctor then brought to a close his exposition of the laws which he affirmed must be the general grounds of the law of England, and invited the Student to explain to him the more particular grounds thereof. This the Student did, and began by naming the six principal grounds of the law of England. First

---

[1] *Ibid.* 10. This description is almost a literal translation of *Decretum*, IV, ii.
[2] Cf. Pecock, *Repressor*, II, 435: 'Wherefore al unleeful thing is forbodun bi Holi Scripture, or bi doom of resoun, or bi mannys law.' All not so forbidden is lawful.
[3] *Ethics*, Lib. iii.

of these was the law of reason; second, the law of God; third, general customs of the realm; fourth, divers principles called maxims; fifth, particular customs; sixth, 'divers statutes made in parliament by the king and by the common council of the realm'.[1]

The law of reason, the Student declared, was kept in England, as in all realms it must of necessity be. What the Doctor called the law of nature was in England called the law of reason. For, as the Student said, 'It is not used among them that be learned in the laws of England to reason what thing is commanded or prohibited by the law of nature, and what not, but all the reasoning in that behalf is in this manner. As when anything is grounded upon the law of nature, they say, that reason will that such a thing be done; and if it be prohibited by the law of nature, they say it is against reason, or that reason will not suffer that to be done'.[2]

The lawyers distinguished two degrees of this law of reason, the law of reason primary and the law of reason secondary. The first of these laws prohibited in the law of England such offences as murder, perjury, deceit, breaking of the peace; by it, it was lawful for every man to defend himself against injury, and by it promises made under menace were void. The secondary law of reason was subdivisible into two, the general and the particular. The secondary law general was itself derived from the 'general law and custom' of property, 'whereby goods moveable and immoveable be brought into a certain property, so that every man may know his own thing'. By the light of this law were prohibited all manner of disseisins, trespasses, rescous,[3] thefts, and detinues; and by it were prescribed the remedies for these wrongs—satisfaction for trespasses, restitution of goods, payment of debts, fulfilment of covenants. All those offences would not,

---

[1] *Dialogue*, 12. In the Latin text this sentence runs thus: '...Sexto ex diuersis statutis per commune consilium regni in parliamentis editis....'

[2] *Ibid.* 12.

[3] *I.e.* the illegal taking away and releasing of a distress taken or a person arrested by due process of law.

according to the Student, have been known, if the law of property had not been ordained. Hence, and because the law of property was generally observed in all countries, everything derivable by reason from this law of property was to be called the law of reason secondary general.[1] The law of reason secondary particular, on the other hand, was the law derived from customs general and particular, from maxims and statutes ordained in the realm. This law was secondary particular, because it was derived from law which obtained only within the realm and not elsewhere.

The Student, thus, seems to have known nothing of a law of reason which was not to be found embodied in or rationally derivable from the positive law of the land. Indeed, the only value of the concept of the law of reason in the Student's exposition, stripped as it is of the moralising, if vague, words of the Doctor's account, seems to lie in its capacity for instilling a sound rational temper into the minds of the lawyers, and for encouraging the pursuit of the ideal that the law of the land ought to be reasonable. The Student did not countenance the idea entertained by some, that the whole law of the land was the equivalent of the law of reason.[2]

In explaining the second ground of the law of England, the Student could not avoid bringing in theological concepts, for this ground was the law of God. This, however, he reduced to a practical concreteness by defining it merely as the ground of such action as the courts would have taken to deal with heresy, and as the ground of the recognition, or admission, or enforcement of such parts of ecclesiastical law as the courts actually did recognise, admit, or enforce. This law of God was also the ground for the voidance of any custom or statute which contravened these portions of ecclesiastical law, or which prohibited the exercise of godly virtues, such as alms-giving.

The third ground of English law, in the Student's enumeration, was found in general customs. These he well defined as 'of old time used through all the realm, which have been accepted and

------

[1] *Dialogue*, 3. [2] *Ibid.* 14.

approved by our sovereign lord the king, and his progenitors, and all his subjects. And because the said customs be neither against the law of God, nor the law of reason, and have been alway taken to be good and necessary for the commonwealth of all the realm, therefore they have obtained the strength of a law, in so much that he that doth against them, doth against justice; and these be the customs that properly be called the common law'.[1] It was always for the judges, not for the jury, to determine what these general customs were.[2] The most part of the law of the land consisted of these general customs, together with certain principles called maxims, which also derived from old custom. Hence it was that the king at his coronation took a solemn oath that he would cause all the customs of his realm to be observed.

These general customs were the very ground of the courts of the realm themselves—chancery, king's bench, common pleas, and exchequer. These were courts of record, the Student thought, because none might sit therein as judges, unless by the king's letters patent.[3] Other courts, though of much less authority, were also grounded on custom, such as the county, sheriff's tourn (*sic*), court-baron, and piepowder. Though some of these might be mentioned in statutes, there was no explanation of their first institution in any statute or written law. But the custom upon which they were founded was of so high an authority that they, their authorities and names, could not be changed, without the action of parliament.[4] No statute treated of the origin of general customs nor of the reason for their being held as law. Custom is its own authority, and custom, the Doctor admitted, was the surest ground of law.[5]

A curious feature of the Student's account of the sources of law is the authority he accorded to maxims. These, he thought,

---

[1] *Dialogue*, 18.   [2] Cf. Thayer, *Treatise on Evidence*, 185–186.
[3] *Dialogue*, 19. This is, of course, a double error on St Germain's part. Courts were of record because their acts were recorded and were incontrovertible, and not all justices were appointed by letters patent.
[4] *Ibid.* 20.   [5] *Ibid.* 25.

were principles which have been always taken for law in the realm, which it was not lawful for any learned in the law to deny, and which were a sufficient authority in themselves. Whether a maxim existed or not was to be determined by the judges and not by the jury. No reason could be offer'd for the reception of such maxims, except that they were not against the laws of reason and of God, and that they had always been accepted as law. Logical inferences from such maxims were equally lawful and binding. Moreover (most astonishing statement of all), maxims, he asserted, were of the same strength and effect in the law as were statutes.[1] Nevertheless, admittedly many old maxims had been changed by statute.[2]

St Germain seems to have been not unaware of the anomaly of this classification of maxims as one of the grounds of the law, and the Student confessed to some hesitations about it. He was made to say that it would be a 'great respite' to show the Doctor 'specially what is the cause of the law in them', and professed that he had mentioned them to him only with the intent that he might perceive that the maxims 'and other like' might conveniently be set for one of the grounds of the laws. Awkwardly enough, however, there were divers matters which might be either maxims or principles grounded in the law of reason.[3]

Actually the Student's fourth ground is unwarranted, and derives from a confusion between the material and the formal sources of law. There is not one maxim in the list he gives that is more than a pithy statement of custom, and general custom at that. Maxims, as Salmond has said,[4] are the proverbs of the

---

[1] *Ibid.* 26.   [2] *Ibid.* 31.   [3] *Ibid.* 31.

[4] *Jurisprudence*, 7th ed. Appendix III. Cf. Blackstone, *Commentaries*, I, 67–69: 'Some have divided the common law into two principal grounds or foundations: 1. Established customs, such as that, where there are three brothers, the eldest brother shall be heir to the second, in exclusion of the youngest; and 2. Established rules and maxims, as that "the king can do no wrong", that "no man shall be bound to accuse himself", and the like. But I take these to be one and the same thing. For the authority of the maxims rests entirely upon general reception and usage; and the only method of proving that this or that maxim is a rule of the common law is by showing that it hath been always the custom to observe it.' Cf. Vinogradoff, 'Les Maximes dans L'Ancien Droit Commun Anglais' (*Collected Papers*, II, 238).

law. The Student seems to have been misled by the fact that (as he himself remarked) general customs were well known throughout the realm, as well to the unlearned as to the learned, whilst the maxims were known only to the king's courts and to the learned and very few others.[1] On the strength, apparently, of this reconditeness, he raised the maxims into a separate and distinct source of law. No such distinction was justifiable, and indeed, in answer to some of the Doctor's rather sceptical questions, the Student, though he seems to think that some maxims were directly derivable from the law of reason, was obliged to admit that the maxims were to be found either in unwritten custom or in the books of the laws of England, called 'Years or Terms', in the records of the courts and of the treasury, and especially in the statutes.[2]

The fifth ground of the laws was found in the particular customs used in divers counties, towns, cities, and lordships in the realm, which not being against the law of reason and the law of God, and even though they were against the general customs or maxims, were held for law. The determination of these particular customs rested with the jury, and not with the judge, unless such a custom were of record in the court. Examples of these customs were gavelkind, burgh English, and the devisability of land by freemen of the city of London.[3]

The sixth and last ground of the law of England lay in the statutes. Statutes were made by the king and the lords spiritual and temporal and the commons in divers parliaments, 'in such cases where the law of reason, the law of God, customs, maxims, ne other grounds of the law seemed not to be sufficient to punish evil men and to reward good ones'.[4] In so far as a statute was

---

[1] *Dialogue*, 26.   [2] *Ibid.* 34.   [3] *Ibid.* 34-35.

[4] The Latin text of this passage reads: 'Sextum fundamentum legis anglie stat in diuersis statutis per dominum regem et progenitores suos et per dominos spirituales et temporales et per communitatem totius regni in parliamentis editis ubi lex rationis, lex divina, consuetudines, maxima sive alia fundamenta legis anglie prius sufficere minime videbantur et ultra haec fundamenta legis Anglie alia me legisse non meminar.' This doctrine seems to be in sharp contrast to Fortescue's view that statutes can only promulgate natural or customary law. *V. supra*, p. 201.

not against the law of God, nor against the law of reason, it must be observed by all those subject to law,[1] for it was ordained by authority of parliament, 'the which is always taken for the most high court in the realm'.[2] A custom or a prescription did not prevail against statute—at any rate, not 'in the law', though it might 'in conscience'.[3] A statute, in the absence of express words to the contrary, was binding on all men, even without proclamation; for 'there is no statute made in this realm but by the assent of the lords spiritual and temporal, and of all the commons, that is to say, by the knights of the shire, citizens and burgesses, that be chosen by assent of the commons, which in the parliament represent the estate of the whole commons; and every statute there made is of as strong effect in the law, as if all the commons were there present at the making thereof. And like as there needed no proclamation, if all were there present in their own person, so the law presumed there needeth no proclamation when it is made by their authority'.[4]

There could thus, in the Student's view, be no doubt of the validity of the maxim *Ignoratio juris neminem excusat*, so far at least as statute-law went. But, though it was not to be thought that a statute made by authority of the whole realm would recite anything 'against truth',[5] there might be difficulties in understanding the precise meaning of a statute. In determining the intent of a statute it might be necessary to go beyond its express words, but it was not permissible to go against the express words.[6]

Here, in the Student's statements, we have the fullest account of the theoretical position of statutes which we have yet met in

---

[1] *Dialogue*, 74–75. [2] *Ibid*. 75.
[3] *Ibid*. 81. [4] *Ibid*. 251.
[5] *Ibid*. 282.
[6] *Ibid*. 85: 'Truth it is, that sometime the intent of a statute shall be taken farther than the express letter stretcheth; but yet there may no intent be taken against the express words of the statute, for that should be rather an interpretation of the statute than an exposition.' Clearly St Germain is here using the word 'interpretation' in a different sense from that of modern usage, and means by it something in the nature of 'construction put upon'. The chapter in which this passage occurs is not part of the Latin version at all.

our sources, and we need not pursue the *Dialogue* any further. Four points stand out clearly in St Germain's theory of statute-law: First, no enactment is a statute which has not been assented to by king, lords, and commons in parliament, and made by parliament's authority. Second, since statutes make law where all other kinds of law are wanting, they can and do create new law. Third, statutes override common law. Fourth, judges must seek the intent of the statute, not against its express words, but beyond them if necessary; judicial interpretation of statutes, that is to say, need not be strict in the sense of being confined to their express words. How far St Germain's theories are borne out by our evidence from the courts of the fifteenth century remains to be seen.

EXCURSUS

LAW OF NATURE OR REASON IN THE COURTS[1]

1. *Y.B.* 15 *Edward III*, Pas. pl. 45.
   R.S., ed. L. O. Pike, ii, 107–127.
   John de Tornerghe *v.* Abbot of Furness. (App. no. 3.)

Cf. *supra*, p. 198.

The case is replevin between John de Tornerghe and the abbot of Furness. The abbot avowed for certain services and John pleaded a conveyance of the tenements in virtue of which he attorned to a third party, William Coucy, of whom he held. The extremely long discussion which arose was mainly upon the question whether William, who acknowledged that John held of him, could join himself with John in the pleading. This question of joinder gave rise to the argument (with which alone we are concerned here) by Mowbray, that law ought to accord with reason. Law ought, said Mowbray, to accord with reason and to take away mischief except where the contrary had been in

---

[1] Cf. Holdsworth, *Hist. Eng. Law*, ii, App. II, 602–604, 'The Law of Nature and the Common Law'.

use as law. The mischief in this case was apparent, and the joinder ought to be allowed. Judges, he argued, had previously amended the law as practised, without the aid of parliament.[1] The court, for example, had viewed heirs as vouched of full age, although grand distress had been the normal process. In this case, where the reverse had never been the usage, *a fortiori* the joinder ought to be allowed.

The decision (if any) is not reported.

2. *Y.B.* 8 *Edward IV*, Mich. pls. 9, 35. (App. no. 50.)
   Duchess of Suffolk *v.* Anon.

Cf. *supra*, p. 198.

It was related in the exchequer chamber by Pigot, Sjt., that the duchess of Suffolk had sued an action of debt on an obligation against *A*. If he, the defendant, were at the arbitrement of the duchess upon all matters in dispute between himself and *B*, the obligation was to be void. The arbitrement had in fact taken place: notice of it had been written, sealed, and delivered to the parties. The defendant, however, pleaded non-receipt of the notice until after the date upon which one of the terms of the arbitrement should have been executed by him. He therefore prayed to be excused, not having received notice in due time. Upon the question of the lawfulness of such an excuse, the whole case turned. Interest for our purpose focuses on the statements from the bench by Billing, J., and Yelverton, J.

Billing, J., argued that receipt of notice was necessary, for by no manner of reason could a man perform something without having had notice of it. When a man was committed to an impossible condition it was said that the obligation was not void. But there was a difference between an impossible condition and a condition against the law. He contended that it was void in either case, which was conceded by Markham, CJ., and Yelverton, J. For that which was impossible was against the law, since the law was based upon possibility and reason.

[1] Cf. 37 *Lib. Assisarum*, pl. 7 (App. no. 9).

Yelverton, J., asserted from the bench that they must act in the case as did the canonists and the civilians when they lacked a law. They resorted to the law of nature which was the ground of all laws. They acted in accordance with whatever the law of nature pronounced to be the most beneficial for the commonweal, and so must they in the case before them. If they (the judges) were to make a positive law on the point, they must see what was most necessary for the commonweal, and must make the law in accordance therewith. He believed that no one would deny that the better course in that case would be to make such a positive law that no man would be charged to perform an arbitrement without having had notice thereof. For an arbitrement was for the commonweal, that was to say, for the appeasement of disputes and wrongs between parties. If a man could be charged even without receipt of notice, people would hesitate to consent to arbitrement. Therefore they gave judgement in this case, weighing as they did the interests of the commonweal, for such a case had not been seen before, and their judgement would thereafter be taken for a precedent.

3. *Y.B.* 13 *Edward IV*, Pas. pl. 5.
Anon *v.* Anon.[1] (App. no. 58.)

Cf. *supra*, p. 198.

In the star chamber before the king's council it was reported that a certain party had bargained with a man to carry certain bales and other articles to Southampton. The carrier had transported the bales to another place, and broken the bales, had taken 'feloniously' the contents and converted them to his own use. The question was, ought this act properly to be considered a felony?

Brian, Sjt., argued in the negative sense. It was neither felony nor trespass, since it was not done with violence, 'vi et armis', nor against the peace. The only action possible in the case was

---

[1] Cf. Pollock, *First Book of Jurisprudence*, 5th ed. 286, n. 1; Carter, *History of Legal Institutions*, 262; and *Select Cases Concerning the Law Merchant*, II, p. lxxv.

on a writ of detinue. Hussey, the king's attorney, argued that felony was to claim property without cause and with intent to steal, 'animo furandi'. Nothwithstanding the bailment, he insisted that the carrier's act was a felony. The chancellor agreed that felony was according to the intent, and intent could be felonious, as it was in the carrier's action. After further discussion along these lines it was represented to the chancellor that the case ought to be determined at common law and not there, in the council.

But the chancellor pointed out that the case was complicated by the fact that the suitor was a merchant alien enjoying the king's safe-conduct, and such persons were not accustomed to sue according to the law of the land, with trial by jury and other solemnities. The merchant ought to sue to them, and it would be determined according to the law of nature in the chancery. Such a merchant, moreover, would not be bound by their statutes, where the statutes were introductory of new law, though they were by statutes declaratory of old law, 'cestassavoir nature, etc.'

The king had jurisdiction over the merchant alien, and could put him to his right, but if he did so, it would be according to the law of nature, which was called by some the law merchant, which was law universal throughout the world. It had been adjudged, the chancellor continued, that notwithstanding the statutes of safe-conducts,[1] which required the enrolment of conducts and the specification therein of the number of sailors and the name of the vessel, an alien with a safe-conduct deficient in those particulars would be allowed its privileges. For the aliens said that they could not be held to know our statutes, and that they came by authority of the king's seal, and if that were insufficient, it ought to be rescinded.

Others of the council said that the statute of forfeiture of merchandise[2] bound as well aliens as denizens. It was said also that a denizen ought not to sue an alien before the council, but

---

[1] Statutes 15 Henry VI, c. 3; 18 Henry VI, c. 8.
[2] Presumably the statute of Merchants, 11 Edward I (1283).

an alien ought so to sue a denizen—and some thought that this difference had a statutory basis.

The question whether the carrier's act was a felony was argued before the justices in the exchequer chamber, and they reported to the chancellor in the council that in the opinion of the majority it was felony. Though it was felony, the goods could not be claimed as waif, for they belonged to him the alien who sued therefor. The king granted to him safe conduct 'tam in corpore quam in bonis', and that was a covenant between the king and him. The alien should not take action against the felon, but sue on his covenant to the king. The king could not have the goods as waif, nor grant them to another, nor could any other claim them by prescription.

§ 2. LEGISLATIVE PROCEDURE[1]

In the previous section it has been shown that by the end, at least, of the fifteenth century, no enactment, even in theory, could be a statute without having received the assent of king, lords, and commons in parliament, and the sanction of parliament's authority. It has been shown also that this statutory law, even in theory, could create new law distinct from and additional to common law. That this statutory law was distinguished into at least three different classes, and that these classes might be held to stand in different relationships to common law, will be shown in our next section. Here our purpose is to survey the normal course of legislation from the time when a proposal appeared as a bill in one of the houses of parliament to the time when it appeared as a statute on the statute book, and to the

---

[1] Throughout this section I am heavily indebted to Professor H. L. Gray's *The Influence of the Commons on Early Legislation.* I have little fresh information to supply on the subject of procedure, and this section provides little more than a digest and criticism of Professor Gray's materials, together with some supplementary materials, mainly from the *Year Books.* For additional criticism of some of his conclusions, *v.* Excursus III, *infra.* Mr Pickthorn (*op. cit.* 107–108, 123 *et seq.*) has a useful brief account of commons' procedure in some of its aspects. The *Fane Fragment of the Lords' Journal of* 1461, admirably edited by Professor W. H. Dunham, Jr. (1935), provides some fresh and valuable information.

time when it was proclaimed in the counties, if it ever attained that dignity, and to the time when it was repealed, if it ever suffered that indignity.[1] The topics for consideration in this section are, therefore, (i) the types of bills and their passage in either house; (ii) amendments; (iii) engrossment, enrolment, enactment, and proclamation.

(i) *Types of bills and their passage in either house.* From the point of view of procedure, only two types of bills need be considered, namely, private bills and public bills.[2] A third type of bill, called official bills, has sometimes been distinguished, but since procedure within the houses upon this type of bill seems not to have differed from that upon other bills introduced into the lords, they need not concern us at this point.[3]

The differences in procedure upon private and public bills were not very marked. A private bill introduced in the lords was addressed, not to the lords themselves, but to the king. If the king assented to it the bill might, and after the early years of Edward IV's reign often did, receive on the margin above the text the royal sign manual. It was then sent, without any other endorsement, to the commons, who, if they assented to it, endorsed it with the words, 'Acest bille les Communes sount assentuz'.[4] The presence of this endorsement on a bill was proof that it had previously received the lords' assent.[5] Final royal response to such a bill took the form of either 'Soit fait comme il est desiré' or 'Le Roi s'advisera'; and until 1439 this assent was normally directly enrolled, not endorsed on the back of the petition itself, as was subsequently the practice.[6]

---

[1] It has, however, been thought best to treat the subject of repeal *infra*, p. 265, in § 4, 'The Effective Scope of Statutes, (i) Duration and Repeal'.

[2] This section, of course, deals only with the antecedents of statutory law, and leaves out of account such bills as subsidy bills and bills of pardon. All bills, however, must always have been either private or public.

[3] For some discussion of official bills, *v. infra*, pp. 239–243. Mr Pickthorn surely exaggerates in saying that public bills introduced into the lords were always government bills (*op. cit.* 124).

[4] Gray, *op. cit.* 49.

[5] *Pilkington's Case, Y.B.* 33 *Henry VI*, Pas. pl. 8 (App. no. 30). (*V.* Excursus I, *infra*.) [6] Gray, *op. cit.* 300, 321.

Almost precisely the same procedure obtained in the case of public bills introduced into the lords. The only differences were the framing of the address to the king in an impersonal form, the omission of the royal sign manual, and the use for the final royal assent of the words 'Le Roi le veult'.[1]

A private bill introduced in the commons, however, was addressed to the commons as a whole, and appealed to them to beseech the king to grant with the advice and assent of the lords. A public bill introduced in the commons, on the contrary, was addressed to the king, and besought him to enact with the advice and assent of the lords. Whether the bill were private or public, if it passed the commons, it was endorsed with no other words than 'Soit baille as Seigneurs'.[2]

Before 1423, bills in the commons were usually drafted in the form of comprehensive petitions, *i.e.* petitions of several different articles each. In the parliament of that year, however, and subsequently, the single petition was invariably used.[3]

We know very little of the methods of dealing with bills after their introduction in either house during the fifteenth century. Obviously there must have been at least one reading and some sort of debate, but how many readings and what manner of debate, we can only guess. A bill once read was seconded; at least two readings were common, and sometimes three occurred as early as 1461. Debate certainly took place but after which reading we do not know. Bills might be referred to a committee, at any rate, by the lords.[4] Probably by the middle of the century, bills in the lords were dealt with in much the way that was usual from 1509.[5] At that time a bill was read

---

[1] Gray, *op. cit.* 56. A bill might be put into the lords by the king's own hand, as in 1461 (*v. Fane Fragment*, 19).

[2] Gray, *op. cit.* 62; and *Pilkington's Case, ut supra.* Cf. Danvers, J., in *Y.B.* 10 *Henry VII*, Pas. pl. 7 (App. no. 97): '...car il est common cours, quand un parlement est tenu, que quand les communs sont agrees, il est mis au Roy, et il escrit Jeo assent, et sur ceo parols est escrit son Act, *Statuit Rex*.'

[3] *Ibid.* 224 *et seq.*

[4] *Fane Fragment*, 70–73.

[5] Gray, *op. cit.* 164; and *Journals of the House of Lords*, I, 4 *et seq.*

once and amended if necessary, and after two more readings was sent down to the commons. There is not, however, any evidence that bills were read as a rule in the lords more than twice, before the last decade of the fifteenth century, nor any evidence of the number of readings in the commons[1]. But we do know that, in the fourteenth century, debate in the commons was conducted at least once by members' standing at a lectern and delivering their speeches from that position,[2] and a good deal is known of the procedure of amendment in both houses. Moreover, it seems a fair inference from Fortescue's concluding remarks in Pilkington's case that the principle of parliament's being the only judge of its own procedure was well-nigh established by the middle of the century.[3]

(ii) *Amendments.* The evidence of the amendment by the commons of lords' bills during the century is so very slender that it is hardly possible to speak of procedure in such cases. Indeed, it seems fair to say that there is quite conclusive evidence of such amendment in the case of only one bill that became a statute.[4] In this instance, the lords' bill received from the commons the addition of a schedule on which their assent was inscribed, conditional on the incorporation therein of certain provisos.[5] In another possible but not certain instance of such amendment, the commons' provisos were written on the face of the bill

---

[1] Gray, *op. cit.* 164–165.

[2] *Anonimalle Chronicle*, 88.

[3] *V. infra*, Excursus I.

[4] Gray states (*op.cit.* 198) that, in the second half of the century, only two amendments by the commons of lords' bills are found and these are appended to a bill of 1454, which appointed five lords to guard the sea. But as these amendments are identified by the handwriting alone, the point can hardly be considered proved. (Cf. *ibid.* 193.) The extraordinary difficulty of following the arrangement of Professor Gray's materials makes such assertions rash, but it seems that the only certain case of commons' amendment comes from the year 1429. (*V. ibid.* 194.) The bill of 1406 which he cites next was introduced first in the commons, and is therefore irrelevant to the present question, and in any case did not become a statute. (*Ibid.* 194–195.)

[5] 'Les Communes sount assentuz a la bille a cest cedule annexe parissint qe les forsprises en cest cedule comprisez soient affirmez come parcelle de la bille.' (*Ibid.* 194.)

itself.[1] The amendment in these cases was trivial, and there is no reason to suppose that they were considered by the lords, or that any bill was ever referred back to the lords by the commons. In short, amendment of lords' bills by the commons throughout the century was so slight as to be negligible; and, though no doubt the commons possessed, in theory, the right to reject a lords' bill altogether, no instance of the exercise of such a right has come to light.

Not so the amendment of commons' bills by the lords or king. This sort of amendment was very common, and its occurrence has important constitutional bearings. Until 1439 the responses to commons' petitions (which, as has been mentioned, were of the comprehensive variety until 1423) were written down in a series, which might and often did contain provisos amending the text of the petitions. After 1439, however, each single commons' petition was endorsed with the response and any proviso added by the lords, until the reign of Edward IV, when it became usual to write provisos on separate strips, and attach them to the petition. Whether these amendments were made by a committee or by the whole house, or by the government or the king, is generally unknown, and whosoever made them made no difference to procedure as between the houses. But a matter of major constitutional importance arises when we ask the question whether the submission of these amendments to the commons for their assent was a normal part of procedure.

The answer to this question must, it is submitted, be in the negative, except in the case of amendments which extended the terms or scope of the commons' proposals. Amended bills, at any rate in the middle of the century, were not sent back to the commons if the amendments were restrictive, but were if the amendments were extensive.

Our evidence for this statement is clear and authoritative, coming as it does direct from Kirkby, in 1455. In the course of Pilkington's case,[2] Kirkby was sent for by Fortescue, CJ.,

---

[1] Gray. *op. cit.* 193.
[2] *V.* Excursus I, *infra*.

and was requested to inform the court of parliamentary procedure. Part of the information he supplied consisted in the statement that if the lords wished to alter a bill from the commons, and the alteration was in harmony with the commons' proposal, the bill was not sent back to them. But if the lords' amendment extended the terms of the bill, it was written on a schedule, or in some way endorsed, and sent back to the commons. If they did not assent to this amendment, the bill could not be enacted. But if they did agree to it, then the bill was endorsed in the bottom margin with the words, 'Les Communes sont assentus al sedule les Seigneurs a meme cel bille annexe', and was delivered to the clerk of parliament. If, for example, the commons granted tonnage and poundage for four years, and the lords reduced this term to two years, the bill would not be delivered back to the commons. But if the commons made a grant for two years, and the lords extended the term to four years, their lordships would inscribe the bill with the words, 'Les Seigneurs sont a durer pur quatre ans', and it must be sent back to the commons.

This principle of procedure reported by Kirkby does not seem to be contradicted at all by the evidence we have of normal practice. Apropos of the subject, Professor Gray says that 'although the commons' assent to changes seem [*sic*] not to have been specifically got in the first parliament after the promise [of 1414, not to change the meaning of commons' petitions without their assent] had been made, the changes [during the period 1414–1421] were few in number, slight in substance, and usually restricted to the fixing of a time-limit for the duration of the statute'.[1] But the triviality of the amendments—if indeed they were trivial—must not be allowed to obscure the fact that they were effective without assent of the commons. Moreover, for the next period, 1422—51, as many as one half of the 162 commons' bills were amended, and amended in ways which Professor Gray classifies into five groups. 'One specifically

[1] *Op. cit.* 285–286.

reserved the king's prerogative; one defined more closely some clause of the bill, perhaps relating it to other statutes; one made some change in the penalties imposed or in the disposition of them; a fourth limited the duration of the statute which it authorised; and a fifth altered in some respect the administrative machinery of the bill.'[1]

We may surmise that amendments falling into any of these groups would necessarily be restrictive in character, and would not, according to Kirkby's principle, require the commons' assent. But Professor Gray believes that for some of them the commons' assent was sought and obtained.[2] Nevertheless, he adduces only two such instances, and the authenticity of one of these is uncertain, and the relevance of the other doubtful.[3]

The matter for the remaining years of the century is not in

---

[1] *Op. cit.* 311.

[2] *Ibid.* 320.

[3] In 1439 an amendment adding details about the method of naming collectors was attached to a commons' bill asking that citizens and burgesses be not appointed collectors of tenths and fifteenths outside their city or borough, unless they held lands and tenements outside. Below this amendment was written, '*A ycest cedule les Comunes sount assentuz*'. But Professor Gray himself admits that this amendment may have been added by the commons themselves (*ibid.* 321); he is hardly warranted, therefore, in calling it an 'unmistakeable instance of the commons' assent to a lords' amendment' (*ibid.* 323). Even if in fact the amendment was by the lords, it is extensive in character, and therefore agrees with Kirkby's rule. The second alleged instance is a petition of 1444 asking for the punishment of a certain John Bolton, who had committed a grave crime but who possessed a charter of pardon antecedent in date to the detection of his crime. This particular request was followed in the petition by a general proposal for the voidance of similar charters in similar cases. The particular request was assented to, but the general proposal rejected, and the commons are said to have agreed to this response. But the rejection of a legislative proposal can hardly be considered an amendment to a petition for the punishment of a specific person, and the case cannot be held to be an instance of normal procedure. (*V. ibid.* 323.) Professor Gray nevertheless infers that 'by 1439 the commons were usually asked to give their approval to any amendment to one of their bills' (*ibid.*). This inference is groundless. Neither can it be said, in the face of Kirkby's testimony, that either all or none of the amended commons' bills were sent back for their assent, as is supposed (*ibid.*). Professor Gray's general conclusion, that 'the commons' control over legislation in the first three decades of the reign of Henry VI was nearly complete', could not follow from this *type* of evidence, even if it were not so flimsy. (Cf. Excursus III, *infra.*)

doubt.[1] No amendment to a commons' bill inscribed with their assent survives from 1444 to 1503, though we know that twenty-seven of the fifty commons' bills passed in the years from 1450 to 1483 were subjected to lords' amendments falling into the same five groups as in the previous three decades.[2] The principle of procedure stated by Kirkby is thus confirmed by our present knowledge of practice. We are entitled to hold that the normal procedure in the amendment of commons' bills by the lords was to send the amended bill back for the commons' assent, which was necessary for enrolment if the amendment extended the commons' proposal;[3] but to enrol the bill forthwith, if the amendment restricted the proposal.

(iii) *Engrossment, enrolment, enactment, and proclamation.* There is some doubt at what stage in the proceedings a bill in either house was engrossed, if it were engrossed at all. In the sixteenth and seventeenth centuries, engrossment appears usually to have come at the second reading of a bill.[4] But at present there seems to be no definite evidence at what stage the original bill was ordered to be put into the formal script on parchment which constituted engrossment. All original bills surviving from the fifteenth century, however, are in engrossed form,[5] and it is natural to surmise that no bill would be engrossed unless there were good reason to suppose that it was going to receive the assent of one or both of the houses.

Those engrossed bills which had received the assent of king, lords, and commons, were passed on to the clerk of parlia-

---

[1] Cf. *Fane Fragment*, 74: 'More certainty exists, however, about the practice of amendment of commons' bills by Lords. This is quite fully established in the Journal. But no subsequent ratification by the Commons of such amendments can be determined.' Professor Dunham's conclusions on this subject (*ibid.* 74–84) confirm the views the present writer reached before he had the advantage of using the evidence of the *Fane Fragment.*

[2] *Gray, op. cit.* 177, 184.

[3] Though we do not know for certain of any instance of an extensive amendment, Kirkby would hardly have alluded to their possibility if they were quite unknown.

[4] Gray, *op. cit.* 20–21, 8–10.

[5] *Ibid.* 34.

ment,[1] with the appropriate assents inscribed thereon.[2] Their
subsequent fate differed according as they were public or private
bills. Public bills were enrolled by the clerk on the rolls of
parliament; private bills were not so enrolled unless by special
request, but were filed.[3] No record was kept of the date of the
receipt of any of them by the clerk, but every bill was held to
date from the first day of the parliament.[4]

Those bills which were destined to become statutes were
generally enrolled together on the rolls of parliament, under a
single caption,[5] but this enrolment did not necessarily come

---

[1] It is time the office and functions of the clerk of parliament were more fully
investigated. A specified clerk of chancery was evidently performing those functions
at least as early as 1315 (*v. Rot. Parl.* I, 350 a); and in 1330, Henry of Edenestowe,
'*clericus Parliamenti*', is described as having delivered into chancery '*recorda et
memoranda de hiis que fiebant in Parliamento*' (*v. ibid.* II, 52 a). A very remarkable
incident in 1346 shows Thomas Drayton, clerk of parliament, commanded to go to
the common bench, and there to order the justices either to render judgement in
a certain plea or to come into the parliament, bringing the records of the case with
them, and there give judgement in the cause. (The justices came into parliament,
and there debate was held on the case until judgement was reached.) (*V. ibid.* II,
123 a.) In the same year, any of the commons who proposed to put into parliament
a petition touching the common profit was required to deliver it to the clerk (*ibid.*
II, 60 a). In 1348, a like command was given, supplemented by one to the effect
that private petitions were to be sent not to the clerk but to the chancellor (*ibid.*
II, 201 b). From time to time the clerk was given a particular record and instructed to
enrol it on the Roll (*ibid.* II, 226 a; III, 75 b, 217 a, 264 b, 585 b; IV, 102 b) or on the files
(*ibid.* III, 50 b). The clerk was nearly, if not quite, always a receiver, and frequently
a trier, of petitions (*ibid.* II, 68 a; III, 98 b, 122 b, 144 b, etc.). Sometimes he would
read to parliament, at the end of the session, such bills as had been answered (*ibid.*
II, 304 a), or take into his charge outstanding bills still to be answered (*ibid.* II,
374 a). He might be commanded to bring a matter before the king and lords at
the beginning of the next parliament (*ibid.* IV, 21 a). From 1489 he might sign his
name at the end of the Roll for the session. He was not allowed, in 1496, to be a
collector of a fifteenth, but to him fell the task of forbidding in Westminster Hall and
in the city and suburbs of London the wearing of arms, and the playing of games in
Westminster Palace during parliament. He had to proclaim, at any rate in 1351,
that no child or other person 'jue en nul lieu du palays de Westm', durant le
parlement que yest somons, as bares, ne as autres jues nient covenables, come a
oustier chaperons des gentz, ne a mettre main en eux, ne autre empechement faire,
purquoi chescun ne puisse peisiblement suir ses busoigne', on pain of imprisonment
(*ibid.* II, 236 b). An under-clerk of parliament receives mention from 1464, and the
reserving to him, at that date, of the wages and rewards of his office suggests that it
was not a new one (*ibid.* V, 517 a).
[2] Gray, *loc. cit.*; and *Pilkington's Case* (*v.* Excursus I, *infra*).
[3] *Ibid.*
[4] *Ibid.*
[5] For some discussion of this caption, *v.* Excursus III, *infra*, p. 244.

before their enrolment on the statute roll.[1] This enrolment on the statute roll was presumably what Kirkby meant when he said commons' bills were enrolled *and* enacted.[2] Enactment would thus mean re-drafting in statutory form and enrolling on the statute roll. Often, it seems, the engrossed bills approved would be directly copied several times over, separately, in re-drafted and engrossed form, for the purposes of dispatch to the sheriffs, the courts, etc.,[3] and the statute roll might be made up from a set of these engrossed sheets, without reference to the parliament rolls. These engrossed statutes might even be in circulation before the parliament roll had been made up.[4]

A bill which had passed through both houses of parliament and had received the royal assent was an act of parliament,[5] even if some slight technical defect in procedure had occurred.[6] No bill which had not received that threefold assent was an act of parliament.[7] But not all acts of parliament were destined to become statutes. Admittedly the chief criterion of a statute was its capacity for permanently modifying the common law, or for being permanently applicable in the courts of justice.[8] But by whom and how was the selection of those acts which were to be statutes made from those which were not? Who decided that a bill was to be enacted and engrossed and circulated?

Our evidence for an answer to these important questions is not very extensive; but such as it is, it suggests that the council was responsible for the selection of the acts which led to the enrolment of some of them as statutes, and that the judges drafted them in statutory form.

---

[1] Gray, *op. cit.* 401 *et seq.*

[2] *Pilkington's Case.* But more probably 'enrolment' and 'enactment' were synonymous in current usage, even though re-drafting in statutory form and enrolment were two distinct processes.

[3] When issued under the great seal, these would be exemplifications.

[4] Gray, *loc. cit.*

[5] On this point *v.* Excursus II, *infra.* Professor Pollard's suggestion that the assent of the commons was not always necessary for statutes seems disposed of by Professor Gray (*op. cit.* 161, n. 50).

[6] This is the inference from *Pilkington's Case* (*v.* Excursus I *infra*).

[7] *V.* Excursus II, *infra.*   [8] Gray, *op. cit.* 97, 381.

A minute of the council meeting on January 26th, 1423, tells us that on that day the acts made in the last parliament were read to the lords of the council by the clerk of parliament, and that he was instructed to show the acts to the justices of both benches, so that those acts which were to be statutes might be seen by them and be rendered into clear language. Afterwards, they were to be shown again to the lords of the council, and proclaimed. Copies of the other acts, touching the governance of the council and of the realm, were to be deposited with the clerk of the council; and all of them, as soon as (*simul*) they had been written out, were to be enrolled in the chancery, as was customary.[1]

This instructive text strongly points to the council as the body responsible for selecting the acts that were to be statutes, and clearly shows that the judges were consulted on the drafting of them. This seems to be the answer to the questions formulated above; for not only is there no evidence that parliament itself determined which of its acts were to be statutes, but also there is no presumption that it would. The selection was essentially an administrative act to be followed by further administrative actions, such as engrossment, enrolment, and proclamation; though, of course, the nature of the measure enacted by parliament would be the deciding factor in the selection. The decision, however, was taken, it seems, not by the parliament but by the council.[2] The council, in this sense, 'made' statutes, while the

---

[1] *Procs. and Ords.* III, 22: 'Eodem die lecti fuerunt per clericum parliamenti coram dominis actus habiti et facti in ultimo parliamento, qui ibidem habuit in mandatis de ostendendo dictos actus justiciis regis utriusque banci ad effectum quod illi actus qui erunt statuti regni per ipsos videantur et redigantur in mundum et postea quod ostendantur dominis et proclamentur, et quod aliorum actuum tangencium gubernacionem dominorum de consilio et regni dimittantur copie cum clerico consilii regis et quod simul omnes redacti in scripto irrotulentur in cancellaria ut moris est.'

[2] As is suggested by Gray, *op. cit.* 403. Professor Pollard states (*History*, XVIII, 262) that 'the statutes were selected for publication, not by the Commons but by the King's Council on the advice of the judges'. No doubt the council would consult the judges on legal questions arising from the selection; but the council minute above cited surely suggests, if it does not prove, that the selection was made by the council before the acts were sent to the judges.

justices edited them.[1] The final stage in procedure was proclamation. Copies of the statute were sent to the sheriffs to be read in the county courts, and, in the fourteenth century and perhaps later, to the justices for the information of the courts.[2] Long before the end of the fourteenth century, however, it was established that proclamation in the counties was not necessary for a statute to possess full binding force.[3] Proclamation was thus not an indispensable part of procedure.[4]

We say that proclamation, though not necessary, was the last stage in the essential procedure of enactment of statutes. But, though it seems safe to hold that no statute was passed in the fifteenth century which was not enrolled on the statute roll (up to 1490),[5] there was still a variety of possible fates awaiting the

[1] The judges sometimes acted as draftsmen of statutes, in their capacity of assistants in the House of Lords, as late as the eighteenth century. (*V.* Sir Courtenay Ilbert, *Legislative Methods and Forms*, 77–78. Cf. Pickthorn, *op. cit.* 132.) It is evident that the judges also had a hand in the make-up of the *Rolls of Parliament*, at any rate if the following entry on the *Rolls* for 1401 is to be taken as typical of procedure: 'Item, mesme le Samedy, les ditz Communes prierent a notre Seigneur le Roy, que les Bosoignes faitz et a faire en cest parlement soient enactez et engrossez devaunt le departir des Justices, tant come ils les aient en leur memoire. A quir leur feust responduz, Qe le Clerk du Parlement ferroit son devoir pur enacter et engrosser la substance le parlement par advis des Justices et puis le monstrer au Roy et as Seigneurs en Parlement, pur savoir leur advis' (*Rot. Parl.* III, 457, no. 21). In 1406 the commons, through the Speaker, petitioned the king and the lords to name certain of the lords spiritual and temporal who, together with certain named members of the commons, 'purroient estre assignez d'estre a l'enactement et l'engrossement du Rolle de Parlement'. They petitioned also that this request should be entered on the Roll itself. Both petitions were granted (*Rot. Parl.* III, 58, no. 65).

[2] Gray, *op. cit.* 391–394.

[3] *Y.B.* 39 *Edward III*, Pas. pl. 3 (App. no. 8); and *infra*, Excursus II. And cf. *Doctor and Student*, cited *supra* (in § 1), to the same effect.

[4] The statement in Gray, *op. cit.* 386, that a statute must be proclaimed is thus unacceptable.

[5] There can be little doubt that acts intended to be statutes were enrolled on the statute roll throughout the fifteenth century up to 1490. Unfortunately, however, there are two gaps in the extant statute rolls. They are complete in two rolls for the reigns of Henry IV and Henry V, and for the reign of Henry VI up to the 8th year. Then a roll is wanting for the 9th, 10th, 11th, 14th, 15th, 18th, 20th, and 23rd years of the reign of Henry VI; the next extant roll includes the statutes from the 25th to the 39th year of the same reign; and the last extant roll covers the first eight years of the reign of Edward IV. No later roll is known to exist, but there is good reason to suppose that the statute roll was continued up to 4 Henry VII. From the next session, 7 Henry VII, public acts were for the first time printed from the several bills passed, and not as parts of one general statute drawn up in the old form. Apart from these two gaps in the statute rolls, only one act for the century was printed as a

statutes which had passed through these stages of procedure. Some of these possible fates have been mentioned already, but a brief survey of them and others serves to complete our account.

First, it should be noted, any statute might be enrolled eventually in other rolls besides those of parliament and of statutes. At any time up to 22 Edward IV they might be included, when necessary, on the Patent, Close, Fine, or Charter Rolls. These together make up a great collection of statutes, though we may justly doubt whether any statute for the fifteenth century is to be found thereon which is not on the statute rolls so far as they are extant. Then, from the time of Richard III every statute is to be found on an enrolment of acts certified and delivered into chancery, an enrolment which in effect takes the place of the statute roll from 5 Henry VII.

The copies of statutes exemplified out of chancery had many fates, and might be dispatched to the sheriffs, the chanceries and the exchequers of England and of Ireland, to the courts, to some municipalities, and, when appropriate, to various institutions such as the universities and cathedrals. In some of these quarters they went to form either directly or indirectly the various books of statutes, of record or not of record, many of which still survive.[1]

statute by the Record Commissioners from a source other than the statute roll. This act, an ordinance of 1417–1418, was taken from the Exchequer Book; and it appears in all the printed editions and translations. But, since the ordinance merely allowed the appointment of attorneys, etc., until the next parliament, it is very doubtful whether the act in question was a statute at all, and this instance cannot justly be said to be an example of the omission to enrol a statute on the statute roll. For the years in which the statute rolls are wanting, the Commissioners used the same *Red Book of the Exchequer*, transcripts sent into chancery, and *B.M. MSS., Cott. Nero*, C, 1, for the gap in Henry VI's reign; the Exchequer Book only, for the gap in Edward IV's reign and for Richard III's reign; and *Lincoln's Inn Petyt MSS.* no. 8, the *Rolls of Parliament*, and the Exchequer Book again, for Henry VII's reign. After 4 Henry VII, the place of the statute roll is in effect taken by the chancery enrolments containing acts certified and delivered into chancery. These extend from 1 Richard III onwards, and up to 25 Henry VIII contain all the acts, public and private, passed in every session. (*V. Statutes of the Realm*, Introduction.)

[1] References to books of statutes at this time are common enough. The Speaker in the Good Parliament is said to have had a book of statutes by him (*Anonimalle Chronicle*, 86). The translator of Livius wrote that 'Manie and fruitefull and profitable statutes he made and enacted in the same Parliament [of 1414], wch because

But all these various dispositions have nothing, of course, to do
with the validity of a statute. In the fifteenth century, a statute
had full statutory force when, and only when, it was on the
statute roll—unless, as is indeed very probable, it already had
that force as soon as it had been engrossed as a statute prior to
enrolment on the statute roll.[1]

EXCURSUS I

Pilkington's Case (*Y.B.* 33 *Henry VI*, Pas. Pl. 8 (App. no. 30))

Fortescue, CJ., related in the exchequer chamber how in the
last parliament a special bill had been passed against a certain
John Pilkington for rape (*i.e.* abduction). By this bill the sheriff
was to proclaim that Pilkington was to appear before the lords
by a certain date, to answer the charges against him. If he did
not so appear, he was to be adjudged for trespass, and was to
pay damages to the party concerned. The proclamations had

they be not necessarie to my purpose, and also for that they be seriouslie recited in
other bookes ordeyned for the same, I shall heare overpasse and leave unwritten'
(*First Life of Henry V*, ed. Kingsford, 27). The Paston Library contained *A Book of
New Statutes* from Edward III (H. S. Bennett, *The Pastons and their England*, 261).
The courts presumably kept a file or made a book of the engrossed statutes sent
them. Certainly the Exchequer did, and its illuminated books of statutes are now
in the P.R.O. Museum. There are occasional references in the *Year Books* to 'les
livres del Statutes' (*e.g.* *Y.B.* 4 *Edward IV*, Pas. pl. 4 (App. no. 45)). There still
survive many collections of statutes made in the several places whither they were
sent; as, *e.g.*, those sent to the Exchequer in Dublin, to the Guildhall (for a list of
the statutes there, extending up to 3 Henry IV, see *Liber Albus*, ed. H. T. Riley,
4th book), to the cathedrals, to the universities, and to various courts and libraries.
The first four printed collections of statutes fall within the 15th century: (1) The
Vieux Abridgement, published in Latin and French before 1481, includes statutes from
Henry III to 33 Henry VI (1455). (2) The *Nova Statuta*, published in Latin and
French about 1482, includes statutes from 1 Edward III to 22 Edward IV. (3) The
first sessional publication was printed in French for the only parliament of Richard
III, by Caxton and/or Machlinia, and this practice was continued thenceforth.
(4) Pynson's *Nova Statuta* printed the statutes from 1 Edward III to 1 Richard III
in Latin or French, and those from 1 to 12 Henry VII in English, about 1497, and
certainly before 1504. For further particulars of these and later editions, *v. Statutes
of the Realm*, Introduction. Cf. H. G. Richardson and G. O. Sayles, 'The Early
Statutes', *L.Q.R.* L (1934).

[1] This seems the proper inference from the fact that the statute roll itself was
often at least made up from the engrossed acts, after they had been put into circulation, and from the terms of the statement made by the commons in the petition of
1414. They asked that no commons' petition should be made into law 'and engrossed as statute and law' (*Rot. Parl.* IV, 22).

been duly made, but the accused had not appeared by the specified date. Later he had been arrested and confined in the prison of the king's bench. But the prisoner alleged, through his counsel, that the act by which he was penalised was insufficient in law, and he prayed to be dismissed. The act was alleged to be void because the lords had postponed the date fixed for his appearance by the commons, without obtaining their assent to the amendment.

Fortescue considered that the act must be deemed good, for the king had sent them a writ which certified that the bill was confirmed by authority of parliament. Illingworth, CB., however, argued that the writ, which was merely written by a clerk in chancery, could not make an act good if it were vitiated in itself.

The justices then sent for Kirkby, 'of the rolls', and Faukes, clerk of parliament, and required them to inform the court of the order and course of parliament. Kirkby reported that the course of parliament was such.... (Unfortunately, the *Year Book* suppresses this part of the recital.) But, he continued, if a bill were particular (private) or were any other kind of bill that was delivered first in the commons, and it passed them, it was endorsed 'Soit baille as Seigneurs'. If then the king and the lords agreed to it, and did not wish to alter it, they did not endorse it, but sent it to the clerk of parliament. A private bill so sent was not enrolled, but was filed on the file, unless the party concerned should, for better surety, sue to have it enrolled. But a common bill[1] was enrolled and enacted.

If the lords wished to alter the bill in such a way as not to exceed the commons' proposal (ceo qe puit estre ove le grant des Communs), the bill was not sent back to the commons. If, however, the lords amended the bill in such a way as to exceed the commons' proposal, the bill was sent back to the commons with a schedule intimating the amendment; the bill could not be enrolled if they did not accept the amendment. But if they

---

[1] Cf. on this point Excursus III, *infra*, pp. 243–245.

did agree to it, they endorsed the bill in the lower margin with the words 'Les Comuns sont assentus al sedule les Seigniors a mesme cel bille annexe', and the bill was then sent to the clerk.

A bill originating in the lords, if agreed to by them, was not endorsed, but was sent straight to the commons, who, if in agreement, endorsed it with the words 'Les Comuns sont assentus'. This endorsement proved that the bill had previously passed the lords.

Kirkby considered that the act in the case before the court was not good, for the lords had enlarged the term of the bill, but there was no mention in it of the commons' assent. Faukes explained that the lords had extended the term from one Pentecost to another, because the next occurrence of that feast, mentioned by the commons in the bill, fell within the time of the parliament itself—since every bill, notwithstanding its presentment at the end of a session, dated from the beginning of the parliament. The lords had therefore changed the term in accordance with the intent of the bill.

Prisot, J., then asked Faukes whether he could state that the bill was delivered [to the lords (?)] after Pentecost or not. Faukes answered in the affirmative, but Markham, J., enquired whether an enrolment was made of the date of the first receipt of bills, and he answered this question in the negative. Markham denounced this omission, and argued that if the lords had received the bill before Pentecost and amended it, it should have been sent back to the commons; but that if the lords had not received it until after the feast, it need not have been sent back to the commons. As it was, the question of the date of receipt could not be determined by the clerk's records.

Fortescue, however, said that the bill was an act of parliament, and they ought to be well advised before they annulled an act of parliament. Perhaps, he suggested, the matter should wait over until the next parliament, when they could be informed for certain about it by the parliament.

EXCURSUS II

THE THREEFOLD ASSENT TO ACTS
OF PARLIAMENT

Several *Year Book* reports are interesting as showing that the threefold assent was considered by the lawyers the essential criterion of an act of parliament. In *Y.B. 7 Henry VII*, Trin. pl. 1, for example, there is a long discussion on the question whether a certain grant in the form of letters patent in favour of the Provost and Scholars of King's College, Cambridge, which had been confirmed in parliament by Henry VII, was to be deemed royal letters patent or an act of parliament. Keble, Sjt., argued that the grant was only letters patent, for, to be an act of parliament, it was necessary that the commons should have granted, the lords assented, and the king have said 'Le Roi le veult',[1] and that it should have been enrolled. Then it would be a good act. A grant by the king by letters patent, with the authority of parliament, was only a royal grant. The commons, lords, and the king must participate in an act, for they were one body entire, and if one member of the body granted without the other, the grant could not be an act. A grant by the king himself in parliament was just the same as a grant by him outside it.

But Read, J., held that the grant was an act because it had been exemplified as such, and he observed that many statutes made no mention of assent. Exemplification,[2] however, according to Fineux, CJ., could not make that an act which was not by law already sufficient. An act of parliament, he said, was only a judgement; but the king, lords, and commons were necessary for making such a judgement, and none of them could be dispensed with. Vavasour, J., terminated this discussion by an account of procedure that he may have derived from Pilking-

---

[1] As the bill in question was private we should expect the royal response to have been 'Soit fait comme il est desiré'. Cf. *supra*, p. 219.

[2] *I.e.* sent out of chancery, under the great seal, usually to sheriffs, the chancellor of England and Ireland, and to the courts. Cf. *supra*, p. 230, n. 1.

ton's case. An act, he contended, was sufficient if it was a grant by the king with the assent of the lords and the commons. For every court was holden as was customary to hold it; thus the exchequer, king's bench, and common pleas were holden, and so was the court of parliament, which was the highest and worthiest court that the king had. The customary manner of making an act would be upheld. He had seen, he said, the clerk of parliament's being required to show the order and course of that court, what made an act and what did not. That order and course might begin with the commons, or with the lords; a bill went from one to the other, and then the king assented. An act affirmed by the king with the assent of the lords and commons was a good act, and the grant in dispute was a good act and could not be in better form.[1]

Four years later, in *Y.B.* 11 *Henry VII*, Trin. pl. 10, Danvers, J., is found asserting that a bill in parliament was endorsed with the royal assent, and was therefore an act of parliament. But Vavasour, J., insisted that the threefold assent was necessary for an act.[2]

Furthermore, the justices were, in 1489, prepared to assert that an act of attainder without the assent of the commons was invalid.

Thorpe's assertion, made a century earlier, to the effect that an ordinance made by the lords would be held for a statute (*Y.B.* 39 *Edward III*, Pas. pl. 3) does not militate against the conclusions of these cases. Whatever the meaning of this assertion, its early date would of course make it irrelevant to the period under discussion. But it can hardly mean that an ordinance of the lords *was* a statute. It merely signifies that such an ordinance would be held as a statute, *i.e.* would be enforced by the courts,[4] especially when (as in that case) it was supported by a royal writ. Moreover, the statement was made to meet a contention that no ordinance could restrain the effect of a statute unless assented to in full parliament by all the commons.[5]

[1] App. no. 90. [2] App. no. 100.
[3] *Y.B.* 4 *Henry VII*, Mich. pl. 11 (App. no. 81).
[4] Cf. Putnam, *The Enforcement of the Statute of Labourers*, where it is shown that it was the ordinance, not the statute of labourers, that was enforced in the courts until the reign of Richard II.
[5] App. no. 8.

EXCURSUS III

CRITICAL MEMORANDUM ON H. L. GRAY'S
THE INFLUENCE OF THE COMMONS
ON EARLY LEGISLATION (Harvard, 1932.)

1. Reviewers of Professor H. L. Gray's *The Influence of the Commons on Early Legislation* have pointed out that its value is not unmixed. It is, indeed, as Dr Lapsley says, 'an important addition to our knowledge of the procedure and institutional development of parliament in the 14th and 15th centuries';[1] and as Professor Pollard observes, 'it is a monument of patient industry devoted to the minute study of the fragmentary remains of the original MSS. of bills and petitions presented by the house of commons during the later middle ages, and to their comparison with the parliament rolls and statutes'.[2] But Dr Lapsley suggests that Professor Gray has not 'either covered the weakest side of his case or made the most of its strength';[3] and Professor Pollard affirms that 'his intense concentration on particular kinds of documents...has severely limited his circumspection and the evidential foundations on which his thesis rests'.[4]

Despite the merits of Professor Gray's analysis of the given documents, these criticisms of the conclusions which he reaches through that analysis are only too clearly and amply justified. To be sure, his demonstration of the identity of bill and petition, his exposure of the error in the accepted view that the bill *formam actus in se continens* was used by the commons before the 16th century, and his indication that the petition of 1414 was the outcome of the parliamentary events of the previous year, are all both convincing and important. Furthermore, a great deal of his statistical material—the material which forms the main body of the book, and which illuminates the relations of the various

---

[1] G. T. Lapsley in *E.H.R.* XLVIII (1933), 656–659.
[2] A. F. Pollard in *History*, XVIII (1933), 262–263. Cf. T. F. T. Plucknett in *Annual Survey of English Law* (1933), p. 23.
[3] *Op. cit.* 656.   [4] *Op. cit.* 262–263.

types of bills and petitions to parliament rolls and statute rolls
and to one another—must be taken into account by the constitutional historian. He states and solves a number of fruitful
problems in the diplomatics of parliamentary documents, during
the course of the investigation.

But statistics and diplomatic are not, after all, identical with
constitutional history, and one feels that Professor Gray funda-
mentally over-simplifies the larger constitutional questions to
which he professes to supply answers. Indeed, an underestimate of the complexity of constitutional history seems to lie
in the very conception of his book, and the unfortunate results
of this are sometimes aggravated by looseness of thought and
expression.

He conceives the book as an enquiry 'into the influence which
the commons as a body exerted upon the legislation of the
period';[1] but he states that his 'restricted objective' is to
'interpret the rolls of parliament in the light of the documents
from which the clerk of parliament compiled them'.[2] It is not
too much to say that an investigation of these materials alone,
despite all the wealth of information accruing from it, does not
and could not constitute the proposed enquiry. Leaving aside,
for the moment, the irrelevant though noteworthy point that the
enquiry, as termed, is really a problem in purely political and
not constitutional history, we need, for its solution, to know not
only what was the relation of parliament and statute rolls to
those documents, but also what were the forces which produced
those documents. In short, it is necessary to know precisely what
influences were at work *before* and *after* a commons' petition
became an approved bill. No amount of ingenuity expended
on the diplomatics of parliamentary records alone will provide
the required information. The most that such an investigation
will tell us is the proportion of bills initiated in the commons to
other bills enacted into statutes, together with sundry auxiliary
details. To establish this proportion, as Professor Gray does, is

[1] *Op. cit.* xiv.   *Ibid.* xvi.

to make a useful contribution to the history of parliamentary and legislative statistics. But it is important to bear in mind that no problem in constitutional history is thereby solved. For the essence of constitutional problems is always some question of rights—governmental rights—and of the relations of different sets of such rights to one another.

Professor Gray sometimes uses exaggerated terms which vitiate many of his widest constitutional generalisations. Thus, for example, he declares that 'The Revolution of 1399 directed against Richard's tyranny should logically have had an influence on the popular control of legislation. As a matter of fact the influence was very marked indeed. The accession of Henry IV ushered in the complete triumph of a movement which had had only discontinuous success during the preceding half-century. Throughout his reign and that of his son practically all legislation arose from commons petitions.'[1] But Professor Gray does not produce any evidence of the existence of a *popular control* of legislation, or of a triumph of any kind by the commons. The statistical summary of the relative *contributions* of commons' petitions and of official bills to legislation can provide no indication of *any* control, still less of a *popular* control, of it. It is idle to speak of a 'triumph' where no conflict between opposing forces has been shown. The mere fact that the number of commons' petitions contributing to legislation greatly exceeded that of any others so contributing is not proof of a popular control of legislation, because the possession and exercise of the right to initiate, however liberally used, is entirely different from the possession and exercise of an *exclusive* right to initiate (which there is no reason to suppose has ever been claimed by the commons),[2] and equally different from the possession and exercise of the right to amend proposals initiated by others than the commons (which there is no reason to suppose was enjoyed by the commons in the period nor for long after-

---

[1] *Op. cit.* 258. Cf. *ibid.* 235.
[2] Except, of course, money bills.

wards). Neither is this fact any proof of a legislative triumph on
the part of the commons, because it does not indicate that the
number of commons' petitions was maintained in the face of
opposition. If there had really been a popular control of
legislation and a legislative triumph for the commons, it would
hardly be necessary for Professor Gray to record the rejection of
large numbers of commons' bills by the king (or government)
and lords.

Moreover, the assumption that the commons' 'influence' was
necessarily 'popular' is inadmissible. Evidence of lordly and
government management of the commons during the period is
too extensive and well known to allow that. The whole questions
of electoral practice and malpractice, of the personnel of the
house, and of vested interests, must be investigated in detail
before the degree of 'popularity' of the commons' action on any
matter can be even estimated. Some of the contents of the
Paston Letters, alone, reveal the *naïveté* of Professor Gray's
statement that 'the origin of a public bill in one house or the
other presumably indicated whether the forces behind it were,
on the one hand, popular, or, on the other, aristocratic or
official'.[1] The forces behind private or public bills cannot be
presumed—they have to be ascertained.

2. A number of points in Professor Gray's conclusions seem
either to be arbitrary or to be arrived at by false logic. For
instance, one of the main themes of the book—the variations in
the alleged 'influence' of the commons in different decades—is
made to rest largely upon the varying proportions of commons'
bills to official bills.[2] To differentiate between bills initiated by
the commons and those initiated by others is sound enough, but
to differentiate between official and other bills is not. One does

[1] *Ibid.* 406. One of the objections against Richard II was that he had interfered
with the freedom of elections of knights of the shires, contrary to statute and
custom. (*Rot. Parl.* III, 420, no. 36.) Bales's *Chronicle* records that in 1452–3 the
commons at the parliament at Reading were displeased 'because they wer re-
strayned from free elecion of the knights of the shir' (*Six Town Chronicles*, 139–
140).

[2] *Op. cit. e.g.* 415.

not feel too confident about the existence of these official bills, or, if they did exist, about distinguishing them from any other lords' bills. They cannot, in any case, be said to have had any constitutional significance, for they were not, so far as we know, distinguished in procedure from any other bills introduced into lords or commons. They seem, at times, to have no existence whatever except in Professor Gray's classification, which, however, may have its legitimate purposes. It may be, as he assures us,[1] that 'it is not so clear that fifteenth-century bills which first appeared in the lords were drafted by that body and expressed its desires'. No doubt, as he says, 'nearly all bills which seem to have originated with the lords were of an administrative or official character'.[2] But because of this character, Professor Gray calls them 'official bills', and he appears to have no means of identifying as 'official' any given bill introduced into the lords, save by satisfying himself that it possesses this character. He of course admits that some bills introduced therein were 'genuine' lords' bills, and states that his nomenclature 'implies no more than that they (*i.e.* official bills) were as a rule drafted in the council rather than in that enlarged council which constituted the lords'.[3]

Now this view gives rise to two questions. In the first place, is there any satisfactory way of distinguishing official bills from other bills of an administrative character introduced into the lords (or, indeed, the commons)? Professor Gray's method of doing so seems rather disquietingly arbitrary. It looks as though he does so by confusing the subject-matter of a bill with its origin. He says, for instance, that because of their subject-matter, public bills originating in the lords may not inappropriately be referred to as official bills.[4] Leaving aside the additional confusion, in this assertion, of origination with presentation, it is difficult to see by what criterion official bills are distinguishable from other public lords' bills. It is not the

---

[1] *Op. cit.* 61.
[3] *Ibid.* 62.
[2] *Ibid. e.g.* 415.
[4] *Ibid.* 65.

impersonal address, for that is common to both; it is not any
verbal form, for neither has any monopoly of terms.[1] Professor
Gray, presumably, would say it is the 'subject-matter'; but the
subject-matter of both is the same or similar, since both dealt with
public affairs. No doubt in fact some public bills would originate
with the government and be presented in the lords; but the possibility of really differentiating them from other public bills is open
to serious doubt. We must remember, too, that probably it was
generally to the interest of the government to make 'official
bills' look as much like public lords' bills as they could.

In the second place, does not even the limited implication of
Professor Gray's view include rather too much?[2] It suggests
a sharper contrast and difference between the lords and the
government than is actually justified; and the unsoundness of this
inference is confirmed by Professor Gray's contrast of commons'
bills to official bills, by his assertion that one 'superseded the other
as the basis of legislation',[3] and by his inference of a 'popular
triumph'. Such language conjures up visions of a struggle between a popular assembly and some sort or other of a *chambre
administrative*. But if we follow Professor Gray too far into these
visions, or take his classification of bills too seriously, we shall
miss one of the fundamental characteristics of our constitutional
history. For a government bill is not, and never has been,
technically distinguishable from any other public bill introduced
into the same house.

We can admit the usefulness of an attempt to identify bills
which were drawn up by the government, in so far as the
identification is genuinely possible, and in so far as the government is distinct from the lords. But the dangers of this attempt
are shown by Professor Gray's readiness to project into a classification unknown to contemporaries ideas of his own equally
unknown to contemporaries. For he sees a constitutional
struggle where there was none. 'Commons bills,' he says, 'came
to supersede officially formulated measures as the basis of

---

[1] *Ibid.* 65 *et seq.*   [2] *V. supra*, 240.   [3] *Op. cit.* 65.

legislation.'[1] 'Royal legislation', he declares, 'had found a rival, and seemed threatened with being superseded by what may henceforth with propriety be called commons' legislation.'[2] 'The triumph of the representative body in initiating legislation', he assures us, 'was nearly complete.'[3] 'The commons', he believes, 'had brought it about that statutory legislation almost never arose except in response to their petitions.'[4] 'If', he avers, 'legislation arising from them (*i.e.* official bills) should prove to be more important than legislation arising from commons bills, we shall be face to face with a significant relation between the commons on the one hand, and the king, the council, and lords on the other.'[5] Furthermore, in a certain parliament, he tells us, the reliance upon official bills as the basis of legislation was so marked that it may correctly be thought of as an accepted procedure[6]—nay, by Henry VII's time, as an established custom. These expressions surely indicate that their author contemplates the existence of a struggle between the government and the commons for the right to initiate legislation. But the existence of this struggle is purely Berkeleian. It is to be found nowhere save in the author's mind.

Professor Gray makes, indeed, two serious mistakes in his treatment of this subject—one a common mistake, the other peculiar to himself. The first is the mistake of anachronism—the reading into records of the fifteenth century the ideas engendered by the constitutional controversies of later centuries. The second is the mistake of unwarrantably assuming that the fluctuations in his statistical results must register the varying fortune of constitutional rivalries. He believes that every bill which he records as having been initiated by the commons is a constitutional triumph for them, and that every bill which he supposes to have

[1] *Op. cit.* 163.   [2] *Ibid.* 223.   [3] *Ibid.* 253.   [4] *Ibid.* 263.
[5] *Ibid.* 118–119. What the significant relation is he does not state, and what it could be is difficult to see—unless merely the relation between one party energetic and enterprising enough to initiate important measures and another party not so energetic and enterprising; and this relation is not *constitutionally* significant, for assuredly either party *could* initiate *if* it wished.
[6] *Op. cit.* 148.

had an official origin is a constitutional disaster for them. But actually his figures record the operation of more humdrum causes. No grand constitutional battles are revealed by the vicissitudes in the proportion of official bills and commons' bills forming the basis of legislation, but merely the obscure workings of laziness, inertia, preoccupation, lack of enterprise, and legislative inefficiency on the part of one side or the other in different epochs. For there was not the slightest doubt throughout the period that both the commons and the government (or lords) had the *right* to initiate. Neither claimed an exclusive right to do so, and both exercised the right on innumerable occasions. The only question was, who was going to trouble to initiate at any given time? But this is decidedly *not* a constitutional question. In point of fact, as Professor Gray conclusively shows, the initiative happened to be taken more frequently by the commons than by the government in the Lancastrian period, and more frequently by the government than by the commons in the Yorkist period. The triumph of the commons, short-lived as it was, was not over any other part of the constitutional system, but merely over legislative inertia.

The question who was going to trouble to initiate is purely a question in political history, and it is very desirable to remember that when Professor Gray says 'the government was largely to replace the commons as the initiator of statutory legislation',[1] he is merely recording the course of political events. This course of political events ought not to be read as a reflection upon the constitutional position of the commons, who all through the period had the *right* to initiate, and *could* initiate whenever they chose to exercise the right. A good deal of confusion in the understanding of the constitutional history of the fifteenth century may be avoided by distinguishing as clearly as possible between the changes in constitutional rights and the trend of political events.

3. One of Professor Gray's minor, though interesting and not

---

[1] *Ibid.* 141.

altogether unimportant points, is his interpretation of the rubric *communes petitiones* found at the head of certain petitions enrolled on the rolls of parliament. He shows that those bills which were destined to become statutes were generally enrolled together under a single caption on the rolls. This rubric nearly always included the words *communes petitiones* or *communes petitions*, and he contends that these words 'point to a time when all or nearly all of the petitions following were probably (*sic*) commons bills'.[1] He therefore suggests that these words refer to the source of the bills. But, in the fifteenth century at least, as he himself indicates, not only commons' bills, but also official and lords' bills, were enrolled under this rubric, and, moreover, some commons' bills were enrolled before or after it. Nevertheless, all those bills —commons', official, or lords'—which were in fact enrolled under the rubric were distinguished from bills enrolled elsewhere by their capacity to become statutes, and most of them, but few if any of the others, appeared on the statute roll. These facts confirm the inherent improbability of Professor Gray's explanation of the caption. For it is, to say the least, unlikely that the clerks would have gone on year after year labelling a bundle of petitions as having originated in the commons when they knew very well a considerable portion of them had not so originated. Besides, it is not too clear that there ever was a time when it was expected that all or nearly all legislation would originate as commons' bills;[2] and the farther back we go, surely the less likely we are to find such a time. But finally, Professor Gray appears to mistake the meaning of the words *communes petitiones*, and his interpretation is open to fatal objections on linguistic grounds alone. For the word *communes*, in this caption, whether in Latin or in French, is certainly an adjective, and hence the caption must mean 'common petitions', instead of 'commons' petitions', as Professor Gray would have it. Thus, since this rubric correctly describes the petitions enrolled under it, whether in origin they were commons', official, or lords'—describes them, namely, as

[1] *Op. cit.* 115.   [2] *Ibid.* 161.

'common' in the sense of affecting the community at large—the rubric must have related not to the source of some of the petitions falling under it, but to the nature and probable future of all of them. The commons' petitions enrolled together were, for all practical purposes, public bills. To use the word 'common' for 'public' was quite usual; Kirkby, for example, when giving a technical description of parliamentary procedure in 1455, used the expression 'commune bill' to distinguish a public from a private bill.[1] Furthermore, the caption in later years became more or less stereotyped to read *communes petitiones exhibite...per communitates*, etc.; and though this description may not always have embraced every petition falling under it—whether any lords' bills are to be found under this particular formula, I do not know—the supposition that it is a mere tautology, as it obviously would be if the first two words meant commons' petitions and not common petitions, is of course absurd.[2]

4. Professor Gray throws considerable fresh light on the famous petition of 1414,[3] but some of his conclusions regarding the subject are questionable, and some of his inferences from them are more than questionable. The general tendency of his discussion of this subject is to reduce the constitutional importance that has hitherto been attached to the petition, and to exhibit it as a document that merely puts into writing an

[1] In Pilkington's case, *Y.B.* 33 *Henry VI*, Pas. pl. 8 (App. no. 30). *V. supra*, Excursus I.

[2] There is perhaps one small exception to Professor Pollard's statement (*loc. cit.* 262) that Professor Gray confuses petitions of the commons with common petitions *throughout* the book. For on p. 48 the antithesis between *petitiones communes* and *petitiones speciales* or *particulares*, at least, appears. But even on this very page the use of the words 'common' and 'commons' is hopelessly muddled. Thus he takes 'commons' petitions' to be synonymous with 'public bills', and contrasts them, as such, to private bills. His misunderstanding of the point is revealed by his explicit statement that 'it will be convenient to call the petitions of the commons commons petitions rather than common petitions', as though these two latter phrases had precisely the same meaning. The confusion is, I think, encouraged by his unfortunate decision to omit the apostrophe in the word *commons'*—an omission which sometimes occurs without any of the justification that its use in a technical expression might confer; *e.g.* 'commons influence' (*ibid.* 380).

[3] On this subject *v. supra*, Excursus IV to Chapter II.

established custom. His findings may be summarised thus: (1) There is no evidence of any marked divergence between the commons' petitions and the statutes based thereon for many years before 1414. (2) The petition of 1414 seems to have been elicited by the legislation of Henry V's first parliament (1413), which in fact did diverge considerably from the petitions upon which it was based. (3) The promise made by the Crown in response to the petition of 1414 was 'largely kept' during the reigns of Henry V and Henry VI. (4) This promise was 'less well kept' during the reign of Edward IV.[1]

Of these four points, I think Professor Gray conclusively establishes the first two, and they put the petition in a clearer perspective than it has been hitherto; but the second two are exceedingly doubtful. These second two points of course turn upon the question of amendments to commons' bills. A valuable part of Professor Gray's researches deals with these amendments, but even though he lucidly classifies them, he appears to underestimate their significance.[2] To limit the duration of a proposed statute, to reconcile it with existing law and obligations, to exempt persons or groups from its operation—such amendments as these, even though not radical, can hardly be considered insignificant;[3] and it is hard to see how any amendments of this kind, without the commons' assent, would not constitute a violation of the spirit, if not indeed of the letter, of the promise of 1414. Yet Professor Gray shows that their assent often was not sought, even in the reigns of Henry V and Henry VI.[4]

The more than questionable inference drawn by Professor Gray in this connexion which I referred to above, is that the petition was in some way bound up with a claim by the commons to an exclusive right of initiation. 'They assumed', he states, 'that no statute would be made except in response to their petitions.'[5] But actually this assumption is made by Professor

---

[1] *Op. cit.* 261 *et seq.*   [2] *Ibid.* 199.

[3] When amendments of exactly the same character were made in 1413, Professor Gray admits the 'change was serious' (*ibid.* 266).

[4] *Ibid.* 334; 168–169.   *Ibid.* 262

Gray himself, not by the commons; and he derives it, not from any objective evidence, but from his own unwarranted notion of the commons' control over legislation. For neither in the petition nor in the response to it is the slightest implication to be found of an *exclusive* right to initiate. In the petition the commons made only two claims, namely, to petition for legislation and to assent to it, with the corollary to assent to alterations in their bills before their enactment.[1] Since these claims do not, either of them, imply the right in question, Professor Gray's assumption must be gratuitous.

Dealing with another aspect of the subject of amendments to commons' bills, Professor Gray shows an unfortunate zeal in formulating wide generalisations on the slenderest evidential basis. He admits that he can discover only two 'unmistakeable instances' of the commons' assent to lords' amendments of their bills,[2] but nevertheless, he feels that this small (and actually dubious) evidence is adequate for a generalisation covering the whole topic. 'Since, however,' he says, 'it is difficult to suppose that some amended bills were sent back to the commons while others were not, it is best to infer that by 1439 the commons were usually asked to give their approval to any amendment to one of their bills'; and hence, he imagines, it follows that the commons' control over legislation in the first three decades of the reign of Henry VI was nearly complete.

The absurdity of such a conclusion is sufficiently obvious, all the more so when in fact the supposition which Professor Gray interposes between it and his alleged evidence for it is entirely unwarranted. This supposition, that either all or no amended bills were sent back to the commons, is flatly con-

---

[1] I omit the historical (or rather unhistorical) claims of having ever possessed these rights and of having ever been a part of parliament.

[2] *Op. cit.* 323. Four alleged instances are mentioned in all (321–324), coming from the years 1439 (2), 1442, 1444. As Professor Gray admits, the second two instances are mere guess-work, and cannot be counted. The first instance, moreover, is identified only by evidence of handwriting, and therefore cannot be altogether 'unmistakeable'; and the fourth instance, since it shows the royal assent to the special but not to the general request contained in the commons' petition, cannot be considered an example of normal procedure.

tradicted by excellent contemporary evidence to be found in no more recondite an authority than Pilkington's case.[1] In the course of that case Kirkby, master of the rolls, specifically stated that some amended commons' bills were sent back and others were not. Amendments which expanded the commons' proposals were sent back, but amendments which restricted such proposals were not sent back. Hence Professor Gray's supposition and conclusion are both quite untenable.

5. On the topic of statute and ordinance Professor Gray has some useful paragraphs, but as often happens in such discussions, he falls into some confusion by not consistently distinguishing names from things. Thus even though the terms 'ordinance' and 'statute' were used, as he says, synonymously, it does not follow, as he also says, that 'the distinctions elaborated by Hallam and Stubbs become inapplicable'.[2] For whatever the term used to designate each, two different types of measure (to employ a neutral word) undoubtedly emerged. The conversion of the ordinance of 1388 into a statute two years later, an incident which Professor Gray himself mentions, alone proves as much. The distinctions elaborated by Hallam and Stubbs—the distinctions between permanence and impermanence, between legislative and executive—if they are not too rigidly applied, still suggest probable disparities between the two types of measure.[3] Professor Gray seems to think that proclamation in the counties was the object aimed at in converting an ordinance into a statute;[4] but he certainly overestimates the importance of such proclamation. As early as 1362 it was definitely established that a statute was binding whether it had been proclaimed in the counties or not;[5] and proclamation cannot, therefore, be deemed a necessary attribute of statutes. The essential difference be-

---

[1] *Y.B.* 33 *Henry VI*, Pas. pl. 8 (App. no. 30), and Excursus I, *supra*.

[2] *Op. cit.* 384.

[3] On the whole subject *v. infra*, p. 269.   [4] *Op. cit.* 385–386.

[5] Thorpe, CJ., in *Y.B.* 39 *Edward III*, Pas. pl. 3 (App. no. 8). Professor Gray says (*loc. cit.*): 'Statutes were still looked upon as closely enough related to the law of the land to require proclamation in the counties.' Surely statutes always have been *part* of the law of the land.

tween the two types of measure lay in the respective degrees to which they were expected to modify the common law and to be applicable in the ordinary routine of the courts. This consideration was what determined the composition of the statute roll, as Professor Gray shows;[1] and the term 'statute', so far from being used less and less in the fifteenth century,[2] was really being used more and more as a technical term in the speech of the lawyers, and meant any act of parliament of which the courts had cognizance. The term 'statute' and the term 'act', which Professor Gray thinks were serious rivals, have both survived to this day; but 'statute' is primarily a word in legal vocabulary and 'act' is primarily a word in parliamentary language—the double usage has not, and never has had, at most, more significance than that. But then, Professor Gray seems fated to observe rivalries and struggles where none exist.

§ 3. THE CLASSIFICATION OF STATUTES

(i) *Statutes introductory of new law and statutes declaratory of old law*

A distinction between these two classes of statute is still common in jurisprudence and is still not entirely devoid of practical consequence. But it was a distinction of even greater importance in the seventeenth and eighteenth centuries than it is now. 'Of acts of parliament', wrote Coke, 'some be introductory of new law, and some be declaratory of the ancient law, and some be of both kinds by addition of greater penalties or the like.'[3] 'The very lock and key to set open the windows of the statute,' he declared, 'whereby it might be known whether the act were introductory of new law or affirmatory of the old, was to know what the common law was before the making of any statute.'[4] This same distinction, and the practical consequences of it, were elaborated a century and a half after Coke's time by Viner in his

---

[1] *E.g. op. cit.* 97.   [2] *Ibid.* 386.
[3] *IV Institute*, i.   [4] *Ibid.* vi.

treatment of statutory law. He stated that an enactment which was made in affirmance of common law, *i.e.* did not enact any new rule but merely enacted what had previously been provided for, though perhaps less clearly, was nevertheless a statute, and could be pleaded as such, even though the defendant had a plea at common law also. For such a statute enacted nothing contrary to common law, and could well stand with it.[1] A statute which introduced new law (and was also in the affirmative) implied the negative of all that was not in its purview, and it possessed, therefore, the force of negative words.[2] Further, such statutes, unlike statutes in the negative, did not repeal previous statutes on the same matter.

Viner further distinguishes between statutes, according as they are in the affirmative or the negative, and this distinction will be discussed in the next subsection of the present chapter. Here our purpose is to consider how far his and Coke's substantive distinction between introductory and declaratory statutes may have been current in the fifteenth century.

There can be no doubt that the distinction has a long history behind it, going back earlier than the fifteenth century, even though there is no evidence of the use of the actual terms of the classification earlier than the reign of Edward IV. Professor Plucknett has shown that during the reigns of the first three Edwards statutes were often admitted to be affirmations of common law. But exactly how often this admission was made is a doubtful and obscure matter. We cannot believe, as has sometimes been contended, that they were always supposed to be such.[3] Indeed Professor Plucknett goes so far as to assert that the use in the courts of the early fourteenth century of the terms 'special' and 'novel' to describe the statutes 'unmistakeably implies' the recognition of the making of new law by statutes. Special law, he argues, must have been something extraordinary, outside of the usual law, and radically different from

[1] *General Abridgement* (2nd ed.), XIX, 439, *s.v.* Statutes (A 2) 4.
[2] *Ibid.* 512.   [3] *V.* citations in Plucknett: *Statutes and their Interpretation*, 30.

it. The frequent occurrence of the term throughout the *Year Books*, he contends, shows how striking the contrast was felt to be between common law and the 'special law' which was then newly appearing. To hold that this statute law merely affirmed the common law is, he urges, to divest the word 'special' of all its meaning.[1]

But these arguments from the use of the words 'special' and 'novel' can be carried too far. We cannot be so certain that statute law was called 'special' because it made new law. The speciality which distinguished every statute from common law was not, after all, its newness, but its enactment, and it is at least likely that the lawyers in calling a statute 'special' were thinking of its enactment rather than its newness. The idea of 'speciality' does not necessarily include the idea of 'novelty' and if they were thinking primarily of the statute as new law, it is difficult to see why they should have called it 'special'.[2] Enactment and not novelty of the law enacted, was the one and only attribute that was shared by all statutes, and this attribute, sharply differentiating, as it did, statutes from common law, was quite sufficient and likely to give rise to the term 'special' law.[3]

Nor can we be too sure that the use of the term *novel ley* is in itself evidence of the recognition of new law-making. For 'law' and 'statute' were undoubtedly often convertible terms, and the phrase *novel ley* may therefore mean only 'new statute'. Since not all new statutes either were or were thought to be new law, it follows that not all allusions to 'novels leys' are to be relied upon as evidence of the recognition of actually new law.

Adequate evidence of the recognition of legislation proper comes only with the explicit contrasting of the new law of the

[1] *Ibid.*
[2] An instance, however, occurs in *Y.B.* 4 *Henry VI*, Mich. pl. 4 (App. no. 21) in which counsel is reported to have referred to 'le ley special, *scilicet*, le statute'.
[3] There seems to be no reason to doubt that the word 'special' had the same meaning in the fourteenth century as it has to-day (*v. N.E.D.*).

statute with ancient common law, though of course this contrasting is not in itself a classification of statutes. The whole subject of early legislation is made more difficult by the fact that in Bracton's time and for long afterwards, no clear distinction was drawn between law-making by judges and law-making by legislators, and we cannot always be sure whether our texts refer to the one or the other.[1] Nevertheless, in 1310, counsel stated in court that 'as one canon defeats many laws, so the statute defeats many things that were at common law',[2] and three decades later a contrast was made in court between common law and the law then in force.[3] Such contrasts were not infrequently made during the fourteenth century,[4] and it was said, although only in the course of political manœuvring, in the parliament of 1388, that the law of the land is made in parliament by the king, the lords spiritual and temporal, and all the community of the land.[5]

It is far from easy to multiply texts from the fifteenth century which show conclusively a recognition of new law-making by statutes. Some of the promising passages prove to be of ambiguous value when examined. For example, Beaufort addressed the parliament of 1414 in these terms: 'Le Roi...desirant tout dis la bone conservacion, governance et maintenance de la Pees, et de les bones leies de sa Terre, sans quelx null Roialme ne Paiis purra longement estere en prosperitee, et auxi pur faire autres leies de novell.'...[6] But we cannot be absolutely sure whether

---

[1] *V.*, for example, the passage quoted by Plucknett, *loc. cit.*, from Bracton, fo. 16.

[2] *Y.B. 4 Edward II*, Mich. pl. 51 (App. no. 1) cited in Plucknett, *op. cit.* 31.

[3] *Y.B. 13 Edward III*, Mich. pl. 15 (App. no. 2).

[4] Plucknett, *loc. cit.*

[5] *Rot. Parl.* III, 243, cited *ibid.* Article XV of the impeachment of Burley, Beauchamp, and their associates begins thus: 'Item la ou la ley de la terre est faite en parlement par le roi, et les seigneurs espirituels et temporels et tout la communalte du Roialme.' But cf. M. V. Clarke, 'Forfeitures and Treasons in 1388', *T.R.H.S.*, 4th series, XIV (1931), 65–95. This most illuminating article puts the whole of these proceedings in their proper political perspective. 'It is clear', Miss Clarke says (94), 'that statute law was not yet strong enough to bear a heavy strain, and that the magnates discarded it when it suited their purpose', and reverted to common law.

[6] *Rot. Parl.* IV, 15.

he was thinking of new law or merely of new statutes. A similar doubt attaches to Bishop Stafford's address in 1442, in which he said that the parliament had been summoned in order, among other objects, 'novas leges condere ac veteres leges ubi necessitas exigitet requirit renovare'....[1]

Bishop Pecock, the rational exegesist, was not very illuminating in such few remarks on legal topics as he made. He thought, however, that it was lawful for 'princis with his comounalte for to make politic and cyvyl lawis and ordinauncis for the better reuel of the people in temporal and cyvyl governauncis, longing unto worldli pees and prosperite and worldli welthe, to be the better therbi kept and contynued'.[2] Statements of this kind are of neutral value for our present purpose. Equally useless, but curious because of its wild exaggeration, is his assertion that parliamentary enactments were the very ground of *all* the laws of England.[3] Pecock, like Gascoigne, seems not to have been overlearned in the laws of the land.[4]

We have seen that Fortescue, unlike St Germain, does not explicitly admit in the theoretical part of his writings the making of actually new law by statutes.[5] But there is little room for doubt that this admission is to be found in the declaration by him on behalf of the judges in Thorpe's case in 1454 that

---

[1] *Ibid.* v, 35.

[2] *The Repressor*, ii, 454.

[3] *Ibid.* i, 21: 'If the king of Ynglond dwellid in Gascony and wolde sende a noble longe letter or epistle into Englond, both to iugis and to othere men, that ech of hem schulde kepe the pointis of the lawe of Englond, and thou3 he wolde reherce the pointis and gouernauncis, vertues and trouthis of the lawe for to remembre the iugis and the peple ther upon, and thou3 he schulde stire and prouoke, and exorte, bidde or counseile hem therto, 3it it ou3te not be seid that thilk epistle groundid eny of the lawis or gouernauncis of Englond, for her ground is had to hem bifore thilk epistle of the King, and that bi acte and decre of the hool parliament of Englond which is verry ground to alle the lawis of Englond, thou3 thilk epistle of the King or of the Duke had not be writun; and at the leest he in thilk bidding presupposeth the deedis to be knowen bifore of hem to whom he biddeth the deedis to be kept as lawis.'

[4] So far as Thorold Rogers's extracts from his MSS. do justice to Gascoigne's views, his interest in legal themes seems to have been confined to deploring the riches and numbers of lawyers. (*Loci e Libro Veritatum*, 109, 127.) Gascoigne was a versatile gossip-writer.

[5] *V. supra*, § 2.

parliament was so high and mighty in its nature that it might make law and unmake that which was law.[1] Further, he certainly admitted that parliament had powers of making law where existing law was defective.[2] The author of *Somnium Vigilantis* clearly stated that where the laws are insufficient to settle disputes, the king should, with the help of his council, make a law to meet the case.[3]

Entirely conclusive evidence, however, of the recognition of this power comes from the *Year Books* themselves. There are reports, shortly to be examined in more detail, which indicate clearly that the courts recognised that some statutes admittedly introduced new law, while others only declared the old.[4] Occasionally counsel spoke of 'this new statute, which makes a new law'.[5] We can thus be quite confident that the fact of law-making by statute was recognised during the century. The ancient notion that law to be good must be old was not merely decayed; it was dead. Poets, however, could still rhyme its dirge, and it seems that more new laws were made than were to every man's taste.

[1] *Rot. Parl.* v, 239. Cf. Pickthorn, *op. cit.* 141–166. Mr Pickthorn's discussion of law-making seems to suffer by an under-estimation of both the fact and the recognition of law-creation before Henry VII's time, and this is partly due to an apparent confusion of terms that occurs on p. 149. He there observes that a change in adjective law is as important as a change in substantive law, but in the very next paragraph he writes, 'The dispensing with indictment was to fifteenth-century minds (at any rate to politically active ones) a matter of this sort, or nearly, an interference with the machinery of law so profound that it was very nearly like an interference with law itself.' Very like indeed, to be sure, since the machinery or procedure of the law is and always has been part of the law.

I doubt very much whether the 'natural way of thinking and feeling' in Henry VII's time was that the state could not alter the law, as Mr Pickthorn implies, *ibid.* 135. The quotation he there gives from Professor Kern, like most of the latter's remarks, applies without modification only to the early middle ages, certainly not to fifteenth-century England. Cf. *supra*, p. 192, n. 2.

[2] *De Laudibus*, liii, 382, 'Et si que in regno illo dilationes in placitis, minus accommode fuerint usitate in omni parliamento amputari ille possunt, eciam et omnes leges alie in regno illo usitate, cum in aliquo claudicaverint in omni parliamento poterunt reformari.'

[3] *Loc. cit.* 518.

[4] *V.* especially *Y.B.* 13 *Edward IV*, Pas. pl. 5 (App. no. 58). *Y.B.* 15 *Edward IV*, Mich. pl. 17 (App. no. 61); 13 *Henry VII*, Mich. pl. 3 (App. no. 102).

[5] *Y.B.* 13 *Henry VII*, Mich. pl. 3 (App. no. 102).

In alle kyngdomes, here lawe is wryten,
For mede ne drede, þey chaung it nouʒt.
In Engeland, as all men wyten,
Lawe as best, is solde and bouʒt.
Eche ʒear newe lawe is wrouʒt,
And cloþe falsed in trouþe wede.
Fern ʒer was lawe, now nes it nouʒt.
We ben newe fangl, vnstable in dede.[1]

Nevertheless, at whatever date the recognition of law-making became common, it remains a matter of great difficulty to discover the existence of any very definite principles settling the relations of statute and common law until late in the fourteenth century, and the further study of the development of those principles is likely to await the modern editing of the later *Year Books*. Professor Plucknett, nevertheless, after his close study of the materials for the first half of the fourteenth century, was able to formulate two important generalisations upon the subject. There is, he finds, ample evidence for the view that the settled opinion of the courts was that a new statutory remedy did not abolish pre-existing common law.[2] Moreover, the general attitude of the courts was one of jealousy for the common law, which was not to be modified by statute more than could be avoided.[3]

---

[1] *Political and other Poems*, ed. Kail, I, 56: 'Deed is Working' (1414). Apparently the difficulty of enforcing statutes was still being felt at the end of the century. A certain rhymester put it thus:

'Many lawys and lytelle ryght,
Many acts of parlament,
And few kept wyth tru entent.'
(*Political Poems and Songs*, ed. T. Wright, II, 252.)

Even the judges (under the stimulus of refreshments) could think of good statutes, already enacted, most profitable to the realm—if only they could be put into operation (*Y.B.* I *Henry VII*, Mich. pl. 3) (App. no. 72). In this connexion it is significant that as late as 1404 such a town as Colchester could be exempted by patent from sending burgesses to parliament *provided* that they kept and supported all statutes and ordinances and charges made and granted in the said parliament. (*Cal. Pat. R.* II, 355, 13th March, 1404.)

[2] *Op. cit.* 131.

[3] *Ibid.* 134. This jealousy may be said still to exist to-day. There is always a presumption against the alteration of the fundamental principles of common law by statute.

With these generalisations from the fourteenth century as our background, we can proceed to survey the fifteenth-century evidence on the subject. This goes to show that the problem of the relation of statutes to common law had, by the end of that century, become intimately connected with the problem of classification. For the relation, whatever it was in earlier time, came to vary according as the statute was considered to be introductory or declaratory, affirmative or negative,[1] general or particular.[2]

The present writer has not found in the *Year Books* the use of the terms 'statutes introductory of new law' and 'statutes declaratory of the old law' earlier than the thirteenth year of Edward IV.[3] In a well-known case of that year the chancellor in the star chamber before the king's council pointed out that the matter then before them was complicated by the fact that the suitor was an alien. Such aliens, he said, were not accustomed to sue according to the law of the land, with trial by jury and other (common law) procedure. The alien merchant, he observed, would not be bound by statutes if they were introductory of new law, though he would be if they were declaratory of the old law, of the law of nature, etc.[4]

The persistence of this distinction between statutes is well illustrated by those cases in which counsel's argument turns on the question whether or not the given statute is in affirmance of common law. Such was a case in 1475 in which the nature of the famous *Statuta Prerogativa* was discussed. It was decided, as we have seen,[5] that these so-called *Statuta* were not statutes at all, though they were affirmances of common law. Discussion upon them does not, therefore, help very much towards the classification of statutes proper, but counsel's

---

[1] *V.* sub-section (ii), *infra.*   [2] *V.* sub-section (iii), *infra.*

[3] *Y.B.* 13 *Edward IV*, Pas. pl. 5 (App. no. 58). *V.* chapter III, § 1, *supra*, and Excursus III (p. 216). I do not find a reference to this case in W. E. Davies, *The English Law relating to Aliens* (1931).

[4] *Y.B. Ibid.*

[5] *Y.B.* 15 *Edward IV*, Mich. pl. 17 (App. no. 61). The case, it will be remembered, was one of wardship disputed between the king and the bishop of Ely.

arguments in the case antecedent to Littleton, J.'s judgement are not without their significance.

The curious feature of these arguments lies in the contention, on the one hand, that the *Statuta* were not statutory because they changed the law, and on the other that they were statutory precisely for that reason. Brian, Sjt., argued that if one of the so-called statutes were taken literally, the king would not have seisin of the lands of his tenant in socage dying without heirs, the contrary of which, he said, was law;[1] the statutes, therefore, were affirmances of common law. Nele, Sjt., on the opposite side, contended that in a previous case an advowson had been held to have passed to the king with a manor to which it was appurtenant, even though no mention had been made of the advowson in the feoffment, but that such practice was restrained by the *Statuta Prerogativa*,[2] which, therefore, were statutory and not in affirmance of the common law. Littleton, however, decided against the statutory character of the articles on grounds other than their relation to the common law. These grounds were, first, the absence of any mention of the time and place of their enactment; and, secondly, the fact that they had not been held effectual in all points as they would have been if they were statutory. These objections, no doubt, were fatal to the view that the articles were statutes in affirmance of common law, and fatal also to the view that they might be statutes introductory of new law.[3]

But this latter class of statute was one that might have to be considered. Thus later on in the century, Mordaunt in the course of argument reminded the court that various statutes were in confirmation of the common law and some of them provided a better remedy where a sufficient one had existed already at common law.[4] Later still, Sedgewick asserted that the common

---

[1] § iii of the *Statuta Prerogativa*.   [2] *Ibid.* § xvii.
[3] Cf. *Y.B.* 8 *Edward IV*, Pas. pl. 9 (App. no. 51) in which Pigot, Sjt., denied that the *Dies Communes in Banco* was a statutory affirmance of common law, though the Court had termed it a statute. Cf. *supra*, p. 44.
[4] *Y.B.* 7 *Henry VII*, Pas. pl. 2 (App. no. 89).

law might be enlarged by statute.[1] After a time, it became possible to question whether an admitted statute was in affirmance of common law or was introductory of new law. Hence, in the last decade of the century, the statute 4 Henry VII, c. 17, seemed to Mordaunt (then Serjeant) to be an affirmance of common law[2] (and therefore to be interpreted as widely as possible),[3] but to Butler it was a new statute which made new law.[4] A similar dispute arose upon statute 1 Henry VII, c. 1, and Serjeant Kingsmill[5] won acceptance for his view that a statute which abridged common law (therefore introductory of new law) was not to be interpreted equitably.[6]

There is thus no doubt of the importance, by the end of the century, of this classification of statute into the two categories of those introductory of new law and those declaratory of old law. We have seen that aliens would not be bound by the one but would be by the other, and, more important, a fundamental difference had arisen in the manner of interpreting the two classes of statute. The former class, it seems, was not to be interpreted equitably, but the latter was.

(ii) *Statutes in the affirmative and statutes in the negative*

Closely akin to this primary and (we may say) 'natural' classification of statutes is the classification of them according as they give a positive or a negative command. Just as any statute, whenever made, must in some sense or other either enact what is law already or enact new law, so also must it direct either that something shall be done or that something shall not be done; and must, accordingly, be couched either in affirmative or in negative words. We should expect, from the nature of the case, as a general rule, though only as a general rule, that those statutes which were intended or thought to be in

---

[1] *Y.B.* 12 *Henry VII*, Trin. pl. 1 (App. no. 101).
[2] *Y.B.* 13 *Henry VII*, Mich. pl. 3 (App. no. 102).
[3] For some discussion of this point, *v.* § 5, *infra.*   [4] *Y.B. ibid.*
[5] *Y.B.* 14 *Henry VII*, Hil. pl. 7 (App. no. 104).
[6] On the subject of equitable interpretation, *v. infra*, § 5.

affirmance of common law, would be expressed in affirmative terms; and that those statutes which were intended or thought to introduce new law, whether by defeating some rule of common law or by creating some fresh rule, would be expressed in negative terms. How often this coincidence between affirmation and affirmance, and between negation and introduction actually occurred is not worth prolonged enquiry. But at least it does seem clear that the time came when statutes in the affirmative were by general rule treated *as if* they were in affirmance of common law, and when statutes in the negative were by general rule treated *as if* they were introductory of new law.

This treatment is, in effect, the rule—and not a recent rule— propounded by Coke and by Viner. Coke considered it a maxim in the common law that a statute in the affirmative, without any negative expressed or implied, did not take away common law,[1] nor repeal previous statutes in the affirmative. Viner repeats and develops Coke's doctrines. A statute in the affirmative, he says, seldom or never worked a change in the common law, unless by addition or confirmation;[2] it did not take away common law,[3] nor the remedies thereby given;[4] nor did it defeat the king's prerogative at common law,[5] nor bind him unless specially named.[6] But a statute in the negative, on the other hand, bound or superseded the common law.[7] Coke, to be sure, had distinguished between negative statutes declaratory of common law and negative statutes introductory of new law, so that negation and introduction did not always go together.[8] But

---

[1] *II Institutes, sub. tit.* Westminster I, c. 20 (4): 'For it is a maxime in the common law, that a statute made in the affirmative without any negative expressed or implied, doth not take away the common law; and therefore in this case the plaintiff may either have his remedy by the common law or upon the statute; if he bring his action of trespass generally without grounding the same upon the statute, then he waiveth the benefit of the statute, or taketh his remedy by the common law.' *V.* also *ibid., sub. tit.* Gloucester, c. 8 (6), Westminster II, c. 38 (9), c. 45 (11), and 6 *Co. Rep.*, 115, 119 (Dr Foster's Case).

[2] *General Abridgement*, XIX, Statutes E 6, 510 (3).   [3] *Ibid.* 511 (2).
[4] *Ibid.* (11).   [5] *Ibid.* 533 n.   [6] *Ibid.* (8).   [7] *Ibid.* 511 (5).
[8] It should, however, also be noted that Matthew Bacon in his *New Abridgement* (1738) mentions that if an *affirmative* statute introductory of a *new* law directs a thing to be done in a certain manner, that thing shall not, even though there are no negative words in the statute, be done in any other manner. (*Sub. tit.* Statutes, 641.)

Viner points out that prescription had been held invalid against both kinds of negative statute,[1] though valid against affirmative statutes.[2] Our proposition that negative statutes were treated *as if* they were introductory of new law is, therefore, not defeated by Coke's differentiation. In short, as Viner observes, negative statutes were 'more strong' than affirmative ones, though, like those, they did not bind the king without express words.[3]

The early history of this classification of statutes is extremely obscure. Professor Plucknett's study of the *Year Books* of the first half of the fourteenth century throws no light on the subject.[4] Perhaps the legal sources of the second half of that century, if suitably examined, would disclose the origin of the differentiation. It is possible that a close investigation of the *Year Books* of the fifteenth century would illustrate its early history. But the present writer, following up the clues that the various abridgements give, has not discovered a definite reference in the *Year Books* to a distinction between statutes in the affirmative and in the negative earlier than the fifth year of Edward IV.[5]

---

[1] *Op. cit.* 522 (102).

[2] *Ibid.* The customs of London, nevertheless, were thought to be of sufficient force to stand against even a negative statute (*ibid.* 511 (10)). Cf. p. 285, n. 4, *infra.*

[3] *Ibid.* 533 (8).

[4] The section therein (42–43) on *Words of Prohibition* does not help for our purpose.

[5] In this connection, as in others, we have to accept with caution, or reject with regret, some of the rubrics which the sixteenth-century compilers of abridgements applied to cases from the earlier *Year Books*. For example, Brooke, in his section on Parliament and Statutes (no. 29), attached to his abridgement of *Y.B.* 36 *Henry VI*, pl. 2 (fo. 2) (App. no. 34) a marginal note and a statement which seem to suggest that this case affords the earliest instance of the distinction between affirmative and negative statutes. His marginal note runs, 'Statutes in affirmative ne tolle le comen ley', and his abridgement runs thus: 'Nota que ou acte de parliament est fait in affirmative, come ou le common ley fuit, que si home recovera debt ou damages et ne sua execucion *infra annum proximum*, etc., il fuit mise a novel original, car nul *scire facias* fuit al comon ley in ceo case, et Lestatut de Westminster 2 cap. 45, *quia de his que recordata sunt*, etc., done *scire facias*, mes pur ceo que ceo est in l'affirmative que il poet aver *scire facias* post annum, ideo ces ne tolle le brief de dette, mes que le partie poet aver brief de dette de ceo arrer *post annum, ut* al common ley, et *sic habetur ibidem*, quar fuit accion de dette parte sur un recognisance et bene, et ne fuit acte a un *scire facias*.' Now this may be a fair statement of the gist of the case, but in the report there is no allusion of any kind to the fact that the statute is in the affirmative. One supposes, therefore, that Brooke added to this abridgement the marginal note, and a reason for the decision, which were familiar to him, but not to the counsel in the case. One cannot, therefore, count this case as evidence for the subject under review.

This instance is to be found in a case which, in its bearings on the question of the royal prerogative, has already been examined in some detail above.[1] In the course of it, Choke, J., discussed some aspects of one of the statutes of safe-conducts.[2] He said that safe-conducts were sometimes issued without the specification of all the particulars required by that act, but they were nevertheless held to be sufficient. The statute, he supposed, had been aimed at the restraint of the issue of general safe-conducts, but, at that time, it was not held to restrict the king. According to some, that was so because the statute was only in the affirmative, and the king could there-fore at his choice do one thing or the other, and either would be good, notwithstanding the statute. But, if the statute had been in the negative, some said that it would have been otherwise.

Choke's language in this case suggests that this is at least a very early instance of the distinction between affirmative and negative statutes. Evidently he was cautious in attributing the reason for the king's option to the verbal differences in statutes. He himself did not even adopt such an explanation. He noted that the king was not held to be restricted by the statute, and merely stated that some people asserted that this freedom was due to the affirmative character of the statute, and that a negative statute would have had the opposite effect. It thus seems that the distinction had not yet been embodied in a definite rule, though obviously it was beginning to make an impression on the judicial mind.

But, only five years later, Choke himself is found formulating one of those rules on the subject that were prominent in the following century. He laid it down that if a statute which gave a process was in the affirmative, a party might choose either this statutory process or process at common law, but if such a statute were in the negative, then there was no choice, and the

---

[1] *Y.B.* 5 *Edward IV*, Pas. fo. 32–34 (App. no. 46). Cf. *supra*, p. 47.
[2] 15 Henry VI, c. 3.

statutory process must be employed.[1] Thus by the 1470's at any rate, affirmative and negative statutes had become sharply differentiated; the former did not abolish remedy at common law,[2] but the latter did. Affirmative statutes, that is to say, were being treated *as if* they were simply declaratory of common law; whereas negative statutes were being treated *as if* they were introductory of new law.

Then, just as we found above that declaratory statutes were being interpreted equitably and introductory statutes interpreted strictly, so we find an opinion, at least, that the same interpretational distinction applied as between affirmative and negative statutes.[3] To this aspect of the classification we must direct attention in a following section. Here we may note that by the end of the century the classification of statutes according as they were affirmative or negative must have been of first-rate importance to litigants.[4]

(iii) *Statutes general and statutes particular*

Statutes were, in Coke's exposition, not only introductory or declaratory, and affirmative or negative, but also general or particular.[5] This, then, is the third and last dividing distinction

---

[1] *Y.B.* 10 *Edward IV*, Pas. pl. 18 (App. no. 55). The case appears in the Selden Society Year Book series in the volume edited by Miss N. Neilson (Selden Society, XLVII, 63–67, pl. 17). The case is Trespass by cattle taken '*vi et armis*'. The defendant avowed the taking for arrears of service; he obtained judgement but there was no execution. The plaintiff in this suit, now defendant in a second suit, pleads that he is lord, and that for him to pay a fine will be against the statute of '*non puniatur dominus*' (Statute of Marlborough, 51 Henry III, c. 3). Since the statute is in the negative, he has not waived his right to appeal to the statute by his pleading to the writ, and the writ abates. Choke went on to assert that if the king appointed a justice of the peace in a town, the authority of a justice of the county would continue in that town, if the second patent were in the affirmative. But this doctrine, according to the reporter, was denied.

[2] Vavasour, J., is found, a few years later, contending that a statute in the affirmative does not defeat anything. (*Y.B.* 4 *Henry VII*, Trin. pl. 6 (App. no. 82)).

[3] *Y.B.* 22 *Edward IV*, Pas. pl. 30 (App. no. 64). Cf. *supra*, p. 258, and *infra*, § 5.

[4] It is interesting to compare with these doctrines Pecock's distinction between the binding force of negative and affirmative commands of God. The former, he held, were binding absolutely, the latter only relatively (*v. Repressor*, II, 505).

[5] *IV Institutes*, iii.

among statutes. As in the case of the first two distinctions, we find this one also well developed by the end of the fifteenth century.

Several reports illustrate both the distinction and its consequential rules. Thus Hody, CJKB., ruled in 1441 that a certain statute was made by authority of parliament, and was general as well within franchises as without, since by its authority a writ could issue to a franchise, notwithstanding the franchise.[1] A few years later Prisot, J., denied that a certain act of resumption was a general act, for it contained exceptions and therefore could not be a general act.[2] A private or particular act (providing for the repayment to the mayor and constables of a Staple of their loan to the king) did not, in the opinion of the court, extend to all men as if it were general.[3] In 1474, the court ruled that it had no cognizance of an act which declared void all incorporations and licences granted by Henry VI, any more than it had of any particular act made for any particular person. The said act was not general, but a 'particular in a generality'. If an act provided for all corporations, or all bishops, or all lords, it was a particular act. But when an act was general, *i.e.* when it extended to every man, it need not be pleaded, for it was common and general law.[4]

Again, as in the other two classifications of statute, a difference in interpretation was involved in this distinction between general and particular statutes. A general act made for the common profit of the realm was to be interpreted equitably, but a particular one strictly.[5]

---

[1] *Y.B.* 19 *Henry VI*, Mich. pl. 2 (App. no. 23 (ii)). The point of this case was the question whether an outlawry was void when the outlawed person lived in a county different from that in which the appeal had been brought, contrary, it was alleged, to the statute of the third year of Henry VI (actually 6 Henry VI, c. 2). It was decided nothing could be done in the matter save on a writ of error. The appellee (apparently pleading in person) seems to have been a trifle dense, judging from his dialogue with Hody.

[2] *Y.B.* 34 *Henry VI*, Pas. pl. 1 (App. no. 32).

[3] *Y.B.* 37 *Henry VI*, Hil. pl. 5 (App. no. 38).

[4] *Y.B.* 13 *Edward IV*, Pas. pl. 4 (App. no. 57).

[5] *Y.B.* 14 *Edward IV*, Mich. pl. 1 (App. no. 59).

The distinguishing marks, from the procedural standpoint, of these two types of statute are thus clear. The court was deemed to have cognizance of general statutes;[1] they did not require pleading; the burden of proving or disproving their existence rested not upon the resource of the pleader, but upon the erudition of the court. But particular (or private) statutes were in exactly the opposite position. The court assumed no knowledge of them; they must be specifically pleaded and their authenticity established by the pleader. Moreover, a general statute could be interpreted equitably by the court, but a particular statute would be interpreted *stricti juris*.

§ 4. The effective scope of statutes

In the foregoing sections a survey has been made of the place of statutes in legal theory, of the processes of statute-making, and of the classification of statutes. We now have to consider what in fact statute-law could do; what its effective duration was; to what extent it possessed binding force over territories and over persons; how it stood in relation to royal letters patent if these conflicted with it; how, in general terms, it stood with the law of the church, with the common law of the land, and with certain other bodies of law.

[1] For the interest of the Pastons in this technical point, see *Paston Letters*, ed. Gairdner, II, no. 540, Clement Paston to John Paston, 18th March, 1466: '...And as for 3our question of the patentes, Grenfeld and Catesby (Serjeants) and Starkey (counsel) holdyn it a good question, for the Statute is, *Patentes dez tenements dount null titill est trouve pur le roy de recorde sount voydez, anno xviii. H. VI, ca. vj*. But I trowe in 3our cas that be ther opiniounis the Acte of Parlement is a tytill of recorde. It is said to the contrary intent, thow the londs be forfetyed of record, yet ther is no certificacion of recorde qwat londes they be, nor wer nor in qwat place they bye; but and thys clawse be in the patents, *Non obstante quod nulla inquisicio pro nobis inde est inventa*, by Grenfelde is consayle the patents xwlde be clerly goode. But me semythe that amendyt not the mater, for be for the makyng of the statute above sayde, patents graunttyd of londs be fore inquisicion were goode and effectuell and the statute is generall: *Patents dount null tytill etc. sount voydez*. Thanne it folowyt well if the Acte of Parlement be no tytill for the Kyng thann is ther no tytill for the Kyng of recorde, for that clawse in the patente is no tytill; than if ther (be) no tytill, *ergo* the patents voyde?'

(i) *Duration and repeal*[1]

As late as 1464 it was still arguable in the courts that, if a statute were no longer put into operation, it ceased to be effective law. But this proposition was flatly overruled by Choke, Illingworth and Yelverton in the exchequer chamber. The mere fact that a certain statute had not yet been enforced, they said, was of no consequence. Even if there were many articles in the statute books that had never been applied, it did not follow that they were void. For they were still law, and could be put into execution by any man who was aggrieved contrary to them.[2]

This ruling established beyond question that a statute could not fall into desuetude. Its binding force did not lapse with the passage of time; it remained effective unless and until repealed. But could a statute once made be repealed at all?

For a decade or so after 1388 this might have been a very grave question for any one attempting to bring about the repeal of certain statutes. The Merciless Parliament of 1388, for the convenience of the party that dominated it, announced that parliament was supreme, and could override all the laws and courts in the land; and equally for the party convenience, it proceeded tacitly to disregard the statute of treasons of 1352, prosecuted its victim by common law powers and procedure, and declared that any persons taking part in the repeal of the provisions of the parliament were traitors and were to be visited with the penalties of treason. It thus simultaneously declared that parliament was supreme and that the next parliament would be guilty of treason if it exercised its supremacy over the measures taken by its predecessors. It perpetrated, that is to say, the constitutional paradox of declaring that parliament was supreme, but could bind its successor, which by definition

---

[1] For an account of this subject, see R. B. Merriman, 'Control by National Assemblies of the Repeal of Legislation in the Later Middle Ages', in *Mélanges D'Histoire offerts à M. Charles Bémont.*

[2] *Y.B.* 4 *Edward IV*, Pas. pl. 4 (App. no. 45).

was also supreme.[1] Again, in 1397, political manœuvring, even though from the opposite side, led the parliament to swear solemn oaths not to repeal its own measures.

But the first parliament of Henry IV, whilst it lost no time in confirming the acts of 1388, including its declaration of supremacy, reserved the right to deliberate on some of those acts and to recommend the repeal of any of them. Before long in the same session, it proceeded to repeal the offensive article which made repeal a treason, 'as a thing dishonest and against the estate of the realm'.[2] The power and the right of parliament to repeal was not again seriously disputed,[3] and we can say that in the fifteenth century every statute was deemed to be effective unless and until it was repealed by parliament,[4] which alone could repeal its own statutes. Parliament might err, but it alone could revise its errors.[5]

(ii) *Binding force : territories*

We cannot suppose that there remained in the fifteenth century any refuges of feudal independence in England that were held to be exempt from the rule of statutory law. Hody, CJ.,

---

[1] *V.* M. V. Clarke, 'Forfeitures and Treasons', *loc. cit.*

[2] *Rot. Parl.* III, 425, 442. Cf. Lapsley, 'Parliamentary Title of Henry IV', *E.H.R.* XLIX, 585.

[3] Or perhaps, we should say, has not been successfully attacked. For example, the Acts of Union with Scotland and Ireland were intended to be unrepealable, but the attempt to make them so, and all other similar attempts have, as Dicey shows, been unsuccessful. (*Law of the Constitution*, 8th ed. 63 *et seq.*)

[4] *V.,* for example, Henry VI's letter to Pope Alexander V, quoted *supra*, pp. 59, 117. The principle stands out clearly in *Y.B.* I *Henry VII*, Hil. pl. 1 (App. no. 75). All the justices in the exchequer chamber, by command of the king, discussed the reversal and destruction of the act which bastardised the children of Edward IV and his wife. This act was considered so scandalous that they were unwilling to rehearse it, and advised against its recital in the repealing act in order to avoid the perpetuation of its terms. '*Nota* icy bien le policy', wrote the reporter. '*Nota* ensement,' he continued, 'que il (*i.e.* the offensive act) ne puissoit estre pris hors del record sans act de le parliament pur l'indemnity et jeopardie d'eux qui avoient les records in lour gard.' The authority of parliament was needed to discharge them. The lords in the parliament chamber thought well of this counsel, and some of them wished to summon the bishop of Bath (Stillington), who had made the false bill, to answer for it, but the king said he had pardoned him and did not wish to proceed against him.

[5] *Y.B.* 21 *Edward III*, Mich. pl. 46 (App. no. 6).

clearly ruled in 1441 that general statutes were valid as well within franchises as without,[1] and the historian of the county palatine of Durham has shown that the validity of statutes was never doubted in that franchise.[2]

But it might not always be so clear that all other parts of the king's domains were equally bound. Brooke, for instance, states in his Abridgement that it was sometimes held that Wales and the counties palatine, which did not send representatives to parliament, were not bound by it. This view, however, he shows was incorrect,[3] even though certain statutes or parts of them were not applied to those territories or were inapplicable to them.[4] Indeed, there is ample evidence to show that parliament could bind all the king's domains, whether or not they were represented in it, and it doubtless did so because it remained as it had begun before it acquired a representative character—the king's council, and the organ of the king's authority.[5] The presentation to parliament of petitions from various domains outside England was common from an early date.

Wales, despite the great statute of 1284,[6] was not regarded as a part of the realm of England before Henry VIII's Act of 1536,[7] and except on two occasions in Edward II's reign, it did

[1] *Y.B.* 19 *Henry VI*, Mich. pl. 2 (App. no. 23 (ii)).

[2] G. T. Lapsley, *The County Palatine of Durham*, 126–127.

[3] *Sub. tit.* 'Parliament and Statutes', no. 101, on *Y.B.* 8 *Henry VI*, Hil. pl. 36 (App. no. 22).

[4] An instance of this technical difficulty is to be found in *Y.B.* 31 *Henry VI*, Mich. pl. 8 (App. no. 28). A writ of *capias* on the statute 6 Henry VI issued to the County Palatine of Chester. But the statute provided that the writ should issue to the sheriff of the county, and Chester, not being a county, was out of the statute.

[5] Professor R. L. Schuyler establishes these facts in the first chapter of his *Parliament and the British Empire*.

[6] The statute of 1284 was not parliamentary. Edward I ordained it with the advice only of his nobles.

[7] *Y.B.* 19 *Henry VI*, Mich. pl. 31 (App. no. 24), includes a discussion of the differences between the legal position of Wales and of counties palatine. Wales, said Fortescue, then serjeant, had once been a kingdom, but Lancaster, Durham, and Chester derived from the crown, and had once been in the common law of all the realm. Hence it was that the king could command a trial to be held according to common law in them, but not in Wales. Ascogh, J., observed that if an erroneous judgement were made in a county palatine, it could be redressed in the king's court, but if the error had occurred in Wales, it could not be amended in any court in the realm, save only in parliament.

not send any representatives to the English parliament in the mediaeval period. Nevertheless, as Professor Schuyler has effectively shown, parliament legislated for Wales on numerous occasions in the fifteenth century,[1] and even the great act of 1536 was passed by a parliament which included no Welsh representatives.

Ireland was in a like case, and many statutes were passed from the end of the thirteenth century expressly naming that country.[2] Gascony was treated in the same way,[3] and so was Calais.[4] There was, in fact, no doubt that Wales, Ireland, Calais, Gascony, and Guienne, so long as their inhabitants were subjects of the king, could be bound by the statutes of the English parliament, and that persons obedient to the English admiral on the high seas were bound.[5]

(iii) *Binding force: persons*

We have seen that there survived well into the fifteenth century a notion that an act of parliament did not necessarily bind everyone. Serjeant Markham argued in 1441 that the rector of Eddington, who possessed a charter of exemption from taxation, was not bound by a grant made by parliament, because acts of a corporation did not override the rights of the individual members in their private capacity.[6] But this theory was not very favourably received by the court; and, although emphatic statements, made from time to time in court that acts or statutes bound everyone, suggest that the contrary opinion was not dead, we cannot doubt that by the middle of the century at least the orthodox view was that statutes bound all

---

[1] *E.g.* statutes 2 Henry IV, c. 17; 5 Henry IV, c. 15; 2 Henry VI, c. 4.

[2] Schuyler, *op. cit.* 33 *et seq.*

[3] *Ibid.*, and statutes 27 Edward III, st. 2, c. 3; 42 Edward III, c. 8; 23 Henry VI, c. 17.

[4] *Ibid.* and statutes 1 Henry V, c. 9; 9 Henry V, st. 2, c. 6; 27 Henry VI, c. 2; 1 Henry VII, cc. 3, 8. Calais, it will be remembered, actually was represented in the English parliament from 1536 (or perhaps 1542) until 1555.

[5] *Y.B.* 2 *Richard III*, Mich. pl. 26 (App. no. 68); *Y.B.* 20 *Henry VI*, Mich. pl. 17 (App. no. 26). The section in the text above should be read in conjunction with the discussion by Professor Schuyler, *op. cit.*

[6] *Y.B.* 19 *Henry VI*, Pas. pl. 1 (App. no. 25).

ordinary persons in those territories admittedly under the jurisdiction of the king in parliament. Serjeant Laicon, in 1463, argued, with the approval of the court, that by such a record as an act of parliament every man was bound, because every man was party to it.[1] A general statute admittedly extended to every man.[2] Every man to whom a statute extended (*i.e.* whether general or not) was bound by it, for every man was party and privy to it.[3]

But not all persons were ordinary, and those who were not, might not be so bound. It was not clear that aliens were bound by all English statutes, nor that they were supposed even to know them.[4] That very extraordinary person, the king, was not bound at all by statutes unless he was expressly named.[5]

(iv) *Statutes and other law*

(*a*) Statutes and ordinances.

Much controversy has centred, during many generations, upon the question of the differences between statutes and ordinances, and in some measure the controversy still continues. Nevertheless, most of the important evidence for the subject has been well known for many years, and it seems hardly likely that much fresh material of fundamental significance will be forthcoming. A reasonable settlement of the controversy, therefore, ought to be well within the bounds of possibility at no distant date, and seems to depend largely upon a clarification of the issues involved. As in many disputes of the kind, part of the difficulty has arisen not so much from the available evidence itself as from the confusion of names with things, from insufficient allowance for the mediaeval habit of indulgence in synonyms,

---

[1] *Y.B.* 3 *Edward IV*. Trin. pl. 1 (App. no. 43).
[2] *Y.B.* 13 *Edward IV*, Pas. pl. 4 (App. no. 57).
[3] *Y.B.* 21 *Edward IV*, Mich. pl. 6 (App. no. 63).
[4] *Y.B.* 13 *Edward IV*, Pas. pl. 5 (App. no. 58).
[5] *Y.B.* 35 *Henry VI*, Trin. pl. 1 (App. no. 33); *Y.B.* 12 *Henry VII*, Trin. pl. 1 (App. no. 101 (ii)).

and from the inadequate appreciation of the fact that though names may remain constant, the things which those names designate often change with the lapse of years.

A detailed review of the controversy is not necessary for the present purpose, but we do need to arrive at some conclusions as to how the matter stands for the fifteenth century, and must therefore take some account of the views that have been held regarding it, and to consider the position of statutes and ordinances as it was in the preceding century.

Stated in the baldest terms, the controversy rages between those who side with Prynne, and those who do not. Prynne took the view that there was no difference between statute and ordinance, but, despite certain modern and even recent tendencies to follow him, the greater weight of authority, from Coke onwards, is against an unqualified acceptance of his opinion.

Hallam, to-day a somewhat neglected, but none the less always a judicious scholar, certainly lent no support to such a view, and the evidence which he adduced appears to be unassailably in favour of part at least of his theory. He pointed out that during the reign of Edward III, though an ordinance could not be defined as a provision made without the assent of the commons, even if such a description was sometimes correct, none the less ordinances, distinct from statutes, did emanate from king, lords, and commons. The fact that the two terms were often used synonymously did not detract from this conclusion. He justly emphasised the reluctance of the time to innovate in the law without necessity, and he saw in this reluctance the root of the distinction between statute and ordinance; indeed, he went so far as to say that if it were not for the intended particular and sometimes temporary operation of ordinances, they could not well be distinguished from statutes. Ordinances, he observed, were often established in great councils, but provisions which altered the common law or any former statute, and were entered on the statute rolls as general obligatory enactments, did require, he was convinced, the assent of the three estates duly summoned.[1]

However correct these distinctions may or may not be, the fact that the commons were asked in 1363 to state whether they would have a certain sumptuary law enacted in the form of statute or ordinance is assuredly conclusive evidence that by that date, at any rate, two different types of enactment were possible, even though the terms continued to be used synonymously; and the reply of the commons to the question is conclusive evidence of the temporary and mutable nature of an ordinance as compared with a statute.[2]

Stubbs adopted, in the main, the same view of the matter as Hallam. He repeated the fact that ordinances might be issued by king and council without assent of the whole parliament, and noticed that the perpetuation of an ordinance by making it a statute had been the subject of a commons' petition. He discerned differences between the two types of enactment that led him to regard an ordinance as generally what we should call an executive or administrative provision, and a statute as generally what we should call a legislative one.[3]

Professor McIlwain followed the same line of argument, and held that, though a distinction could not be traced back beyond Edward I's time, statute and ordinance were clearly differentiated by Edward III's reign.[4] But he proceeded to overstate the distinction by asserting that not only were statutes the more permanent of the two, but that they also enacted new law, whereas ordinances merely declared old law, and he added to this view a further untenable proposition to the effect that though all enactments on the statute roll were statutes, all other enactments were ordinances. Professor McIlwain's views incurred the criticism—stated perhaps with insufficient discrimination—of

[1] *View of the State of Europe during the Middle Ages*, VIII, pt. II, § 12 (ii).
[2] *Rot. Parl.* II, 280.
[3] *Const. Hist.* II, 221, 232, 259, 292.
[4] *High Court of Parliament*, 313 *et seq*. Cf. *Magna Carta Commemoration Essays*, 161 *et seq*.

Professor Plucknett, who not only abandoned them but also strongly asserted that 'there is no contrast expressed or distinction visible between statute and ordinance in our period'.[1] Professor Plucknett, however, was careful to add that he spoke of nothing outside of his period, which he appears to have rigidly terminated, for this subject, at 1350; and he added also, in a footnote, that there were traces of a distinction shortly after that period, a distinction which he attributed to the growth of differentiation between great councils and parliament.[2] For the period 1300–50, therefore, he regarded statute and ordinance as no more than synonymous terms.

But, as Professor Hazeltine observed, Professors McIlwain and Plucknett based their views on quite different materials,[3] and we may well add, were apparently thinking of different periods. Even so, we perhaps feel that Professor Plucknett's strong statement that 'no contrast is expressed or distinction visible' between statute and ordinance, 'during the period', should be qualified by the addition of the words 'in the *Year Books*'. For it is perfectly clear that the contrast was expressed and a distinction *was* visible, very shortly indeed after 1350, and we can scarcely suppose that these occurrences were sudden and totally unprecedented during the previous half-century.

Yet Tout was inclined to believe that there was something comparatively sudden in the emergence of the distinction. He noticed the use of the term 'statute' for the household ordinance of 1300, and justly considered this should make us chary of pushing back the distinction earlier than the reign of Edward III,[4] though indeed, in a previous work he stated (rather more reasonably) that the growing distinction during Edward II's reign between parliament as the legislative and the council as the executive body would tend to differentiate more sharply the sphere of statute from the sphere of ordinance.[5] But in his latest

[1] *Statutes and their Interpretation*, 32–34.   [2] *Ibid.* 32, n. 2.
[3] *Ibid.* Preface, pp. xix–xx.   [4] *Chapters*, II, 49, n.
[5] *The Place of Edward II*, 158. This view is adopted by Holdsworth, *Hist. Eng. Law*, II, 309.

pronouncement he was convinced that Professor Plucknett had
shown the equivalence of the terms before 1350, and actually
suggested the year 1354 as something like an exact date for the
distinction. 'When this stage (of 1354) was reached,' he wrote,
'we can without hesitation use the modern distinction between
statute and ordinance, without being guilty of a gross anticipa-
tion of later history. Thus law received its final definition, and the
process of differentiation between administrative and legislative
action became complete.'[1] This definition, he considered, was
only one example of a general stiffening at that date of differentiation between institutions and principles, such as between
common law and statute, law and equity, council, parliament
and chancery.

Tout's judgement on this matter, provided his suggestion of
the exact date for the distinction is not taken too seriously,
seems to be the soundest available and sufficiently definitive.
Recently, however, Professor H. L. Gray has re-opened the
discussion, with, indeed, scant reference to the views of his
predecessors, and he comes to a conclusion, which, though
apparently a revival of a view held by Professor McIlwain,[2] is
startling and incredible enough to require careful examination.
In his view the differentiation was short-lived, very short-lived.
'In the course of the fifteenth century', he says, 'men ceased to
attempt to maintain the distinction. Ordinances and statutes
came to be terms used synonymously, and for this reason the
distinctions elaborated by Hallam and Stubbs became inapplicable.'[3]

Now, if this statement were true, it would be very remarkable.
For it seems most unusual for men ever to abandon differentia-
tions once made, and it would be very difficult indeed to point
to any reversal of the normal process of differentiation in
institutional or constitutional history. The cessation of any
distinction between statute and ordinance, which Professor

[1] *Chapters*, III, 182. [2] *Magna Carta Essays*, 161, 164. *Cf. infra*, p. 276.
[3] *Influence of the Commons*, 384.

Gray fully admits was made in the fourteenth century, would therefore be something like a unique phenomenon in history.

Before, however, Professor Gray's conclusions are examined, it is desirable to recall briefly the outstanding items of evidence upon which the views of Hallam and later scholars were based. As early as 1340 an indication occurs[1] of the notion of the permanent quality of statutes, even though it was not coupled with any allusion to ordinances. In that year a committee of lords and commons was appointed to make into a statute such articles, already agreed upon by common assent, as were perpetual. Then in 1354—in Tout's estimation the crucial year in the history of the differentiation—came an ordinance of the Staple, which was formulated outside of a full parliament, but which, when parliament met, the commons petitioned should be enrolled, since ordinances made in councils were not of record, as they were if made by 'common parliament'; and in response to this request, it was agreed that the ordinance should be published in the counties and wherever Staples were established, and be enrolled on the rolls of parliament for greater security, and, as was afterwards said, should be held *pur Estatut* for ever.[2]

Even more instructive is the incident of 1363, when the commons were actually asked whether they would have certain sumptuary provisions enacted by ordinance or by statute.[3] To this unequivocal question[4] they replied that they thought it better to have the provisions by ordinance and not by statute because, if anything therein required amendment, it could be dealt with in the next parliament.[5] Richard II's arbitrariness in the use of ordinances seems to have emphasised the distinction, for in 1390 the commons petitioned that neither the chancellor

---

[1] *Rot. Parl.* ii, 113, no. 7.   [2] *Ibid.* 253, 257.

[3] *Ibid.* 280.

[4] The words: 'per voie de ordinance ou de Statuyt' in this question do not seem to me to diminish its significance as they did to Professor McIlwain (*Essays*, 164).

[5] These words of course imply that to change an ordinance was easier than to change a statute once made—as we should expect. But it does not follow that the actual immutability or strict permanence of a statute was also implied.

nor the king's council should, after the rising of parliament, make
ordinances contrary to the common law, ancient customs, or
statutes ordained before or during the then parliament.[1] This
petition obviously suggests that an ordinance was coming to
signify something like a definitely extra-parliamentary measure,
and as such a possible rival to statute-law; but it received no
cordial response from the king, who replied merely that what
was customary should be observed, saving to the king his
regality, and that if anyone were thereby aggrieved, he should
complain, and right would be done to him.

A statement of Thorpe, CJ., in 1366, to the effect that an
ordinance made by the lords would be held as a statute implies
that the two were not the same thing, even though the courts
might enforce such an ordinance as they would a statute.[2]

Thus, by the end of the fourteenth century, people could
distinguish between statutes and ordinances, although the terms
were still often used synonymously.[3] What, then, are the reasons
put forward by Professor Gray for the inherently improbable
conclusion that this differentiation was dropped during the
following century?

The reasons appear to be two only, and both seem to be
inadequate or irrelevant. One of these reasons is that statutes,
coming to be recognised as repealable, were no longer permanent, and the other is that the terms 'statutes' and 'ordinances'
were used synonymously. The first of these reasons is inadequate,
because it is doubtful whether there ever was a time, except in
the stress of political crisis, when a statute was supposed to be
permanent in the sense of being absolutely unrepealable. It is
also partially irrelevant because it relates to only one, and that
a secondary, distinction between statutes and ordinances. Even

---

[1] *Rot. Parl.* III, 266.   [2] *Y.B.* 39 *Edward III*, Pas. pl. 3 (App. no. 8).

[3] No doubt the elaborate business of proclaiming statutes in the counties and
elsewhere—not usually involved in the promulgation of ordinances—would dis-
courage the use of statutory forms for enactments intended to be temporary.
Nothing seems to be known as to the lapse of ordinances. When did an ordinance
cease to be binding? Presumably ordinances (like blockades after the Crimean
War) to be binding must be effective.

though statutes were impermanent in the sense of being repealable, and were also sometimes enacted for short specified periods, it does not follow that all distinctions between statute and ordinance disappeared. Moreover, when Hallam and Stubbs elaborated their distinctions between the two types of enactment they did not imply that a statute was eternal and immutable or that a repealable statute was indistinguishable from an ordinance.

The second reason is inadequate because there never was a time when the terms 'statute' and 'ordinance' were not sometimes used synonymously. There was nothing new in this usage in the fifteenth century; it was common throughout the fourteenth century, in the latter part of which Professor Gray himself admits the distinction existed. His reason is also irrelevant because, even though the terms were used synonymously, it does not follow at all that they were always so used, nor that two differing types of enactments did not exist, one an ordinance type, and the other a statute type.

Neither of these reasons, therefore, can be considered to have established Professor Gray's contention,[1] which we submit is inherently improbable. Moreover, there is positive evidence to the contrary which goes far to prove its impossibility. What Professor Gray and others have failed to take into account, preoccupied as they are with the synonymous usages of the terms 'statute' and 'ordinance', are the instances of the use of the term 'ordinance' independently, without its being coupled with the term 'statute' at all, and this use is quite common during the fifteenth century. Some instances of this use, and other evidence, call for review.

Thus the ordinance of 1399 declaring Prince Henry to be

---

[1] Professor McIlwain's view to a like effect was briefly stated in the *Essay* cited above (164, 166), and was based mainly upon the same evidence, especially on the point that statutes themselves came to be enacted for short periods. The number of instances which he cites (164, n. 4) from the statute rolls or parliament rolls are all examples either of such temporary enactments or of the synonymous usage of the terms. It is interesting to notice that a good many of these statutes, though temporary, did constitute an alteration of the law of the land whilst in operation.

heir-apparent was entered on the rolls of parliament but was not called a statute.[1] In the parliament of 1400–1 an ordinance made and enrolled on the rolls in the previous parliament was ordered to be held and kept, notwithstanding a statute made in a parliament of Richard II's time, and the king required that it should be made a statute and proclaimed in the counties.[2] The commons petitioned in 1414 for authority of parliament to be given to the king for making an ordinance with the council to regulate the coinage matters until the next parliament, when the provisions might be established as a statute perpetually to endure.[3] In 1420 an ordinance providing that parliament should not be dissolved on the king's return from abroad was assented to by all the estates, having been delivered in parliament by the commons among their common petitions.[4]

These examples make clear the fact that the distinction between statute and ordinance was by no means dead in the earlier part of the century, and others go to show that it was actually becoming sharper. More and more, it seems, ordinances were becoming the enactments of king and council rather than enactments of the full parliament. Time and again the commons petitioned that the council should make an ordinance for one object or another, and not infrequently the authority of parliament was given them for the purpose.[5] This fact helps to corroborate the views of Stubbs and Tout, that statute and ordinance were distinguished chiefly by their origin in parliament and great council respectively, and in that case the further differentiation of the continual from the great council would facilitate the growth of the distinction.

There is no reason to believe that provisions of the king and council (great or lesser) were normally called statutes in the fifteenth century, whatever may have been the case in earlier times. Indeed, we can be pretty confident that by that century

---

[1] *Rot. Parl.* III, 434 a.   [2] *Ibid.* 478 b.   [3] *Rot. Parl.* IV, 35 b.   [4] *Ibid.* 128 b.
[5] *Rot. Parl.* III, 506 b, 627 a; IV, 20 b, 35 b, 130 b; V, 62 a, etc.

the term statute was never applied to enactments other than those assented to by king, lords, and commons duly summoned (apart of course from the application of it to such documents as the *Statuta Prerogativa*, an application admitted to be erroneous during the century[1]). Further, as we have seen, and as is generally agreed, there was a close connection between statutory enactments and modification or extension of the law as administered in the courts. But few, if any, of the enactments described as ordinances have this connexion; or, if they have it at all, it is only with a limited scope or for a limited time. Otherwise they appear to be measures of an administrative, not a legislative character, concerned with good governance rather than with good laws; they relate to men's apparel, regulations for their professions, rules of the household, and countless other matters which had little or nothing to do with alterations in men's legal status, were unlikely to give rise to litigation, and were the business of the king's bailiffs rather than his justices.

Doubtless an ordinance of the king and his council would be duly enforced by the courts should it come within their cognisance at any time, and certainly an ordinance agreed to by the three estates would be so enforced. But, though we find a great deal about statutes in the Year Books of the fifteenth century, and a good deal also about acts, the allusions therein to ordinances are very slight indeed. Consequently there is no known instance of a conflict of any sort between statute and ordinance in the courts; the rivalry between them feared in Richard II's reign did not develop, no doubt partly because the spheres of the two enactments became different. Normally king and council did not attempt to alter statute and custom by ordinances of their own; there could be no conflict between statutes and ordinances which were agreed upon by the three estates, whatever the nature of their provisions, because of course their legislative authority was the same. There could be no doubt of the full authority of such ordinances as were made by the king

[1] *V. supra,* pp. 44, 256–57.

and council, unless they conflicted with statute and custom of the land; but any ordinances which did not so conflict could hardly be by nature more than administrative measures, so that the essential difference between statute and ordinance, indicated by Stubbs, the difference between legislative and executive acts, is by no means inapplicable in the fifteenth century. Whether or not we speak of ordinances as law will naturally depend upon our view of law. If we regard law as the body of rules obligatory upon the subject, certainly we shall call them law. But if we wish to define law as the body of rules normally enforced in the courts of the realm, then we may hesitate to do so.

(*b*) Statutes and royal prerogative.

We have seen that royal prerogatives might and often did suffer restrictive definition in the course of litigation. The same process, though far less in evidence, was carried on in the courts by the enforcement of statutes. Not often, indeed, did an occasion occur when the king's prerogative was in direct conflict with statutes. No such instances of conflict as Professor Plucknett found in the early fourteenth century have come to light from our period. He showed that the supremacy of statute was by no means always assured at that time, but for the fifteenth century, though the evidence is not very striking, we can feel confident, in view of such cases as are known and of the general temper of the courts, that statutes were not to be overridden by any exercise or privileges of prerogative, and that a statute would be upheld even if in conflict with prerogative.[1] Nevertheless the king admittedly could and did, within limits, grant exemption by his letters patent from the provisions of statutes, though he could not, by any exercise of prerogative, repeal or revoke any statute.[2]

---

[1] For some discussion of the question whether the king was bound by statutory restriction of his own prerogative, as distinct from the restriction of his powers of making grants to other persons (with which we were concerned in this section), *v. supra*, pp. 55–58.

[2] *V. supra*, p. 58.

That the king's prerogative had been actually enlarged by statute was at least arguable as late as the early years of Henry VII, but against this were the opinion that a prerogative could not commence at a recent date, and the inveterate tendency of the lawyers to regard prerogatives as merely common law rights of the king.[1]

There is slight, if any, reason to believe that any king in the fifteenth century interfered directly with a statute and its enforcement. But grants made by letters patent to individuals were sometimes found to be in conflict with statutes; if the terms of grants of this kind which came before the courts had been allowed, the provisions of statutes would in effect have been overridden. The general attitude of the courts, however, did not permit such overriding, and letters patent were sometimes disallowed, thus vindicating the supremacy of statute-law over royal prerogative. This attitude may well have been connected in part with the rule that letters patent were to be executed strictly and to the benefit of the king,[2] and it is worth remembering that although the king no doubt wished to enjoy the exercise of his prerogative, he was not likely to be the loser when a grant from him was disallowed by the courts.

We find this attitude of the courts well illustrated by the fate accorded to letters of protection issued by the king in excess of the limits laid down by statute.[3] These letters of protection were sometimes made use of by their grantees to escape litigation, and this abuse no doubt attracted the particular hostility of the lawyer. For example, in 1411 a certain man had been outlawed

---

[1] The outstanding cases on this point are *Y.B.* 12 *Henry VII*, Trin. pl. 1 (App. no. 101) and *Y.B.* 13 *Henry VII*, Mich. pl. 3 (App. no. 102).

[2] *Y.B.* 21 *Henry VII*, Hil. pl. 6 (App. no. 111).

[3] According to Cowell, there were two main classes of royal protections. (*a*) *cum clausula volumus*; of this class there were four kinds: (i) *quia profecturus*, (ii) *quia moraturus*, (iii) for the king's debtors, (iv) for those in the king's military or naval service; (*b*) *cum clausula nolumus*; these were usually granted to a spiritual community for immunity from seizure of their chattels by the royal officers, but they might be granted to an individual lay or spiritual. None of these protections extended against actions of dower, *quare impedit*, *novel disseisin*, *darrein presentment*, or attaints and pleas before justices in eyre.

on a writ of debt, and had had his 'charter of pardon', but a *scire facias* was sued thereon, and he sent into the court a royal protection, 'quia profecturus est en le company Thomas fitz du roy en Ireland'. But this protection was attacked as being contrary to statute 13 Richard II, c. 16, which disallowed protections to persons other than those going in the company of the king himself, or in a royal voyage, or as king's messengers. Since the defendant was doing none of these things, but was merely accompanying the prince to Ireland, and not in a voyage royal—for no army was going—the protection it was argued ought to be disallowed, and it was in fact disallowed.[1]

Similarly, fifty years later, another letter of protection fell foul of statutes. A defendant in a case of *Quare impedit*[2] pleaded a protection granted him for three years because he was setting out to the court of Rome in the king's service. Counsel attacked the protection and piled up arguments against its validity. The form should be, it was argued, not *profecturus est*, but *profectus est*. Any protection would last only for one year and not for three. The words of the grant were too general. An exemption from all pleas and actions was contrary to form. The place of the grantee's sojourn must be stated; a protection to the court of Rome was unheard of; if it were admissible, all the king's proctors at Rome would have been obtaining such protections long before. Besides, it was against statutes 13 Richard II, c. 16,[3] and 9 Henry V, st. 1, c. 3.[4] The words, 'any statute notwithstanding', were utterly inadmissible, for the king could not take anyone into protection against the law. In law, moreover, the

[1] *Y.B.* 11 *Henry IV*, Mich. pl. 17 (App. no. 16). Cf. Vinogradoff, *Collected Papers*, I, 204.
[2] *Y.B.* 39 *Henry VI*. Hil. pl. 3 (App. no. 42).
[3] By this statute no protection *quia profecturus* was allowed in any plea whereof the suit was commenced before the date of the protection except in the case of a royal voyage or message.
[4] By this statute, *novel disseisin* was included in the scope of protection, provided that judgements in such actions were not prejudicial to reversioners being in the king's service; but this protection was to endure only till the parliament holden next after the king's return to England.

protection could last only for one year, since otherwise the king might grant one for thirty, or a hundred, or a thousand years.

But against these arguments it was urged that the king could by his prerogative take a man into his protection so long as another was not thereby disinherited. Choke, Sjt., agreed with this contention, but only in cases when the protection was for one year, and was in accordance with convenience. For if the king exempted a man from serving on an inquest, and then another also, it was good, but to exempt all who lived in a county would be a void grant. Finally, it was the opinion of the court that a protection lay only for one year, and the protection in question was disallowed.

Similarly a grant of a general pardon for felonies would not, without express words, be upheld;[1] indeed no pardon at all would be valid unless it contained the necessary *non obstante* clause.[2] Moreover, letters patent which had been ratified by parliament must adhere to the terms of the parliamentary confirmation, otherwise they would be void.[3]

These cases encourage the belief that letters patent conflicting with a statute would not be upheld in the courts. But a royal letter patent might and did have the effect of dispensing with a statute. The king could give licence of exemption from statute.[4] He could give a licence with a *non obstante* clause, and, providing the territory involved was specified, it would be good, unless it exempted from a statutory felony, for which the king could grant not dispensation, but only pardon.[5]

In time, this principle of dispensation came to be expressed in a doctrine which allowed such power only in the case of statutes which dealt with *mala prohibita*, and disallowed it in the case of

---

[1] *Y.B.* 36 *Henry VI*, pl. 21, fo. 24 (App. no. 35); *Y.B.* 37 *Henry VI*, Pas. pl. 9 (App. no. 39).

[2] *Y.B.* 2 *Henry VII*, Mich. pl. 20 (App. no. 80). The justices in the exchequer chamber upheld this rule.

[3] *Y.B.* 10 *Henry VII*, Mich. pl. 20 (App. no. 93).

[4] The case of the Waterford merchants cited above, p. 268. *Y.B.* 2 *Richard III*, Mich. pl. 26 (App. no. 68).

[5] *Ibid.*: *Y.B.* 1 *Henry VII*, Mich. pl. 2 (App. no. 71).

those dealing with *mala in se*. Such offences as counterfeiting, shipping wool elsewhere than to Calais, holding of more than one benefice, a bastard's becoming a priest, were all *mala prohibita,* and could be dispensed from by the king. But such offences as homicide or committing a nuisance on the highway could not be licensed by the king, though they might be pardoned.[1] Nor could a man who had been bound over to keep the peace be released from his obligation before making forfeit. Neither the king nor bishop nor priest could license anyone to act lecherously,[2] for such a deed was *malum in se* in the law of nature, though one guilty of it could be absolved.[3]

Royal letters patent, therefore, would not defeat a statute, though, rightly worded, they might dispense with it, *i.e.* confer exemption upon the grantee from its provisions, provided the offence involved was neither a felony nor *malum in se.*

(*c*) Statutes and common law.

None of the doubt about the supremacy of statute-law over common law which is found in the earlier fourteenth century appears during the fifteenth century.[4] Statute-law had, of course, in common law a rival older than itself, better known to the lawyers, and more adaptable to changing needs of the day than itself. Common law was, as has often been said, tough law, not easily to be broken by the latest addition to the statute roll, and its relations with statute-law were not always simple and obvious. The history of these relations is necessarily intricate, and much difficult investigation will be needed before that history can be fully worked out.

---

[1] To-day a public nuisance cannot be pardoned until abated.

[2] This is clearly what Fineux, CJ., said, according to the report, even if he thereby committed himself to the assertion that the king could dispense with portions of the canon law, and to the denial of the papal theory of Indulgences.

[3] *Y.B.* 11 *Henry VII*, Mich. pl. 35 (App. no. 99).

This case was cited by Herbert, CJ., in the famous Hales's case (*Godden v. Hales,* (1686) 11 St. Tr. 1165) on the dispensing power in 1686. (See Keir and Lawson, *Cases in Constitutional Law,* 2nd ed. 55–56.)

[4] See Plucknett, *Statutes and their Interpretation.*

Professor Plucknett has exposed the fallacy in the old view—cherished by Coke—that common law was regarded in the mediaeval period as fundamental law which could not be altered even by statute.[1] But Professor Plucknett also noticed, as we have seen,[2] that the general attitude of the courts in the first half of the fourteenth century was one of jealousy for the common law, and until late in that century the supremacy of every statute over a rule of common law was by no means axiomatic.

During our period, however, this supremacy appears to have been unquestioned. The attitude of the courts is clearly shown by the discussions that took place from time to time as to what was law before the making of statutes and what afterwards.[3] No one, the judges held, could prescribe against statute.[4] Statute not only broke the custom of the realm,[5] but also the custom of an administrative department such as the Exchequer.[6]

In a previous section[7] we have submitted that the problem of the relation of statute to common law is, for the fifteenth century, closely connected with the classification of statutes, and varied with the class of statute. The judges and counsel themselves indicate in terms this connexion, and we need do no more for our purpose than restate here the principles of the relation.

A statute (or part of a statute) admittedly in affirmance of common law obviously differed from the common law only in being written and enacted. No question of the one's overriding the other could arise, and so far from a relation existing between the two, they were necessarily identical in substance. How far statutes were in fact thus absorbed, as it were, into common law, and their capacity to innovate thus curbed, is an interesting and important question which nothing but the most meticulous study of the *Year Books* will ever answer.

---

[1] Plucknett, *op. cit.*   [2] *Supra*, p. 250.
[3] *E.g. Y.B.* 7 *Henry IV*, Mich. pl. 19 (App. no. 12); *Y.B.* 7 *Henry VII*, Mich. pl. 9 (App. no. 88); 10 *Henry VII*, Mich. pl. 24 (App. no. 94).
[4] *Y.B.* 8 *Henry VII*, Trin. pl. 1 (App. no. 91).
[5] *Y.B.* 21 *Henry VII*, Hil. pl. 28 (App. no. 112).
[6] *Y.B.* 1 *Henry VII*, Mich. pl. 4 (App. no. 73).
[7] *Supra*, § 3 (i).

Again, a statute might be in the affirmative, and if it were it would not abolish remedies pre-existing at common law,[1] so that such a statute would be no more than alternative to common law and stand to it in a merely supplementary relation.

But all other types of statute, if in conflict with common law, would break it and override it. Statutes providing remedies and couched in the negative would abolish remedies at common law.[2] Most statutes introducing new law in the affirmative would not, perhaps, conflict with any existing rule of common law, but if they did, they overrode it just as they did if they introduced new law in the negative.[3]

Thus, though a certain jealousy for the common law might continue, and though an uncertain discretion on the part of the judges might modify the effect of a statute, common law during the fifteenth century was not so tough that it could withstand the authority of statute. Common law had found its master,[4] and not even the championship of Coke was going to be able to release it.

(d) Statutes and canon law.

However dubious the precise relations of church and state may have been at different periods, the church courts were at no time expected or required to enforce within their jurisdiction the statute-law of the state.[5] The law enforced within those courts was always the canon law and no other, unless, indeed, it was secular law for the good of the church which had been approved by the church.[6] But it did not follow that statute-law could not

[1] *Y.B.* 10 *Edward IV*, Pas. pl. 18 (App. no. 55).   [2] *Ibid.*
[3] See generally above, § 3 (i) and (ii).
[4] According to Viner, however, the customs of London were of such strength that they prevailed even against statutes in the negative. (*Op. cit.* XIX, *sub. tit.* Statutes, E 6, 511, no. 10.) But apparently as early as Henry VII's reign the lawyers held a different view. A number of serjeants held in 1505–6 that the 'prescription' enjoyed by the citizens of London that no attaint lay against any servant in the city was defeated by statute. (*Y.B.* 21 *Henry VII*, Hil. pl. 28 (App. no. 112).)
[5] *V.* Maitland, *Canon Law in the Church of England*, especially 78–79; Pollock and Maitland, *Hist. Eng. Law*; Z. N. Brooke, *English Church and the Papacy*.
[6] *V.* Lyndwood, *Provinciale*, lib. III, tit. 28. The Tabula on this reads: 'Statutum factum per laicos etiam ad utilitatem ecclesiae non tenet nisi Ecclesia illud approbaverit.'

and did not defeat the law of the church. On the contrary statutes not only restricted the very jurisdiction of the church courts, but also, by preventing the application of canons, superseded parts of substantive ecclesiastical law. Certain matters such as temporalities, particularly advowsons, sanctuaries, benefit of clergy, legitimacy, and even heresy, were not left by the secular state entirely to the rulings of Holy Church. Such matters, on the borders as it were between church and state, were, however, few in number and limited in scope even in the fifteenth century; and, though these, as time passed, had become more definitely within the sphere of secular legislation and jurisdiction, canon law as a whole was not encroached upon by secular law. Canon law was admittedly supreme in its own proper sphere, and so was statute-law. The proper sphere of statute-law did not include undoubted *spiritualia*. No act of parliament could make the king a parson, nor confer upon a layman rights of spiritual jurisdiction, nor usurp the powers of the Supreme Head of the Church.[1] On the other hand, the pope could not change the laws of the land,[2] nor act in derogation of the king and his crown;[3] excommunication, the severest of spiritual penalties, was not deemed a disability in the law of the land.[4] Moreover, the principle established since Henry II's time, that the king's court had exclusive jurisdiction over real property, necessarily brought many borderline cases within the domain of secular law.

For our present purpose, we need only to recall illustrations of the fact that, however mutually independent statutes and canons were within their own proper sphere of judicature, statute could and did break and suppress canon law if the two overlapped.

Thus, even though the judges in the fifteenth century

[1] *Y.B.* 21 *Henry VII*, Hil. pl. 1 (App. no. 110).
[2] *Y.B.* 11 *Henry IV*, Mich. pl. 67 (App. no. 19 (i)).
[3] *Y.B.* 1 *Henry VII*, Hil. pl. 10 (App. no. 77).
[4] *Y.B.* 2 *Richard III*, Mich. pl. 51 (App. no. 70); 4 *Henry VII*, Trin. pl. 12 (App. no. 83). Cf. Pollock and Maitland, *Hist. Eng. Law*, I, 480.

scrupulously avoided encroachment upon papal rights and recognised the authority of certain papal bulls,[1] none the less that century and the preceding saw a number of statutes passed which set limits to the exercise of papal authority,[2] and therefore to the maintenance of canon law in England. Of these the most celebrated were the statutes of *provisors* and *praemunire*, and though even the 'great' statute of *praemunire* of 1393 was intended to prohibit the exercise of papal authority only on certain specific points prejudicial to the rights and interests of the king, there was no doubt that these statutes, when enforced, defeated canon law. When the pope tried to obtain the repeal of some of these measures, he was told, even by Richard II, that this could be done only by parliament.[3]

Moreover, statutes of no political import were passed from time to time which had a like effect, restricting the scope of ecclesiastical jurisdiction[4] or superseding the canons on certain subjects. The law of advowsons was subjected to statutory revision from the time of the statute of Westminster I in 1285. As for rights of sanctuary, the most extensive of these were based, not on canon law but on royal grants, and as such were successfully attacked by king and judges in Henry VII's time.[5] Far more thorny was the question of benefit of clergy, but this canon law right by no means escaped statutory definition and modification during the fourteenth century.[6] The canon law of legitimacy—so far as it concerned the rule of *legitimatio per subsequens matrimonium*—was defeated by the baronial refusal 'leges terrae mutari' and the statute of Merton. The heresy

[1] See the references given by W. T. Waugh in his article 'The Great Statute of Praemunire' (*E.H.R.* (1922), xxxvii). Furthermore, if an action already commenced in a court christian raised an issue triable at common law, the issue nevertheless was to be tried by canon law (*Y.B.* 1 *Richard III*, Mich. pl. 7 (App. no. 66)).

[2] See Waugh, *op. cit.*, and also in *History* (1924), viii, 289.

[3] *Cont. Polychronicon*, ix, 247.

[4] *E.g.*, 15 Edward III, st. 1, cc. 5, 6; 25 Edward III, st. 6, cc. 1, 4; 5 Richard II, st. 2, c. 5.

[5] *V.* Pickthorn, *op. cit.* i, 178–179; I. D. Thornley, 'The Destruction of Sanctuary', in *Tudor Studies*, ed. R. W. Seton-Watson, 182 *et seq.*

[6] *V.* Pickthorn, *op. cit.* 180; L. C. Gabel, *Benefit of Clergy in England.*

laws,[1] though they did not actually defeat any canons—the first condemnation of a heretic in the fifteenth century was carried through before the statute *De Heretico Comburendo* was passed[2]— certainly modified church law in the sense of supplementing it. They brought arrest and punishment for heresy within the purview of secular jurisdiction.

Then, further, statutes were sometimes passed which protected the church courts in their administration of canon law, and confirmed the liberties of the church.[3] What statute confirmed, statute could one day take away,[4] and even though that day had not yet fully arrived, there could be no doubt in the fifteenth century that the state could and did, by its statutes, supersede and defeat such parts of canon law as it determined dealt with matters more properly secular than spiritual.

(*e*) Statutes and law merchant.

Even before the fourteenth century the law merchant was regarded as distinct from the common law, and though its rules were supposed to be specially known to merchants, it was law relating to a particular class of transactions rather than to a class of men.[5] Though this law was unwritten (except in so far as it came to be partly embodied in certain codifications), customary, and international in character, it was, from Edward I's day at least, modified by legislation. The statutes of Acton Burnell (1283) and of Merchants (1285)[6] revised the law of debt and encroached

---

[1] 5 Richard II, st. 2, c. 5; 2 Henry IV, c. 15; 5 Henry VI, st. 2, c. 7. An interesting case in which an excess of episcopal zeal in applying the statute *De Heretico Comburendo* was restrained by the justices occurs in *Y.B.* 10 *Henry VII*, Hil. pl. 17 (App. no. 96). The judges argued what was properly heresy and what not, and overruled the bishops' opinion.

[2] See Maitland, *Canon Law in the Church of England.*

[3] *Circumspecte agatis*, 13 Edward I, st. 2, c. 1; *Consultationes*, 24 Edward I; *Articuli cleri*, 9 Edward II; 26 Edward III, st. 6; 2 Henry VI, c. 1.

[4] Unless this idea is too modern to be held in the fifteenth century. I cannot prove its existence then, but it can hardly have been wholly lacking.

[5] Pollock and Maitland, *Hist. Eng. Law*, 1, 467. Cf. E. Lipson, *Economic History of England*, 1, 230; W. Mitchell, *The Law Merchant.*

[6] 11 Edward I; 13 Edward I. Cf. Bland, Brown and Tawney, *English Economic History, Select Documents*, 162.

upon the mercantile customs concerning fairs, and those statutes were actually enforced in the mercantile courts.[1] These provisions were further strengthened by enactments, as in 1311, and in 1353 by the great statute of the Staple.[2] This latter enactment, conferring as it did statutory recognition upon law merchant as a whole, brought that law under its sway, since, at least in theory, what statute gave, statute could take away.[3] Furthermore, even though the statutes merchant and statutes staple which abound in the records were bonds and not enactments, their only claim to existence was statutory. The power of statute to override the law merchant in the fifteenth century was thus beyond doubt.

§ 5. Statutes and judicial discretion

We have seen in the foregoing sections of this chapter ample evidence of the supremacy of statute law in all the spheres to which it could apply. We can, therefore, agree with Mr Pickthorn when he says that 'to any question which English law or government could properly raise statute could give a decisive answer, and the answer would generally be effective in practice as well as decisive in law...'.[4] But, as he also observes, 'every judge of the later fifteenth century knew that acts of parliament were not all the law in England and that he himself had very wide powers of interpreting statutes...' even to the extent of nullifying a statute altogether on certain grounds.[5]

Now it is obvious that if judges in the fifteenth century really did exercise such wide powers as these, some statutes might not only fail to be effective in practice, but might also be indecisive in law. Hence, before the true position of statute-law in the century can be appreciated even tentatively, some conclusion as to the measure of judicial discretion employed in the applica-

---

[1] See *Select Cases in the Law Merchant*, Selden Society, *passim*, esp. I, 19, 63.
[2] 5 Edward II, c. 32; 25 Edward III; for further regulation of fairs, *v.* 17 Edward IV, c. 2, and 1 Richard III, c. 6.
[3] But *v.* p. 288, n. 4, *supra*.
[4] *Early Tudor Government*, I, 141.   [5] *Ibid.* 134.

tion of statutes must be reached. This crucial question is all the more in need of fresh consideration in view of the apparent discrepancy between Mr Pickthorn's observation and the conclusions come to by Professor Plucknett upon the subject. The latter, after his extensive study of the *Year Books* of the early fourteenth century, found that the scope of judicial discretion became much restricted about the middle of that century. 'As our period advances,' he says, 'the judges begin to show a decided preference for one policy, namely, that of strict interpretation, examples of which steadily became more numerous, while at the same time there is a marked diminution of cases of expansion and restriction.'[1] By 1342–43 Thorpe, CJ., was declaring that 'Privelegia statuti sunt stricti juris',[2] and soon Shareshulle, J., is found announcing that 'Nous ne poms prendre lestatut plus avant qe les paroles en ycele ne parlent.'[3] Professor Plucknett naturally inferred that by that time the days of judicial discretion were, to say the least, numbered. We should not, therefore, expect to find in the fifteenth century any considerable exercise of judicial discretion. Yet we do find it to a certain extent, and the conclusion arises that the restriction of judicial discretion was at any rate a much slower process than might have been supposed.

Any estimate of the measure of judicial discretion allowed at any time in the application of statutes must take account of the possibility of actual nullification of statute by the judges as well as the permissible latitude in the interpretation of particular statutes.

Now, as regards the nullification of statutes, there is no room at all for doubt that judges in the fifteenth century were *theoretically* justified in nullifying statute law on certain grounds. Both Fortescue and St Germain agreed in maintaining that any law was void if it were contrary to the law of nature (or reason)

[1] *Statutes and their Interpretation.*
[2] *Y.B.* 17 *Edward III*, Hil. pl. 29 (App. no. 4).
[3] *Y.B.* 20 *Edward III*, Mich. pl. 9 (App. no. 5).

or law of God.[1] Theoretically, therefore, a statute in conflict with those laws was *ipso facto* void, whether nullified by judges or not. But whether judges in the fourteenth and fifteenth centuries ever did nullify a statute on such grounds is very doubtful. True, occasionally in the fourteenth century the justices did nullify statutes, but never on such grounds. When they did so, it was for more technical reasons.[2] With the increased differentiation between the institutions of government, between the legislative and the judicial functions, and as statutes became more definitely acts of the parliament, the judges inevitably became more chary of exercising their discretion to the extreme of nullification.

Consequently we do not know of any clear case of the nullification of a statute by judges in the fifteenth century, on any of the grounds admitted in theory as sufficient for voidance, and in face of Fortescue's obvious reluctance, in Pilkington's case, to nullify even a statute the technical authenticity of which was dubious, we cannot assert, with Professor McIlwain, that 'statutes are void entirely because against reason or the fundamental law'.[3] The one and only clear case of the voidance of a statute which Professor McIlwain could cite[4]—and no other instance is forthcoming from the fifteenth century—was based on no such general theory. The case in question was that in which the bench held one of the articles of the statute of Carlisle to be void. No doubt Professor McIlwain was right in pointing out that modern commentators[5] who have found the reason for this voidance in the impossibility of fulfilling the terms of the statute are not justified, and in rejecting Sir Frederick Pollock's statement that the statute was voided because unintelligible.[6] But though, as Professor McIlwain says, the judges seem to have found an excuse for their treatment of the statute in a mere verbal quibble, the reason for their voidance of it seems genuinely to have been the sheer impracticability of its provision and the

---

[1] *V. supra*, § 1.   [2] See Plucknett, *op. cit.*
[3] *High Court of Parliament*, 270 *et seq.*
[4] *Ibid.* 273.   [5] *E.g.* Blackstone, *Commentaries*, I, 91.
[6] *Expansion of the Common Law*, 122.

opportunity it gave for chicanery. At any rate the bench, so far as our brief and indirect report shows,[1] was moved only by special and particular reasons, and did not resort to any general theory of voidance on grounds of conflict with law of nature, reason, or law of God. Moreover, they relied on an extremely literal interpretation of the words of the statute in order to gain their end.

The other two cases which Professor McIlwain cited as evidence for his sweeping generalisation cannot be accepted as relevant. These were the case in the course of which it was said that an act of parliament could not make the king a parson,[2] and Taltarum's case.[3] The dictum in the earlier case merely states an admitted principle, for parliament cannot confer *spiritualia*.[4] But Taltarum's case, even though it 'repealed by a judicial sentence the principal enactment of *De Donis*, did so not by direct nullification, but by acceptance of a complicated fiction'—a course which clearly proves the extreme reluctance of the judges to void the statute openly.[5]

In the absence, therefore, of any further evidence, we conclude that though the possibility of nullification of statute by the judges was admitted in theory, in practice such an extreme exercise of discretion has, in the fifteenth century, still to be sought. But, short of actual voidance, the necessity of interpreting statutes when the meaning was ambiguous might, and did, leave room for the exercise of judicial discretion. In such a contingency the judge to-day is guided by reference to the intention of the legislature, and interpretation guided by such reference may take one of two forms. It may be either restrictive, limiting the operation of the statute to its express words, on the assumption that the legislature, if it had intended more, would

---

[1] In Fitzherbert's *Abridgement, sub tit.* Annuity, 41. The Easter term of 27 Henry VI is lacking in all printed versions of the *Year Books* (App. no. 27).

[2] *Y.B.* 21 *Henry VII*, Hil. pl. 1 (App. no. 110).

[3] *Y.B.* 12 *Edward IV*, Mich. pl. 25 (App. no. 56).

[4] *V. supra*, § 4 (d), p. 285.

[5] See Sir K. E. Digby, *Introduction to the History of the Law of Real Property*, 5th ed. 205–258; Holdsworth, *Hist. Eng. Law*, III, 119.

have said so; or it may be extensive, being extended to include more than is included in the express words of the statute.[1] This latter form, this extensive interpretation, affords, short of extension amounting to actual judicial legislation, the widest possible opportunity for the exercise of judicial discretion; and this form of interpretation—extension 'by the equity[2] of the statute' as it was called—was by no means unknown in the fifteenth century.

The rule of reference to the intention[3] of the legislators—limiting, as it does, the absolute discretion of the judges but relieving them, as it does, of rigid adherence to the express words of a statute—was certainly established by the second half of the fifteenth century. The leading case on the subject came before all the justices (except the chief justices, who were absent) in the exchequer chamber, in the fourth year of Edward IV's reign.[4] A certain merchant had shipped wool without having provided the surety required of him by statute 14 Edward III, c. 5. His defence for his action was that statute 36 Edward III had given the king a subsidy on wool for three years, and had included in its terms an agreement that after three years no imposition or charge would be taken or asked from the commons, except the customary subsidy; and further, that statute 45 Edward III had declared that no tax would be put upon wool apart from the usual custom without the assent of the commons. On the strength of this agreement the merchant claimed immunity from the obligation of giving surety. After discussion by the king's attorney, the serjeants, and the counsel for the defendant, the justices gave judgement. Nedham and Arderne were of the

---

[1] See Sir P. B. Maxwell, *On the Interpretation of Statutes*, 7th ed., and W. F. Craies, *A Treatise on Statute Law*, 3rd ed.

[2] The term 'equitable construction' can be taken either (1) as synonymous with the intention of the legislature, or (2) as signifying the extension to general cases of a statute where its words taken literally are specific. The second of these meanings, or any extension of a statute, is the sense in which the term is used in the text above. 'Equity of a statute' has sometimes meant the principle or ground of a rule adopted from analogy to a statute (see Maxwell, *op. cit.* 219–220).

[3] Speaking of 'intention' (in a different connexion) it is worth noting that Brian, C.J., repudiated in 1479 the idea that the court could try intent, for the Devil himself knew not the intent of man. (*Y.B.* 17 *Edward IV*, Pas. pl. 2 (App. no. 62).)

[4] *Y.B.* 4 *Edward IV*, Pas. pl. 4 (App. no. 45).

opinion that the merchant was excused and that the duty of giving surety was repealed by the two later statutes. But Choke, Illingworth, and Yelverton held that such was not the case, 'for', they said, 'every statute made must be taken according to the intent of those that made it, when its words are doubtful or ambiguous, and according to its preamble'. On the principle here enunciated, that of interpretation in the case of ambiguity by reference to the intention of the legislature—decision was given against the defendant.

By Henry VII's reign this principle had become sufficiently established to be clearly stated several times from the bench. Thus Frowike, on the first day he argued (on the bench) after having been made chief justice—so says the report at any rate— had occasion to refer to methods of interpretation.[1] He had to discuss whether a feoffor on confidence had, as *cestui que use*, an interest in land which he had enfeoffed to his own use. He denied that the interest was proved by the fact that the feoffor had been empanelled on a jury. Such a feoffor would have been empanelled in accordance with the construction of statute 1 Richard III, c. 4, by reference to the intention of its makers. For the statute was made to avoid the mischief caused by sheriffs empanelling persons 'de small conscience', and therefore ordered them to empanel persons of substance and good conscience. At the time when the statute was made, the greater part of England was in feoffments on confidence, so that the intention of its makers could not have been to exclude feoffors to uses from being sworn, since otherwise only a few men would pass on to juries. The statute was therefore to be construed according to the intent of its makers.

A few years later, all the justices again laid down the principle that 'in any statute one must construe the intent of those that made the statute'. In this case the question at issue was whether the exaction of a small sum of money as bar-fee[2] by an under-

---

[1] *Y.B.* 15 *Henry VII*, Mich. pl. 1 (App. no. 105).

[2] *I.e.* a fee that every prisoner acquitted of felony paid to the gaoler.

sheriff from a prisoner was contrary to the statute 23 Henry VI, c. 9, which forbade extortions by sheriffs. All the justices agreed that the exaction was outside of the statute.[1] For the statute's intention, they said, was to provide against the extortion of large sums by the sheriffs from prisoners at their release, and to limit the sums that gaolers could take from the prisoners in their custody. The sum of money in point had been claimed by the sheriff as bar-fee, and had been awarded to him by the order and discretion of the court, and could not be included within the statute, and had not been intended to be included by those who had been the makers of the statute. 'Et en chescun statut on covient de construir l'entent de eux que fesoient le statut.'[2]

Alongside of these cases, enunciating as they do the principle of restrictive interpretation according to the intention of the legislature, must be placed cases which assert that statutes should be interpreted strictly or 'without equity'. In the case last mentioned above, Read, J., followed up the ruling by stating that such statutes as were in abridgement of the common law could not be taken equitably.[3] Cases have been noted above[4] which indicate the growing strength of the principle that statutes introductory of new law, or in the negative, or particular, should be interpreted strictly. Similarly, every penal statute would, it was held by 1506 at least, be taken strictly. By such strict interpretation, the statute forbidding sheriffs to empanel their servants would not prevent them from empanelling their friends and cousins, nor would the statute forbidding them to lease their counties prevent their leasing only a part of them.[5]

No doubt these examples of the restrictive interpretation of statutes by reference to the intention of the legislature could be multiplied; and the more numerous such examples, the fewer the opportunities must have been for the exercise of judicial discretion. But that such opportunities did exist, and were used,

---

[1] *Y.B.* 21 *Henry VII*, Hil. pl. 28 (App. no. 112).
[2] Cf. *Y.B.* 12 *Henry VII*, Trin. pl. 1 (App. no. 101).
[3] *Ibid.*   [4] § 3 (i), (ii) and (iii).
[5] *Y.B.* 21 *Henry VII*, Mich. pl. 45 (App. no. 109).

is amply shown by other cases in which the words of statutes are extended by the judges on grounds of equity or discretion. This interpretation 'by the equity' of the statute, was due, in part at least, Sir Peter Maxwell suggests, to the lax and over-concise construction of early statutes; furthermore, 'the ancient practice of having the statutes drawn by judges from the petitions of the commons and the answers of the king may also account for the latitude of their interpretation. The judges would be disposed to construe the language with freedom, knowing, like Hengham, CJ., and Lord Nottingham, what they meant when framing them.' This mode of extensive interpretation is not tolerated to-day.[1]

Thus in 1466 it was argued in a case of formedon in the remainder that a statute giving remedy in such cases against the plea of *nontenure* was by equity extended to include the plea of *joint tenancy*, notwithstanding the fact that the statute made no express mention thereof—because the mischief arising from such pleas was the same.[2]

An outstanding example of the exercise of judicial discretion is to be found in a case in the second year of Richard III.[3] The king had occasion to put to all the judges in the Star Chamber three questions. Their response to the third question was one that involved a generous exercise of discretion.

This third question had arisen from these circumstances. A certain John Barrett had been sued for debt and outlawed. Afterwards, an attorney approached Thomas Darby, keeper of writs, and caused all the writs against John Barrett to be erased, and the record against him to be destroyed, and a new one made out against W. Barrett. The problem now was how to punish this audacious contempt of justice. The judges determined to take a high line, and, it seems, to exceed their statutory powers in order to bring the offenders to book. Statute 8 Henry VI, c. 12, was brought and read before the king and council in the

---

[1] *Op. cit.* 219.   [2] *Y.B.* 5 *Edward IV*, fo. 44–45 (App. no. 47).
[3] *Y.B.* 2 *Richard III*, Mich. pl. 22 (App. no. 67).

Star Chamber, and, notwithstanding the fact that the statute made a felony only the embezzlement of a record whereby judgement was reversed,[1] they all decided that the action of the offenders was felony. But difficulties of procedure at once arose. The whole record against John Barrett having been destroyed, correction for error could not proceed; five persons, moreover, had been implicated in the destruction of the record, and they had done it partly in the county of London, and partly in the county of Middlesex. All had been committed to jail, but one and the same felony could not be tried in two different counties. Further, when 'rasatores' of records were indicted of felony, according to the literal words of the statute, the officials of both benches, the chancellor, and the treasurer, and others were to deliberate; and the magistrates of London ought to be but could not be associated with these; again, by the express words of the statute, justices of either bench had authority to hear such a case, if the felony was committed in Westminster or Middlesex, wherein the benches were located. But when the felony occurred in London, a commission, with the mayor as principal, should be appointed; the statute, however, did not appoint to such a commission anyone but the justices of either bench, who themselves had no authority in such cases except by the statute, and in a case of felony, the statute ought to be construed strictly and not by any manner of equity.

This somewhat belated allusion to strict construction did not prevent the justices from disposing of the case at discretion. They all assembled in the church of St Andrew's in Holborn, and ruled that those convicted of misprision of felony should make fine, and that all persons convicted of misprision, trespass, and the like, should give security to the judges before whom they were convicted; the justices—not the king himself nor anyone else—should then assess the fine at their discretion. Finally, the king's will in the matter, the reporter tells us, was 'per justicios suos et legem suam unum est dicere'.

---

[1] *V.* the statute.

This case is a good example of the extension of a statute by judicial discretion to include an offence closely analogous to, but not actually identical with, one made into a felony by statute.

The same principle is illustrated by other cases. For example, in 1490, Fisher, in replying to Keble, who argued that a certain statute should be taken strictly, said that, on the contrary, it should be taken 'according to a good construction', and observed that many things would be taken in a statute that were not therein named. Thus the statute of Gloucester, c. 7, which gave a writ of entry where a tenant in dower alienated, was extended to include a tenant for life and a tenant by the courtesy. The statute which gave formedon gave a writ only, but a process was added by equity. The reasonableness of a statute, he seems to have said, depended on accuracy in its drafting, and would not be abandoned for want of words not expressly mentioned therein.[1]

Again, in 1500, the justices held[2] that the statute 1 Henry VII would, by equity, include the pernor of profits, although he was not seised of the land in question. Frowike, CJ., in the same year, observed that divers statutes were construed in other form than that of their express words,[3] and, as we have seen above,[4] statutes open to equitable construction included statutes declaratory of the common law, statutes in the affirmative, and statutes general.

We must, therefore, conclude that the possibility of the exercise of judicial discretion in the interpretation of statutes had not, by the end of the fifteenth century, been entirely precluded. There is not, indeed, visible in that period, that large latitude

---

[1] *Y.B.* 5 *Henry VII*, Pas. pl. 12 (App. no. 84); cf. *Y.B.* 10 *Henry VII*, Mich. pl. 3 (App. no. 92).

[2] *Y.B.* 15 *Henry VII*, Trin. pl. 2 (App. no. 106).

[3] *Y.B.* 15 *Henry VII*, Mich. pl. 1 (App. no. 105). Cf. *Y.B.* 14 *Henry VII*, Hil. pl. 2 (App. no. 103). This case suggests that there may have been in some instances a connexion between equitable construction and action on the cases authorised by statute Westminster II (*Consimili casu*).

[4] See above § 3 (i), (ii) and (iii).

of discretion and that arbitrary power enjoyed by the judges of the early fourteenth century. Institutional development had gone too far, the principle of reference to the intention of the legislature had become too matured, for the maintenance of that latitude and that power. But manifestly the judicial power of equitable construction was still something to be reckoned with by litigants, and still a significant element in the constitutional position of the judiciary.[1]

---

[1] For a unique reference to judicial discretion in the sense of law-giving, *v. supra*, p. 198.

Chapter IV

THE THEORY OF THE STATE

The traditional intellectual barrenness of fifteenth-century England cannot be explained by the equally traditional notion that times of turbulence and strife are also necessarily times of sterility in thought. The barrenness of the century cannot be laid to the account of the Percies and of the Wars of the Roses, any more than the far more widespread civil wars of the seventeenth century prevented the originality and mental ferment of that age. True, the Wars of the Roses were not exactly wars of ideas, as those of the seventeenth century to a great extent were, but there does not appear to be any inevitable connection between times of physical conflict and times of mental inertia. The spirit moveth as it listeth—that is the safest generalisation the historian of ideas can venture upon in such a matter.

No doubt the fifteenth century saw more of feats of arms, alarums, excursions, and bewildering vicissitudes of fortune, than adventures in ideas. No doubt we look in vain through its years for the presence of outstanding minds—unless we except Reginald Pecock (who was perhaps the only man of the century who was born before his time), Fortescue, and the many great figures of Henry VIII's reign who spent their youth within the limits of the century. But it would be a mistake to suppose that the times were entirely out of joint and entirely given over to faction without principle, to bloodshed without let, to litigiousness without scruple, and to materialism without heed.

The century that created Eton and King's College, that laid the foundations of general education in the grammar schools endowed by the public-spirited new rich, that brought reading and writing within the reach of more sorts and conditions of men than ever before, that produced vernacular histories as well as the Bedford Book of Hours, that could receive the first-fruits of humanism, and that produced a man who even in the bitterness of exile and at the height of faction-fury could write an unreserved panegyric of his country and its institutions,[1]* could not have been totally devoid of the qualities that enrich the spiritual heritage of mankind.

But whatever deficiencies we may discern in fifteenth-century England, one above all seems to lie at the root of its lack of intellectual distinction. That was its insularity. The stream of stimulus and inspiration from the continent, which has at all times irrigated the seeds of English intellectual movements, seems to have dried up until the end of the century, when the trickle began to widen, to flow, and to enrich the harvest once again. Despite—or rather perhaps because of—the *ignis fatuus* of the French war, despite Duke Humphrey's literary, and Secretary Bekynton's diplomatic correspondence abroad, despite the foreign education of butcher Tiptoft and his imitators, despite the English Channel's being regarded not as a moat defensive to a house, but as a barrier to friendly help,[2] the fifteenth-century intellect remained insular.

One would suppose, for example, in reading the sources cited in these studies, that the average Englishman had scarcely heard of the outstanding development of the century in the political and religious sphere on the continent—the Conciliar movement. The council of Constance of 1414 may have been the culmination of mediaeval constitutionalism; its decree may have been the most revolutionary document in the world; it may have definitely put the question, Is the sovereignty of the community inherently in the ruler or in the representative organ of the people?[3] but the Englishman was quite unaware of it and unmoved by it. No doubt there were exceptions to this general rule; the University of Oxford, academic circles generally, and

---

* As many of the footnotes to this Chapter are lengthy, they have been relegated to the end of it.

ecclesiastics like Robert Hallam, no doubt took their share in the movement. But even they, it seems, were interested only in the restoration of the unity of the Church, not in the political and constitutional implications of Conciliar theory.[4] The chroniclers, if they mentioned the councils at all, did so with the briefest allusions, and passed on without heed to more absorbing parochial matters. Even Fortescue, who lived through all the councils from that of Pisa to that of Ferrara, shows not the slightest impression of any aspect of the Conciliar movement other than that of the expense to the crown involved in sending ambassadors to the assemblies. The constitutional questions raised by the Conciliar theorists made no stir in the political intelligences of contemporary England.

The native of England, in fact, was then, as nearly always, a great beggar of questions. He could depose his lawful king Richard and set up a Henry, not, indeed, entirely without reference to justification, foreign example, sanctions of Holy Church, nor without much legalistic formality, but with a minimum of interrogation; just as sixty years later he could upset a new dynasty, and thereby upset parliamentary claims to settle the succession, not indeed without some theorising, nor even without theoretical hesitations, but with a minimum of consistency.

Limited monarchy may have been in the air—and on the throne, in fifteenth-century England. But mostly it remained there. It did not, with one striking, and a few occasional exceptions, find its way into black and white on paper or parchment. Theorists did not flourish, and consequently the century has very little political theory of its own. It had, of course, the heritage of the past, and it had Sir John Fortescue, who once or twice in his travels stumbled into the domain of political thought. Moreover, even though it had no great thinker, it had the ideas of a host of practical men, politicians, administrators, and above all, lawyers, who carried on the actual work of government, and who must needs have had some concept of the

State and its machinery, and these were not as inarticulate as their predecessors had been. But it was not, indeed, the State that was the main focus of fifteenth-century thought. Rather the focus, if any, was government—good and politic governance. Only by courtesy, therefore, may we say that the fifteenth century, as such, had a theory of the State, and thus head this present study with that title.

I

If an attempt were made to define the tendency of political thought in England during the fifteenth century, it would be destined to failure unless it gave expression to opposing views of the character of the time. Here, as elsewhere, the historian's most difficult task is to form not merely generalisations that will sum up part of the facts, but generalisations that will take account of all the facts, however irreconcilable they may seem. The task of formulating general statements about the fifteenth century is especially troublesome, for the character of no century in English history is more open to conflicting interpretation. The reason for this conflict is not the so-called transitional aspect of the period, for every century is transitional, and every historical generalisation must express a transition of some sort. The source of the conflict goes much deeper than that, and is to be found rather in the sheer contradictoriness of our evidence, which is itself due in part to the seminal nature of the times. It was the seed-time of ideas that were one day to be incompatible. From one standpoint the most remarkable features of the century seem to be its conservatism, its lack of originality, its old-fashioned-ness. We see in it the absence of new theories to explain new facts, and the vain effort to accommodate new facts to old theories. We see the leading figures of the time struggling like old men in a new world, forced to grapple fresh problems with old mentalities. The period then seems to us, as it did to Stubbs, 'a worn-out helpless age, that calls for pity without sympathy, and yet balances weariness with something like regret',[5] we are led to regard it as a mere degenerate continuation of the fourteenth century, and see it as the bleak and barren winter of the mediaeval epoch. But from another standpoint its most striking features seem to be quite different. Its many anticipations of later ways of thought, its abundance of fruitful precedents, the novelty of many of its problems, are impressive. Its turbulent restlessness we feel must have been mental as well as practical. We note its literary activity, its intellectual contacts abroad, and the seeming modernity of many of its governmental forms, and we are thus led to think of it as the century of *Frühhumanismus*, of constitutional experiment and new monarchy, as the seed-time of the modern epoch.

But there is perhaps one tendency in the political thought of the fifteenth century a definition of which reflects both these interpretations, and that tendency was towards a change in its subject-matter. Political thought was becoming less exclusively a theory of monarchy, and rather more a theory of the State. This tendency is noticeable in many expressions of political concepts made by active politicians, even though theory was still shot through and through with notions of kingship. It is true that the theory of the only outstanding political thinker of the century, Fortescue, is essentially a theory of kingship rather than of the State, and of dominion rather than of kingship; yet it is also closely connected with a theory of what we should call the origin of the State, and there are indications, from the century as a whole, of the currency of a conception of the *respublica*, commonweal, or State, which transcends theory of a purely monarchical derivation. Talk of the body politic, elaborate anthropomorphic conceits,[6] concern for the *respublica Angliae*[7] and the 'whole weal publique', and questions of 'politic governance'[8] are all characteristic of the period, and all are significant commonplaces of everyday political thought. The king's advisers are the *reipublicae servitores*.[9] Speculation on the mutual duties of king and subject was no less prominent then than before,[10] but other topics were being canvassed: topics the

discussion of which might one day radically affect that speculation. The *utilitas regni*, the commonweal, and the public good[11]
were being mooted, and these considerations were not far removed from the corrosive yet creative Reason of State, which it
has been justly said, 'has its roots deeper in time than we often
imagine'.[12] We can see, therefore, in the fifteenth century, the
beginnings, at least, of a process that was to merge the sacred
mystery of kingship into a theory of the State which might be
sacred but was not mysterious.

We must not, however, over-emphasise this change in tendency. The characteristic theme is government rather than the
State as an entity. Governance, not the Republic, is the common
word and concern.

Moreover, political thinking was becoming less abstract and
universal, and more concrete and particular. Discussion was
concerning itself not simply with *respublica* and kingship, but
with the *respublica Angliae* and the English kingship. Far-
reaching theoretical assertions were being bandied about in the
English tongue—in rebellious manifestos,[13] and in political
tracts.[14] The era of English political pamphleteering had begun.
Besides, a central clearing-house was now available for the
exchange of political notions of all kinds, commonplace or
original. In the parliament house at Westminster,[15] many men
—country squires and burgesses of rural towns, whose book-
lore was small, and whose acquaintance with learned doctrines
was very distant—heard the language and learnt the terms of
political theorising, often, perhaps, for the very first time.
Chancellor after chancellor preached sermons to the parliament, and few of the faithful commons could have escaped these
homilies without some political edification.[16] Doubtless most of
these parliamentary sermons contained little but orthodox and
trite thought, but their important result was the diffusion of
political concepts, phrases, and words among people from diverse parts of the country, many of whom had never before
heard a political theory formulated, or concept enunciated, or

formal contention stated. The theoretical education in politics of the plain man had begun.

Moreover, fundamental questions—questions that would one day embroil the political life of the country—were occasionally, very occasionally, being raised. In this respect the unknown author of *Somnium Vigilantis* took the lead. He put, and answered to his own satisfaction, the most essential among all constitutional questions. Admitting that the realm may have needed reform, he asked the question by what authority and power did the rebels (of 1459?) set about reforming it, in the absence of any commission from the king? It was not, he asserted, for any member of the community to act as a reformer—not when authority was lacking.[17] On the contrary, every one owed subjection and obedience to the king's high commands—which are reason.[18] The king's laws should decide all disputes, civil and criminal, real and personal; and if they do not, then the king, with the help of his council, should make a law to meet the case, so that nothing should be done by force of the will of one man nor by force of vested interests.[19]

The political theories of the plain man might one day move mountains; but as yet there was little systematic thought in politics. There may have been a good deal of informal thinking, undoubtedly there was much repetition of political clichés. But only one man, so far as we know, set out, in a more or less systematic way, the results of his meditation on the political phenomenon, and he was no professional theorist, but a practising lawyer, an active politician, and a zealous dynastic partisan. The political theorising of Sir John Fortescue has to be taken as representative of the thought of his time, and as such needs close examination. For our estimate of the state of political ideas in fifteenth-century England must very largely rest upon our understanding of his work, and upon it as it really was, not as it seemed to the controversialists of the seventeenth and later centuries. The use made of Fortescue by both parties in the constitutional struggles of later centuries is standing testimony to the Janus-facedness of a publicist of a 'transitional' era,[20] but the historian has too often assumed that the views of the winning party in those struggles were also substantially the views of Fortescue himself.

How, in modern terms, are Fortescue's views to be understood?[21]

II

The theory of dominion had a long history behind it at the time when Fortescue was writing, and we are bound to regard him as one in a series of exponents of that theory, and to set his doctrines in the perspective of antecedent usage and thought. The mediaeval theory of dominion was a theory maintaining the pre-ordained rightness of the relation of superior to inferior. It envisaged the whole of creation as the sum of parts which either served or were being served by one another. The sources of this theory were ancient. Its root was to be found in Aristotle's theory of slavery and subjection, and its growth was profoundly influenced by doctrines of a feudal character. Germanic notions of land-tenure contributed to its development, and the theory thus modified went far to explain the fusion of government with landownership characteristic of feudalism, and to resolve the paradox involved in the common circumstance of the king's being supreme landlord without thereby destroying the proprietary rights of his subjects.[22] Many subtle distinctions could be drawn from such a theory. All property might be considered as dominion, but it did not follow that all dominion conferred proprietary rights in the fullest sense, though it did in a restricted sense. Every dominion was a right of use, but not every right of use was dominion. Possession, which was the fruit of dominion, had to be distinguished from dominion or the right of use itself; for a man might grant a thing to the use of another whilst retaining the dominion to himself, and no one could exercise his dominion, that is, use the thing over which he had dominion, unless he had possession of that thing. Thus both a king and his

baron had dominion over a barony, but the barony was not
their property equally; for the king's right of use of the barony
was different from the baron's, and was restricted to what we
should call public purposes. Nevertheless, the king had a
proprietary right to his dominion, and there was a distinction
between property that was dominion and property or right of
use that was conferred by dominion, and also between dominion
that was the right of use and possession that was actual use. It
was thus possible to accord to the king *proprietas dominii* without prejudice to the *proprietas rei dominatae* of his subjects. The
theory of dominion, in short, could reconcile the proprietary
right of the king to rule with the proprietary rights of his
subjects to possess. The king's dominion might limit for his
subjects the exercise of their dominion, but not their dominion
itself.[23]

Such, in essence, was the fruitful theory of dominion as
expounded by Richard Fitzralph, archbishop of Armagh, about
a century before Fortescue wrote. Earlier still it had been
elaborated, in more metaphysical and less juristic form, by
Egidius Romanus, whom Fortescue actually cited as one of the
authorities for his own classification of dominions. Wycliffe had
made a version of the theory notorious about the time of
Fortescue's birth. It is true that Fortescue did not provide any
definition of the term 'dominion' in his usage; but he gave a
clear indication that dominion in the polities which he described
had in it a strong element of full-blooded lordship over others *ut
servis* to the use and benefit of the dominator. This, he said,
citing St Thomas, was the only dominion known outside the
state of innocence. There were, indeed, on his own showing,
three types of dominion, each with diverse beneficial effects,
but obviously none of these could be *dominium in statu innocentiae*.[24]
We cannot doubt that Fortescue used the term in much the
same sense as his predecessors used it; to him its meaning was
sufficiently obvious to call for no definition. To him, as to
Fitzralph, it must have meant *dominium ad bona unius regni sive*

regiminis unius domini super multos minores dominos. His use of the term, to be sure, was not entirely consistent; he sometimes substituted for it '*regimen*', '*principatus*', or '*regnum*'.[25] But 'dominion' is the typical word in his writings, and his political theory is a theory of dominion.

III

Fortescue's political thought is descriptive rather than analytical, and its substance is a differentiation of types of dominion and an explanation of their origin. He distinguished three types, and explained the origins of two of them.[26] An analysis of these two themes exhausts all that is important in his political theory, and with him classification came before explanation. He particularised the characteristics of the three dominions in varying detail. The regal dominion and the dominion regal and political were described with some fulness, but the political dominion was sketched very meagrely, and figures very much as a drone in the hive ruled by the mixed dominion as queen-bee.

The *differentiae* of the regal dominion were these. The head (*ille preest*) ruled according to such laws as he made himself, and his own thought was law. He possessed the realm in hereditary right; the people could not legislate without his authority, and they were subject to his dignity. He could change the law and impose taxation without consulting them.[27] He was free to sin in the exercise of his dominion.[28] Regal dominions such as this (*regna tantum regaliter regulata*) were exemplified in the ancient histories of Nimrod, Belus, and Ninus; in part of the history of the Roman empire; and in the monarchy desired by the Israelites.[29] In more recent times, the kingdom of France afforded a most instructive example of this type.[30] This dominion under good princes was like the kingdom of God, and many Christian princes ruled by its laws.[31]

But these features were lacking in the political dominion. Here the head ruled according to laws which the people had instituted (*leges quas cives instituerunt*).[32] The political dominion, alone, admitted of a plurality of rulers; a regal dominion never did.[33] Rome under the consuls was an example of this type of dominion.[34]

The third type was a combination of some of the features— nay, of the merits—of both the regal and the political dominions.[35] Such a combination varied in its constituent elements. Rome under the emperors was at one time a regal and political dominion; for though the emperor's wish was law for all his subjects, and though he did not always consult the senate nor inherit by hereditary right, yet he did rule for the benefit of the many (*ad plurium usum*).[36] Israel, too, was a dominion political and legal, since it was ruled by the king of kings and also by the judges, for the common good.[37] Many kingdoms in early times, such as Egypt, Ethiopia, and Arabia, had been similar examples. So was Scotland, and so was England. In England the people could not legislate without the authority of the head, who was a king and possessed the realm in hereditary right, and to whom the people were subject; yet even there the dominion was regulated by the dispensation of many. For the king could not change the law nor impose taxation without the consent of his subjects, and the judges were sworn not to give judgements against the laws, even if the king commanded them to do so.[38]

Finally, even Heaven itself was an example of this dominion, since, indeed, there the consent of all its citizens was not lacking to every judgement of the king.[39]

Though there were fundamental differences in the dominions exercised by the king ruling regally and by the king ruling politically, nevertheless certain affinities between the two were discernible.[40] The king reigning *tantum regaliter* would sometimes in practice find it advisable to rule politically, *i.e.* with a *regimen plurium consilio ministratum*, as in the case of the Roman king's consulting the senate.[41] Likewise, a king ruling *politice* would for some purposes find it desirable to act royally, and for other purposes would find it necessary to do so. In the sphere of judicature, for instance, a residuum of cases would be at his will;

criminal cases, questions of punishment, and matters of equity would be at his discretion; and when laws were lacking, he, the lord, would make provision.[42] He would necessarily act royally in the event of military emergency arising from rebellion or invasion.[43] But in the sphere of legislation he should neither make law nor introduce foreign law, without the assent of his chief subjects; in this sphere the political king should never act regally.

Both kings were equally to be likened to God, and the regal king was not to pride himself on being superior to the political king.[44] For the power of each was the same.[45] To be sure, the political king could not change the law without assent; but the regal king's freedom from restraint in this respect was no more than a liberty to sin, and that was not power at all.[46] For all action sprang from two forces; will and power. Since man ever wished for good, the failure to attain it came not from will but from lack of power or impotence. Therefore, the regal king who sinned by forsaking the natural good of consent to laws could not be deemed more powerful than the king who did not so sin; and on the other hand, the good realised by the latter in obtaining consent to laws must be held to derive not only from his will, but also from his power.[47] Nevertheless, though the two kings were equal in *power*, they certainly differed in the *authority* they had over their subjects.[48] The explanation of this important difference was to be sought in the different origins of the two dominions.[49]

Both types of monarchy, Fortescue thought, originated under natural law. The law of nature was a divine law arising from the very earliest beginnings of human nature; under it and by it the *dignitas regia* originated and has ever since been ruled.[50] All rights of kings (*jura regum*) were ultimately derived not from the prince's authority, but from the law of nature.[51] This law not only established the royal dignity, but also—since there is less virtue in ruling than in creating—governed it.[52] Both the *ius tantum regale* and the *ius regale et politicum* were subject to natural law.[53]

Nevertheless, these two sets of kingly rights originated differently. The regal dominion was established by force, but the political and regal dominion by consent,[54] and of the two the former was the more ancient. Regal dominion was first set up by unjust men for the sake of ambition, though, indeed, the law of nature none the less worked through them for man's good.[55] Men impelled by power, greedy of dignity and glory, had subjugated their neighbours by force, had compelled their service, and had obliged them to obey commands which obtained the sanctity of laws. These subjugated peoples in time assented to their yoke, thinking themselves fortunate by submission to one, to enjoy protection from the injury and violence threatened them by numerous powerful men. The dominator eventually usurped to himself the name of king. Such had been Nimrod, first of all, then Belus, Ninus, and many other pagans; and so originated the kingdoms ruled by a *dominium tantum regale*.[56]

But at a later stage of civilisation, large communities of their own accord willed to unite and form themselves into a body politic by establishing one ruler as king. At the time of this incorporation and institution, both the king and the people ordained that the kingdom should be ruled by such laws as they all would assent unto.[57] Such a union into a body politic as this could not be made without the elevation of one to rule. For the body politic was similarly constituted as the body natural. Just as the natural body without a head was a mere trunk, so in political life a community could not be incorporated without a head to govern it. Any people, therefore, desiring to erect itself into a kingdom or any other body politic must needs prefer one man into the ruler's place. The creation of the mystical body of the state was like the development of an embryo into a natural body regulated by one head. As in the natural body the beginning of life was in the heart, which transmitted blood to all the members, so in the politic body the beginning was in the intention of the people, which provided for their benefit, and transmitted itself to the head and all the members. As the nerves in the natural body bound both head and members, and were immutable by the head, and the members could not be denied by it their due sustenance, so in the body politic the king could not change its law, nor could he deprive his subjects of their substance against their will. This being the manner in which the regal and political dominion originated, the scope of the royal power in realms thereby governed was obvious. The king was established (*erectus est*) for the protection of his subjects' laws, bodies, and goods, and his power was authorised by the people for this purpose and for no other (*hanc potestatem a populo effluxam ipse habet*).[58]

Authority, or the sanction of power, for the two kings was thus quite different. The right of the king ruling *tantum regaliter* was merely might,[59] he had no authority save that conferred by force; his power, Richard Fitzralph would have said, was in no better category than the mere brute strength of irrational creatures.[60] But the power of the king ruling *politice*, though it was no less, was derived from the very union of a community into a body politic; it was authorised by the foundation of society and state; its sanction was conferred by the will of the whole people; it was, Fitzralph would have said, the authority that belongs to rational creatures alone.

IV

Three main questions arise from this analysis of Fortescue's doctrines. First, from what sources, if any other than practical experience, did he derive his conception of the dominion regal and political? Secondly, precisely how is his account of the origin of this dominion to be interpreted? Thirdly, how far is his attribution of the mixed dominion to England justified by the facts of the fifteenth century? On our answer to each of these questions depends our estimate of Fortescue's originality as a theorist, his significance in the history of political ideas, and his value as a publicist.

A good deal of difficulty has been made out of the fact that Fortescue's citations of St Thomas Aquinas or his continuator, Ptolemy of Lucca, and of Egidius Romanus as authorities for his doctrine of the regal and political dominion appear to be unwarranted. It seems that if we turn up his references to those works, or even search through their pages, we do not find any statement about such a dominion.[61] This discrepancy between Fortescue and his authorities caused Lord Carlingford, the editor of the *De Natura* in Lord Clermont's collection, to conclude that Fortescue 'really derived his doctrines from his own liberal sentiments and the happy experience of his own country'; this conclusion Mr Plummer also embraced.[62] A first note of scepticism on this point, however, has been sounded by Professor McIlwain, who puts the pertinent question: Did Fortescue misunderstand his authorities, or have we misunderstood him?— and who suggests that even though we do not find anything about constitutional monarchy in those works, yet Fortescue may have cited them legitimately, since perhaps he did not mean by dominion regal and political what we mean by constitutional monarchy. For, to say the least, it is improbable that Fortescue cited these authorities again and again unless he supposed they gave some support or other to his doctrines.[63]

Professor McIlwain's query undoubtedly indicates one of the errors that has confused the issue in this matter. Whether or not the dominion regal and political can be thought of as constitutional monarchy must be discussed later; but in either case, we ought not to expect to find a highly modernised interpretation of Fortescue's fifteenth-century doctrine written very plainly in the texts of the thirteenth century. Yet this seems to be what Lord Carlingford, Plummer, and others have been surprised in not finding. Moreover, Fortescue's citations themselves have been regarded with excessive literalness, partly owing to preoccupation with the works subsequent to the *De Natura*, which is far more explanatory than those. We have expected to find in his authorities just the same doctrine as his own, though citation is not necessarily reproduction. We have not considered that he might have found certain statements in his authorities, and have combined some of them together into a whole differing from any of its parts. Yet this seems to be precisely what in fact he did do; and if the *De Natura* does not explicitly say so, it comes very near to it. In the sixteenth chapter of that work, which gives his earliest and fullest account of the classification of dominions, Fortescue did not directly attribute the mixed dominion to St Thomas. On the contrary, he stated that, among various kinds of government, St Thomas commended *dominium regale* and *dominium politicum*, and that Egidius Romanus did likewise. But, wrote Fortescue, there was a third kind of dominion not inferior to these in dignity and praiseworthiness, which was called political and regal (*sed et tertium esse dominium, non minus his dignitate et laude, quod politicum et regale nominatur*). We not only learnt of this dominion from experience and histories of the ancients, but we also understood it to be taught by the doctrine of St Thomas (*nedum experientia et veterum historiis edocemur, sed et dicti Sancti Thomae doctrina edoctum esse cognoscimus*). The important words in this statement are *doctrina edoctum esse*; those scholars who think that Fortescue cited St Thomas inaccurately must, presumably, interpret these words to mean 'is to be found written literally in the doctrine'. But a strict translation of them is surely 'is taught in the doctrine'. This comparatively vague assertion does not amount to any very precise citation, and seems a not unfair statement of the possibilities of St Thomas's or Ptolemy's text. For Fortescue merely took what he supposed to be some of the features of St Thomas's *dominium politicum* and *dominium regale* and joined them together, just as he specifically combined the two dominions out of Egidius Romanus's treatise. He found in the *De Regimine Principum* of St Thomas (and Ptolemy) and in that of Egidius a characterisation of *dominium politicum* as a rule according to laws that have been made not by one man alone, but by the many. Presumably he saw that the principle of this rule could be joined to the principles of *dominium regale*, without more loss to the latter than the prince's monopoly of legislative capacity; and that the resulting combination made a fair description of certain polities of which *experientia et veterum historiis edocemur*. He thus improved on his authorities simply by combining certain features of their work for his own purposes. But, having their authority for the parts of the whole he had made himself, he seems sometimes to have assumed that he had their authority also for the whole. This assumption—and before it is said to be insincere, we ought to know a great deal about mediaeval methods of literary citation—appears in several passages. For instance, in the chapter just mentioned he stated that St Thomas affirmed that the Israelites were ruled *politice et regaliter* under God and the judges, whereas the author of the *De Regimine* merely said they were ruled *politice* at one time and *regaliter* at another. In *The Governance* St Thomas was represented as having praised dominion political and regal, whereas actually he praised merely the two separate dominions.[64]

But what if, when he cited St Thomas's *De Regimine*, he was really thinking of the *Summa Theologica*? May not the difficulties, or a large part of them, involved in interpreting Fortescue's use of his sources be resolved, if authority can be found for his statements elsewhere in St Thomas's writings? Now, though it is quite clear that no mixed dominion appears in the *De Regimine*, it is equally clear that such a dominion does occur in the *Summa*. True, in two places in that work, St Thomas asserted that two possible forms of legislation exist; either by the people, or by the prince; and if these are the only alternative legislative authorities, there can be no room for a mixed polity. But elsewhere in the *Summa* St Thomas declared that the best form of polity was a mixture of monarchy, aristocracy, and democracy. In such a polity law was sanctioned by the *majores natu* as well as by the *plebs*, as Isidore, following Roman jurists, had said; moreover, therein one man was given the power to preside over all, while under him others had governing powers, yet the government was shared by all, because all were eligible to govern and because the rulers were chosen by all. The polity was thus a mixture, partly monarchy, because one presided, partly aristocracy, because a number of persons were set in authority, and partly democracy, because the rulers could be chosen from among the people, and because the people had the right to elect those rulers.[65]

There is, therefore, unquestionable authority for a mixed polity in the *Summa*, and we know that Fortescue was acquainted with part at least of the *Summa*, because he cites it by name and quotes from it in his *De Natura Legis Naturae*. Assuming that he was aware of this mixed dominion in the *Summa*, the chief problem is to account for the fact that he does not cite the *Summa*, which contains an authority for his purpose, but did cite the *De Regimine*, which does not contain such authority. The reason is not far to seek. For it is very doubtful whether this *politia bene commixta* of St Thomas's is really monarchy at all in the ordinary sense of the term. Rather its description would fit a republic in which the president and senate were elected by the people. Hereditary kingship figures in it too little, and popular election and government too much, to suit Fortescue's purposes. He may, of course, have derived from it the notion of a 'mixture' of polities, but it seems not too much to say that Fortescue's *dominium regale et politicum* is emphatically not St Thomas's *politia commixta*. We are, therefore, driven back to our supposition that Fortescue made use of the *De Regimine* in some such way as we have suggested above, and the conjecture derives no small support from the fact that his terminology is clearly derived from the *De Regimine*, and not from the *Summa*, where the words *dominium*, *regale*, and *politicum* do not appear at all.

If we ask why Fortescue made this combination and formulated his mixed dominion, there are clues for an answer. For we note that he placed first among the sources of the theory experience and ancient histories: St Thomas and the other theorists were placed second. Furthermore, immediately after his allusion to what could be learnt from St Thomas, he passed on to the kingdom of England. *In regno namque Angliae* is the conjunctive phrase between these topics. These facts suggest that he wanted a theory to cover the facts of the English polity as he knew them. He saw that the English polity could not be described as either a political or a regal dominion merely, nor yet as an elective republic. But a combination of the two dominions not only substantially provided the desired theoretical category, but also brought in the authority of the great St Thomas and his successors. He therefore made the combination. Hence we may say that Fortescue found the theoretical explanation of the English polity as he had experienced it, in his own combination of certain features of the *dominium politicum* and *dominium regale* which were described in two works, both entitled *De Regimine Principum*—of which one was by Egidius Romanus, and the other by St Thomas and a continuator usually deemed to have been Ptolemy of Lucca.[66]

In answering our second question—Precisely how is Fortescue's account of the origin of the political and regal dominion to be interpreted?—our chief object of attention must be the thirteenth chapter of the *De Laudibus*. Doubts, indeed, have been raised whether this chapter really does describe the origin of the mixed dominion, but these doubts cannot be upheld. It is true that the text says that the chapter narrates the manner of institution of the political kingdom (*institutionis regni politici formam*), and that later on in the text of the chapter occur the terms *dominium regale et politicum* and *regnum regale et politicum*; and it has therefore been suggested that the *regnum politicum* therein described is really the *dominium politicum*, which was not a mixed dominion at all nor equivalent to the *dominium* or *regnum regale et politicum* of England and Scotland mentioned at the end of the chapter. But this purely verbal discrepancy—merely apparent as it is—is quite insufficient to support this theory. For it is undeniable that the chapter relates to the establishment not only of a dominion, but also of a kingdom; so that *regnum politicum* is a literal term for the theme of the chapter. There cannot be a kingdom without a king; every *regnum* is necessarily *regale*, whether it be also *politicum* or not. The word *regale* is always redundant in the phrase *regnum regale et politicum*, though it is not redundant in the phrase *dominium regale et politicum*; and therefore no inference can be drawn from its omission from the phrase in question. Moreover, either the statements towards the end of the chapter which commence *Sic namque regnum Angliae* and *Sic Scotia* are meaningless verbiage, or they mean that the dominion regal and political of England and the kingdom regal and political of Scotland originated as the political kingdom is said to have done in the previous part of the chapter. All three phrases must therefore mean the same kind of dominion, and the chapter must relate to the origin of the mixed dominion, regal and political.

It is the interpretation of this chapter that has been responsible for most of the modern constitutionalism that has been attributed to Fortescue. For this description of the origin of the *regnum politicum* has been understood as an account of the origin of constitutional monarchy, and on the strength of it he has been hailed as the precursor of Sidney and of Locke.[67] But it is easy to read back into early texts the ideas of a later date, and Fortescue has been a ready prey for constitutional controversialists and liberal sentimentalists. Actually, no theory of constitutional monarchy[68] is propounded or implied in Fortescue's account of the origin of the *regnum politicum*, or anywhere else in his writings; and if he was the precursor of anyone, it was of Hobbes rather than of Locke.[69] For close attention to Fortescue's own words makes it clear that he completely confused the origin of political society and the formation of the monarchical state by treating them as one phenomenon. In his view, the people, when joining together in political society, necessarily (*semper oportet*) established at the same time one ruler over them, and this ruler was king. He did not conceive, as Locke did, that the people might agree to unite first, and later, by some further compact, appoint a ruler to rule according to an agreed code of laws. His social contract was also itself the political one. The body politic and the monarchy were created at one and the same time, and by the same act of union. Fortescue's *regnum politicum* was established in exactly the same manner as Hobbes's *Leviathan*.

There was no room, in Fortescue's view of this establishment, for a choice among various forms of government. Once the initial act of incorporation had been performed, all else followed with the same immutability as an embryo developed into a physical organism with one head. The act of incorporation was engendered by the intention of the people to provide for their political welfare, and this provision necessarily involved the maintenance of law; or rather, their political welfare *was* the maintenance of law by all members. There was thus no question of agreements between people and ruler to do or not to do this or that; there was no question of surrendering, retaining, or conferring rights. The act of incorporation and the establishment of the monarch were part and parcel of the maintenance of law; there could be none of these without the others, any more than in a physical organism the head, heart, and nerves could live without one another. Nor did it follow that law existed before this incorporation, any more than the nerves existed before the development of the embryo into the physical organism. Without the incorporation of the people and the establishment of the ruler, law could not be maintained; and law unmaintained is not law. But the purpose of law was to protect the people in their lives and goods, and therefore the king, when established, had no power to change the law or to seize the property of the people. King and law were bound up together; no king, no law—no law, no king. Hence if the law were to be altered, or the goods of the people confiscated by taxation, their assent had to be obtained. For the only power the king had was from them, and he had it for the maintenance of law. But he did have this power, and he had it absolutely. Once given, it could not be taken away without the dissolution of the body politic; there was no control over it, no system of checks or balances upon it; for the purposes of his establishment the king was an absolute monarch. He was limited only by the necessity of procuring the assent of the people for an alteration in their legal and proprietary *status*. He was not, in short, a constitutional monarch; for he was uncontrolled, and there were no means of restraining him or of disposing of him. He was an absolute autocrat in his own proper sphere.[70] Yet he was not above the law, for it was the law that made him ruler, just as the head of the physical organism was not above the biological law that made it. The maintenance of the laws and property of the people was his very *raison d'être*, and the exercise of his power was thus limited by the need for the assent of the people, from whom his power originally came.[71]

Fortescue's theory of regal and political dominion is thus in no sense a theory of constitutional monarchy. It is essentially a theory in line with the typical mediaeval theory of the kingship that was not tyranny, of the king ruling according to law. It is impossible—unless we ignore the Roman law theory of 'lex regia'— to find in it any important innovation in the theory of kingship, except the vivid explanation of its origin. This explanation was obviously suggested, with perhaps some help from Vincent of Beauvais,[72] by the two passages which Fortescue quoted from St Augustine and Aristotle respectively. St Augustine said that a people is a body of men associated together by a consent to law and a community of interest; Aristotle affirmed that when a multitude is reduced to a unity, one will rule and the others be ruled. Fortescue again exercised his talents for combining theories, and produced his account of the origin of limited monarchy. If, as seems clear, he held that this king originally derived his power from the consent of the people, this was saying no more than was to be found in the very first section of the first book of the Institutes. If his premises be granted, his theory is not an unreasonable one. But no more striking evidence of his conservatism can be mentioned than the very restricted conclusion he drew from his theory. If he had been a constitutionalist it would have been easy for him to deduce a whole system of checked, balanced, responsible, and controlled monarchy from a few modifications of his account of origins. But he did not do so, for to him the king was absolute, even though limited. It never occurred to him that the king was accountable to any less remote authority than that of the divine wrath.[73] The people had established the monarch, but this act exhausted their initiative. They had established, for their own good, a master who was to be obeyed, unless, indeed, he altered the law or seized their goods without their assent. But even if he did these things without their assent, they had no remedy against him unless they could overpower him. The king's council was not a check upon, but an instrument of, the royal power, and Fortescue thought it should be made more efficient.[74]

The third and last of our questions—How far was Fortescue's attribution of the mixed dominion to England justified?—involves a preliminary determination of precisely what the attribution implied. This determination is easy, for Fortescue's specific references to the polity of England were few, definite, and unambiguous. The kingdom of England was a dominion regal and political, and the king of England's authority was that of a king ruling politically. For the kingdom had been founded by the community that had come long ago from Italy and Greece with Brutus; this community had willed to unite and form a body politic called a realm, and had chosen Brutus to be its head and king. They and he, at the time of this incorporation and institution, had ordained the realm to be ruled and 'justified' by such laws as they all would assent to. The 'law' of England was therefore political because it was made by the counsel of many, and it was also regal because it was administered by a king.[75] Hence it came about that in Fortescue's time the king and his ministers could not, or at least did not, change the laws or impose taxes on his subjects, without their assent. This assent he specified in one place as that of the Three Estates, and in another as that of parliament. Furthermore, in England, he said, the judges were sworn to render judgment according to the laws, even if the prince commanded them to the contrary.[76] Apart from the statement of the historical origins—and even that is not without foundation in the then received Brutus legend—it ought not to be necessary to argue that Fortescue's very brief and matter-of-fact description of the monarchy of his day is a just one. But it has been said in a well-known work on the evolution of parliament that 'the constitutional ideal which Sir John Fortescue depicted at the close of the middle ages had little more relevance to the practice of his day than More's Utopia had to the government of Cardinal Wolsey'.[77] These words are picturesque, and create a vivid impression of Fortescue's work; but unfortunately, they give a totally wrong impression of it. For if Fortescue depicted an ideal at all, it was not constitutional; and if he depicted anything constitutional, it was not ideal. It is true that he depicted in one passage a more or less Utopian ideal for England—a state in which 'this (England) shal be a collage, in whiche shul syng and pray for evermore al the men of England spirituel and temporel'[78]—but this ideal was based merely upon certain administrative reforms tending to strengthen the executive, and had nothing whatever to do with constitutional matters. He contemplated no sort of constitutional reforms or ideals. His remarks on what we call the constitution are in no sense Utopian—they simply reflect the facts; so far from being irrelevant to the practice of his day, they state it. For there can be no serious doubt that the normal practice of the king in the fifteenth century was neither to alter the law of the land nor to impose taxes without the assent of parliament. Even the theory that his practice might be different was mentioned only to be refuted. The rebels of 1450, for instance, alleged that there were some people who said the king was above law and might break it as he wished, and that he should live on the commons, whose bodies and goods were his. But the contrary, they insisted, was the truth; otherwise the king would not swear at his coronation to keep the laws, nor would he ever need to summon parliament to ask the commons for their money.[79] Moreover, King Henry IV himself informed the pope that statutes could not be revoked or changed without the assent of the estates,[80] and the lords of parliament affirmed in the minority of Henry VI that the law of the land could not have been altered by the late king without the same assent.[81] The king of England, Philip de Commynes observed, took a long time to raise money, for he could not do it without the assent of parliament.[82]

Practice and theory in these constitutional matters thus coincided. Fortescue, in stating them, was but voicing the common opinion and describing the ordinary fact of his time. His originality lay not in any exceptional constitutional enlightenment nor in liberal sentiments, but in his attempt to array bare constitutional facts in the imposing raiment of political theory.

EXCURSUS I

FORTESCUE AND BRACTON

The absence of any definite influence on Fortescue's doctrine of the work of Bracton and the other early legal writers is remarkable. No reference to them is found in any of Fortescue's writings. It is hardly possible to suppose that the chief justice of the king's bench from 1442 to 1462 can have been entirely unacquainted with the works of Bracton and his successors, Fleta and Britton. However, it has to be remembered that the popularity of these works was at its lowest ebb in the fifteenth century. Nearly all of the known MSS. of Bracton's text were written during the century of its original composition; many of them within fifty years of it; very few after 1350; and none at all after 1400.[83] Apparently legal opinion in fifteenth-century England did not hold Bracton as an authority in the law.[84] Fleta, who reproduced most of Bracton's doctrines on the kingship[85], is supposed never to have been much read.[86] Britton was a more popular work, but the Bractonian doctrines of kingship scarcely appear in it at all.

True, the general views of Bracton that the English king was below the law, and that sovereignty lay in the law, are also broadly the views of Fortescue. But there the similarity in their doctrines ceases. A comparison between the component parts of their doctrines of kingship makes it unlikely that Fortescue, despite all his zeal for citation and authorities, made any use of Bracton's work.

There are four main points in Fortescue's doctrine of English kingship and it is interesting to see what analogies to them, if any, are to be found in Bracton, Fleta, or Britton. These four points are, briefly: (1) the king's legislative and fiscal capacity is limited by assent of parliament; (2) the king's power is not thereby diminished; (3) the king, with the assent of parliament, can change and add to the law; (4) the civilian principle of *Quod principi placet legis habet vigorem* does not obtain in England.

(1) Bracton conceived of the king as legislating or adjudicating with the co-operation of the magnates, but placed no emphasis on the *necessity* of the *assent* of such a body for valid legislation. The limitation on the king, in his view, is not so much an assenting body as the very law itself. On the other hand, his view that the law makes the king, and that the king ought to attribute to the law what the law attributes to him, namely, dominion and power, is also, at least implicitly, Fortescue's.[88]

Fo. 5b: 'Ipse autem rex non debet esse sub homine sed sub deo et sub lege, quia lex facit regem. Attribuat igitur rex legi, quod lex attribuat ei, videlicet, dominationem et potestatem. Non est enim rex ubi dominatur voluntas et non lex.'

Fo. 107b: 'Temperet igitur potentiam suam per legem quae frenum est potentiae quod secundum leges vivat, quod hoc sanxit lex humana quod leges suum ligent latorem, et alibi in eadem, digna vox maiestate regnantis est legibus, scilicet alligatum se principem profiteri.'

(2) Bracton certainly held that, although the king was bridled

by the law, his true power was not thereby diminished. For in so far as the king was the servant of the law, he was the vicar of God, and in so far as he acted contrary to the law, he was the minister of the Devil. This is in essence the same argument as Fortescue used in contending that the *rex regalis et politicus* was restrained only from sinning. But the form and structure of the two arguments are entirely different, and show no connexion with each other.

(3) Bracton of course wrote too early to insist on parliament's assent as being necessary for law-giving. He did not say even that the assent of any body was essential for the purpose, but he attributed legislative capacity by adjudication to the king and a more or less vague counsel and advice of magnates and acceptance by the community.

Ibid. fo. 1 a: 'Sed non erit absurdum leges Anglicanas licet non scriptas leges appellare cum legis vigorem habeat quidquid de consilio et consensu magnatum et rei publicae communi sponsione, auctoritate regis sive principis praecedente, iuste fuerit definitum et approbatum.'

This idea was substantially repeated in Britton's preamble, where the legislative authority is attributed to the king, his earls, barons, and others of his council.[89]

'Desiraintz pes entre le poeple qe est en nostre proteccioun par la suffraunce de Dieu, la quele pes ne poet mie ben estre sauntz ley, si avoms les leyes qe hom ad use en nostier reaume avaunt ces hores fet mettre en escrit solum ceo qe cy est ordeyne. Et volums et comaundums qe par tut Engleterre et tut Hyrelande soint usetz et tenuz en toutz pointz, sauve a nous de repeler les et de enoyter et de amenuser et de amender a totes les foiz que nous verums que bon serra, par le assent de nos Countes et Barouns et autres de noster conseyl, sauve les usages a ceux que par prescripcioun de tens ount autrement use en taunt qe lour usages ne soynt mie descordantz a dreiture.'

But in Fleta the equivalent of these statements takes the form: 'Habet enim rex curiam suam in consilio suo in parliamentis suis, presentibus praelatis, comitibus, baronibus et aliis viris peritis, terminatae sunt dubitationes judiciorum et novis injuriis emersis nova constituuntur remedia, et unicuique justitia prout meruit, retribuetur ibidem.'[90]

These are the nearest approaches to be found in the thirteenth- and fourteenth-century legal writers to Fortescue's statement that 'in regno Angliae reges sine Trium Statuum Regni illius consensu leges non condunt'.[91] But the wide differences between the theories involved in the several views of legislation are obvious.

4. Comparison on the three foregoing points has shown at most only a vague similarity between the doctrines of Fortescue and Bracton and the others. Comparison on the fourth point shows a striking contrast between them. Bracton, unlike Fortescue, did not totally reject for the English king the principle of *Quod principi placet legis habet vigorem.* Instead, he interpreted it in such a way that he attributed it to the king whilst nevertheless withholding from him autocratic power. He arrived at this result by assuming, unwarrantably, that the expression 'what is pleasing to the prince' really meant 'what is agreed upon after deliberation with his council of magnates'.

Fo. 107b: 'Nihil enim aliud potest rex in terris, cum sit dei minister et vicarius, nisi id solum quod de iure potest, nec obstat quod dicitur quod principi placet legis habet vigorem, quia sequitur in fine legis cum lege regia quae de imperio eius lata est, id est non quidquid de voluntate regis temere praesumptum est, sed quod magnatum suorum consilio, rege auctoritatem prae- stante et habita super hoc deliberatione et tractatu recte fuerit definitum.'

This interpretation was adopted by Fleta.[92]

'Nec obstat quod dicitur quod Principi placet legis habet potestatem, quia sequitur cum lege regia quae de eius imperio lata est, quod est non quicquid de voluntate regis tantopere praesumptum, sed quod magnatum suorum consilio rege auctoritatem praestante, et habita super hoc deliberatione et tractatu recte fuerit definitum.'

A significant comment to the same general effect is to be found written on the margin of an early fourteenth-century MS. of Britton, against the preamble to the text above-quoted. 'This preamble or prologue', it is commented, 'is divided into two parts; first the regal style where he says "Edward, etc." and the salutation, where he says, "And we will and command, etc.", affirming a prerogative in his person that what he thinks right ought to be held to be law, according to the saying, "*Quod principi placuit pro lege habetur*". Because peace cannot be without law, nor law without a king, who can change the laws and establish others, but not without the assent of the earls and others of his council, *quia ubi voluntas unius in toto dominatur, ratio plurimum succumbit.*'[93]

Fortescue, on the contrary, always flatly rejected this civilian principle for the king of England—though he said many Christian princes used it.[94] Bracton's interpretation, nevertheless, would have been very apposite to his purpose.

The famous 'addicio' to Bracton's text, which accords, as superiors to the king, not only God but also the law and his court, '*videlicet comites et barones, quia comites dicuntur quasi socii regis et qui socium habet magistratum*, etc.', has no equivalent in Fortescue. That this passage was an addition to Bracton's text is now sufficiently established,[95] but it was fully reproduced in Fleta.[96] Fortescue, however, does not seem to have contemplated any superior to the king other than God, or the pope, or the law of nature.

On the whole, therefore, though in a few points Fortescue's doctrines are paralleled in the texts of Bracton, Fleta, and Britton, there is no evidence of direct relation between them. But all of them, of course, had a common background—the principles of the common law.

EXCURSUS II

FORTESCUE'S ADMINISTRATIVE PROPOSALS

Strictly speaking, Fortescue's proposals for administrative reform are irrelevant to the themes of the present work. But in the course of the above studies some account has been given of every main subject touched on by Fortescue, and it is desirable for the convenience of the reader to round off the picture by providing a concise analysis of these administrative proposals. They are of great interest as being the practical expression of Fortescue's political experience, and of great historical importance as being a programme of reform which was partly that adopted and carried out by the Yorkists and the Tudors.

Fortescue's proposals relate first to the increase of the royal revenue, and secondly to the strengthening of the king's council. He insists that the revenue must be made greater than in fact it was at the time of his writing,[97] and must exceed that of any of the king's subjects.[98] The evils ensuing from an inadequate revenue were manifest, and were highly prejudicial to the royal prestige and power. The king was thereby driven to living on credit and to borrowing; the necessity of paying interest on loans continually increased his poverty; he was forced to reward services not in cash but in assignments, to the dissatisfaction of all concerned; and he was compelled to find 'exquisite means' of getting money.[99] The revenue must be made to exceed the annual charges, both ordinary and extraordinary, and these should be estimated as far as possible in advance. The ordinary charges included the expenses of the royal household and wardrobe, the salaries of the great officers, the maintenance of the courts and of the council, the costs of keeping the Marches and Calais, the financing of the royal works. The keeping of the sea also had to be provided for, and tonnage and poundage should be strictly applied to this purpose.[100] The extraordinary charges were so casual that they could not be accurately estimated in advance, but none the less a rough maximum computation of them ought to be made. They included the costs of sending embassies and envoys, and of receiving, maintaining and making gifts to representatives of other powers; rewards for faithful services, the expenses of special commissions and visitations within the realm, the expense of buildings and clothing, and provision against the event of invasions.[101]

The best way to secure revenue sufficient for all these and any other needs was to keep in the royal hands the greatest possible amount of land.[102] Royal lands should never be sold nor alienated for more than a term of years and lands that had been alienated should be resumed by authority of parliament.[103] The great increase in the permanent royal revenue by such resumption would perpetually relieve the realm from taxation in future, and a large immediate subsidy could be granted with which the holders of resumed lands could be compensated, and from which future services could be rewarded in cash. The greatest care should be given to the judicious bestowal of rewards. These should take the form of cash, office, marriage, franchise, or privilege, and, as infrequently as possible, of lands, and then only for a term of years or at most for life, never in perpetuity.[104] Offices at the king's disposal were very numerous, and his power could be much augmented by bestowing only one office on any man, and by ensuring that office-holders served only the king and no other master.[105] Corrodies and pensions should be given only to royal servants as a reward for their services, and not to any suitor who might seek them.[106] Above all, rewards of every kind should be granted by the advice of the council, which could deliberate on the merits of every reward and could relieve the king of the incessant importunities of petitioners.[107] By these measures the crown could be strongly endowed, and the people relieved of the great part of recurrent taxation.

The king's council hitherto had been composed mostly of great magnates who had overawed the lesser councillors and were frequently too much pre-occupied in advancing their own and their friends' interests to attend adequately to the king's business, or to preserve properly the secrets of the council. Yet a well-constituted council could deal with every case of difficulty, and with its help the king could 'do anything'[108]. The king should select twelve spiritual men and twelve temporal men from the wisest and best-disposed that could be found, and appoint them to form his council; to them should be added every year, at the king's choice, four spiritual lords and four temporal lords, or only two of each if the expense of four were too great. The councillors should swear to take no gift or rewards except from the king himself, and should devote themselves entirely to the work of the council, without any very great payment. At their meetings the chancellor, the treasurer, and the lord privy seal might attend when they wished or were invited, and the chancellor, in that event, should be the president of the council. A chief councillor to act as head of the council should be appointed by the king to serve during pleasure. The judges, barons of the exchequer, the clerk of the rolls, and other lords should attend the council when requested by it to do so. The council should draw up in writing rules for its procedure, and preserve them in a book to be kept as a register. Such a council as this could debate all matters of difficulty, all questions of policy, and the amendment of the law. Parliament would do more for the improvement of the law in a month than it otherwise would in a year, if the council were to draft legislation. The council should also deliberate on the bestowal of every office, and advise on the grant of other rewards.[109]

These proposals, it should be noted, are in no sense constitutional in character, and deal solely with the strengthening of the executive, without touching the question of rights. The statement, therefore, of Lord Fortescue of Credan, in his 1714 edition of the *Governance*, to the effect that 'the subject of this piece is the most excellent and curious part of the law, the English Constitution'[110] is misleading. Nevertheless, the administrative proposals set out in it, if thoroughly carried out, would have had far-reaching constitutional consequences which Fortescue's Whiggish eulogists have seldom noticed. For instance, the suggested endowment of the crown[111] was partly designed to relieve the people from the burden of recurrent taxation. If this had been accomplished parliament would have lost control of supplies; this deprivation, coupled with the proposed vast increase in the power of the council, would have reduced it, apart from its judicial work, to the business of registering supplies. Thus the most important part of Fortescue's scheme of reform would have involved the atrophy of English constitutional development if it had been carried out.

NOTES CHAPTER IV

1 Fortescue in the *De Laudibus*, written whilst he was in exile in St Mighel-en-Barrois. On the subject touched on in the text above, cf. Kingsford, *Promise and Prejudice*.

2 Fortescue, *Governance*, 115: 'Yf the reaume of Englonde, wich is an Ile, and therfor mey not lyghtly geyte soucore of other landes....'

3 Figgis, *Political Thought from Gerson to Grotius*, i.

4 *V.* especially E. F. Jacob, 'Some English Documents of the Conciliar Movement', *Bull. J.R.L.* (1931), xv, 358–394. He admits (390) that the 'examples of conciliar zeal and activity' which he there adduces are insufficient to disprove Stubbs's implication that the country as a whole was not interested in the movement.

5 *Const. Hist.* 5th ed. iii, 638.

6 Bishop Beaufort of Lincoln, the chancellor at the parliament of 1404, compared any realm to the body of a man, of which the left part resembled Holy Church, and the right part resembled the temporality, and the other members resembled the commonalty (*Rot. Parl.* iii, 522). Thomas Chaundler, warden of New College and chancellor of Oxford, quoted Plutarch's comparison of the state to a body, and applied it to England, in a letter to Bekynton dated 6th January, 1452 (*Official Correspondence of Thomas Bekynton*, i, 267–268): 'Quod cum advertissem eleganter descriptum, traduci formam volui, et velut ex simili simile, desideravi Angliae communitatem Plutarchi simulacro fecisse parem. Ast tandem eo bene ventum est ut illustrissimum Regem et benignissimum Principem contemplarer Henricum, et qui locum animae tenent pontifices almos; ceterosque duces et comites, omnem deinceps militiam, usque ad plebeium aratrum. Sed cum hujus nostrae rei publicae corpus instituerem, ut caput sursum, pedes deorsum, concordantia aeque latera, ut cor, item manus, cetera quoque membra, apte suis starent locis, mira mihi Anglici Regni componebatur effigies.' Bishop Russell, in his parliamentary drafts of 1483, frequently uses the phrase 'public body'; and he also elaborates an anthropomorphic analogy (*Grants of Edward V*, p. xlvi; and Chapter II, Excursus VI, *supra*): 'What', he asks, 'ys the bely or where ys the wombe of thys grete publick body of Englonde but that and there where the kyng ys him self, hys court and hys counselle? For there must be dijested alle maner metes, not onely servyng to commyn foode, but alleso to dent... and some tyme to medicines, such as be appropred to remedye

the excesses and surfettes comitted at large....' Cf. his paragraph (*ibid.*) on the 'mistyk or politike body of the congregacione of peuple'. Cf. Fortescue's 'corpus politicum' (*De Laudibus*, xiii, cited *infra*, n. 25). The elaboration of anthropomorphic analogies was common at this period. *V.* Gierke, *Political Theories of the Middle Age* (ed. and trans. F. W. Maitland).

7 *Official Correspondence of Thomas Bekynton,* I, 78 (Henry VI to John de Lastic, grand master of St John of Jerusalem, May 10th, 1440): '...eo praecipue quod prior hujusmodi quicumque, juxta regni nostri consuetudines et jura, esse debeat unus ex dominis parliamenti nostri et magnorum consiliorum nostrorum, quotiens et quando ea pro bono rei publicae regnorum nostrorum fuerint ineunda....' *V.* Chaundler's letter cited, *supra,* n. 6. Beaufort, in the parliament of 1416, referred (*Gesta Henrici Quinti,* ed. Williams, 73) to 'materias quas tangebat in genere pro re publica regni...'; and the earl of Dorset was said (*ibid.* 107) to be made duke 'propter illustrissimos labores et agones suos pro regno et republica intus et extra.' *V. Vita Henrici Quinti,* ed. Hearne, 5: 'Hinc tanto principi per concionem publicam totius regni, quam parliamentum vocant, elato regi post triduum fidelitatis jusjurandum singuli proceres obtulerunt, priusquam ipse coronatus de bene regendo jusjurandum praestitisset. Quod antehac in nullo Anglico principe factum invenitur. Quibus habitis debitis gratis, ipsos hortatus est, ad rei publicae salutem et honorem.'

8 *V. Scrope's Articles* (1406), *Inner Temple, Petyt MSS.,* 583, 17, fo. 237a: 'Wherefore wee seeing and perceiving divers horrible crimes and great enormities daily without ceasing to bee committed by the children of the divill and Satan's souldiers against the supremacy of ye Church of Rome and the liberty of the Church of England and the Laws of the Realm of England, against the person of king Richard and his heires, against the prelates, noblemen, religion, and commonalty, and finally against the whole weale publique of the Realme of England....' *V. Rot. Parl.* v, 246: '...for the politique and restfull rule of this said land'; *ibid.* 280: '...and the good publique, restfull and politique rule and governance of his said land and people'; *ibid.* 290: '...concerne the good and politique rule and governance of this land'; and *Rot. Parl.* VI, 168: '...the poletyk governance of thys noble Realme standith and owith to be in the noble persones born of high blode....' Cf. Bishop Russell's parliamentary sermons, *loc. cit. passim.*

9 Richard II was charged with having proceeded against certain lords and *reipublicae servitores,* against the king's peace. But these were the lords appellant. (*V. Rot. Parl.* III, 417.)

10 For discourses, in parliamentary sermons, on duties of kings and subjects, *v. Rot. Parl.* III, 662; IV, 261, 295, 316. Cf. *Official Correspondence of Thomas Bekynton,* I, 290–291 (bishop of Bayeux to Humphrey of Gloucester, *c.* 1435): 'Etenim cum multa sint quae regibus debentur a subditis; velut obsequium, fides, vectigal, et quae sunt ejusdem generis legibus instituta, certe aliquid est quod humano divinoque jure subjectis debetur a principe. Quid igitur hoc aliud est, quam cura rerum publicarum? Quae demum nulla esse potest si vacat pietate et justitia; quae, cum maxime regiam majestatem exornent et illustrent, profecto non minus utiles et optandae sunt quam praeclarae. Siquidem omnis amplitudo et imperii gloria hinc exorta est; nec ulla tanta potestas imperii, quae sine his possit esse diuturna. Quare summa ope omni principi enitendum est, ut subjectam multitudinem praeservet et foveat; nec minus de utilitate publica quam de privata cogitet; quoniam populi fundamenta sunt ex quibus omnia prominent imperia; nec ulli ambigendum est tam magna fore dominia, quam dives subest populi multitudo. Quapropter non satis utilitati propriae consulit, qui publicam negligit; nec satis curare videntur amplitudinis suae culmina, qui negligunt vel avertunt fundamenta.'

11 *V.* references cited *supra,* n. 8; and also *Scrope's Articles* (1406), no. iii, in Gascoigne, *Loci e Libro Veritatum,* 230–231: '...eo quod stant pro veritate

coronae et utilitate regni.' Cf. *ibid.*, in *Inner Temple, Petyt MSS., loc. cit.*: '...and to the utility and profitt of the weale publique.' As early as 1292 the judges held that the king's prerogative was above law and custom 'pro communi utilitate' (*v. Rot. Parl.* I, 71). Cf. also the sarcastic allusions to the Yorkist pretensions, made by the author of *Somnium Vigilantis* (*loc. cit.* 519): 'Trow ye', he asks, 'thay will have procured the commone wealth?' He also uses the phrases 'good publique' and 'public prosperite'.

12 E. F. Jacob, 'Changing Views of the Renaissance', *History* (1931), XVI, 209.

13 *V. Scrope's Articles*, in Gascoigne, *loc. cit.*, and in *Inner Temple, Petyt MSS., loc. cit.* For the important articles of Kent in 1450, *v. Magdalen College, Oxford, MSS.*, in *Hist. MSS. Commission*, 8th Report, 266–267, and 271, n. 6. Kingsford, in *Eng. Hist. Literature* (359–360), omits the valuable articles enunciating theory.

14 *V.*, for example, Fortescue's tracts on the succession question; and also *Somnium Vigilantis* (*loc. cit.*), which is attributed to him, and is called by Kingsford (*op. cit.* 168) 'perhaps the earliest political pamphlet in English prose'.

15 About three-quarters of the parliamentary meetings between 1399 and 1497 occurred at Westminster (*v. Interim Report on House of Commons Personnel and Politics* (1932)).

16 For the texts of these parliamentary sermons during the century, *v.* Chapter II, Excursus V, *supra.*

17 *Somnium Vigilantis, loc. cit.* 519: 'In case it hadd be so that the good publique of þis royame hath ben vacillant in ony wyse and in perill of decay, what auctorite and power had thay to reforme it, þe kyng present and not yevynge thaim commyssioun tharof? Ye say perhaps that it longeth to every persoune of þe commynalte to oppose himselfe to þe ruyne of the good publique. But it is not so whann autoryte laketh.'

18 *Ibid.* 522: 'As for the fyrste, it were an hard worlde yf thay myght be comparable to þe kynges pouer, to the whiche euery subjecte oghte naturaly due subjectioun and obeyssaunce and promitytude of jeopard of his body and goodes for the fulfyllynge of his highe and dredefull commaundements made by reason....'

19 *Ibid.* 518: 'Singular wylle and senceall affecion....'

20 C. A. J. Skeel, 'The Influence of the Writings of Sir John Fortescue', *T.R.H.S.* (1916), 3rd series, X, 77–114.

21 All references hereinafter to Fortescue's works are to Lord Clermont's edition of the complete *Works*, except those to the *Governance*, for which Plummer's edition is cited.

22 *V.* the standard histories of mediaeval political theory, especially McIlwain's *The Growth of Political Thought in the West* (1932).

23 *V.* McIlwain, *op. cit.* 356–357; and Ricardi Armachani, *De Pauperie Salvatoris*, lib. I, ii, in Johannis Wycliffe, *De Dominio Divino*, ed. R. L. Poole, 280: 'Omni proprio correspondet proprietas; igitur, sicut quisque istorum habet dominium proprium, ita in quocunque ipsorum est una proprietas. Set forsitan non advertis quod alia est proprietas dominii, alia rei dominate proprietas. Habet enim quisque istorum proprietatem sive solitudinem aut singularitatem unius in ipso existentis dominii, et ita eciam habet baro; set preter hanc proprietatem baro habet solitudinem, singularitatem, sive proprietatem baronie, quia pro voto suo racionabili potest omne genus usus in baronia libere exercere.' The quotation from Fitzralph given by McIlwain (*loc. cit.*) shows that the archbishop's work on this topic is of great interest to students of political and legal concepts. Fitzralph's text has many significant points which McIlwain had no occasion to cite. Fitzralph distinguished three classes of dominion: the divine, the angelic, and the human. The human class was subdivided into two genera: the natural or original, and the adventitious or political. And the latter genus was of three species: the domestic, the civil, and the regal: 'Que tria debes ita

distinguere ut domesticum dominium ad bona unius familie unius immediati domini, civile ad bona civitatis seu communitatis multorum dominorum immediatorum, et regnum ad bona unius regni sive regiminis unius domini super multos minores dominos aut unum inferiorem dominum referantur.' What here applied to a kingdom applied also to a duchy, a marquisate, an earldom, a principality, a barony, a knighthood, 'et omni dominio sub se plura dominia minora et minores dominos continenti.' (*Ibid.*)

24 What seems to be the nearest approach to a definition of dominion in Fortescue's writings is the following (*N.L.N.* I, xxxiv): 'Qualiter soli viro promissa est Prelatura mundi antequam homo crearetur.' But the point made herein is that the rule over the world accorded to man at creation ought to be called 'prelacy' rather than 'dominion'; for man was appointed to preside, not to lord it, over nature. He says, however—following the *De Regimine Principum*—that the word 'dominion' may be taken in either of two senses. One sense is that in which the dominator, for his own benefit, lords it over another, as a slave; and dominion in this sense was introduced by sin, and did not exist in the state of innocence. The other sense is that in which the dominator governs and directs free men for their own or the common good; and dominion in this sense was natural, and belonged to the state of innocence. Clearly, Fortescue's theories of dominion regal, dominion political, and dominion regal and political do not relate to the state of innocence; and hence we are bound to suppose that it was the former sense of the word that he had in mind in writing of these three types of dominion. The passage in the present chapter runs thus: 'Unde soli viro hoc officium regendi orbem concessum est; nec officium illud dominium, sed prelaturam congruit appellare, cum ex Dei decreto vir ad illud non ut dominaretur sed ut preesset fuerat tunc prelatus. Sic namque et Ecclesia regentes ejus dominia prelatos nominat, et non dominos, cum dominia illa Ecclesiae constent, et non sint domini eorum omnes illi qui ea regunt aut qui eisdem praeferuntur. Tamen Sanctus Thomas in Prima Secunda Quaestione lxxxxvj, Articulo iiij°, et etiam in tertio libro *De Regimine Principum*, dicit quod dominium duplicitur potest accipi: uno modo prout quis dominatur alteri ut servo, quod sit quando eo utitur ad utilitatem et bonum ipsius dominantis, et istud dominium introductum fuit per peccatum, quare tale dominium non habuisset homo super hominem in statu innocentiae; alio modo potest accipi dominium prout est officium gubernandi et dirigendi liberos ad eorum bonum, vel ad bonum commune, et illud dominium est naturale, quale dominium habuisset homo in statu innocentiae, eo quod homo est animal sociale et politicum, et non potest in societate vivere sine aliquo praesidente et regente, ut tradit Philosophus in primo Politicorum.'

25 For the term 'regimen', *v.* 'regimen politicum' (*N.L.N.* I, xvi, xxvi, and *De Laudibus*, xxxvi); 'regimen plurium' (*ibid.* xxiii); 'regimen regale et politicum' (*ibid.* xxvi, and *Governance*, i, ii); 'regimen tantum regale' (*De Laudibus*, xiv, and *Governance*, i, ii). For the term '*principatus*', *v.* 'principatu nedum regali sed et politico' (*De Laudibus*, ix); 'principatu politico et regali' (*N.L.N.* I, 63, 188); 'principatu tantum regali' (*ibid.*). For the term 'regnum', *v.* 'regnum politicum' (*De Laudibus*, xiii); 'regnum crevit politicum et regale' (*ibid.*).

26 Cf. *Governance*, 109: There are two kinds of kingdoms, 'of the wich that on is a lordship callid in laten "dominium regale", and that other is callid "dominium politicum et regale"'; and *ibid.* iii: '...whi on reaume is a lordeshippe only roialle,...and a nother kingdome is a lordeshippe roiall and politike....'

27 *N.L.N.* I, xvi: 'S. Thomas in predicto libro quem regi Cipri scripserat, diversa dominandi genera quae docet Philosophus commemorans, dominium regale et dominium politicum precipue ipse commendat, quas dominandi species, Egidius Romanus in libro quem ipse *De Regimine Principum* scripserat, discribens ait, quod ille preest dominio regali qui preest secundum leges quas ipsemet statuit, et

secundum arbitrium suum, sed dominio politico preest qui secundum leges quas cives instituerunt eis dominatur.'

28 *N.L.N.* i, xxvi. (Cf. *infra*, n. 46.)

29 *Ibid.* xvi; *De Laudibus*, xii; *Governance*, ii.

30 *Ibid.* iii.

31 *Ibid.* ii.

32 *N.L.N.* i, xvi. (Cf. *supra*, n. 27.)

33 *Ibid.* ii, iv: '...politicum solum dominium est quod plures recipit rectores, sed regale nunquam.'

34 *Ibid.* i, xvi. (Cf. *infra*, n. 36.)

35 *De Laudibus*, xxxvii: 'Combinacio meritorum utriusque regiminis'.

36 *N.L.N.* i, xvi: 'Sed et tertium esse dominium non minus his dignitate et laude, quod politicum et regale nominatur, nedum experientia et veterum historiis edocemur, sed et dicti St. Thomae doctrina edoctum esse cognoscimus. In regno namque Angliae reges sine Trium Statuum regni illius consensu leges non condunt, nec subsidia imponunt subditis suis, sed et judices regni illius ne ipsi contra leges terrae quamvis mandata principis ad contrarium audierint, judicia reddant, omnes suis astringuntur sacramentis. Numquid tunc hoc dominium politicum, id est, plurium dispensatione regulatum, dici possit, verum etiam et regale dominium nominari mereatur, cum nec ipsi subditi sine regia auctoritate leges condere valeant, et cum regnum illud regiae dignitati suppositum per reges et eorum heredes successive hereditario jure possideatur, qualiter non possidentur dominia aliqua politice tantum regulata. Et in Romanorum historiis erudimur qualiter populus ille primitus sub septem regibus regale regimen expertus, deinde, quia regum inheritias luxus et rapinas diutius sufferre non poterat, regale excuciens jugum, Tarquinium eorum regem septimum simul et regale regimen proscripserunt, ac se deinceps politico regimini submittentes sub Consulibus et Dictatoribus Senatorum consultu regulatis plusquam quingentis annis regebantur. Sed demum Julius alter ibidem Consulum socialis dominii impatiens tam urbis quam orbis sibi soli arripuit monarchiam, quo ipse ex tunc regaliter vivere arbitratus est, non tamen Regis nomine, quod Romanis exosum fuit, voluit insigniri sed Imperator nominari maluit, ut quidam Consulum appellari affectabant antea Dictatores. Sed eo hujus arrogantiae causa demum interfecto, Octavianus, vir mansuetissimus in totius mundi monarchiam erectus mundum universum nedum regaliter, sed et politice Senatorum consilio gubernavit; consimiliterque fecerunt nonnulli sibi succedentes Imperatores, quorum dominium regale et politicum nominat St. Thomas in libro suo predicto, regale, quia eorum placita lex erant omnibus subditis suis, sed politicum, non quia per Senatores semper consulti sunt, nam eorum consilium multi Imperatorum in eorum perniciem contempserunt, sed quia ad plurium usum videlicet Romanorum regebant rempublicam, nec ad proprios heredes, ut solent regna, imperium Romanum descendebat.'

37 *Ibid.*: 'Sic et filii Israel, ut dicit Sanctus ille, ante postulatum regem politice regebantur; quo dominium eorum politicum erat et regale....'

38 *De Laudibus*, xiii: 'Sic namque regnum Angliae, quod ex Bruti comitiva Trojanorum, quam ex Italie et Graecorum finibus perduxit, in dominium politicum et regale prorupit. [For England as an example of the mixed dominion, cf. *supra*, n. 27, and *infra*, n. 76.] Sic et Scotia, que ei quondam ut ducatus obedivit, in regnum crevit politicum et regale. Alia quoque quam plurima regna nedum regaliter sed et politice regulari, tali origine jus sortita sunt. Unde Diodorus Siculus in secundo libro Historiarum Priscarum, de Egipciis sic scribit: "Suam primum Egipcii reges vitam non aliorum regnancium quibus voluntas pro lege est traducebant licentia, sed veluti privati tenebantur legibus; neque id egre ferebant, existimantes parendo legibus se beatos fore, nam ab hiis, qui suis indulgerent cupiditatibus, multa censebant fieri, quibus dampna periculaque subirent." Et in

quarto libro sic scribit: "Assumptus in regem Ethiopum vitam ducit statutam legibus, omniaque agit juxta patrios mores, neque premio neque pena afficiens quemquam preter per traditam a superioribus legem." Consimiliter loquitur de rege Saba in felici Arabia, et aliis quibusdam regibus, qui priscis temporibus feliciter regnabant.'

39 *N.L.N.* 1, xxii. How Fortescue reconciled this assertion with his other assertion that the regal dominion was like the kingdom of God is a delicate point.

40 Cf. Peter von Andlau's discussion, 'An conveniat imperium et quodlibet regnum magis regaliter quam politice gubernavi', *Libellus de Cesarea Monarchia*, lib. iii, tit. 8—whether, that is to say, it is better to be ruled by one or by many. The Hebrews before Saul, he says (*ibid.* lib. ii), were ruled not 'regaliter' but 'politice'. Many people believe, he states, that the 'regimen politicum' is the better system, and that under a monarchy the common good is more slowly served. But he decides that kingship is the better. Cf. J. Hürbin, *Peter von Andlau* (Strassburg, 1897).

41 *N.L.N.*, 1, xxiii.

42 *Ibid.* xxiv.

43 *Ibid.* xxv.

44 *Ibid.* xxii.

45 *Ibid.* xxvi.

46 *Ibid.*: 'Ut quamvis Rex politice dominans non possit sine assensu procerum regni sui mutare leges suas, sed tamen cum leges deficiant supplere vices legum, non propter hoc extollat se Lex Regia, putans se in hoc potentiorem liberiorem ve esse lege politica aut regem suum potentiorem liberiorem ve esse rege politice populum gubernante, cum peccare posse potestatis non sit, sed impotentiae servitutis que periculum, ut orbari visu vel posse virtutes ignorare.'

47 *Ibid.* The source of the argument is Boethius's *De Consolatione Philosophiae*, lib. iv.

48 *De Laudibus*, x and xi: '*Princeps*: "Unde hoc, Cancellarie, quod rex unus plebem suam regaliter tantum regere valeat, et regi alteri potestas hujusmodi denegatur? Equalis fastigii cum sint reges ambo, cur in potestate sint ipsi dispares nequeo non admirari." *Cancellarius*: "Non minoris esse potestatis regem politice imperantem, quam qui ut vult regaliter regit populum suum, in supradicto opusculo sufficienter est ostensum [*N.L.N.* 1, xxvi]; diverse tamen autoritatis eos esse in subditos suos ibidem aut jam nullatenus denegavi, cujus diversitatis causam, ut potero, tibi pandam."'

49 *Ibid.* xiii: 'Quare ut postulationi tue, qua certiorari cupis, unde hoc provenit quod potestates regum tam diversimode variantur, succinctius satisfaciam. Firme conjector, quod diversitates institucionum dignitatum illarum quas propalavi, predictam discrepanciam solummodo operantur, prout rationis discursu tu ex premissis poteris exhaurire.' Cf. *Governance*, ii: 'The first institucion of thes ij realmes upon the incorporacion of thaim is cause of this diversite.'

50 *N.L.N.* 1, 63. V. E. F. Jacob, 'Sir John Fortescue and the Law of Nature', *Bull. J.R.L.* (1934), xviii.

51 *N.L.N.* 1, v.

52 *Ibid.* vii, ix, xxix.

53 *Ibid.* xxix.

54 *Governance*, 113: 'ffor that on kyngedome beganne of and bi the might of the prince, and that oþer beganne bi the desire and institucion of the peple of the same prince.'

55 *N.L.N.* 1, xviii.

56 *De Laudibus*, xii: '*Qualiter regna tantum regaliter regulata primitus inchoata sunt.* Homines quondam potencia prepollentes, avidi dignitatis et glorie, vicinas saepe gentes sibi viribus subjugarunt, ac ipsis servire, obtemperare quoque jussionibus suis

compulerunt, quas jussiones extunc leges hominibus illis esse ipsi sancierunt. Quarum perpecione diutina, subjectus sic populus, dum per subjicientes ceterorum injuriis defendebatur, in subjiciencium dominium consenserunt; opportunius esse arbitrantes, se unius subdi imperio quo erga alios defenderentur, quam omnium eos infestare volencium oppressionibus exponi. Sic que regna quedam inchoata sunt, et subjicientes illi, dum subjectum populum sic rexerunt, a regendo sibi nomen regis usurparunt, eorum quoque dominatus tantum regalis dictus est. Sic Nembroth...Habes nunc ni fallor, Princeps, formam exordii regnorum regaliter possessorum. Quare, quomodo regnum politice regulatum primitus erupit eciam propalare conabor, ut cognitis amborum regnorum initiis causam diversitatis quam tu queris inde elicere tibi faccillimum sit.'

57 *Governance*, ii; *De Laudibus*, xiii.

58 *De Laudibus*, xiii: '*Qualiter regna politice regulata primitus inceperunt.* Sanctus Augustinus, in Libro xix, *de Civitate Dei*, cap. xxiii, dixit quod "populus est cetus hominum, juris consensu et utilitatis communione sociatus". Nec tamen populus hujusmodi dum acephalus, id est sine capite est, corpus vocari meretur. Quia ut in naturalibus, capite detruncato, residuum non corpus, sed truncum appellamus, sic et in politicis, sine capite communitas nullatenus corporatur. Quo primo politicorum dixit Philosophus quod "quandocunque ex pluribus constituitur unum inter illa, unum erit regens, et alia erunt recta". Quare populum, se in regnum aliudve corpus politicum erigere volentem, semper oportet unum preficere tocius corporis illius regitivum, quem per analogiam in regnis, a regendo regem nominare solitum est. Hoc ordine, sicut ex embrione corpus surgit phisicum uno capite regulatum, sic ex populo erumpit regnum, quod corpus extat misticum uno homine ut capite gubernatum. Et sicut in naturali corpore, ut dixit Philosophus, cor est primum vivens, habens in se sanguinem quem emittit in omnia ejus membra unde illa vegetantur et vivunt, sic in corpore politico intencio populi primum vivens est, habens in se sanguinem, viz.: provisionem politicam utilitati populi illius quam in caput et in omnia membra ejusdem corporis ipsa transmittit, quo corpus illud alitur et vegetatur. Lex vero, sub qua cetus hominum populus efficitur, nervorum corporis phisici tenet racionem, quia sicut per nervos compago corporis solidatur, sic per legem, quae a ligando dicitur, corpus hujusmodi misticum ligatur et servatur in unum, et ejusdem corporis membra ac ossa, que veritatis qua communitas illa sustentatur soliditatem denotant, per legem, ut corpus naturale per nervos propria retinent jura. Et ut non potest caput corporis phisici nervos suos commutare, neque membris suis proprias vires, et propria sanguinis alimenta denegare, nec rex, qui caput corporis politici est, mutare potest leges corporis illius, nec ejusdem populi substancias proprias subtrahere, reclamantibus eis aut invitis. Habes ex hoc jam, Princeps, institutionis regni politici formam, ex qua metiri poteris potestatem, quam rex ejus in leges ipsius aut subditos valeat exercere. Ad tutelam namque legis subditorum, ac eorum corporum et bonorum Rex hujusmodi erectus est, et hanc potestatem a populo effluxam ipse habet, quo ei non licet potestate alia suo populo dominari.'

59 *N.L.N.* xxvii.

60 Richard Fitzralph of Armagh, *op. cit.* 338. After giving a description of man's original lordship in the world, Richard is asked why he used therein the word 'authority' rather than the word 'power'. He replies: 'Auctoritas seu ius soli racionali convenit creature; potestas sive facultas irracionabilibus competit ex sua institucione primaria; quoniam iuxta supra posita verba de Genese, i, 29, 30.'

61 Plummer, *op. cit.* 171 *et seq.*; McIlwain, *op. cit.* 358 *et seq.* The present writer hopes to give more detailed attention to the question of Fortescue's sources, and of his education—which is closely connected therewith—in his forthcoming edition of the *De Laudibus*. But the question will never be fully cleared up until the *De Natura*

is thoroughly investigated, for the citations therein are vastly more extensive than those in any of his other works.

62 *Works*, ed. Clermont, 360; Plummer, *loc. cit.*

63 McIlwain, *loc. cit.*

64 *N.L.N.* I, xvi; *Governance*, i. For the various passages in the *De Regimine Principum* of St Thomas and Ptolemy, and of Egidius, *v.* the references and citations given by Plummer, *loc. cit.* Fortescue's citation of the *Compendium Morale Rogeri de Waltham*, which he says (*Governance*, i) 'more openly treats' of dominion political and regal than does St Thomas's work, shows that he was content to regard even nebulous allusions as good authority; for Roger's treatment of monarchy is of a merely moral character (*v.* Plummer, *op. cit.* 175).

65 For the two alternative legislative authorities, *v. Summa*, pt. II, i, Q. 90, art. 3, and Q. 97, art. 3. For the mixed polity, *v. ibid.*, Q. 95, art. 4: 'Est etiam aliquod regimen ex istis commixtum, quod est optimum, et secundum hoc sumitur lex quam majores natu simul cum plebibus sanxerunt, ut Isidorus dicit (*Etym.* v, 10)'; and Q. 105, art. 1: 'Unde optima ordinatio principum est in aliqua civitate vel regno in quo unus preficitur secundum virtutem qui omnibus presit, et sub ipso sunt aliqui principantes secundum virtutem, et tamen talis principatus ad omnes pertinet, tum quia ex omnibus eligi possunt, tum quia etiam ab omnibus eliguntur. Talis vero est omnis politia bene commixta ex regno, in quantum unus praeest, ex aristocratia in quantum multi principantur secundum virtutem, et ex democratia, id est, potestate populi in quantum ex popularibus possunt eligi principes et ad populum pertinet electio principum.' (Cf. Carlyle, *Mediaeval Political Theory*, v.) For Fortescue's references to the *Summa*, *v. N.L.N.* I, v, xxxiv, xlii (by name), II, xviii, xlii. It is remarkable that he refers to Qs. 91 and 96 (three times), but not to any of the above.

66 I entirely agree with A. P. D'Entrèves when he remarks on the absence of any visible influence on Fortescue's writings of his legal predecessors, Glanville and Bracton ('San Tommaso d' Aquino e la Costituzione Inglese nell' Opera di Sir John Fortescue', *Atti della Reale Accademia delle Scienze di Torino* (1927), LXII, 264). I am indebted to Mr H. O. Evennett, Fellow of Trinity College, Cambridge, for calling my attention to and lending me this suggestive essay. Sig. D'Entrèves does not, I think, add substantially to the conclusions arrived at by Plummer in regard to the relation of Fortescue to St Thomas's texts.

67 Carlingford, *Works*, 361. Lord Carlingford seems to suggest that Hallam also thought of Fortescue in this light, but I do not find any warrant for this in Hallam's text.

68 It is essential to maintain a clear distinction between the terms 'limited monarchy' and 'constitutional monarchy'. Plummer, and indeed Professor McIlwain also, use these terms as though they were synonymous, and this confusion is most misleading. A limited monarch is one whose power is absolute except in certain spheres delimited by law and custom. A constitutional monarch is limited but not absolute, for his power is controlled by some other co-existent power whose authority he cannot lawfully override. An absolute monarch is not necessarily also despotic; for though he may be restrained only by custom or by moral and material forces, yet his power need not be arbitrary, as a despot's is.

69 The present writer arrived at this conclusion independently, but notes with pleasure that Amos, as long ago as 1825, made a suggestion to the same effect, in his edition of the *De Laudibus* (38).

70 Jovian Hicks, in his *Passive Obedience Defended* (1683), noted this point: 'Thus', he said, 'the learned chancellor Fortescue grants the king of England to have regal or Imperial power, although it be under the restraint and regulation of the power political as to the exercise thereof. And as a Fountain, which hath channels or Pipes made for it, within which its waters are bounded in their passage, and through which they are to flow, is nevertheless as perfect a fountain, and hath

its waters as fully and entirely within itself, as any other Fountain whose waters flow from it at liberty, without any such regulation; so a king, whose Imperial power is limited by humane constitutions in the exercise of it, is nevertheless as compleat a Soveraign and hath the Soveraign Power as fully and entirely within himself, as he who is at liberty to exercise his authority as he will.'

71 Waterhous, in his *Commentaries on the De Laudibus* (1663), observes (200) that the phrase 'potestatem a populo effluxam ipse habet' is not to be understood as applying to the government of England, 'which is an Imperial Crown, and is not alloyed by the politique admissions into it, but that that, as to the integrals and essentials of regality, retains its independency'. Such phrases he held to relate to the 'first ages of the world'.

72 Plummer suggests (*op. cit.* 84) that the account of the origin of the two forms of government was derived from Vincent of Beauvais's *De Morali Principis Institutione*. But he brings hardly any evidence to the support of this suggestion (*v. ibid.* ii, notes). He merely quotes a passage from that work bearing on Nimrod and Ninus, which is, of course, quite irrelevant to the theory of origins; and in any case, Fortescue cites St Augustine for his authority on those two monarchs. The present writer has not examined the *De Morali*, a copy of which, known to have belonged to Fortescue, is now in the Bodleian (*Rawl.* c. 398).

73 *N.L.N.* I, xxvii. He repudiated tyrannicide (*ibid.* vii).

74 *Governance*, xv, xvi.

75 *De Laudibus*, xiii: 'Sic namque regnum Anglie, quod ex Bruti comitiva Trojanorum, quam ex Italie et Graecorum finibus perduxit, in dominium politicum et regale prorupit.' Cf. *Governance*, ii. Fortescue seems to have had a certain amount of authority for his version of Brutus's elevation, at any rate in so far as the legend tells of his being chosen as leader of the Trojans. Thus, in the *Nova Chronica* of Rede —a copy of which is known to have been in Fortescue's possession—it is said (185) that Brutus was elected leader before the migration from Greece. Geoffrey of Monmouth's own version (in *Historia Regum Brittanie*, ed. A. Griscom (1929)) is to the effect that the Trojans besought Brutus to be their 'dux' and free them from their servitude to the Greeks. He uses the same words that Fortescue does, to describe this elevation—*i.e.* 'erectum est'. He writes (*ibid.* 225): '...troiani ceperant ad eum confluere, orantes ut ipso duce a servitute Grecorum liberarentur'; and (*ibid.* 226): 'Erectus igitur in ducem.' There appears to be no evidence that Brutus was supposed to be of royal birth or that he was called king. On the contrary, it seems that after the settlement in England, his descendants became kings (*ibid.* 239):

> 'Insula in occeano est habitata gigantibus olim
> Nunc deserta quidem gentibus apta tuis.
> Illa tibi fietque tuis locus aptus in aeuum.
> Hec erit et natis altera troia tuis,
> Hic de prole tua reges nascentur et ipsis
> Totius terrae subditus orbis erit.'

76 The texts for these statements are as follows: (i) *N.L.N.* I, xvi, quoted *supra*, n. 27. (ii) *De Laudibus*, ix: 'Nam non potest Rex Anglie ad libitum suum leges mutare regni sui, principatu nedum regali sed et politico, ipse suo populo dominatur.' (iii) *Ibid.* xxxvi: 'Neque rex ibidem (in Anglia) per se, aut ministros suos, tallagia, subsidia, aut quevis onera alia imponit legiis suis aut leges eorum mutat vel novas condit, sine concessione vel assensu tocius regni sui in Parliamento suo expresso.' (iv) *Ibid.* xviii: 'Sed non sic Anglie statuta oriri possunt, dum nedum principis voluntate, sed et tocius regni assensu, ipsa conduntur....'

77 A. F. Pollard, *The Evolution of Parliament* (1926), 133.

78 *Governance*, xix. These proposals are in no sense Utopian. As the German translator of *The Governance* says (*Über die Regierung Englands*, übers. u. hsgb. v. Dr

Walter Parow (1897), 9): 'Was Fortescue in der "Regierung Englands" schreibt, ist der Niederschlag der Erfahrungen, die er unter den Lancasters gemacht.'

79 Articles of Kent, *Magdalen College, Oxford, MSS.*, in *Hist. MSS. Commission,* 8th Report, 266–267: '(ii) Item, they say that oure Sovereigne lorde is above his lawe and that the lawe is made to his plesure, and that he may breke hit as ofte as hym lyst withouten any discucsione; the contraire is trew and elles he schuld not have bene swerane in his Coronacione to kepe hit, the weche we conceyve far the higheste poynt of tresone that any subject may do azenst his prynse for to make hym reygne in perjurie. (iii) Item, they seye the Kynge schuld lyve upon his comyns, and that her bodyes and goodes ern his; the contraire is trew, ffor than nedid hym nevir to set parlements and to aske good of hem.'

80 *V.* letter to Alexander V, printed by E. F. Jacob, *Bull. J.R.L.* xv, 379.

81 *Rot. Parl.* iv, 326.

82 *Mémoires,* i, 266: 'Mais les choses y sont longues, car le roy ne peult entre-prendre une telle oeuvre sans assembler son parlement.'

83 Bracton, ed. Woodbine, i, 24–25.

88 *Ibid.* citing Fitzherbert's *Abridgement, sub tit. Garde,* 17.

85 Lib. i, cap. 17.

86 Holdsworth, *Hist. Eng. Law,* ii, 321–322.

87 Ed. Nichols, i, xxxiv.

88 *V.* Bracton, ed. Woodbine.

89 Ed. Nichols, i, i.

90 Ed. Selden, lib. ii, cap. 2.

91 *N.L.N.* i, 77.

92 Lib. i, cap. 17, § 7. Cf. Selden, *Dissertatio ad Fletam,* ed. Ogg, 25 *et seq.*

93 Ed. Nichols, 2, n. B.

94 *De Laudibus,* 363; *Governance,* ii.

95 Ed. Woodbine, i, 333: 'That this particular *addicio* is a very old one there can be no doubt—it seems to be a not very distant echo of the trouble between Henry III and his barons, but the authority on which it rests is far too insufficient to allow us to regard Bracton as the author of it.' Ehrlich to the contrary, in *Proceedings against the Crown* (20–25), is no longer convincing.

96 Lib. i, cap. 17, § 9.

97 *Governance,* iv.

98 *Ibid.* ix.

99 *Ibid.* v.

100 *Ibid.* vi.

101 *Ibid.* vii.

102 *Ibid.* x.

103 *Ibid.* xi.

104 *Ibid.* vii, xx.

105 *Ibid.* xvii.

106 *Ibid.* xviii.

107 *Ibid.* xiv.

108 *Ibid.* The statement in Baldwin, *The King's Council* (206), that 'as to the composition of the council Fortescue takes the strongly aristocratic point of view', appears to be entirely erroneous, and indeed exactly contrary to the facts.

109 *Ibid.* xv.

110 *Op. cit.* 3.

111 Pecock, in his *Repressor* (1394), speaks of the unwisdom of allowing rulers to be dependent financially on the grants of the governed.

Conclusion

THE "SPIRIT" OF THE CONSTITUTION

In the immemorial past, or so it seemed to the 'constitutional' man of the fifteenth century, the people willed to unite themselves together into a body politic by submitting themselves to the rule of a king. This action of theirs was in accordance with all divine and natural laws, for the purpose of their union and their submission was in harmony with the scheme of things, with the will of the Almighty, with the immediate and the ultimate well-being of mankind. It was both natural and right.

The authority of the king is therefore sanctioned by its source in the will of the people obeying the divine impulse. The king is at once the minister of his people and the vicegerent of God. He is the special channel and instrument of the divine power and favour. The kingship is sacred, immortal, the very head of the body politic, which cannot exist without it. But the king himself is necessarily mortal, like all men. His office, nevertheless, must be filled. Successors must be found for it. God moves in mysterious ways, and His vicegerent may arrive by divers routes. Hereditary descent is the best and surest indication of His wishes for the succession to this office, as it is in respect of succession to real property, but it is not the only one. Other signs may serve. The might of the conqueror, or the voice of the people, may reveal the Chosen. But whatever be the sign, the kingship itself remains as it always has been. God and His will for the people do not change with a mere change of dynasty.

God's will it is that the king shall serve the divine ends, and of these Justice above all. The king must seek to secure, and he has sworn solemn and sacred oaths to secure, Justice for his people. This end is his duty, and for the performance of it he is endowed with all necessary rights.

The king has the right to command in his ordinances, his writs, his letters, and his words, and his subjects ought to obey his commands, so long as they are not incompatible with the true ends of kingship. He has the right to be provided with sufficient material resources for the due discharge of that great and all-embracing duty of pursuing Justice, but that right does not mean that he may take what is not his own, for that would be to encroach on the rights of others, which it is his duty to protect; the rights of others may be encroached on only with their free consent; this is an axiom of morality, and a rule of custom; those rights are secured to them by the law and the king is below the law.

He has also the right to have the counsel of any of his subjects that he may choose, and certain of his subjects contend that he has no right to dispense with the counsel of themselves or their nominees. He has the right to take any measures in the defence of his own rights, and of the rights and lives of his people. But the defender of Justice has no right to make of Justice merely his own will. He is human, mortal, short-lived, fallible, perhaps capricious, even malicious; he wills Justice, but Justice is more than the king's will. Justice is beyond the dictates of personal motive, Justice is the maintenance of the Law. Law is the good old custom in virtue of which everyone has come to have the status he has and to possess his own. It is the sum total of everyone's rights, including the king's. But not all old customs are good, and not all good customs are old. Yet the king ought to further Justice, and he may therefore change or add to the law. He may legislate. He alone may do this, but he may not do it alone. He may command a man to do this or that, and he ought to be obeyed. But he is the maintainer, not the creator, of Law. Law is not one man's will only, but something that ought to be sanctioned by those whose rights it determines. The king, therefore, if he legislates, ought to do so with the assent of others, of those whose assent is customary for the purpose.

The beginnings of kingship are very remote, but rights of property are very near and very important. The king, it seems, is not only sovereign lord of his people, but lord of the land also. He is the great lord of whom all land is ultimately held. His is all property in the realm not belonging to any of his subjects; he is, on earth, God's residuary beneficiary. He retains much property in his own hand and has special ways and means of so doing, though he is also a great grantor of lands, a giver of good gifts, and the fountain of honour. Perhaps he is not only lord of all, but God's freeholder of all the land. Perhaps the whole realm is his fief, and his franchises differ from those of other lords only in their magnitude, their universality. Perhaps the grants of his people made in his parliaments are no more than rent-services due to their landlord. Perhaps even his court of parliament is but a court-baron for all the land; and its acts merely judgements.

The king is the maintainer of the Law, and must therefore respect it himself. So must his officers, whom he appoints to exercise his powers or some of them, and they cannot avoid responsibility to the Law even if the king has commanded them to the contrary. Indeed the king cannot be deemed to have commanded a breach of the Law, nor to depart from the justice upheld by his predecessors the kings of England. He may not infringe the common law which protects everyone's rights; to do so would be to reverse the purpose of his existence. But with the new law that he has made himself, with the due assent of his subjects or some of them, it is different. He has made it and is not necessarily himself bound by all of it, unless he has expressed his agreement to be so bound in the law itself; nor need he always enforce this new law, especially when it is not a prohibition, and he may sometimes grant exemption from its ruling, so long as no man thereby loses his inheritance and right. For he is the judge of what is good for his people. When custom, old or new, ends, he

in the last resort is the source of discretion. He is the residuary
beneficiary on earth not only of God's good things, but of His
will also. He is the governor to choose or reject, to command
or forbid, to act or not to act.

The king is no ordinary or common person. His powers
remain constant, no matter whether he be an infant, or invalid,
or imbecile. He is all-absorbed by his office; he can do no wrong,
cannot be attainted, cannot be sued; he may delegate his powers,
but cannot give them away. He is not a person at all, but an
impersonality, an office in himself. He is at once the very
commonwealth, its supreme head, and its unifying principle.

He cannot even transfer his powers to a successor, nor divest
himself of his office, of his own will alone. Even though he
abdicate, his abdication is not valid unless accepted by his
people, or some of them. Even then there may be regality
enough left in him to require a deposition before it be finally
extinguished. His people, or some of them, may perhaps depose
him if he offend against Justice, but it is better—even necessary—that he abdicate first. Perhaps his own parliament might
depose him if it were to try, but it does not try.

Parliament is the king's highest court and has power to bind
all the king's subjects because all are party to it. It is a court,
and its members are therefore free from arrest during its session.
It is also the place where what is amiss is mended, the place of
worldly policy, and its members therefore have more freedom of
speech than other persons. It may make law that which is not
law, and may unmake that which is law. It is sustained by the
authority of the king, whose court it is; it speaks with the voice
of the people, whom it represents. The temporal lords are part
of it—the most important part of it, because they are the natural
leaders of the people and the natural counsellors of the king; they
are summoned to it singly by name by the king, and some of
these peers think the king has no right to refuse to summon the
heirs of those of their number who have passed away. The
spiritual lords are part of it, too, on their own behalf and on

behalf of Holy Church. The commons also are part and parcel of it, summoned by the force of the king's writ to the sheriffs, on behalf of their cities and towns and counties, with power to act in the name of those who sent them—of the commons of England, even if they are chosen by the interest of the local magnates rather than by the will of the people. The natural orders of the community, the three estates of the realm, old as time out of memory, seem somehow to be there.

The king in parliament is the inexhaustible source of remedies. All aggrieved may there petition the king for redress, or petition the parliament to petition the king for remedy of their wrongs. The petitions that touch the public as a whole, and even some others, may be adopted by the whole of the commons and be sent up to the lords' House in the name of the commons with the backing of the whole, or of the majority of the commons' House. The commons (and the lords, too, for that matter) have the right to petition the king about anything, to initiate any measure that may or may not become legislation. They, the commons, have the exclusive right to initiate those money grants to the king which seem to be sometimes the spontaneous gifts of the people and sometimes only his dues, but which are always necessary to the king for the carrying on of governance, though indeed he ought to live of his own as far as possible and even further.

Whatever proposals the commons make the lords may reject, but they have no right to amend them without obtaining the commons' assent before sending them up to the king, unless their amendments restrict and do not enlarge the proposals. But the king may reject them altogether, and may also amend them and enact them without obtaining their assent, so long as he does not actually reverse their intent, though the commons do not approve of the exercise of this royal right.

Parliament, including, of course, the commons, has the right to participate in all legislation intended to change or add to the permanent law of the land as administered in the courts.

Legislation of this sort, statute-law, cannot be established without the assent of both houses of parliament, and such law once made cannot be abolished save with the same assent. These statutes once made, whether they have been proclaimed or not, are perpetually binding on all the king's subjects wherever they be, on sea or on land, unless repealed by king in parliament. They are not only law: they are also the command of the prince, and must be obeyed under greater penalties for that reason.

They are not the only law that has to be obeyed, but in the last resort they are the most obligatory. If they conflict with some other human law, they break it, unless it be some canon of Holy Church regulating purely spiritual matters; they break it whether it be the king's command otherwise expressed, or his prerogative, or common law, or the law of the church touching temporal matters, or the law of the merchants, or those strong customs of London. All must give way to the law made by the king with the advice and assent of his lords spiritual and temporal, and of his commons, in parliament assembled, and by the authority of parliament. This is true of any sort of statute, unless it be simply a declaration of common law, when no conflict can be deemed to exist.

It is the right and sworn duty of the king's justices, to whom he has delegated his powers of doing justice according to law, to maintain and enforce the law, including the law that has been declared or made in parliament. They may, moreover, number among their duties that of sharing in the final making of statutes; not indeed in the sense of initiating, but in the sense of helping the king's council—they have been themselves serjeants at law and therefore givers of counsel—to decide which of the acts of parliament are fit and proper to become statutes; in the sense also of ensuring that the drafting of those acts which are to be statutes is suitable and correctly expresses parliament's intention, before their irrevocable engrossment as statutes and enrolment on the parliament or statute rolls, occur.

It is the intention of parliament that the judges must discover and enforce in the courts, if the meaning of the express words of a statute, which they may themselves have helped to edit, is ambiguous or otherwise not clear. But the judges are the ministers of the king's justice and not merely of the letter of the law. They ought not, in any circumstance, to be obliged to uphold what is manifest injustice nor to fail to do justice for want of a word in a statute. Therefore should even a statute be contrary to justice according to revelation, nature, or reason, they may, indeed they must, nullify it; if it be manifestly deficient according to the same standards, they may exercise the residuary discretion of the king whose justice they do, and may extend its express words, however unambiguous or clear, by a construction according to equity, especially when the statute can be treated as declaratory of the common law, of which they the judges are the only interpreters.

The king may indeed be deposed, if not by parliament, at least by the 'people' or 'estates' of the realm, but only if he fail to discharge the duties of his office. Such deposition is all the surer if his abdication precedes it. Otherwise he cannot be coerced, except by force. He alone can authorise reform; all resistance to him is rebellion and unlawful. There is no control over him, except the restraint of custom and conscience, common sense and, perhaps, vague contractual concept. Parliament, to be sure, has an authority of its own as the assembly of the estates, as the agent of the public weal, and perhaps of the public will, if there be any; it is entitled to speak and act for the people. But it may not resist the king, whose court it is. It ought not to refuse to grant him resources, for the people are bound to provide for the king's governance; and permanent endowment for him would be better than dependence upon grants, which in any case should be infrequent, as parliaments themselves should be, although annual sessions would be very convenient for redressing grievances irremediable at common law.

Nevertheless action by the king in parliament is the safest and surest way of securing the acceptance and approval of the people at large, and of disarming in advance popular sedition. The king in parliament has the most incontestable right to the people's obedience. The king in parliament possesses the most solemn, strongest, and best-sanctioned rights of governance. But in the last resort conflict between king and parliament is unthinkable. No king, no parliament. The king's displeasure is enough to dissolve parliament's pretension, as his will is enough to dissolve its session. His demise is the demise of the parliament. His abdication invalidates writs for its summons. Parliament has no rights save by the grace of the king's majesty, who, so long as he remains a true king, maintaining the law, pursuing justice, defending his realm, is responsible to no human authority. The sovereign lord king has the right to expect no coercion less remote nor more positive than that of Him whose Viceroy he is.

APPENDIX

EXTRACTS FROM YEAR BOOK CASES CITED IN THE TEXT

(1) 4 Edward II, Mich. pl. 51.   p. 252[1]
     (*Selden Soc.* XXII, ed. Maitland and Turner, 162.)
     Venour *v.* Blount.   Replevin.

 Ingham: ...'car un canoun defet plussours leis, auxi le statut[2] defet
 plussours choses qe sunt a la commune lei.'
 ......

(2) 13 Edward III, Mich. pl. 15.   p. 252
     (*Rolls Series*, ed. L. O. Pike, II, 25.)
     Staunton *v.* Staunton.   Formedon.

 Blayk: ...'il apiert qe eux averount ceo voucher.'
 Pole: 'A la commune ley ne a la ley qore court, etc.'

(3) 15 Edward III, Pas. pl. 45.   pp. 198, 214
     (*Rolls Series*, ed. L. O. Pike, II, 127.)
     John de Tornerghe *v.* Abbot of Furness.   Replevin.

 Mowbray: 'Lei deit accorder a resoun, et oster meschief, si le reverse neit
 este use pur lei; et ore le meschief est apparent, et unque nul
 fut forjuge del joindre en tiel cas, par quei par lei vous le devez
 suffrir; et home veit qe chose qe fut auncienement use pur lei,
 put le meschief vous lamendes de vous mesmes saunz parlement,
 come ou heir est vouche come deinz age, et le demandant en
 haste de sa suyte die q'il est de pleyn age, et prie q'il soit vew
 de court la ou le proces soleit estre toutz jours par graunt
 destresse, vous le changes ore et dones *Sequatur suo periculo* pur le
 meschief de ley; a plus foitz, poetz ouster meschief en ceo cas ou
 le reverse ne fut unques usee.'

(4) 17 Edward III, Hil. pl. 29.   p. 290
     (*Rolls Series*, ed. L. O. Pike, I, 143.)
     Warde *v.* Anon.   Detinue.

 Thorpe: ...'Ceo nest forseque forme; mes les accions sount diverses;
 et *Privelegia Statuti sunt stricti juris.*...'

---

[1] These numbers refer to the pages of the text above on which the case is cited.
[2] Stat. Marlborough, c. 9.

(5) 20 Edward III, Mich. pl. 9.   p. 290
(*Rolls Series*, ed. L. O. Pike, 11, 199.)
Waghan *v.* Anon.   Scire facias.

Shareshulle J: ...'Lestatute[1] ne parle mes qe proces serra amende par
tielx defautes et ne parle mye qe defautes en briefs par tiele
manere soient amendes, par quei nous ne poms prendre
lestatut plus avant qe les paroules en ycele ne parlent....'

(6) 21 Edward III, Mich. pl. 46.   p. 266
Brooke's Abridgement, Parliament and Statutes, no. 16.

...'patet ibidem que le parliament poet errer, come ou ils reuerce
le statut J.N. in certeins terres et le charter de ceo, et ne appel le
partie a ceo per proces devant le repelle, et *videtur ibidem* que error in
parliament ne poet este reverce, mes perauter parliament, et que
erronious iudgement la est bon, tanque soyt reverce.

(7) 22 Edward III, Hil. pl. 25.   p. 155
'Brief vient a Sir Wm. Thorp Chief de Banc du Roy de faire venir
le record et proces en Parliament d'un jugement qe fut rendu pour
le roy a la suite Edmond Hadelow et sa feme. Et *nota* que peticio
fut suy au roy devant ce qe le brief fut grante. Pourquoy le roll en
qui le proces et le jugement fut, fut porte par le dit Sir W. Thorpe
en Parliament. Sur qe le Roy assigna certeins Counts et barons, et
aveq les Justices, etc., de terminer le dit besoings. Et devant ce qe
rien fut fait, le parliament fut fini, et les deputies demeurrent, me
le roy meme fut ale; devant queux allege fut qe le jugement ne peut
estre revers, si non en Parliament. Et depuis qe ce est finy *ulterius*
en cest besoing *nihil agendum est.* Et fut dit qe le roy fit les leyes par
assent de Pers et de la Commune, et non par les Pers et le Commune.
Et qe navoit nul Per en sa terre demesne; et qe le roy par eux ne
doit estre adjudge. Et qe en temps le roy H et devant le roy fut
emplede comme seroit autre homme de people. Mes Ed. Roy son
fils ordonna qe homme suiroit vers Roy per peticion; mes onques
Rois ne serroit adjudge si non par eux memes et leurs Justices.'

(8) 39 Edward III, Pas. pl. 3.   pp. 76, 156, 229, 235, 248, 275
Rex *v.* Bishop of Chichester.   Provisors.
        ......
Caundish (?): ...'Sir, le breve fuit port long temps devant cel statut[2] fait,
et nous entendons que il y ad nul tiel statut.'
Thorpe CJ: 'Nous voulons aviser de cecy et auxy de l'autre challenge;
et puis a un autre jour breve vient a les Justices que l'ordi-

_____

[1] 14 Edward III, st. 1, c. 6.   [2] 26 Edward III.

nance fuit, qe si ascun trahist ples hors del Royalme, il viendra cy en propre person; purqei comandons qe vous allowes per statut.'

Caundish (?): 'Vous scaves bien qe terre ne fuit unques statut, ne publi en conte; et comment qe vous soies comander de allower ceo per statut, s'il ne soit ley, uncore ne deves ce allower par breve.'

Thorpe CJ: 'Comment per proclamation ne soit mi fait en le conte chescun est tenu de le scaver maintenant quand il est fait en Parliament, car tantost ad conclude ascun chose, le ley entende qe chescun person ad conusance de ce; car le Parliament represent le corps de tout le Royalme; et parce il nest requisite aver *proclamatio* ou le statut prist son effect adevant.'

Caundish (?): 'Devant ore il ne fuit my statut; mes ore le roy l'ad affirme; purquoi a ore commence le statut estre de force, et ce breve es pris sur un statut fait an xvij[1] et par cel statut nest il pas restreint qe il ne poit apparer per atturney; et nul ordinance fait puis ne poit restreiner cela, s'il ne fuit agreer en plein Parlement par tout les Communes.'

Thorpe CJ: 'Quand touts les Seigneurs sont assembles, ils poient faire un ordinance, et cel sera tenu pur statut, et pur cel cause le Roy nous ad mande de tenir ce pur statut.'

......

(9) 37 Liber Assisarum, pl. 7.   pp. 75, 215
Brooke's Abridgement, Parliament and Statutes, no. 33.
Rex *v.* Anon.   Scire facias.

...ou matter est encounter reason, et le partie nad remedy al comon ley, il suera pur remedy in parliament, et *nota* que a ce jour plures de ceux suets sont en le court de chancerie.

(10) 49 Liber Assisarum, pl. 8.   p. 55
Rex *v.* Anon.   Scire facias.
......

Bell: 'Le roy ne purra my grant cel par son chartes sans parliament, ne faire tenements devisable per son chartre ou ils ne furent pas devisable devant.'

(11) 6 Henry IV, Hil. pl. 2.   p. 35
Rex *v.* Anon.

Nota per Thirning CJ et Gascoigne CJ qe nostre seigneur le roy en ascun suit pur ascun chose que appertaine al corone, ne monstre en

---

[1] 17 Edward III.

certaine son cosinage, mes des choses touchant son duchie de Lancaster ou auter tiel duchie, il covient de faire son cosinage come auter person, etc.

(12) 7 Henry IV, Mich. pl. 19.   p. 284
     Rex *v.* Earl of Kent.   Livery.

......

Skrene Sjt: 'Avant le statute de Donis Conditionalibus, l'heire averoit de tiel possession le mort d'ancestor, et le roy averoit le terre par le forfeiture, et par le fesans de treason de tiel tenant le sank est issint corrupt, que son issue ne poit estre droiturel heire a luy mes il est droiturel heire a luy per forme de done, et al comon ley le roy duist seisier, donques entant que le roy seisist en ce case, et son seisier n'est pas tolle par le statute....'

......

Hankford J: 'Il est voier que devant le statute apres issue il avait fee-simple, et poiast forfeiter et aliener; qu'il ore formedon est done; mes par parols en l'statut le tenant en le taille ad auter maner d'estate, qe il avait devant le statute, car ore il n'avera forsque fee tail a nul temps, purquei, etc.'

......

(13) 8 Henry IV, Mich. pl. 2.   p. 45
     Rex *v.* Anon.

Gascoigne CJ: 'Touts les biens qe sont en Engleterre, en quex nul home ad propertie serra ajudges al roy per son prerogative, et en cest cas quant les felons estoierent mutes, et fuerent mis a lour penance, ils refuseront daver propertie en ascuns biens; issint par cel cause ne poit estre ajudge nul propertie a eux des biens, mes al roy per son prerogative. Purquei, etc.'

......

(14) 8 Henry IV, Mich. pl. 13.   pp. 74, 75
     Chedder *v.* Savage.   Trespass.

......

Tirwhit J: 'Moy semble qe Chedder recovera ses damages, car l'ordinance del Parliament voyt que si apres proclamation, *ut supra,* J.S. n'ust pas venus deins le quarter, que adonques il serra convicte, que est un judgement done en Parlement, que ne poit estre reverse, ou revoke en court pluis base,'...

Gascoigne CJ: 'Quant a ceo que vous dits, que l'ordinance fuit un judgement en le Parliament il nest my issint....'

......

(15) 9 Henry IV, Mich. pl. 20.   p. 45
      Simon B. *v.* Andrew   Scire facias.

      ......

Lodington Sjt: 'Le roy poit prender issue auterfoits sur un des auters
      points.'
Gascoigne CJ: 'Non sans tiels novel office trove.'

      ......

(16) 11 Henry IV, Mich. pl. 17.   pp. 54, 281
      Anon. *v.* Anon.   Debt.
      For extract *v.* Lodge and Thornton, *English Constitutional
      Documents*, 33.

(17) 11 Henry IV, Mich. pl. 20.   pp. 45, 139
      Rex *v.* Bishop of Coventry and Lichfield.   Quare impedit.
      (i)   ......

Hankford J: 'Le statute voit que les justices tiendront nul plee sur tiels
      titles; *ergo* le court ne puit my conustre en tiel plee, et mesque
      le party voil accepter votre title bon, uncore le court ne le
      suffre pas. Et mittomus qe le roy nous maund' breve, qe
      nous ne duissomus aler avant en cest plee, nous surcesseromus
      a pluisfort duissomus a ore, quant nostre poiar est restreint
      par authority de Parliament.'

      (ii)   ......

Skrene Sjt: 'Nous ferromus auter title pur le roy en cest briefe.'

Hill J: 'Il est bon qe vous issint faits, car vostre title est trop feble.'

(18) 11 Henry IV, Mich. pl. 66.   pp. 54, 77
      Abbot of Glastonbury *v.* A Purveyor.   Trespass.
      (i)   ......

Culpepper J: 'Si le XV ad estre levie torciousement devant ore, ceo ne
      don nul title a roy;....'

      (ii)   ......

Hill J: 'Le XV n'est my enheritance a roy, car il ne puit le aver sans le
      grant de son people.'

Norton Sjt: 'Voyer est, que il ne le puit aver sans le grant de son people;
      mes quant il est issint que il est graunt, donques l'usage del
      terre est de distreiner pur levier de money que est enheritance
      a luy.'

      (iii)   ......

Hill J: 'S'ils fierent treate ovesque autres, ils le fierent sans garrant et sans
      authority.'

Hankford J: 'Home ne scaveroit de quel metal un campane fuit si ce ne fuit bien batuz; *quasi diceret,* le ley per bon disputacion serra bien conuz.'

(19) 11 Henry IV, Mich. pl. 67, Pas. pl. 10, Trin. pl. 18.   pp. 45, 53, 286
 Rex *v.* Bishop of St David's.   Quare impedit.
 ......

Thirning J: 'Ceo grant del appostle en cest case ne puit my changer le
(i)   ley de terre, car si le roy ad title per cause d'un voidance,
       l'appostle ne luy puit faire perdre per reason de son droit.'

Hankford J: '*Papa omnia potest.*'
 ......

Thirning J: 'Ceo fuit en ancien temps et jeo ne serra disputation del
       poiar l'appostle, mes jeo ne scay veier comment il per ses
       bulles changera le ley d'Engleterre.'
 ......

(ii)   Norton Sjt. count de novel pur le roy,...
 ......

(20) 14 Henry IV, Mich. pl. 6.   pp. 55, 58
 Brooke's Abridgement, Prerogative le roy, no. 18.
 Mayn *v.* Cros.   Recordari facias.

 Recordare, fuit dit per Hill iustice que le roy ad prerogatife que il
 avera le gard de corps son tenant comment que il tient de luy per
 posterioritie, et uncore il ne poet graunt ceo a vn autre per graunt
 del seignorie a un subiect, car il navera le prerogatife et le roy per
 son graunt ne poet alter un ley ne chaunge un ley.

(21) 4 Henry VI, Mich. pl. 4.   p. 251
 Laurence *v.* Cheney.   Account.

Babington J: 'Me semble que ceo n'est my ple en abatement de brefe; car
       donque ceo peut estre per le common ley, ou per le ley
       special, *s.* le statut.'
 ......

(22) 8 Henry VI, Hil. pl. 36.   p. 267
 Brooke's Abridgement, Parliament and Statutes, no. 101.
 Anon. *v.* Anon.   Waste.

 Nota quod sepissime invenitur qe Gales ne les Counties palentines
 qe ne veigne al parliament ne sera lies par le parliament d'engliter,
 quar aunciet demesne est bon plee in accion de wast done par estatute et uncor auncien demesne nest excepte.... Mes *vide tit.* County
 palentine, 17 and 20, que ascun acte extenda al countie palentine.

356 *Appendix*

(23) 19 Henry VI, Mich. pl. 2.   pp. 140, 263, 267
      Anon. *v.* Anon.   Appeal.

Appellee: 'Nous disons que al temps del utlary prononce nous fumous icy
(i)   devant vous en prison, et prions qe le utlare soit reverse.'

Hody CJ: 'Tout que fustes en xx prisons al temps, etc., vous ne reversez
      l'utlare icy per tiel manere come vous pensez, sans suir breve de
      Error.'

Appellee: 'Il est de record que nous fumes en prison al temps, etc., auxi si
      nous fussions en autre prison al temps de utlare, il seroit reverse.'

Hody CJ: 'Vous estes un mervilous home; vous ne serez jamais rec', car
      nous ne poioms ceo reverser sans breve de error.' *Et sic fuit
      opinio totius curiae.*

      . . . . . .

Hody CJ: 'A le comen ley pur certein choses un breve issera al Franchise
(ii)   de Chestre, come pur treason, et statute est fait par autorite de
      parlement, et est general si bien deins Franchise come dehors,
      purquei adonque quand par autorite de parlement, breve peut
      issuer al Franchise nient obstant le Franchise; cest act de parle-
      ment est general, et sera pris general accordant al le statute.'
      Quod conceditur.

      . . . . . .

(24) 19 Henry VI, Mich. pl. 31.   p. 267
      Anon. *v.* Anon.   Debt.
      . . . . . .

Fortescue Sjt: 'Sir, il est grand diversite parentre Gales, que fuit un
      royalme aperluy a un temps, et Lanc', Chester, et Duresme,
      que furent derives hors del corone, et furent un fois a Com-
      mun ley tout un royaulme, et or sont county palais, car a
      ceux le roy put bien mander le record estre trie, pur ceo
      que il issint purrait devant le derivacion; mes a Gales ne peut
      mander pur ceo que al common ley il ne peut issint faire;
      et ce est la cause que le statut veut de choses pledes en
      Gales, come releas port date la, etc., serra trie en le county
      adjoynant. . . .'
      . . . . . .

Ascogh J: 'A ma entent touts fois al comon ley les Justices le roy purroit
      mander al County paleis a trier aucun chose fait la, mes pur ce
      que par tiel triel le party avoit long delay par le circum-
      stances del triel, le statut fuit ordonne anno 9 Ed. 3,[1] que lou
      aucun fait porte date en aucun Franchise de royaulme, ou
      breve de roy ne court soit plede, ce serra trie ou le brefe est
      porte, mes touts autres issues des choses faits en county-paleis

---
[1] 9 Edward III, st. 1, c. 4.

serra tries la come ils furent devant le fesance de cel statute; et
meme le statut pruve en luy meme qu'il ne s'extend pas a fait
port date en Gales, mes touts tiels faits et touts autres choses
alleges en Gales serront tries en le county prochein adjoynant
par le Common Ley, pur ceo que auterment droit failera al
party, entant que il ne peut estre trie en Gales par autorite de
cest court; mes cest court ad pouvoir de mander al seigneur de
county-paleis a luy faire trier un chose fait deins son county-
paleis et a certifier icy, et ceo ad souvent fois ete fait; purquei
ne peut estre semble a county-paleis.'

. . . . . .

(25) 19 Henry VI, Pas. pl 1.   pp. 13, 39, 74, 77, 137, 153, 268
      Rex *v.* Rector of Eddington.   In the Exchequer Chamber.

. . . . . .

Fray CB: 'Sir, me semble que le grant est bon, et ce est chose en le roy al
temps del grant, car le parlement est la court du roy, et le plus
haut court que il ad, et la ley est le plus haut inheritance que
le roy ad, car par la ley il meme et touts ses subjects sont rules;
et si son ley ne fuit, nul roy ny nul inheritance seroit; donc par
son ley il est a aver touts amerciments et revenues de ses courts,
come en banc le roy, common place, etc.; et par son autorite et
son brief les parties son estre appelle en sa court a respondre,
issint sont les seigniors par son breve appelles a venir a son
parlement, et autres, come chevaliers et burgesses, etc., estre
eleus per son brief; et attainders et forfaitours qui sont adjuges
en meme le parlement sont revenues de cel court, et aussi sont
les xv par cest grant de revenues come serra autre person a que
le roy ad grant les fines et amerciments des ses tenants faits en
autres courts que sont revenues de cel court.' *Quasi dicere, nulla
est ratio,* quand est inheritance auxy fortement en le ley a aver
lun court come lautre.

. . . . . .

Hody CJ: . . . 'Et cest fine ou due au roy est un profit de sa court dont il
est inheriter par droit de sa court, come est des autres issues et
cest par ma livre, issint icy mesque le xv ne fuit en luy al temps
del grant, uncore le grant voult bien. Et auxy est un profit de
son court de Parlement, mesque ne soit due a luy forsque par le
grant de son people ove l'assent des seigniors ensemble en un
lieu a ces deputes, que fait le Parlement; et issint a ma entent le
roy peut granter les profits de sa court de Parlement come il peut
de ses autres courts devant que le chose grant soit en luy, pur
ceo que le droit cest court est inheritance a luy. . . .'

Newton CJ: 'Sir, *gratia argumenti,* ce xv grant au roy per son people ne peut
estre dit perquisitions ne profit de sa court de Parliament; car
issues ou perquisitiones de ses courts sont choses a luy accrues

par cause d'un forfaitour fait a sa ley, come des issue perdus par ma disobedience al commandement du roy a apperer en court, par cause d'aver licence aucun chose, come fine pur fine leve, mes cest xv est un grant de *voluntate populi sui spontanea*, qui prove que il nest droit en luy devant le grant par inheritance que il ad en ses courts come issues et autre profits sont....'

......

Hody CJ: ...'Et auxy, sir, le parlement est le pluis haut court que le roi ad et est inheritance en cel court a aver tiel xv come est en autre court a aver ses issues; car mesme la ley que veut que le Roy defendra son people, meme la ley veut que le people grantera a luy de lour bons en aid de cel defence, que prove inheritance. Et ou est dit que tiel grant prend son effect de son people; jeo dit que non, mes covient apres tiel grant eu par son people, que les seigniors du Royaulme approuvent ceo, et auxy que le roy accept.' Pur quei.

Markham Sjt: 'Sir, ou est dit que le general grant fuit fait par le Parlement dun xv au roy, en quel tout le clergy du royaulme fuit party, et issint *per consequens* le Rector fuit party a son grant, ceo exclura l'especial grant par quel le Rector fuit discharge, jeo di que non, car mesque un grant dun xv au roy soit fait en Parlement, uncore chaqun ne serra lie par cel. Et auxy mettons que un del communalte de Londres soit disseisi par un estranger de son franctenement, et puis le Maior et le communalte release al disseisor, cest release fait par tout le Communalte ne barre cestuy de son especial inheritance, pur ce que il ne claime ce inheritance come un del communalte mes come private person; et ceo pruve, car si le communalte fuit disseisi, puis chaqun person aperluy release al disseisor ce ne vault, mes covient que ils release par lour common seel. Et issint est si certain recovery soit tail' envers le communalte les biens de nul private person ne serront mis en execution, mes les biens de communalte; issint icy, mesque le Rector fuit party a cest general grant del xv, uncore cest special grant que fuit fait a luy nest oste par ce, si non par special parol fait, *scilicet*, nient obstante aucun special grant grante adevant.'

......

(26) 20 Henry VI, Mich. pl. 17.   p. 268
    Pilkington *v.* Anon.   Scire facias.

......

Fortescue CJ: ...'Et aussi la terre de Ireland est severe del Roiaume d'Angleterre; car si un disme ou quinzisme soit grant icy, ceo ne liera ceux d'Ireland, mesque le roy mandera meme cel estat en Ireland, soubz son grand seel, sinon que ils veulent en lour parlement ceo approver; mes s'ils veut allower ceo, donque sera tenu la et ils seront lies par icel;....'

Portington Sjt: ...'Et auxi quant a ce que Fortescue a dit, que si un disme soit grant en parlement icy, ce ne liera ceux d'Ireland; jeo veut bien, pur ce que ils n'ont commandement ove nous par breve de venir al parlement; mes n'est prove que le terre est severe d'Angleterre, car un disme grant ne liera ceux de Duresme, del county-paleis de Chestre, et uncore ils ne sont severes de cest Roiaume. Purquei, etc.'

. . . . . .

(27) 27 Henry VI, Pas.   p. 292

Fitzherbert's Abridgement, Annuity, no. 41.

Anon. *v.* An Abbot.

Nota que l'estatute de Carlisle[1] voit que le ordre de cieustrz et austens que ount couent et comen seale, que le comen seale serra en la garde le prior que est de south l'abbe et iiij auters les pluis sages del meason, et que ascun fait enseale oue le comen seale que nest issint en garde serra voide; et l'oppinion del court que cest estatut est void car est inpartin' destre observe, car esteant le seal en lour garde l'abbe ne puit riens ensealer ove ceo, et quant il est en mainz l'abbe il est hors de lour gard *ipso facto*, et si l'estatute serra observe chescun comen seale serra defeit par un simple surmise que ne puit estre trie, etc.

(28) 31 Henry VI, Mich. pl. 8.   p. 267

Anon. *v.* Anon.   Appeal de Mort.

Et un capias fuit agarde autrefois al county Paleis de Chester accordant a le statute cest roy an. 6[2], contenant le space de vj semaines, et nul *capias* est or retorne, ne nul chose par le chancellor certifie de Counte-Palais. Purquei *Laicon* pria un Exigent al Vicont de Lincoln; car ceux del County Palais ne voile jamais executer le brefe. Et cest court ne poit eux punir mesque ils ne voilent rien faire. Et le statut est, que les brefes serront directes al Viconte des Counties dont il sont nomes. Et de Chestre est nul Viconte; issint hors de cas le statut. Et pur ceo me semble que vous purres agarder un Exigent assez bon, etc.

Fortescue CJ: 'Vous dites verity, le statut est comme vous dites, mes nienobstant le proces ad ete agarde plusors fois illonque cy devant; et issint il covient icy, car il est un egal mischief, purquei le statut fuit fait; et pur ceo vous covient de suir illonque. Purquei sues, etc., en le County ou l'appel est porte, etc.'

[1] 35 Edward I.

[2] 6 Henry VI, c. 2. The time limit in the statute is six days, not six weeks.

(29) 32 Henry VI, Hil. pl. 13.   p. 55
     Anon. *v.* Anon.   Debt.

      . . . . . .

   Fortescue CJ: . . . 'mes ascuns foiz Chestr, Lancaster, et Durham furent
            al Common Ley, et coment que le roy ad eux fait Countie-
            Paleis comme bien poit sans Parlement; uncore le roy sans
            parlement ne poit prendre son lige homme de droit. . . .'

(30) 33 Henry VI, Pas. pl. 8.   pp. 75, 154, 219, 220, 226, 227,
                                     231–233, 245, 248

     Pilkington *v.* Anon.   In the Exchequer Chamber.

En l'Exchequer Chambre Fortescue CJ rehersa comment en Parlement darrein passe, un special Act passa encounter John Pylkington
Esquier pur rape d'un femme hors de N. etc., et rehersa l'effect del
Act, et comment par mesme l'Act fuit grante, qe proces sera fait al
Viconte de E. de faire certein proclamacioun en un ville, cestassavoir, qe le dit John doit apperer devant les Seigniours a W. a un
certein jour, etc., a respondre transgression contenus en le dit Act,
etc., et sil ne voil, etc., adonques il sera atteint de *transgressio*, etc.,
et paieroit un certein somme al party, etc., et il disoit comment les
proclamaciouns furent fait et returnes en le Chauncerie, et le dit J.
n'apparust my, etc., et puis apres le dit J. fuit pris et mis en le Bank
le Roy en le gard del Marshal pur certein causes, pur quei un
transcript del dit acte ove un *Mittimus* fuit mande hors del Chauncerie direct a nos, etc. Parquei le Marshall fuit charge fuit ove luy
pur meme le condemnacioun contenu en mesme l'Acte, et or il
vient et allege par son conseil qe le dit Acte n'est my sufficent en ley
et pria etre dismys, etc., car la bill qe fuit en direct as Communes
passa eux bien et fuit endosse en tiel fourme, 'Soit baille as Seigniors',
et meme la bill passa le Roy et les Seigniours mes ou la bill voiloit qe le
dit John respond, etc., devant le Feste de Pentecost adonqe prochein
ensuant par qe les Seigniors endosseront la bill en tiel forme, 'Les
Seigniors grantent en cas qil nappert devant le Feste de Pentecost
que sera Anno domini millesimo ccccli', etc., al Pentecost prochein
apres l'auter Feste contenu en la bille. Et pource les Seigniors
granteront plus long jour qe fuit grante par les Comunes en quel cas
les Comunes devoient aver le bille areremayn et de assent al grant
les Seigniors et issint ne fuit my par qe il semble l'Acte voide, etc. Et
sur ceo le brefe de *Mittimus* et l'acte furent leus, etc., et le brefe fuit
tiele. *Rex justiciis suis, etc. Transcripcionem cujusdam billae coram nobis
in Cancellaria nostra in filacione, etc., exhibitam et auctoritate ultimi parliamenti nostri, etc., confirmatam versus J.P., etc., vobis mittimus, etc.*

   Fortescue CJ: 'Me semble qe nos poimus autrement entendre, mes qe
            l'acte est bon icy; car le Roy ad escripte a nos par son brefe,
            ad nous certefie qe la bille est conferme per auctorite de
            Parliament. Purquei.'

Illingworth CB: 'Ceo ne fuit estre entendu icy comme vos ditez; car le brief qui est fait forsque par un Clerk del Chancery ne fuit faire un Acte de Parliament bon, si soit vicious en luy meme, etc. Et si ilz del Chancery mandent as Justices de Comen Bank un transcript d'un fine par un *Mittimus*, et en fait est nul tiel fine, par qe ils de Comen Bank fesoient brief de *Scire facias* hors del transcript, etc., ne serra la party receu adire qe est nul tiel fine; *quasi dicere sic*, pur ce qe le brefe qe il ad fait ne fera un bon fyn ou ne fuit nul fine, etc. Purquei.' Et puis ils manderent pur *Kirkby* des rolles et pur *Faukes* Clerk del Parlament pur estre pris del fourm et cours del Parlement, etc. (*Fortescue CJ*) rehersa le mattre a eux, purquei,

Kirkby: 'Sir le cours del Parlement est tiel, etc. Mes si ascun bill soit particuler ou autre bille qe soit primerment delivre a les Communes et sil passe eux ils usent endosser la bille en tiel forme, cestassavoir, "Soit baille as Seigniours", et si le roy et les Seigniours agreent a meme le bill et ne voilloit alterer ne changer la bill, adonque ils ne ussent endosser la bill, mes est baille al clerk del Parlement pour estre enrolle; et si soit un commune bill il sera enrolle et enacte; mes si soit un particuler bill, il ne sera enrolle, mes sera file sur le filacion et est assez bien; mes si la party veut suir pur l'entre pour estre le mieux suer, il purroit estre enrolle, etc. Et si les Seigniours voillant alterer le bille, ceo qe puit estre ove le grant des Communs ceo ne sera delivre as Communes. Come si les Comuns grantent pondage ou tonnage pour quatre ans, etc., et les Seigniors grantent mes pur deux ans, ceo ne serra relivre a Communs pource qe ceo puit estre ove lour grant, mes *via versa* si les Comuns grantent lour tonnage et pondage ou tiel, etc., a durer pur ij ans; et les Seigniors grantent a durer pur quatre ans; en cest cas le bill covient etre relivre as Communs et en cest cas les Seigniors doivent faire un Scedule de lour entent, ou autrement endosser le Bill comme adire issint "Les Seigniors sont assentus a durer pour quatre ans, etc." Et quand les Comuns ont le bill arreremain et ne voillent assentir a ce, ceo ne puit estre enacte, mes si les Comuns voillent assentir a Seigniors adonque les Comuns endosseront lour respouns sur le marge de bas deins de bill en tiel forme "Les Comuns sont assentus al sedule les Seigniors a mesme cel bille annexe" et donque serra baille al Clarke du Parlement *ut supra*. Et si un bill soit primerment livrer as Seigniors et la bille passe eux, etc., donque en cest cas ils ne usent de faire nul manner d'endossement, mes de mettre le bill a les Comuns. Et dit en cest cas si la bille passe les Comuns est endosse par eux en tiel form "Les Comuns sont assentus", et par ce prove qe la bil ad passe les Seigniors a devant. Purquei en vostre cas pur ce que les Comuns granterent cest bill, et que la proclamacion donna un certein jour, et appert par l'endossement que les Seigniours ont varie, et auxint enlarge le jour, et nul mencion fait en la bill del assent des Comuns apres, purquei semble qe cest Acte n'est my bone, etc.'

Faukes: 'Sir, le cas fuist tiel, qe la bill fuit mis eins a les Comuns puis le Feste de Pentecost, qe fuist en le temps del Parlement; et l'entent de la bill fuist qe la proclamacion doit durer jusques al Feste de Pentecost adonque prochein ensuant, que feust en le dit Anno millesimo ccccli; etc., mes chescun bill de Parlement aura relacioun al premier jour de Parlement nonobstant qe soit mys eins al fin del Parlement. Purquei les Seigniors granterent accordaunt al entent del bill.'

Prisot J: 'Estes vos verament assertes si le bill fuit livre apres la Feste de Pentecost que fuit en le temps del Parlement ou nemy?'

Faukes: 'Verament entend' icy, etc.'

Markham J: 'Uses vous de faire enrollement de jour quand les bills sont primerment receus?'

Faukes: 'Non, sir.'

Markham J: 'Verament ce est perylous chose, car le court de parlement est la plus haut court le Roy ad, et si bien seroit chescun maner chose au Acte que est materiel et fait illonque, la reason seroit estre enroll, etc. Car en cest cas or si bill passe les Comuns et les Seigniors par la forme avandit devant le primer Feste de Pentecost, adonques cest Acte ne voult pur ceo as l'endossement des Seigniors del jour, etc., vary del bill, etc., et ne fuit mis arere as Comuns, mes s'il fuit livre apres le dit Feste de Pentecost, adonques me semble qe ils sont accorde; car tout est un jour, et ne besoigne my a relivrer la bill arere as Communz, purquei cest matter or ne purra estre determine l'un nel autre par vostre record, qe estes le Clerk, etc. Et or nous ne poimus doner nul auter credence quand la bill est en le file, mesque fuit livre al primer jour de Parlement, etc.'

Fortescue CJ: 'C'est un Acte de parlement, et nos voillomus etre bien avise devant qe nos anullomus ascun Acte fait en le Parlement; et peraventure le matter doit attendre jusques al prochein Parlement, adonque nos poimus etre certifier par eux del certainte del matier; mes non obstant nos voillomus etre avises qe serra fait, etc.'

(31) 34 Henry VI, Mich. pl. 16.   p. 51
Heuster *v.* Corbet.   Waste.
     . . . . . .

Et auxi fuit dit per Prisot J que en ce case ou le roy grante a moy le reversion per ses lettres patentes, que jeo aura brefe de Wast sans attornement etc. Car les lettres patentes sont de record.

(32) 34 Henry VI, Pas. pl. 1.   p. 263
    Master of the House of God *v.* Abbess of Sion. Quare impedit.
    . . . . . .
    Prisot J: 'Nous sumus apris de nul tiel general resumption, mesque soient
        divers provisions come vous parles; purquei l'act n'est general.
        Mes si soit ascun general acte come vous parles sans ascuns
        provisions, allege ceo pur ple, ou autrement sicome soit provide
        a ceo pur ple, mes *prima facie*, il ad bon count, etc.'
    . . . . . .

(33) 35 Henry VI, Trin. pl. 1.   pp. 6, 45, 269
    Rex *v.* Radcliffe.   Quare impedit.
    . . . . . .
    Ashton J: . . . 'donque jeo conceoy que le remedy de statut de W. second
    (i)   ne puit estre entend' encontre le roy, car jeo entend que si un
            remedy soit fait par un Statut, ce ne sera entend' encontre le roy,
            sinon que il soit expressement reherce. . . .'
    . . . . . .
    Moile J: . . . 'Et quand al second point, me semble que le roy n'est en le
    (ii)   case del statut, nienobstant que le statute soit general; car le roy
            ne semble a un comon person.'

(34) 36 Henry VI, pl. 2, fo. 2.   p. 260
    Anon. *v.* Anon.   Debt.
    V. supra, p. 260, n. 5.

(35) 36 Henry VI, pl. 21, fo. 24.   p. 282
    Rex *v.* Quatermain.   Scire facias.
    . . . . . .
    Choke Sjt: . . . 'La seconde cause est, que le chartre n'est my sufficient en
        luy mesme; car les parols de le chartre sont general, par les
        queux le roy ne sera my forbarre des choses dont ascun home
        est Attaint; sinon que il soit per parol especial. Come si home
        soit attaint de felony, come per utlagare ou autrement et il plede
        un pardon general de touts felonies, ceo ne vault sinon que il soit
        expressement reherce, et un *indictus est*, vel *convictus est*. . . .'
    . . . . . .

(36) 37 Henry VI, Pas. pl. 9.[1]   p. 282
    Rex *v.* Quatermain.   In the Exchequer Chamber.
    . . . . . .
    Et opinio Omnium Justiciorum, que la party aura advantage per son
    chartre (de pardon). *Et adjournantur in Banco*, etc. Queux paroles
    sont requisite en chartre de pardon pur offence ou trangression
    encontre statuts, et as queux choses ils extend. . . .

    [1] Continued from 36 Henry VI, pl. 21, *v. supra*, no. 35.

(37) 37 Henry VI, Mich. pl. 20.　　　　　　　　　p. 50
　　　Anon. *v.* Anon.　　　　　　　　　　　　　　Trespass.
　　　. . . . . .

　　　Choke Sjt dit non; car nul chose poit passer hors du roy sinon per
　　　matter de record, *scilicet scriptum*, car tout ce que le roy fait est
　　　record, sicome vos faits car vous ne poies commander un homme a
　　　arrester un homme par ley pur surete de paix hors de vestre presence
　　　sans matter de record, *scilicet*, briefe ou garrant; pur que [par quei]
　　　vous estes a recover' [de record] issint du roy car, il [ne] poet
　　　commander un officer darrester un homme hors de sa presence [sans
　　　brief] ou garrant.[1]

(38) 37 Henry VI, Hil. pl. 5.　　　　　　　　　　p. 263
　　　Anon. *v.* Anon.　　　　　　　　　　　　　　Error.
　　　. . . . . .

　　　Et l'opinion del court fuit que le ple fuit bon. Et fuit dit que tiel
　　　privie acte ne conclut touts homes si come un general acte.
　　　. . . . . .

(39) 37 Henry VI, Pas. pl. 9.　　　　　　　　　　p. 282
　　　V. supra, no. 36.

(40) 37 Henry VI, Trin. pl. 3.　　　　　　　　　p. 54
　　　Anon. *v.* Anon.　　　　　　　　　Praecipe in capite.
　　　. . . . . .

　Littleton Sjt: . . . 'et uncore le roy ne poet faire ne grant ancien demesne ce
　　　　　　jour, on poet prescriber des terres devisables, et uncore le
　　　　　　roy ne poet faire terres devisables a cest jour, et ensement que
　　　　　　le puisne fits sera enheritable sicome il est la deins la dit ville,
　　　　　　et uncore le roy ne poet granter ceo a cest jour, purce que le
　　　　　　roy ne poet granter ceo a cest jour, ne prove pas mes que le
　　　　　　prescripcion ne sera assez, et en Londres il pledera al juris-
　　　　　　diction et uncore il nest ancient demesne.'
　　　. . . . . .

(41) 39 Henry VI, Mich. pl. 21.　　　　　　　　p. 54
　　　Anon. *v.* Anon.　　　　　　　　　　　　　Trespass.

　　　Trespass en Bank le Roy. Le plaintiff counta de ses biens a tort pris.
　　　Jenny pur le defendant justifia le prisel per le commandement le roy
　　　pur ce q'il fuit utlage. Et pria aid du roy. Et *opinio curiae* fuit qe il

---

[1] I am indebted to Professor C. H. Williams for suggesting some emendations to
this passage in the Black-Letter edition. These suggestions are bracketed above. The
insertion of the negative receives some support, additional to the requirement from the
text, from the fact that in the Tables at the back of the Year Book the case is listed
under the caption 'Roy', and reads '*ne* poet commander officer darester un homme
hors de sa presence sans garrent, etc.'

naura aid de roy pur ce que il ne monstre qe il est officer al roy, come baill' al roy, vicomte, eschetor, et *huius modi* que ont authority a seiser en le droit le roy. Purquei il fuit oustre del aid.

......

(42) 39 Henry VI, Hil. pl. 3. pp. 54, 281
Anon. *v.* Anon. Quare impedit.

......

Laicon Sjt: ...'car le roy per son prerogative puit prendre un homme en sa protection ou l'autre ne sera pas par ceo disherite.'

......

Choke Sjt: 'Sicome le roy puit grant a un chartre dexemption que il ne sera mis en Enquest, etc., et puis a un auter, et ceux chartres sont bons; mes s'il grante par son chartre a touts que demeurent en le county, qu'ils ne seront mis en l'enquest, cest grant est void pur l'inconvenience.'

......

Et l'opinio *curiae* fuit clerement, que le protection ne gisoit forsque pur un [an], et oustre que il ne gist en ceo case. *Et ad alium diem le Protection fuit disallowe. Quod nota.*

(43) 3 Edward IV, Trin. pl. 1. pp. 78, 269
Woodlac *v.* Sewer. Trespass.

......

Laicon Sjt: 'Le pleder est assets bon, car en ceo case ne besoigne a le defendant a doner colour al plaintiff ne possession, sinon que il mesme voille, car en ce case le defendant ad plede un act de Parliament envers le plaintiff, quel est de pluis hault recorde en le ley; car per tiel recorde chescun home est lye, car chescun home est party a ceo; issint que le plaintiff est party et privie a cest recorde, quel luy liera auxibien....'

......

Littleton J: ...'car tiel record et act de Parlement est pluis hault en le ley, et est de tiel nature come recordes ou fines en courts le roy, car hors d'un act de Parliament home poit aver *Habere facias seisinam* et *scire facias* auxy a aver execution per force de cel record, ou a entre per force de cel, sicome il ferra sur un recovery ou fine.'

(44) 4 Edward IV, Hil. pls. 3, 4. p. 75
Rex *v.* Paston. In the Exchequer Chamber.
Cf. Lodge and Thornton, *English Constitutional Documents*, 36.

......

...'que ceo que ne poet estre amend ne aid per le comen ley, uncore reason est in ceo, la ceo serra aid per act de parliament.'

(45) 4 Edward IV, Pas. pl. 4.   pp. 38, 231, 265, 293
     Rex *v.* Anon.   In the Exchequer Chamber.

. . . . . .

Et l'opinion de Choke J, Illingworth CB, et Yelverton J fuit que par les statutes avandits le suerty n'est pas repelle, car chescun statute fait, covient estre pris solonque l'entent de ceu que ce feceront, la ou les parolx de ce sont doutes et nemy en certain et solonque le rehercel de le statute, . . . et coment que cel statut ici n'ad pas estre mis en ure, ceo ne fait matter, car si sont en les livres del statutes multes articules, queux ne ont my estre mis en ure, mes ce ne fait matter, car uncore ils sont ley, et poient estre execute par chescun home que est greve contraire a eux, et issint devant assets bien.

. . . . . .

(46) 5 Edward IV, Pas. fo. 32–34.   pp. 48, 261
     Anon. *v.* Anon.   In the Exchequer Chamber.

. . . . . .

Choke J: 'Est un statute[1] que en safeconduct grant que le nosme del maistre del nief et les nosmes de mariners a certain number serront mises en le safeconduct, etc., et si auterment soit fait, le statute voet que eux soient voides, uncore puis cest statutes a divers temps, et ore a cest jour safeconducts sont faits fesant nul tiel mention, et uncore eux sont tenus estre assets bon. Et uncore cel statute un foits come semble fuit fait pur restreiner general safeconducts en cel point. Mes nienobstant a cest jour n'est tenus restreint al roy. Et solonque ascuns ceo est tenus le cause pur ce que le statute n'est forsque en le affirmative, issint que le roy poet a son election, nienobstant cel statute, faire l'un ou l'auter, et chescun de eux assets bon. Mes si le statute ust este fait en le negative est dit per divers homes que outerment ust este etc. Issint semble en le case devant lou enditement est, ceo est le suit le Roy. Et pur ceo semble pur le roy l'enditement assets bon, car cel statute ne lieroit luy come semble, nient pluis que l'auter statute, issint que il est al election le roy la aver l'addition eins ou dehors, sicome fuit al commun ley etc.'

Illingworth CB: 'Ceux statutes ne sont pas semblables, car l'un strech forsque al roy meme, quel le roy poet eslier a user a son volunt, car il est a son election de user la ley de prerogative, ou a user la ley especial ley del statute, car nul home est prejudice par ceo, car tiel ley appent al roy mesme. Mes d'un ley que appent a common person, soit ce common ley ou especial ley, come de statute de Addition[2] avandit, per cel ley chescun home avera avantage, issint que ce touche liege home le roy, quel le roy ne poet defeter de common droit etc.'

[1] 15 Henry VI, c. 3.   [2] 1 Henry V, c. 5.

Danby CJ: 'Chescun home est enherite a cel common ley de addition sicome de autre common ley, quel le roy de droit ne defetera sans Parliament, car par cel ley chescun home avera advantage, etc.'

Et a ce accorderont touts les Justices que l'addition covient estre auxibien en les actions le roy, si l'endictments, lou process utlagery gist auxibien come en det, transgressions, appeales, et autres tiels originals lou proces d'utlagerie gist, etc.

Markham CJ: 'Il est bon pur estre sure a faire *Melius inquirendo* par le roy, etc., et issint pur estre certain.'

Et a ce accorderont tout les justices et le attorny le roy avandit.

(47) 5 Edward IV, fo. 44–45.   p. 296

Anon. *v.* Anon.   Formedon in remainder.

......

Et cel plee en maintenance de breve fuit challenge quant al moitie del terre, *scilicet*, de cel part a que le disclaimer est pled, car a maintenir le breve per le statute per prender des profits encounter disclaimer et nosment icy lou il ne recover damages, ne poit estre pris, car per le statut nest done le maintenance del breve pur prendre des profits forsque encounter nontenure general. Et per l'equitie de mesme le statute au tiel ley est encounter le jointenancy car tout est un egal mischief, mes de disclaimer ceo est hors de les ij cases, etc. Solonque ascuns del court, que sur disclaimer home avera benefite de le statute per prendre des profits, come enconter nontenure ou jointenancie, car disclaimer nest forsque nontenure del terre en droit en possession et en fait, et issint disclaime en tout le title et possession de ceo, et pur ceo si le demandant voile, il poit maintenir son brefe per l'equite de le statute enconter disclaimer, auxibien come envers nontenure generalment plede, car auxybien come jointenancie est pris per l'equite de le statute a maintenance que il est tenant per prendre des profits, auxibien serra pris remedie per l'equity de disclaimer, et tout serra un equitie, comment que le statute ne remedie per expresse parols forsque de nontenure generalment, etc.... Solonque ascuns et divers de les Justices, et per le melior opinion que ceo n'est pas deins le remedie del equity de le statute, sinon que ceo fuit al meins en tiel accion en que recovery des damages serra.....

Mes jointenancie et non tenure sont pris deins le statut, l'un per parolx de le statute, l'autre per l'equite....

......

(48) 5 Edward IV, Mich. fo. 118–123.   pp. 35, 58
     Rex *v.* Abbot of Leicester.   In the Exchequer Chamber.
     ......

    Yelverton J: ...'car ceo est le prerogative le roy, quel ne poit estre
         dismember del person le roy, etc.'
     ......

(49) 7 Edward IV, Mich. pl. 11.   pp. 51, 54
     Bagot *v.* Anon.   In the Exchequer Chamber.
     ......

    Markham CJ: 'Chescun home poit le monstre al court come *amicus curiae*,
         etc., et dit oustre que si l'Eschetor seisit ascun terre per
         title de office, qe nest pas sufficeant l'ou office nest pas pris
         forsque *virtute officii*, il est come disseisor. Et sir, le roy ne
         poit estre entitle per fait de feoffement, sinon que il soit
         enrolle de record.' *Ad quod tota curia concordatur.*
     ......

(50) 8 Edward IV, Mich. pls. 9, 35.   pp. 198, 215
     Duchess of Suffolk *v.* Anon.   Debt.
     ......

    Billing J: 'Le notice est necessary, car par nul maner reason home ne
         poet performe chose sans notice aver de ceo, et sir, j'entend
         que lou home est oblige sur condition impossible que l'obliga-
         tion n'est voide, mes ascun metter diversity enter condition
         impossible et condition encounter ley, mes j'entend qe en l'un
         et l'auter il est void, etc. *Quod Markham CJ. et Yelverton J.*
         concesserunt. Car ce que est impossible est enconter ley, issint
         jeo provera, car le ley est sur possibility, et reason, donques ce
         qe est impossible est encounter ley....'

    Yelverton J: 'Et sir nous ferromus a ore en ce case sicome les savonists et
         civilliones face quant un novel case anient de que ils n'ont
         nul ley adevant, donques il resorter al ley de natur que est le
         ground de touts leys, et solonque ce que est avise a eux estre
         pluis beneficial a le Common Weale etc., ils font, et issint ore
         ferromus nous. Si nous ferromus un positive ley sur cel point,
         nous devomus voier ce que est pluis necessary a le Common
         Weale et solonque ce faire nostre ley, et jeo croy que nul voet
         denier mes le meliour serra en ce case de faire tiel positive ley,
         que nul homme serra charge de performer l'arbitrement sans
         notice ent aver etc., car arbitrement est use pur le Common
         Weale, cestascavoir pur appeser debates, et tortes enter les
         peoples, et issint sont fines, et si l'arbitrement purra charge
         le party sans notice faire, donques le people voet timer et

doubter de eux mettre en arbitrement etc., parce que le plus beneficial voy pur le Common Weale est, q'ils ne serront charges, sinon qu'ils eient notice etc. Donques en mesme le maner a ore est nostre judgment icy en ce case devomus poiser le Common Weale, car ce case n'ad estre view a devant, par quei nostre judgment a ore serra prise pur un president en apres, purquei etc., et sir come ad este touch est diversity, lou homme est oblige a chose certeine et a chose noncerteine de quel il poit aver notice per choses ou outward et ou nemy, et devant que il ait fine son reason, les justices surrexerunt etc.'

(51) 8 Edward IV, Pas. pl. 9.   pp. 44, 257
      Anon. *v.* Anon.   Formedon.
      . . . . . .

Pigot Sjt: Il (le statute de dies communes in banco)[1] n'est statute eins affirmative del comen ley, *ut* les justices disoient que ce fuit statute, etc.,...
      . . . . . .

(52) 8 Edward IV, Trin. pl. 1.   p. 75
      Anon *v.* Anon.   Sub Poena.
      . . . . . .

Et l'opinion de la chancellor et les Justices que il ne gist pas envers le heire, pur que il sua un bill al Parliament, etc.
      . . . . . .

(53) 9 Edward IV, Pas. pls. 2, 20, Trin. pl. 3.   pp. 4, 16, 31, 55, 56
      Bagot *v.* Anon.   Assise.

(i)   Pluis d'assise Bagot, ore fuit le matter reherce et touche que non obstante cel act des patentes de legitimation sont bones, car le roy H. fuist roy en possession, et il covient que le roialme eit un roy south que les leyes serront tenus et maintenus, donque par ce que il ne fuist eins forsque par usurpacion, uncore chescun act judicial fait per luy que touche jurisdiction roial serra bon, et liera le roy de droit, quant il fait regresse, etc.
      . . . . . .

Counsel: ...'Et sir, le dit roy H. ne fuit merement come usurpar car le
(ii)   corone fuist taile a luy per parliament....'
      . . . . . .

Et de l'auter part per les serjeants et apprentices fuit touche que lettres patentes serront voides, car le roy ne serra de pluis *peior*

[1] *Stat. R.* I, 208.

condition que autre commen person. Et si commen person soit disseise, et fait regresse, il defetera tout mesme actes, issint ore le roy est eins accorde a son droit discendi del roy Richard et cel act nest forsque l'affirmance de common ley, issint per son regresse il ad voide touts acts faits par le usurpor etc.

. . . . . .

Billing CJ: 'A chescun roy par reason de son office il appent a faire
(iii)   justice et grace; justice en executer des leyes, etc., et grace de granter pardon as felons et tiel legitimation come c'est, etc.'

. . . . . .

Pigot Sjt: 'Jeo voille bien qe les Masters et Bouchers, etc., covient estre
(iv)   admittes et jures, etc., car ils n'ont auter maner *creationis* en l'offices, eins *per electionem* del court, parcequ'il la ils usent per eux jure, mes Bagot ad cel office per letters patents le roy, en quel case maintenant per le lettres patent il est officer, etc., et nos avomus monstre en evidence que apres l'office a luy graunt, il vient en le chancery et la il escria un briefe dappell en son nosme demesne, et prist le fee pur ce, issint ce est un sufficient seisin.' *Quod Laken Sjt. et tota curia concederunt.*

Brian Sjt: 'En le case Winter il y avait les lettres patents del clerk del coron icy et uncore il ne fuit par ce que vos ne luy admittastes.'

Billing CJ: 'Le cause est par ce qe ceux lettres fueront voides, car quant le roy graunt l'office a l'un que ne savoit ce occupier, tiel patent est voide et issint en tiel case fuit Winter.'

Brian Sjt: 'Comment saves vous ce sinon *per examinationem* per luy?'

Billing CJ: 'Nous savomus bien de nous mesmes qe nul ne savoit occupier cel office si non tiel qe ad este instrue en l'office tout son vie, car xx ou xxx ans est assets petit pur home destre erudite en cel office.'

. . . . . .

(v)   Et les justices disoient que ils avaient communer de touts ceux points ove les Justices del comen bank et il semble a eux que ceux mattres sont a nul purpose pur arrester le judgement, et issint semble a nous, parquei agardi fuist que le plaintiff recovera l'offices et ses damages, taxes, etc., et ses costages, etc., et le defendant en le mercie, etc.

(54) 10 Edward IV, Pas. pl. 9.   p. 202
     Anon. *v.* Anon.   Trespass.

. . . . . .

Catesby Sjt: . . . 'Commen ley ad estre tout temps puis le creacion de monde.'

(55) 10 Edward IV, Pas. pl. 18.   pp. 262, 285
     Selden Society, ed. Neilson, XLVII, pl. 17.   Trespass.
     Dokemaster *v.* Abbot of Leicester.
     . . . . . .
     Choke J: 'Lou le statute que done process est in l'affirmative, donqe il
         puit eslier dauer cell process etc., ou le proces del comen ley
         mesque autrement si soit en le negatif, setassauer, qu'il auera
         tiel proces et nul autre.'
     . . . . . .

(56) 12 Edward IV, Mich. pl. 25.   p. 292
     Taltarum's case.
     For analysis and translation, *v.* Sir Kenneth Digby, *Introduction
     to the History of Real Property*, 5th ed. 255–258.

(57) 13 Edward IV, Pas. pl. 4.   pp. 263, 269
     Lord Say *v.* Borough of Nottingham.
     En le Bank, le roy en le case de le Seignoir Say vers ceux de Notting-
     ham, fuit tenus que un act de Parliament que touts corporations et
     licences grauntes per le roy Henry, etc., serront voides, que ils
     covient estre pledes, et le court n'est tenus d'aver conusance de eux,
     nient plus que un particuler act pur un particuler person. Et le dit
     act nest general, mes est particular en un generalitie, cest assavoir,
     que touts corporations, etc., sicome un act soit fait que touts
     Evesques ou touts Seigniors averont tiel chose, etc., cest particular
     act, etc., mes ou un act est general que extende a chescun home, ceo
     ne besoigne d'estre plede, car il est un general et commen ley, etc.
     . . . . . .

(58) 13 Edward IV, Pas. pl. 5.   pp. 13, 198, 216, 254, 256, 269
     Anon. *v.* Anon.
     V. Selden Society, *Select Cases concerning the Law Merchant*, II,
     p. lxxv.
     Bishop Stillington,[1] *Chancellor:* 'Cest suit est pris per un marchant alien, que est
                         venus par safe conduit icy, et il n'est tenus de
                         suer solonques le ley del terre a tarier le trial
                         de xij homes et auters solempnities del ley de
                         Terre, mes doit suer icy, et serra determine
                         solonque le ley de nature en le Chancery, et il
                         doyt suer la de heur en heur et de jour pur le
                         sped des Marchants etc. Et dit oustre que
                         marchants (aliens?) etc. ne sera lies par notre

---

[1] The identity of this chancellor is doubtful, but of the chancellors in office
about this date, Stillington seems the most likely to have expressed the ideas in
the report.

statutes, lou les statutes sont *introductiva novae legis,* mes ils sont *declarativa antiqui juris* cestassavoir, nature etc. Et coment que ils sont venus deyns le royalme par ce le Roy ad jurisdiccion d'eux de mitter d'estoyer al droyt, etc. mes ce serra *secundum legem naturae* que est appelle per ascuns ley Marchant, que est ley universal per tout le monde, et il dysoyt que il ad este ajudge que non obstant le statute que voet que safe conduits soyent enroll' et le nombre des mariners et le nosme del vessel etc. que lou alien avoit safe conduit, et n'avoit les dites circumstances en cel, et tamen il fuit allowe, car l'alleyns disoyent que ils ne sont tenus de conustre nostre statutes, et ils venoyent per cause del seale de Roy, cestassavoir, son conduit, et s'il ne serra sufficient, donques il serra resceu etc. Et *tamen* ascuns disoient que le statute fait de forfaiture de merchandise lia aliens auxibien come denizens etc. Et fuit dit que un denizen, ne duist suer alien devant le Counsaille, mes l'alien doit suer le denizen, *tamen* ascuns disoient que ceo fuit per statut.'

Et puis les Justices fiereront report al Chancellor en le Counsaill qe l'opinion de les plusors de eux fuit que il fuit felonie. Et comment qe il est felonie, uncore les biens ne purra estre claime comme waife, car il appert icy qe cesty qe sua icy pur les biens est alien et le Roy ad grant a luy *salvum et securum conductum, tam in corpore quam in bonis,* et cest un covenant entre le Roy et luy, donques si un felon eux preigne, il n'est reason qe cesty alien eux prendre et de luy mitter a suer vers le felon, mes il suera al Roy sur cest covenant, et issint il semble le Roy meme ne poit aver tiels biens comme waif, et per mesme le reason il ne poit grant a auter, ne nul auter poit eux claimer per prescription.

(59)　14 Edward IV, Mich. pl. 1.　　　　　　　　p. 263
　　　　Brian *v.* Anon.　　　　　　　　　　　　Sub poena.
　　　　　　. . . . . .

Littleton J: 'Semble que le breve bon, car l'act[1] serra construe solonque l'entent, etc. Et il ne poit estre suppose que les fesors del act entendraient auterment, mes que il avera general breve. . . .'
　　. . . . . .

---

[1] 28 Henry VI, c. 5 (?).

Et l'opinio de le chancellor et touts les Justices forsque Littleton que le breve ne fuit bon, mes que il avera un especial breve sur son cas, et matter, etc.; et quant al statute de xxviij etc., la les Justices ne sont forsque counsells, mes en cest act il sont judges, et on auxi grand power come le chancellor, et ceo appiert par l'act que ils sont judges, et ont, etc., que donne power a eux; issint l'entent appiert clerement que serront judges en le matter, etc.; auxi le dit statut de xxviij est que le chancellor per son discretion, etc., auxi quant un act est fait pur le comen profit de realme, ce serra interpretate largement, mes un particuler act serra interpretate strictement, etc.

. . . . . .

(60) 15 Edward IV, Mich. pl. 2.   p. 137
    Kedwelly *v.* An Abbot.   Debt.

. . . . . .

Littleton J: ...'Et sir, si en le parliament si le greindre party des chivallers des counties assentent al feasans d'un act du parliament, et le meindre party ne voille my agreer a cel act, uncore ce serra bon statute a durer en perpetuity....'

(61) 15 Edward IV, Mich. pl. 17.   pp. 44, 254, 256
    Rex *v.* Bishop of Ely.   Wardship.

. . . . . .

Littleton J: 'Moy semble le contrarie, et sir, come moy semble cest statute est en affirmance del commen ley, car en chescun statute est limit un certein temps quant ceo fuit fait et en temps de quel Roy et un quel lieu, *quia magna carta* ne fuit statute a commencement tanque ce fuit confirm par Marlebridge cap. 5, et la est le temps limit en certain quant ce fuit fait, et auxi Westm' 2 est *quia emptores terrarum,* etc. et divers autres statutes ont un temps certein en escript quant ils fuerant faits, mes cest statute nad pas tiel jour limit, par quil nest pas statute nient plus que *dies communes in banco, dies communes in dote, expositiones vocabulorum,* ceux sont escriptes en nostre livers et uncore ne sont statutes mes fuerant faits a tiel entent, que ceo que fuit en dout al common ley serra mis en certeine, sic est le statute *de prerogativa Regis*; et sur ceo serra statute a un entent, tout les points deins le dit statute serront tenus comme comme effectuel, et ceo nest pas issint, car jeo voy un foits devant mon Seigneur Markham, que le temps le roy morust, et avoit issue un file, la fille marie soy mesme sans licence de roy et el ne fesoit fine, mes si le widow le roy mary soy mesme sans licence elle fera fine al roy, et le statute *de prerogativa Regis* voet que en ambideux cases il ferra fine, *ergo* ceo ne poet estre dit come un statute, mes come un affirmance del comon ley.'

. . . . . .

(62) 17 Edward IV, Pas. pl. 2.　　　　　　　　　p. 293
　　　Anon. *v.* Anon.　　　　　　　　　　　　　Trespass.

．．．．．．

Brian Sjt: 'Pur l'auter conceyt moy semble le plee n'est bon sans monstre
　　　　que il ad certifie l'auter de son pleasure, car comen erudition
　　　　est que l'intent d'un home ne serra trie, car le Diable n'ad
　　　　conusance de l'entent de home. . . .'

(63) 21 Edward IV, Mich. pl. 6.　　　pp. 13, 14, 42, 78, 154, 269
　　　Abbot of Waltham *v.* Anon.　　　In the Exchequer Chamber.

．．．．．．

Nottingham CB: 'Semble que ce chartre ne serra allowe, car ce disme
　　　　quant il est grant est un enheritance et duty al roy, etc.'

．．．．．．

Starkey Sjt: 'Semble que le chartre serra allowe. Et quant al entent que
　　　　ad ete pris quant il serra pris pur le melior avantage pur le
　　　　roy que le chartre ne serra my allowe, sir, vous n'estes pas
　　　　venus icy pur arguer pur le lucre le roy, mes pur ministre
　　　　Justice entre le party et le roy, *scilicet* darguer le quel ceo
　　　　patent serra allow ou non. Et, sir, il covient en ce cas destre
　　　　allowe, ou autrement vos covient affirmer laucthority et le
　　　　jurisdiction del convocation destre plus haut et de grand
　　　　aucthorite que l'aucthorite et jurisdiction del roy en son
　　　　prerogatife, *cuius contrarium est verum.* Et le roy ad excepte l'Abbe
　　　　par ces lettres patentes, queux sont mere temporel, et rien est
　　　　monstre mesque ils serra allowe, forsque un act fait en le
　　　　convocation que est desoubs le power et authorite del roy.'
　　　　Quod Vavisour et Browne concordant.

．．．．．．

Redmayn: 'Me semble le contraire, et que le chartre serra voide, car jeo
　　　　entend que auxibien que le roy per son prerogative et son
　　　　roial power est nostre seignior, et aver ces services et duties de
　　　　ses subjects, sibien sont ces subjects enherites d'aver avantage
　　　　de ces leies et customes, et d'aver lour service de ceux que sont
　　　　de soubz eux, et l'Evesque est enherite de faire le collector et
　　　　de luy eslier deins son Diocese et de luy certifier al roy come luy
　　　　pleirait, donque si le roy poit luy discharger par meme le reason
　　　　il poit discharger tout le clergie, etc.[1] . . .'

．．．．．．

Pigot Sjt: 'Le XV n'est unque grant, mes per *communitatem Angliae,*
　　　　autrement est des dismes que *per clerum,* car la est *clerus pro-*
　　　　vinciae Cantuariensis et clerus provinciae Eburaciencis, parquei sont

_____
[1] On fo. 47 occurs a rare indication of the reporter's own movements. '*Ad alium*
diem,' he writes, 'plusieurs des Serjeants argueront, mes jeo ne fue la a lour
arguments.'

divers, et XV poit estre grant en Parliament sans l'assent des seigniors et est assets bon.'

Et puis touts les Justices fuerunt agrees que le patent serra assets bon quant a ceo entent.

. . . . . .

Et issint fuit l'opinion de touts le Justices. Et puis fuit issint adjudge en le Eschequer, et l'Abbe charge del Collection a ceo temps. Mais fuit dit que autrefoits il avera avantage des patents, etc.

(64) 22 Edward IV, Pas. pl. 30.   p. 262
      Anon. *v.* Anon.   Trespass.

      . . . . . .

Pigot Sjt: 'Moy semble que il ne poit justifier en tiel maner, car il est restreint par le statute,[1] que est en le negative, que voet que *nullus de caetero,* issint le statute ne poit estre construe sinon *stricti juris*. . . . .'

      . . . . . .

Hussey CJ: 'Moy semble que il ne poit justifier, par ce que le statute est en le negative. . . .'

      . . . . . .

(65) 1 Edward V, Trin. pl. 13.   p. 45

Nota que fuit dit a mesme le jour en le chancery et agre par touts les juges et serjeants la estants qe le roy ne poet estre dit unqe fist tort, car si un veut disseisir un autre al oeps le roy, ou le roy n'ad droit, le roy ne poet estre dit disseisor. *Quod nota.*

(66) 1 Richard III, Mich. pl. 7.   p. 287
      Anon. *v.* Anon.

Nota per Hussey CJ que quand original doit commencer en Court chrestien, et commence la, comment que apres chose vient en issue que est triable par notre ley, uncore serra trie per lour ley. . . .

(67) 2 Richard III, Mich. pl. 22.   p. 296
                              In the Star Chamber.

Dominus Rex interiori Camera Stellata appellavit se omnes justicios suos, et ab eis petiit tres quaestiones. . . . 'Si quis tulerit falsum breve et actionem versus aliquem, per quem captus est et imprisonetur, et moritur in prisona, si aliquod remedium sit in casu illo pro parte sive pro rege, etc.

Si aliquis justicius pacis ceperit billam de indictamento non invenitur per Jur', et illam rotulat inter alia indictamenta bene et veraciter invenita, etc., si aliqua punitio proinde sit versus talem

---

[1] Stat. Marlborough, c. 4.

justicium si facientem.'....Ad quod justicii responderunt quod nulla
sequatur poena, pro prosecutione falsae accionis, etc., quia non intelligitur etc., quousque terminetur et tunc amerciamentur Regi, etc.
Et quod ad contemptum contra judicium, etc., respondetur sic,
idem T.S. habuit notiam de judicio, etc., toto tempore postea cancellarius Angliae potest eum compellare per imprisonamentum....
Et quidem eorum dicebant quod justiciis non potest puniri....Et ad
ultimum, omnes concordati fuerunt quod si aliquis justicius ceperit
aliquod indictamentum, et illud fecerit irrotulari et non per juratum
inventum, falso et contra sacrum suum fecerit, et magna misprisio
est.

Alia quaestio fuit quod quidem Johannes Barret de Bury Sancti
Edmundi prosecutus fuit per brevem de debitum in London..et
fecit rasari omnia brevia predicta, et fecerunt W.B. utlagari...Et
statutum de anno 8 H. 6, ca. 12.[1] visum et lectum fuit coram rege et
consilio suo in camera stellata et ibidem per Willelmum Hussey et
per consensum omnium justiciorum declaratus totum actum illud
fore feloniam, etc., per haec verba, etc., "Si ascun record, brief,
retourne, processe, panel, etc., ou parcel dicell' soit emble, emport,
retrahi, ou avoide a causa de quel ascun jugement soit revers, etc."
Et quia apparet quod W.B. pro Johanne B non bene sed falso
fraudulenter sine errore utlagetur est, sic quod recordum illud non
potest corrigi per errorem, et totum recordum versus J.B. etc.,
adnihilatum et vacuatum per rasuram et magis falsum extitit ad
adnihilandum et adnullandum totum record quam parcellum inde
et verba sufficientes sunt in statuto quoniam dicit quod emble
record ou parcell dicell, etc. paront, etc.

......

(68) 2 Richard III, Mich. pl. 26.[2]   pp. 268, 282
Treasurer of Calais *v.* Merchants of Waterford. In the Exchequer Chamber.

......

Una (quaestio) si villae corporatae in Hibernia, et alii habitantes in
Hibernia erunt ligati per statutum factum in Anglia; secunda
quaestio fuit, si rex possit dare licentiam contra statutum, etc.,
et specialiter ubi nunc ordinatur per statutum quod inventor
habebit medietatem et rex aliam. Et pro solutione istarum, etc.,
omnes justicii associati fuerunt in camera scaccaria. Et ibi quoad

---

[1] 'That if any record or parcel of the same, writ, return, panel, process, or
warrant of attorney in the king's courts of Chancery, Exchequer, the one Bench or
the other, or in his treasury, be wilfully stolen, taken away, withdrawn, or avoided
by any clerk, or by other person by cause whereof any judgment shall be reversed,
that such stealer, taker away, withdrawer, or avoider, their procurators, counsellers,
and abettors thereof indicted, by process thereupon made thereof duly convict...
shall be judged felons and shall incur the pain of felony....'
[2] Continued in 1 Henry VII, Mich. pl. 2, no. 71, *infra.*

primam quaestionem dicebatur, quod illi Hibernicae inter se habent
parliamentum, et omnimodo curiae prout in Anglia, et per idem
parliamentum faciunt leges et mutant leges, et non obligantur per
statutum in Anglia, quia non hic habent milites parliamenti, sed
hoc intelligitur de terris et rebus in terris illius tantum efficiendo, sed
personae illae sunt subjectae regis, et tanquam subjecti erunt
obligati ad aliquam rem extra terra illa faciendam contra statutum
sicut habitantes in Calesia, Gascoignie, Guienne, etc., dum fuerunt
subjecti, et similiter obedientes erunt sub admirall' Angliae de re
fact' super altum mare, et similiter breve de errore de judicio reddi-
tur in Hibernia in banco regis hic in Anglia, etc.
Et pro secunda quaestione, rex potest dare licentiam satis bene cum
clausula non obstante, prout patet ubi per statutum H. 4. ordinatur
quod non faciat aliquas litteras patentes alicui de aliqua re nisi
specialem mentionem terrarum, etc., et similiter valorem inde,
recitantur in litteris illius, et tamen cum clausula non obstante satis
bonam est.

. . . . . .

(69) 2 Richard III, Mich. pl. 49.   p. 75
      Anon. *v.* Anon.   Error.

. . . . . .

Hussey CJ: . . . 'issint me semble que vous devez suir al parlement.'

Fairfax J: A meme l'entent. Car, il dit, que ce ordeine bien per statut
      que le parliament seroit chescun an un fois, et ce fuit bien
      ordein pur tiels cases. . . .

. . . . . .

(70) 2 Richard III, Mich. pl. 51.   p. 286
      Anon. *v.* Anon.   Trespass.

. . . . . .

Vavasour Sjt: . . . 'Et auxy tiel jugement del court de Rome ne sera pre-
      judice a ascun al comen ley; car si un Excommengement soit
      certifice icy que tiel home et excommenge en le court de
      Rome, ou, pur ascun chose qui append al court de Rome, ce
      ne sera ascun disablement icy. . . .'

. . . . . .

(71) 1 Henry VII, Mich. pl. 2.[1]   p. 282
      Treasurer of Calais *v.* Merchants of Waterford.

. . . . . .

Hussey CJ: disoit que les statutes faits en Engleterre liera ceux d'Ireland,
      que ne fuit moult dedit des autres Justices, nient obstant que

---

[1] Continued from 2 Richard III, Mich. pl. 26, *v. supra*, no. 68.

ascun de eux fuerunt en *contraria opinione* le darrein term en son
absence. Donque disoit que est a voir les statutes, et comment
les statuts et lour lettres poient estre ensemble; et si il y ad un
statut que face ceo felony, de ceo ne poet le Roy granter
licence sicome d'autres felonies; mes le Roy poet pardoner son
interest qu'il est fait.

. . . . . .

(72)   1 Henry VII, Mich. pl. 3.   p. 255

Et puis manger touts les Justices furent a l'Black Friers pur les
matters le Roy encontre le Parliament. Et la fust move plusors
bons statuts moult profitables al Royaume s'ilz puissent estre
execute.... Mes comment ceux serront executes, ceo fuist le
Question.

. . . . . .

(73)   1 Henry VII, Mich. pl. 4.   p. 284

Touts les Justices fuerunt a White Friers pur lour fees que furent
areres de les Customers et Controllers de Londres, etc., et avoient
l'acte fait pur eux en temps le Roy H. le vj, qui veut que les
customers paieront as Justices de les premiers deniers provenants de
les customes, etc., lour gages.... Et al derrein fuit agre per eux que
les Customers seront charge de ceo.... Mes Radcliffe, et les autres
Barons (except le Chief Baron) et les clerks d'Eschequer furent en
grand opinion, pur ce que un de customers fuit discharge le F. de
Michael que fuit le jour de payment, que l'auters customers, que
avoient Patent de novel Roy H. le 7 seront discharges envers les
Justices de tout temps encourru a le fest de Pasce, tanque al 26 jour
d' Aoust, que novel Patents et customers furent faites, et disaient que
ce avoit este le comen cours del Place. *Ad quod omnes Justiciari
responderunt dicentes, quod hoc nec fuit nec potest esse Lex*, car l'act est, que
les Justices auront lour rate pur chescun jour, comment qu'ils
devient ou sont remues devant le jour de paiement.

(74)   1 Henry VII, Mich. pl. 5.   p. 51
                              In the Exchequer Chamber.

. . . . . .

Et si fuit mouve un Question que serra dit pur le Roy mesme pur
ceo que il fuit attaint et puis communication eue enter eux Touts
accorderent que le Roy fuist personable et discharge dascun
attainder eo facto que il prist sur le Raigne et estre roy. Et issint
fuit *Opinio Sir Richard Choke* et de autres Juges devant, come fuit dit.
Townsend dit, que le roy H. 6 in son redemption teignoit son
parlement et uncore il fuit attaint, et ne fuit reverse. Et lez autres
Justices disent que il ne fuit attaint, mes disable de son coron,

Regne, dignite, terres, et tenements; et disent que *eo facto* que il prist
sur luy le Roial dignite estre roy, tout ce fuit void et issint icy le Roy
puit luy mesme inabler et ne besoigne ascun act de le reversel de
son atteindre.

(75) 1 Henry VII, Hil. pl. 1.   p. 266
                                   In the Exchequer Chamber.

......

Nota icy bien le policy. *Nota* ensement, que il ne puissoit estre pris
hors del record sans act de le parliament pur l'indemnity et jeopardie
d'eux qui avoient les records in lour gard, qui fuerent assent' a ce,
per tout discharges il fuit par authority del Parliament....

......

(76) 1 Henry VII, Hil. pl. 5.   pp. 13, 56
                                   In the Exchequer Chamber.

En L'Eschequier Chambre fuit demand' un Question per le Chief
Baron, qui devoit estre fait de ceux qui avoit assignements sur les
Collectors des dismes grantes au Roy Richard; payable, l'un moity
al Feste de Nativite de St John Baptist derrein pas', et l'auter moity
al Fest de Saint Michael derrein passe. Et Touts les Justices except
Catesby et *Townsend*, tenirent clerement, que les assignements furent
bons, et que les coilours seront compelle a paier les assignements,
si bien pur le Feste de St John, come pur le Feste de St Michael,
nient obstant que le Roy Richard mourust en aoust long temps
devant le dit Feste de St Michael.

......

(77) 1 Henry VII, Hil. pl. 10.[1]   pp. 53, 286

Die sabbatie proxima post Festum Purificationis Beatae Mariae[2] en le
Parlement Chambre, le Chancelier demanda de les Justices, qui
sera fait de le alom' que fuit pris par Anglais des Florences cy en
Angleterre pur ce que le Saint Pier' le Pape avoid mande a ex-
commenger touts ceux qui attach' le dit alome de les Florences[3] etc.
Et fuit dit per plusiours des Justices, que quand les marchandizes
viennent en le terre per le sauf conduit le Roy, le Roy doit estre

---

[1] This case was printed by A. F. Pollard in *The Reign of Henry VII from contemporary sources*, III, 154–155, and is translated in part by Pickthorn, *op. cit.* I,
181.

[2] 4th February, 1486.

[3] Apparently the Pope owned alum mines in Italy, and the alum transported by
these Florentines may have been derived therefrom. A long and interesting letter
dated 19th February, 1486, which must refer to this seizure of alum, was sent to
Pope Innocent VIII by an unknown correspondent. (*V. Venetian Calendar*, I, 160.)

saufgard' a les marchants, que ils ne serront despoiles deins sa terre, et principalment per ses liges. *Et Monseigniour Hussey*[1] disoit, que en temps Ed. le IV un Legat fuit a Calice,[2] et mist au Roy a aver son gard pur vener en sa terre, et donque en le plein' Counsell devant les Seigniours et Justices fuit demande, qui sera fait. Qui dissoient que serra mande al Legat, et si qu'il voil' jurer que il nad rien porte ove luy qui serra en derogation du Roy et de sa Corone, il aura licence, ou autrement nemy. Et l'Evesque de Ely issint fait son Legat, qui est icy a or,[3] a jurer a Calice qu'il n'avoit ascun chose qui sera prejudicial au Roy et a son Corone. Et dit oustre que un grand commodite en cet terre est per le fesance de les draps que ne poient estre performes sans allomes. Purque, etc. Et *le Chief Justice* dit, que en le temps E. le premier, le Pape mist lettres au dit Roy qu'il prendra paix ove Scotland, que fuit tenu de luy, et que il mettra le mattre a luy. Et le Roy per advis de son Consel escrit al Pape que il ny avoit en le temporalte ascuns persons sus luy eins qu'il est immediat a Dieu.[4] Purque, etc. Et touts les Seigniors escriver' al Pape que comment que le Roy voile donner son droit que il ad en Scotland de luy, il ne sera; car cestuy que est Roy d'Angleterre est tout paramount Seigneur de Escoce.[5] Et l'Evesque de Londres[6] disoit qu'il veia en temps le Roy H. 6 que quand le Pape mist lettres que furent en derogation du Roy, etc., et les espirituels n'osent parler de ce, Humfrey Duc de Gloucestre prist les lettres et mist eux en feu, et ils furent ars.[7] Et donque en conclus tind' que les biens seront restores; mes il voill' estre advises.

[1] Sir William Hussey (d. 1495), attorney-general 1471; conducted impeachment of Clarence; serjeant, 1478; 7th May, 1481, chief justice of the king's bench. He protested successfully against the king's practice of consulting the judges beforehand on crown cases which they were to try. (*V. Y.B.* 1 *Henry VII*, p. 26.)

[2] It is a hard matter to identify this legate. The *Calendar of Papal Letters* only goes up to the year 1481, and further research will be needed to indicate the legate's name, if indeed it can be done at all.

[3] Bishop of Ely; presumably John Morton (1420?–1500); bishop of Ely 1478/9, archbishop of Canterbury and chancellor of England 1486, cardinal 1493.

[4] This must refer to the letter sent by Boniface VIII to Edward I, dated 27th June, 1299. (*V.* Ramsay, *Dawn of the Constitution*, 471.)

[5] The barons' letter was drawn up on 12th February, 1301 (*v.* Ramsay, *op. cit.* 478, and *Foedera*, I, 926) but it was never dispatched.

[6] Presumably Thomas Kemp, bishop of London 1450–89, nephew of Archbishop Kemp. Thomas had procured the bishopric through his uncle's interest with the king, who recommended the Pope to provide him notwithstanding the statute.

[7] There seem to be small means of identifying which papal letters Humphrey was said to have burnt. There appears to be no allusion to such an incident elsewhere, not even in the *Calendar of Papal Registers*. But the most likely occasion for it to have occurred was in 1427. On the 13th October of that year, the Pope dispatched a severe letter to Gloucester with reference to the violence that had been done to Master John de Obizis, nuncio and collector, and in it, allusion was made to a rumour that Gloucester himself had been responsible for his imprisonment—though his Holiness refused to believe this until he had received Gloucester's own reply. A

(78) 1 Henry VII, Hil. pl. 25. pp. 55, 130

'Un grande question fuit demande per le Chancelier de Angleterre de touts les justices de ceo que ou bill fuit mis en le Common hous a les seigniours en le Parlement eux priant d'asentir. Et leffect de le dit bill fuit qe lenheritance de le Corone d'Angleterre et de France, ove touts pre-eminences et prerogatives soit a nostre seignour le Roy H le vii et as ses heires de son corps loialment engendres etc. Et in effect solonque l'Act fait an 7 H 4 ca. 2. Et le question fuit, si les Franchises et Liberties de touts maners persons soient per cel resumes ou nemy. Et dit fuit que non.'

(79) 1 Henry VII, Trin. pl. 1. p. 58
Rex *v.* Abbot of Abingdon. Franchise.

Le Cas fuit tiel; Humfrey Stafford Esquire, qui fuit atteint de Haute Treason al Parliament tenu xxvij die Januarii lan premer le roy H. vij. prist sanctuary a Colchester, etc.
......

Townsend J: ...'car nul Franches poet estre sans grants des Roys; car nul poet granter tiel Franches, que on doit aver tiel tuicion sinon le Roy meme....'

Suliard J: disoit que le Roy ne poit ceo granter mes pur term de sa vie, car son heir ne sera lie par ceo grante l'ancestre; et parce il entend que ceux grants ne poient estre sans Parliament.
......

Et fuit tenu per eux touts (Justices et Serjeants) que prescripcion de tiels lieux privileges de tuicions ne puit estre en ceux cases, come de Treason, que est si haut, et touche le person le Roy sans ple et fondation, et ce covient estre del grant le Roy; car nul person poit granter tiel privilege sinon le Roy meme. Et al derrein ils touts ceo grantent; mes le quelle de Roy poit granter a ce jour, ou nemy, ils furent en divers opinions....Et quant al cest parol (Sanctuary) ils ne vouloient arguer moult de ceo, mes ils tenirent que le sentence le Pape ne poit exceder le grant le roy.
......

similar letter was addressed to the 'bishops and nobles, the parliament of England', and both epistles were apparently items in the vigorous papal endeavour at that date to procure the repeal of the 'execrable statute against ecclesiastical liberty'. (*V. Cal. Pap. Registers*, vii, 36–37. K. Vickers, *Humphrey Duke of Gloucester*, 325.) In May of the same year the Council debated the question of bail for a papal collector imprisoned for delivery of a bull against statute. (*Procs. and Ords.* ii, 263.) This occasion may very likely have been the same as that which witnessed the letter-burning incident. It is true Bedford was in England, and was therefore Protector, in 1427, but he returned to France in March of that year, and Gloucester was, in the summer and autumn, at least nominally at the head of the administration.

(80) 2 Henry VII, Mich. pl. 20. pp. 58, 282
   Rex *v.* Earl of Norfolk(?). In the Exchequer Chamber.
   ......
   Donque fuit monstre un resumpcion, et donque fuit monstre un Proviso pur H. Cont. de. N., issint que le Patent demeine en sa force.

   Radcliffe B: monstra le statut de an. 28. E. 3, c. 7, et an. 42 Ed. 3, c. 5. que nul Vicomte sera oustre un an, etc., comment que il y ad un *non Obstante*, et ce nonobstant que le Roy avoit tout dits son prerogative, sibien comme de valu et le certeinte del terres, autres choses grants par le roy et de lainz eskippes, et des chartres de murders et plusors autres cases, ou les statuts sont que Patents que fautent ceux choses, sera voids; uncore les Patents le roy sont bons ove *Non obstante*, mes sans *Non Obstante* sont voids par cause de les Statutes; issint icy le Patent ove un *Non Obstante*. Purquei, etc.
   ......

   Hussey CJ: disoit que cest especial matter que vient a la terre, et le grant le Roy sera pris strict envers luy....

(81) 4 Henry VII, Mich. pl. 11. p. 235
   En le Parlement le Roy voul' que un tiel soit attaint, et prendre ses terres, et les Seigniors assenterent, et rien fuit parle des Commons. Purquei touts les Justices tenirent clerement, que ceo ne fuit Act. Purquei il fuit restore etc.

(82) 4 Henry VII, Trin. pl. 6. p. 262
   Anon. *v.* Anon. Trespass.
   ......
   Vavasour J: 'Semble que l'action gist bien....Et, Sir, un Statut en le affirmative ne defetera ascun chose; car est un statute qui voille, que les Vicomtes del Counties delivreront les enditements aux Justices de paix par endenture, uncore si ils ne issint fait, ceo nest void....'
   ......

(83) 4 Henry VII, Trin. pl. 12. p. 286
   Sands *v.* Peckham.
   ......
   Fairfax J: 'Et coment que cel Judgement soit donne per autorite del Pape, uncore ceo barre en nostre ley, mes un excommengement de l'Evesque de Rome n'est disablement en nostre ley, pur ceo que le court le Roy ne poit escrire a luy a faire absolution....'
   ......

(84) 5 Henry VII, Pas. pl. 12.   p. 298
      Colt *v.* Anon.   Assise.

      . . . . . .

Fisher Sjt: 'Et quant a ce que est dit qu'il (le statut) sera pris strict, et que
      l'estat l'heir ne sera my void, pur ceo que il est heir al miere:
      Sir, me semble que si, car l'estatute sera pris solonque un bon
      constructio, et divers choses seront pris deins un statut, le quel
      n'est my nosme. Come par le Statut de Glouc., c. 7, ou le
      tenant in dower alien, gist in brief d'entre *in casu provisio*, et per
      equity de mesme le statut est pris pur le terme de vie, et le
      curtesi. Et in Formedon n'est donc forsque le brief, mes uncore
      le proces est pris per l'equity. Et que les Justices per ceo doient
      donc Jugement apres ceo que les parties ont pled, et que
      apres jugement que le demandant poit suer execution; et issint
      touts reasonables choses depend' sur le fesans d'un estatut
      et sera pris nient contristant que il ne soit express et issint
      icy....'

      . . . . . .

(85) 6 Henry VII, Hil. pl. 9.   p. 16
      Rex *v.* Merchants of the Steelyard. In the Exchequer Chamber.

      . . . . . .

Keble¹ Sjt (?): 'Et sir, le party defendant n'est pas tenu a faire les Justices
      venir in l'Eschiquier Chambre, car le Roy est tenu a faire
      droit al parties, et le Juge nest tenu a venir al request des
      plaintiff in le breve d'Error, ne ils ne sont tenus a eux doner
      fee, ne argent, mes ils sont appoints Juges in cel matter per
      Act de Parlement....'

      . . . . . .

(86) 6 Henry VII, Trin. pl. 4.   p. 58
      Rex *v.* Anon.   Certiorari.

      . . . . . .

      Et si le roy grant prochein garde, cest bon, etc. Et issint le roy poit
      grant conusance de touts maners d'actions avenir, et c'est bon. Mes
      icy le Roy ne poit granter un Leet forsque come le Court de Leet
      est use, et ad este use, car il mesme ne poit aver Leet, et ce user
      auterment que ad este use. Purque de touts choses que sont faits per
      le statut, qui ne furent al Comen ley, on ne poit enquerer en Leet,
      pur ce que ne furent jamais uses estre enquis en son Leet; mes de
      tiels choses qui furent al comen ley enquere; et sont grand punitions
      per statut fait, in cest cas il sont enquere, mes nemy come le statut
      veut, mes solonques le Comen ley.......

      . . . . . .

      ¹ A Walter Keble became serjeant in 1481, and a Thomas Keble in 1494. The
      identity of the counsel in the report is uncertain.

(87) 7 Henry VII, Mich. pl. 6.   p. 33
     Eliot *v*. Anon.   Trespass.

......

Le Court dit come si le roy morust cest jour, et mesme le jour un autre est esleu, in cest cas il sera pris le jour de cesty qui est mort.

(88) 7 Henry VII, Mich. pl. 9.   p. 284
     Anon. *v*. Anon.   Trespass.

......

Keble[1] *Sjt:* 'Me semble que cest ple n'est bon pur ij causes. Un, car le statute est auxibien de chose devant le statut fait come puis, et donq tiel execucion fuit bon per le statut fait....'

......

(89) 7 Henry VII, Pas. pl. 2.   p. 257
     Rede *v*. Capel.   Subpoena.

......

Mordaunt: ...'car divers Statuts sont in confirmacion de Comen Ley, et ou suffis remedy fuit al Comen Ley, mes pur meliour remedy....'

(90) 7 Henry VII, Trin. pl. 1.   pp. 74, 75, 234, 235
     King's College, Cambridge *v*. Vicar of Cambridge. Trespass.

Keble Sjt: ...'Et oustre me semble que ceo qu'ils ont allege pur un Act, n'est forsque grant per lettres patentes del Roy Henry, et nemy un Act de Parlement, car ils n'ont monstres mes que le roy Henry le 6 a son parlement tenu, etc., per ses lettres patentes ore l'assent, etc.; ceo nest forsque grant et patent le Roy. Car s'il soit un Act de Parlement, il covient que le Communalte grant, et les Seigniors, etc. Et donc le Roy dira, le Roy le veut, et donq ceo sera entre en le roll accord et donq cest bon Act, ou autrement nest Act. Car si ils disent que le Roy per authorite de Parlement per ses lettres patentes grant, ce n'est forsque un grant de Roy; car le communalty doit granter, et seigneurs auxy bien come le Roy, car ce est l'entiers corps ensemble. Et si ascun del corps grant, et nemy les autres, n'est Act, et si le Roy sans Communalty grant, ou *e contra*, le grant n'est bon; donques comment que le Roy grant in son Parlement, ce n'est forsque come ou il grant dehors, pur ceo que nest Acte....'

Read Sjt: ...'Sir, ceo est bon Acte a ma entent, car ceo est exemplifie pur bon Act. Et l'ordre de faire un Act est d'aver l'assent del Communalty, et des Seigneurs et du Roy, et issint est ce plede et

[1] *V*. note on p. 383 *supra*.

comment qu'il ne soit entre in le Rolle, uncore ce est assez suffis, car in moults des Statutes, est *quod Dominus Rex statuit....*'

Fineux Sjt: ...'Car exemplification ne poit faire ceo un Act que ne purroit estre per ley un suffisant Act....Car un Act de Parlement n'est forsque *judicium,* et un Act come un judgement, et le Roy, Seigneurs, et Communalty requirent a faire cest Judgement, et nul d'eux poit estre enterlasse....'

......

Vavasour J: 'Et quant al Act, ou ce est un Act ou nemy, me semble que ce est suffisant Act, que le Roy ove l'assent del Communalty et Seigneurs grant; car chescun Court serra pris solonque ce que ad ete use come ce court, come ad ete use, et issint l'Eschequier, et Banc le Roy et Chancery, et issint del Court de Parlement, le quel est le pluiz haut et digne court que le Roy ad; et donq come ad ete use a faire un Act, issint il sera pris. Et j'ay veu ou le Clerc du Parlement ad este demande a monster le cours et l'ordre del court, le quel chose fait un Act, et quel nemy; et jeo conceoy que l'ordre est a commencer ove le communalty, et donq les Seigneurs pur request au Roy, et donq le Roy dit, le Roy le veut; et issint al request del Communalty et seigneurs, et aucun fois le bil est primes monstre al Seigneurz et donq as Communs; et issint il prove que l'Act est suffisant per assent de Seigneurs et Communalty, et le Roy affirm le mesme; pur quel cause ce icy bon Act, et ne poit estre in melior forme....'

(91) 8 Henry VII, Trin. pl. 1.   pp. 16, 284
       Anon. *v.* Abbot of Tewkesbury.   Replevin.
       ......

Brian CJ: 'Et Quare, si le statut soit issint, ou on a poit prescriber 2 fois a tener ceo (leet). Jeo croy que non; car on ne poit prescriber encontre un Statut, sinon que il soit save per auter Statut, come ceux de Londres purroit doner sans licence terre al mortmain, et ceo est per le Statut de *Magna Carta,* c. 9, que est confirme, et per le quel lour franchises et custome est grant....Uncore le leet ne passera, pur ceo que n'est express deins le grant, et purceo que nest express il ne passera, purceo que le grant le Roy sera pris plus beneficial pur le Roy, et plus fort encontre le grantee, pur ceo que le Roy est Conservator del Ley, le quel est le Common Weal, et pur ceo que est le Souvern' de ceo, il sera plus faveur que un common person...pur ceo que il est Conservator del comon weal, *et scilicet* le ley, et pur cel cause il sera plus faveur que ascun estranger, qui n'est forsque privat person.'

......

(92) 10 Henry VII, Mich. pl. 3.   p. 298
      Anon. *v.* Anon.   Waste.
      ......

Frowike Sjt: ...'Mes si un Abbe recovert per defalt, *Quale ius* issera par
le Statute W. 2, c. 32, et per l'equite de meme le statute sera
enquis par meme l'Enquest, ou trove est pur le plaintiff per
verdict, et si le plaintiff avera case de recov' per defalt ou per
verdit, il aura jugement maintenant. Uncore les parols de
mesme le statute sont, *Inquiratur per Patriam, utrum Petens
habeat jus in sua Petitione an non. Et in compertum fuerit quod
Petens jus habeat, procedatur ut Judicium....*'
......

(93) 10 Henry VII, Mich. pl. 20.   pp. 58, 282
      Anon. *v.* Anon.   ......
      ......

Frowike Sjt: ...Et oustre il appert sur meme la mattre, que fuit ordonne
par meme l'act, que le Roy fera grant par ses lettres solonque
la forme de meme l'acte donqe si le Roy fuit un grant et
omission est de firme performance del condicion compris
deins l'act, ceux Lettres patents sont voides, car chescun des
conditions deins l'act doivent estre expressez deinz le grant.
......

(94) 10 Henry VII, Mich. pl. 24.   p. 284
      Rex *v.* Delawar.   Wardship.
      ......

Frowike Sjt: 'Quant al premier [question, si le roy aura la gard], semble
que il sera in gard, car le novel statut in temps ie Roy que or
est veut,' *etc.*
......

(95) 10 Henry VII, Hil. pl. 6.   p. 58

Hussey CJ dit, et l'opinio del court fuit: Ou un ancien grant est fait,
ceo sera pris selonque le ancien allowance. Car per ascun entent si
le roy avoit grante a un auter *Omnia jura sua regalia*, et en ascun cas
son grant est, *As free as tongue can speak, or heart can think*, uncore
ceux grants ne seront pris solonque le purport des parols, eins
solonque le ancien allowance, car en ascun lieu per reason de cest
grant ils avoient pouvoir tantum tenir ples, et en ascun lieu d'aver
conisance, et in ascun lieu ambideux. Et auxi est diversite ou un tiel
grant ad estre allowe en *Quo Warranto*, et ou en autre court le Roy,
car si le grant fuit allowe en *Quo Warranto*, le roy est conclu' par ceo;
autre est, sil soit en le Common Banc, ou autre Court le Roy; car
c'est le suit' le Roy a trier le Franchise. Et issint est, ou tiel grant est
allowe devant les Justices en Eire.

(96) 10 Henry VII, Hil. pl. 17.   pp. 8, 288
        Anon. *v.* A Bishop, etc.   False imprisonment.

Faux imprisonment vers plusors. Qui disent, que anno quarto
Henrici 4.[1] fuit ordone et enacte per l'authorite de Parlement,
que Si ascun soit defame de Heresie, ou si ascun prend ascun
opinion contrary a les Leys de Saint Esglise, l'Evesque del Dioces
luy doit arrester, et saufment garder, issint que il procedera a sa
purgation, ou abjuration del party, deins iij mois procheins apres
l'arrest.

. . . . . .

Frowike Sjt: 'Al auter entent la mater de ple nest bon; car l'entent de
          ceux qui firent le statut fuit, si ou fuit deleet', ou diffame
          d'ascun heresie, ou dascun point encountre le Faith, l'Evesque
          poit arrester; et devant le Statut ils n'avoient auter pouvoir
          que de faire proces envers eux per Citations, mes l'entent de
          eux qui firent le statut ne fuit que l'Evesque arrest ascun qui
          prend opinion enconter lour constitutions; car ils avoient un
          constitution, que nul Prestre seroit emplede per Commun Ley
          pur nul cause, si home prend' opinion enconter tiels consti-
          tutions, il nest deins le remedy de cest statute. Et en cest cas
          paradventure il poit bien, et per lour reason issint dire; car
          poit estre que le Pape grant' a luy que il ne payer dismes; ou
          paraventure un auter ad un portion des dismes deins mesme
          le paroisse, ou poet estre que il ad poie les dismes en les queux
          cases sil ne doit paier ses dismes a son curate, il est bien
          dit. . . .'

Keble Sjt: . . . 'Et al autre entent, le Statut ne parle solement ou un home
          prend ascun opinion de heresie, mes le statut est en le disjunctive;
          "ou il tien ascun opinion enconter lour constitution de S.
          Esglise". Donque devant le Conseil de Latrouens chescun
          puissoit donner ses dismes al ascun Curate, a quel temps fuit
          decrete par meme le Conseil que de Temps avenir nul home
          grant ou don' ses dismes sinon a son propre curate; en quel cas
          quand il tient opinion del contrary, c'est deins le cas de Statut.
          Mes le ple est, *quod dixit quod non tenebatur solvere decimum, etc.,*
          Curato suo; et il n'est tout un, a dire qu'il doit paier dismes, et
          qu'il ne voïlle paier dismes.

Brian CJ: disoit en ce cas, que un sage Docteur de Ley a luy disoit un
          fois, Prestres et Clerks poient estre enpledes al Common Ley
          assez bien par reason de usage de ceo; car il dit, *quod Rex est*
          persona mixta, car est *persona unita cum sacerdotibus* saint Eglise; en
          quel cas le Roy poit maintenir son jurisdiction per prescription.

[1] ? 2 Henry IV, c. 15.

25-2

(97) 10 Henry VII, Pas. pl. 7.   p. 220
   Anon. *v.* Anon.   Action on the Statute.
        ......

Danvers J: semble que quand est plede que l'Union fuit fait per assent,
        il est suffis; car il est common cours, quand un parlement est
        tenu, que quand les communs sont agrees, il est mis au Roy,
        et il escrit Jeo assent, et sur ceo parols est escrit son Act,
        Statuit Rex. . . .
        ......

(98) 10 Henry VII, Pas. pl. 26.   p. 58
   Rex *v.* Abbot of Barking.   In the Exchequer Chamber.
        ......

   Et fuit touch' que le Roy ne fuit lie per le Statut de *Quia Emptores
   terrae,* et que il poit changer ses services. Et fuit touche oustre que les
   6 marks reserves per le roy furent voides, car il ne poit reserver un
   rent hors de terre in quelle il n'ad pouvoir. Et *nihil aliud* de ce
   mattre a ce jour.
        ......

(99) 11 Henry VII, Mich. pl. 35.   p. 283
   Diversite entre malum prohibitum et malum per se. Car malum
   prohibitum est, ou le Statut prohibite que on ne fera monnoie, et sil
   face, que il sera pendue, ceo est malum prohibitum; car devant le dit
   Statut fuit loyal acte, faire monnoie mes or nient; et pur cest mal le
   Roy poit dispenser. Issint si on eskippe laine in autre lieu que al
   Calice, ce est malum prohibitum; car est prohibite par Statut, et
   pur cest malum le Roy poit dispenser. Issint le Roy poit dispenser
   ove un presbiter que il aura deux benefices; et que bastard serra
   Presbytre; et ce est malum prohibitum; et in tiels cases semblables.
   Mes malum in se le Roy, ne nul autre poit dispenser. Sicome le Roy
   veut perdonner a occire un autre, ou luy licence a faire nusance in
   le haut-chemin, ce est void; et uncore quand ils sont faits le Roy poit
   eux perdonner. Issint est si on soit oblige in un recognisaunce in
   Chancery au Roy sur le paix garder al suit d'un homme, le Roy ne
   poit relesser cel dutie pur le prejudice que poit avenir al autre; et
   uncore quand il est forfait, il poit bien relesser, et devant nemy. Et
   issint le Roy, ne nul Evesque, ou Presbiter poit donner licence a un
   a faire lecherie, *quia est malum in se* en ley de nature; mes quand il
   est fait, ils poient assoiler assez bien. *Quod nota* per *Fineux, C.J.*

(100) 11 Henry VII, Trin. pl. 10.   p. 235
   Anon. *v.* Anon.   Replevin.
        ......

Danvers J. 'Sir, un bill in Parlement est indosse, que le Roy est assent et
        ce fait un Act de Parlement.'

Vavasour J: 'Si un Act de Parlement soit de tiel maniere, que par l'assent du Roy, et les Seigneurs Espirituels et Temporels, et les Communes est ordonne et enacte, ce est un bon Act de Parlement, et uncore ce nest pas Act, si le Roy, et les Seigneurs et les Communes ne font pas l'Act; mes parce qu'il dit que il fuit ordonne par lour assent, il est entend' que ils font l'Act.'

. . . . . .

(101) 12 Henry VII, Trin. pl. 1. pp. 45, 258, 269, 280, 295
       Rex *v.* Anon. Wardship.
(i)   . . . . . .

Marowe: . . . 'Donques le prerogative le Roy ne tiend' lieu la; car a ma entent le Roy ne poit aver nul prerogative sinon de chose que ad ete touts temps done a luy per Prerogative, car un Prerogative ne poit commencer a cest jour. . . .'

. . . . . .

Sedgewick: 'Et a ma conceit veut estre diversite ou un chose est per le commen ley, in le quel le Roy aura prerogative, et cest chose est inlarge per Statut; in cest cas le Roy aura prerogative in la chose que est inlarge per le statut. . . .'

Mordaunt Sjt: *e contra;* 'Car quand un Statut est fait, le Statut serra
(ii)   construe solonque l'entent de ceux qui firent le Statut, nient tous fois apres les parolz del estatut. Donques le Statut voet, Que les Seigniors auront la garde et auxy relief; sicome lour tenants eussent moru seisis; donq lour entent n'est que le Roy sera de peior condicion que comoen person sera, come il est Comon diversite, ou un Statut est fait, que restreine le liberte de touts gens; uncore le Roy ne sera lie per cel estatute, sinon que il soit nome in le statut. . . .'

. . . . . .

Keble Sjt: a meme l'entent. . . 'Donque quand cest statute est fait, que est
(iii)   doubteous, il sera construe solonque l'entent del fesors de meme le statute. . . .'

. . . . . .

(102) 13 Henry VII, Mich. pl. 3. pp. 254, 258, 280
       Rex *v.* Stonor. Wardship.

. . . . . .

Mordaunt Sjt: . . . 'Et il semble que cest Statut[1] sera pris auxy large come
(i)   il peut estre, car il est in affirmance del common ley. . . .'

. . . . . .

Butler Sjt: . . . 'purque il est clerement mention fait in le statut qui
(ii)   aura le garde, et nul mention est fait de Prerogative, ne

---

[1] *I.e.* the *Statuta Prerogativa.*

poit estre pris deins cest novel statute qui fait un novel
ley....'

......

Sedgewick: '...*Posito* que un Statut fuit fait que chescun q'est passe l'age
(iii)   de 80 ans sera in garde; in cest cas le Roy n'aura son prero-
             gative; car il nest gardein al comon ley, eins per un statut, que
             ne sera pris mes solonques les parols...'.

......

(103) 14 Henry VII, Hil. pl. 2.   p. 298
                        In the Exchequer Chamber.

'Auter jour in l'Eschiquier Chambre fuit debatu et argue entre les
Justices de l'un Banc et de l'autre ove touts les Serjeants. Et
plusiors des Juges arguerent, a quel jour *non interfui*; mes or fuit argue
per divers Juges....Et or un Enquest fuit pris deins le Cite de
Nicol' et per ceux del cite devant *Justicii de Nisi Prius*, si l'atteint or
sera de ceux del ville de Nicol' ou auterment de forainers, come le
statute est; ceo fuit auter fois debat.'

Tremaile J: 'Semble que l'atteint sera des forainers; ...semble que sera
             remedy per l'equite de cest statut. Et ceo nest inconvenient,
             car issint est in plusieurs cases quand une chose ad este
             purveue per Statut, chose in mesme le mischief ad este remedy
             pur l'equite de cel statut. Come per le statut de Glocester
             cap. 7 est ordonne, que "l'un terre in dower alien", cesty in
             le reversion aura brief de *Casu proviso*; et per cel statut est
             solement parle de tenant in dowre, uncore per equite de cel
             est pris que de alienation fait per le tenant per le Curtesie,
             ou a terme de vie, il en le reversion aura brief d'Entre
             in *Consimili casu*, pur ceque est in ovel mischief. Meme, la
             ley est, ou executor per le Statute de Anno 4 E. 3, cap. 7,
             avoit brefe de Trespass *de bonis asportatis in vita testatoris*, ad-
             ministrators sont pris per l'equite de cel, et uncore le statute ne
             parle de administrators; mes pur ceo que est in ouell mischief,
             est reason que il sera pris pur l'equite de cel....'

Hody CB: al contrary, 'et que l'atteint ne sera pris come le statut veut,
           sinon que l'Enquest ust este pris devant le Mayor et le Vicomte;
           car jeo n'ay veu ou Statut est fait, que est penal, que ascun
           chose sera pris per l'equite de cel....'

Fineux CJ: ...'Et jeo agre in ascun cas que ascuns choses seront pris per
             l'equite d'un statut, que sont in mesme mischief; et ceo a ma
             entente sera ou est in mesme le mischief; et si ne soit pris per
             l'equite de ceo, la party de tiel tort n'ad remedy. Come ou est
             done per Statute Anno 4 Ed. 3, c. 7, *etc*.,...tenent per le
             curtesie, *etc*., *etc*. [(as per *Tremaile, supra*)],...sont un et in
             mesme le mischief come ceux purquoi le Statuts furent faits,

et s'ils ne seront pris per l'equite de ceux statuts, ils faudront remedy; purquei il est reasonable, que soient pris per l'equite de eux. Mes tiels mischief nest pas icy, car il ad autre remedy, cestascavoir le party aver attaint al Comon Ley de remuer le rec' icy, et donque d'aver atteint. Purquei me semble que l'Atteint ne poit gesir icy, ni per expres parols, ni per l'equite. Purquei, *etc.* ' *Quod nota.*

(104) 14 Henry VII, Hil. pl. 7.   p. 258
      Digby *v.* Anon.   Scire facias.

      ......

Kingsmill Sjt: ...'Mes per divers Statuts or est ordine, que brief sera maintenu vers le pernor des profits, que ne sont a reciter, car nul statut mainteint cest brief sinon le Statut de Ann. 1. le Roy qui or est,'[1] qui est Formedon in descender, et in remainder, ou tail est demand; donque coment que cest *Scire facias* soit per execut' le tail, terme nest Formedon in descender et in remainder, de que le statut parle, et ne sera pris per equite. Car ou un Statut est fait, que abrige le Comen Ley, nul chose sera pris per equite de ceo; cest statut abridge le Ley pur lez t', et est in lour disadvantage. Purquei, *etc....*'

Coningsby Sjt: Al contrary...'car il enlarge le comon ley....Et cases que sont in mesme le mischief, pris per l'equite de ceo; come le statut de An. 4 Ed. 3, c. 7, que "Exec' auront brief de *Transgressio de bonis asportatis in vita testatoris*", cest Statute enlarge le Comon Ley, et pur ceo que administrators sont in mesme le mischief, ils auront meme le remedy; mes si un Statut abrige le comon Ley, ou soit penal, la nul equite sera pris, come est in attaint; et issint diversite....'

      ......

(105) 15 Henry VII, Mich. pl. 1.   pp. 294, 298
      Anon. *v.* Anon.

      ......

Frowike:[2] ...'Et comment que le feoffer sera jure in Enquest par cause de cest use, ce ne prove qu'il ad interest en la terre; mes le cause est, parce qu'ils qui firent le statut,[3] donerent que "Un que sera jure en Enquest expend' XL s." construrent in tiel forme, car le

---

[1] 1 Henry VI, c. 1.
[2] This report begins thus: 'Le premier cas que Thomas Frowike argue apres que il fuit fait Chief Justice fuit', etc. According to Foss's *Judges of England*, however, this statement is erroneous, as Frowike was not appointed chief justice until September 30th, 1502.
[3] 1 Richard III, c. 4.

statut fuit fait pur le mischief qe le viconte impanell' simple persons et de small conscience, et pur ceo ils ordonnent le statute, que on de substance serra impanell', qui intend de bon conscience. Et al fesance de le Statut le grand part del terre de Angleterre fuit in feoffements sur confidence, et par ce l'entent de eux qui firent le statut ne fuit, que ceux a que use ils furent seisis ne sera jurez, car donque sera forsque peu d'hommes qui passeront sur Juries, et pur ceo ils construirent le statut in tiels forme que cesty a qui use ils sont seisis, serront jures etc. Et comment que cest construction est encountre les parties del statut, uncore nous devons admettre ceo, par ce que ceo fuit l'entent des fesors. Et sont divers statutes que sont construis in autre forme que les parols sont, purquei ceo ne prove', *etc.*

(106) 15 Henry VII, Trin. pl. 2.   p. 298
      Anon. *v.* Anon.   Scire facias.

...Et tenu clerement par les Justices, que il sera pris par l'equitie del Statut, comment que le Statut[1] parle solement de Formedon in rem' et descend'; uncore quand l'action est done pur l'avantage le terre in tail, et est done in l'original brefe, l'equity done ceo in le brefe dexecucion; et par cause il est bon icy vers le pernor des profits. Purquei les Justices furent in clere opinion, que le brefe est bon.

(107) 16 Henry VII, Trin. pl. 17.   p. 58
      Anon. *v.* Abbot of Battle.   Replevin.
      . . . . . .

Et pur ceo semble al *Hussey CJ* que il (l' allowance) n'est pas bon. Et il mist un diversite ou un conusance lier a le roy et ou nemy; car il dit, in un *Quo Warranto* si le chartre soit allowe, il liera le roy comment que de droit le chartre ne doit estre allowe; car auterment le party serra plusors temps vexe, ce que nest reason quand il est un fois allowe; et sur un original al suit du roy; mes si le chartre ne soit pas allowe devant les Justices in Eyre, puis temps de memory, *etc.*, le grant ad perdu sa force, et donque ne liera le Roy, *etc.*

(108) 20 Henry VII, Mich. pl. 17.   pp. 16, 58
      Anon. *v.* Anon.   Endictment.
      . . . . . .

L'Atturney: dit que non; 'car cest le prerogative le roy, et il ne peut granter son prerogative comme il ne poit granter *Quod nullum tempus occurrit ei,* et sic icy.'
      . . . . . .

[1] 1 Henry VII, c. 1.

Brudenell Sjt: 'Et oustre le Roy ne poit granter a moy de faire mes Justices
de paix, nient plus qu'il poit granter a moy de prendre felons,
car il est le Chief Justice et est annexe a son person, que ne
peut estre severe....'

. . . . . .

(109) 21 Henry VII, Mich. pl. 45.   p. 295
    Tost *v.* Cromer.   Debt.

Eliot Sjt: ...'et chescun Statute penal sera pris strict. Car il est un
statute, "nul home fera paten de Aspe"; le mischief de ce
Statut fuit, pur ceo que ils occupy tants des meresmes, que les
fletchers ne feurent faire sagits, et uncore si ils feront autres
choses que patens, il nest deins le cas de Statut; issint si il voille
ard' ceux meresmes. Et il y ad un Statut, que le vicomte ne
impanel ses servantes; uncore il puit impanell' ses amis et
cousins, et il nest deins le statut. Issint icy ce statut sera pris
strict; car il est, sil lesse son County, mes icy il n'ad lesse forsque
parcel; in quel cas il nest deins le Statut, sinon que il ust lesse
l'entier county.'

(110) 21 Henry VII, Hil. pl. 1.   pp. 79, 286, 292
    Anon. *v.* Anon.   Annuity.

. . . . . .

Butler Sjt: ...'Uncore plus fort matier appiert icy; car par cel Act de
Parlement le annuite de fine force covient estre determine; car
ceo est un de les plus haut records que est in le ley, et tiel record
a quel chescun in Angleterre est prive, et sera lye per ceo....'

. . . . . .

Kingsmill J: ...'Mes, Sir, l'act de Parliament ne peut faire le Roy d'estre
person; Car nous per nostre ley ne pouvons faire ascun
temporel home d'aver Jurisdiction spirituel; car nul poit ceo
faire sinon le supreme teste....'

. . . . . .

(111) 21 Henry VII, Hil. pl. 6.   pp. 58, 280
    Anon. *v.* Anon.

Frowike CJ: 'Et, Sir, quand le Roy ad fait ascun grant ou licence, ceo
covient estre execute accordant et strict, et ceo varie del
cas des commons persons....'

Vavasour J: fuit de meme l'opinion....'Et icy,' il dit, 'que un common
person ne puit faire feoffement sur tiel condition que le feoffe
ne alienera, mes le roy puit; car chescun fait que le Roy fait
sera pris plus beneficial pur luy, et plus forts envers cesty que
fist le fait.'

. . . . . .

(112) 21 Henry VII, Hil. pl. 28.   pp. 284, 285, 295
     Coste *v.* An Undersheriff.   Extortion.

    . . . . . .

    Car fuit mouve que cest prescription ne eux aidera, car le Statut ad
ceo defait, comment que ils avoient en prescription devant. Come
ceux de Londres avoient un prescription que nul attaint gist de
ascun serment la; mes or per le Statut de ano. 11 H. 7, c. 21 ceo est
defait, issint icy. . . . Et l'opinio de Touts les Justices fuit, que ceo
est hors del cas de Statut. Car l'entent de le Statut fuit, que ou
viconte, *etc.*, prindrent grand damage des prisoners quand ils
furent delivrez, pur ce le statut ordeine, et limit' quel summe le
Viconte ou ascun auter gaoler prendre de eux estant in lour garde.
. . . Et en chescun statut on covient de construir l'entent de eux que
fesoient le statut. . . .

Read CJ: dit que nul equite peut estre pris de tiels Statuts que sont in
    abridgement de le common ley; come Forcible entre est done per
    Statute de terre; mes il nest issint de rente; issint Forcible entre
    in rent ne peut estre pris per l'equite; per ce que le statut est in
    abrigement del Comon Ley. Et issint clere opinion des Justices
    que le prisel de cest barre fee est dispunissable per Statut. *Quod
    nota.*

BIBLIOGRAPHY[1]

A. ORIGINAL SOURCES

ANDLAU, PETER VON. Libellus de Cesarea Monarchia. Ed. J. Hürbin. *Zeitschrift der Savigny-Stiftung für Rechtsgeschichte, Germanistische Abteilung*, XVIII, 1897. [337]

ANNALES HENRICI QUARTI. Ed. H. T. Riley. *Johannis de Trokelowe Chronica et Annales, Rolls Series*, 1866. [7, 107, 113]

ANONIMALLE CHRONICLE. Ed. V. H. Galbraith. *Manchester Historical Series*, XLV, 1927. [126, 221, 230]

AQUINAS, ST THOMAS. De Regimine Principum. Paris, 1509. [335]

—— Summa Theologica. Ed. Migne, Patrologiae Cursus Completus, 4 vols. 1845. [200, 339]

ARMACHANI, RICARDUS. De Pauperie Salvatoris. Ed. R. L. Poole. *Wycliffe: De Dominio Divino*, London, 1890. [334, 338]

BEAUVAIS, VINCENT OF. De Morali Principis Institutione. *Bodleian MSS. C.* 398. [340]

BEKYNTON, T. Official Correspondence. Ed. B. Williams. *Rolls Series*, 2 vols. 1872. [332, 333]

BOETHIUS. De Consolatione Philosophiae, trans. King Alfred. Ed. J. S. Cardale. London, 1829. [95, 337]

BRACTON, H. DE. De Legibus et Consuetudinibus Angliae. Ed. G. E. Woodbine. *Yale Historical MS. and Texts*, III, 2 vols. 1918. [15, 57, 65, 324–328, 341]

BRITISH MUSEUM MSS. Cottonian. Cleopatra, F. IV. [149]

—— Cottonian. Nero, C. I. [230]

—— Cottonian. Titus, E. IV. [149]

—— Harleian, 431. [59, 117]

BRITTON. Ed. and trans. F. M. Nichols. 2 vols. London, 1865. [341]

BROOKE, SIR ROBERT. La Graunde Abridgement. London, 1573. [55, 58, 267, 351, 352, 355]

BRUT, THE. Ed. F. D. Brie. *E.E.T.S.* Old Series, 2 vols. CXXI, CXXXVI, 1906, 1908. [94, 129, 139]

CAMBRIDGE UNIV. LIBRARY MSS. Ii, I, 33. [95]

---

[1] The numbers in square brackets after each item in the Bibliography refer to the pages on which the work is cited in the text above.

CAXTON, W. Continuation of Ranulph Higden's Polychronicon. Ed. J. R. Lumby. *Rolls Series*, 1882. [287]

COKE, SIR EDWARD. Reports. 13 vols. London, 1600–1659. [195, 201, 259]

—— Institutes of the Laws of England. 4 vols. London, 1628–1644. [43, 126, 249, 259, 262]

COMMYNES, PHILIP DE. Mémoires. Ed. B. de Mandrot. 2 vols. Paris, 1901–1903. [59, 341]

CORAM REGE ROLLS. William Salt Society Collections, VI. London, 1885. [34]

CORPUS JURIS CANONICI. [106, 199, 200, 207]

DIPLOMATIC CORRESPONDENCE OF RICHARD II. Ed. E. Perroy. *Camden Society*, 3rd Series, XLVIII, 1933. [118]

EGIDIUS ROMANUS. De Regimine Principum. Rome, 1482. [308, 314, 315, 318]

ENGLISH CONSTITUTIONAL DOCUMENTS, 1307–1485. Ed. E. Lodge and G. Thornton. Cambridge, 1935. [35, 38, 59, 162, 164]

ENGLISH CORONATION RECORDS. Ed. L. G. W. Legg. London, 1901. [17, 18, 19]

ENGLISH ECONOMIC HISTORY. Select Documents. Ed. A. E. Bland, P. Brown, R. H. Tawney. London, 1914. [288]

EULOGII CONTINUATIO. Ed. F. Haydon. *Rolls Series*, 1863. [24]

FANE FRAGMENT OF THE 1461 LORDS' JOURNAL. Ed. W. H. Dunham Jr. London, 1935. [63, 126, 129, 139, 163, 218, 220, 225]

FITZHERBERT, SIR ANTHONY. La Graunde Abridgement. London, 1576. [292, 341, 359]

FLETA SEU COMMENTARIUS JURIS ANGLICANI. Ed. J. Selden. London, 1647. [70, 341]

FORTESCUE, SIR JOHN. De Laudibus Legum Angliae. Ed. A. Amos. Cambridge, 1825.

—— Complete Works. Ed. Lord Clermont. 2 vols. London, 1869.

—— Governance of England. Ed. C. Plummer. Oxford, 1885.

[For references *v.* Index, *sub* Fortescue, Works]

GASCOIGNE, T. Loci e Libro Veritatum. Ed. T. Rogers. Oxford, 1881. [26, 253, 333]

GESTA HENRICI QUINTI. Ed. B. Williams. *English History Society*, 1850. [333]

GRANTS OF EDWARD V. Ed. J. Nichols. *Camden Society*, LX, 1854. [For references *v.* Index, *sub* Russell]

GREGORY, W. Chronicle. Ed. J. Gairdner. *Collections of a London Citizen, Camden Society,* New Series, XVII, 1876. [31]

HALL, E. Chronicle. Ed. H. Ellis. London, 1809. [31]

HARDYNG, J. Chronicle. Ed. H. Ellis. London, 1812. [116, 127]

HOCCLEVE, T. The Regement of Princes. Ed. F. J. Furnivall. *E.E.T.S.* Extra Series, LXXII, 1892–1897. [3, 14, 17, 21, 40]

INNER TEMPLE MSS. Petyt 538, 17f. [26, 126, 333, 334]

ITALIAN RELATION, THE. Ed. C. A. Sneyd. *Camden Society,* XXXVII, 1847. [22, 98, 195]

JOURNALS OF THE HOUSE OF LORDS, 1509–1714. 19 vols. London, 1846. [220]

JUSTINIAN. Institutes. [205]

KELHAM, J. Dictionary of the Norman and old French Language. London, 1779. [88]

LETTERS AND PAPERS OF HENRY VI. Ed. J. Stevenson. *Rolls Series,* 2 vols. 1861. [128]

LIBER ALBUS. Trans H. T. Riley. London, 1861. [231]

LINCOLN'S INN MSS. Petyt, 8. [230]

LIVIO DA FORLI, TITO. Vita Henrici Quinti. Ed. T. Hearne. Oxford, 1716. [125, 333]

LONDON, CHRONICLES OF. Ed. C. L. Kingsford. Oxford, 1905. [108, 139]

LYNDWOOD, W. Provinciale, etc. Oxford, 1679. [8, 285]

MARSIGLIO OF PADUA. Defensor Pacis. Ed. C. Previté-Orton. Cambridge, 1928. [135]

MONMOUTH, GEOFFREY OF. Historia Regum Brittanie. Ed. A. Griscom. New York, 1929. [340]

NEW ENGLISH DICTIONARY. Ed. J. Murray, etc. Oxford, 1888–1928. [87, 105, 197, 251]

NOVA STATUTA. London, c. 1482. [231]

—— London, pub. Pynson, c. 1497. [231]

PALINGENESIA JURIS CIVILIS. Ed. O. Lenel. 2 vols. Leipzig, 1889. [179]

PAPAL REGISTERS, CALENDAR OF. Ed. W. Bliss, etc., *Rolls Series,* 10 vols. 1893–1912. [380, 381]

PASTON LETTERS. Ed. J. Gairdner. 3 vols. London, 1874. [121, 127, 129, 264]

PATENT ROLLS, CALENDAR OF. P.R.O. London, 1891–   . [255]

PECOCK, R. The Repressor of over-much Blaming of the Clergy.

Ed. T. Babington. *Rolls Series*, 2 vols. 1860.   [4, 197, 207, 253, 262, 341]

PEMBROKE COLLEGE, CAMBRIDGE MSS. 237.   [95]

POLITICAL AND OTHER POEMS, TWENTY-SIX. Ed. J. Kail. *E.E.T.S.* Old Series, CXXIV, 1904.   [14, 20, 145, 255]

POLITICAL POEMS AND SONGS. Ed. T. Wright. *Camden Society*, VI, 1859.   [95, 255]

PROCEEDINGS AND ORDINANCES OF THE PRIVY COUNCIL. Ed. Sir Harris Nicolas. *Record Comm.* 7 vols. 1834–37.   [17, 36, 66, 70, 142, 148, 149, 151, 152, 228]

RED BOOK OF THE EXCHEQUER. Ed. H. Hall. *Rolls Series*, 1896.   [230]

RED PAPER BOOK OF COLCHESTER. Ed. W. Gurney Benham. Colchester, 1902.   [130, 133]

REDE, R. Nova Chronica. *Bodleian MSS. Rawl. C.* 398.   [340]

ROTULI PARLIAMENTORUM. *Record Comm.* 6 vols. 1767–1777.   [*passim*]

RYMER, T. Foedera, Conventiones, etc., 20 vols. London, 1704–1735.   [118, 380]

ST GERMAIN, CHRISTOPHER. Doctor and Student. London, 1815.   [200, 203–214, 229]

—— Dialogus de fundamentis Regum et conscientia. London, 1523.   [212, 213]

SELECT CASES CONCERNING THE LAW MERCHANT. Ed. C. Gross and H. Hall. 3 vols. *Selden Society*, XXIII, 1908; XLVI, 1929; XLIX, 1932.   [216, 289]

SELECT CHARTERS. Ed. W. Stubbs. Ed. H. W. C. Davis. Oxford, 9th ed. 1921.   [18, 135, 193]

SELECT DOCUMENTS OF ENGLISH CONSTITUTIONAL HISTORY. Ed. G.B. Adams and H. M. Stephens. New York, 1926.   [152, 159]

SIX TOWN CHRONICLES. Ed. R. Flenley. Oxford, 1911.   [131, 239]

SOMNIUM VIGILANTIS or A Defence of the Proscription of the Yorkists. Ed. J. Gilson. *E.H.R.* XXVI, 1911.   [94, 122, 197, 202, 334]

STATUTES OF THE REALM. *Record Commission.* 11 vols. 1810–1828.   [*passim*]

TRANSLATOR OF LIVIUS. First English Life of Henry V. Ed. C. L. Kingsford. Oxford, 1911.   [230]

USK, ADAM OF. Chronicon. Ed. Sir Edward Thompson. *Royal Society of Literature*, 2nd ed. 1904.   [58, 106]

VENETIAN STATE PAPERS, CALENDAR OF. 9 vols. London, 1864–1898.   [379]

VIEUX ABRIDGEMENT DES STATUTES. London, ?1481. [19, 231]

WALSINGHAM, T. Historia Anglicana. Ed. H. T. Riley. *Rolls Series*, 1869. [39, 152]

WALTHAM, ROGERUS DE. Compendium Morale. *Bodleian MSS. Laud Misc.* 616; *Bodl.* 805. [339]

WHETHAMSTEDE JOHANNIS REGISTRUM. Ed. H. T. Riley. *Rolls Series*, 1872. [128]

WORCESTER, W. Annales Rerum Anglicarum. Ed. J. Stevenson. *Letters of Henry VI, Rolls Series*, 1864. [28]

WYCLIFFE, J. De Officio Regis. Ed. A. W. Pollard and C. Sayles. London, 1887. [15, 96]

—— Select English Works. T. Arnold, 1869–1871. [84, 96, 197]

YEAR BOOKS or LES REPORTS DES CASES. 10 vols. London, 1679. [*v.* Appendix]

YEAR BOOK OF 1 HENRY VI. Ed. C. H. Williams. *Selden Society*, L, 1933. [xi]

—— 10 EDWARD IV and of 49 HENRY VI. Ed. N. Neilson. *Selden Society*, XLVII, 1931. [x, 262, 371]

B. SECONDARY AUTHORITIES

ADAMS, G. B. Constitutional History of England. London, 1935. [xvii]

ALLEN, C. K. Law in the Making. Oxford, 2nd ed. 1931. [49]

ANSON, Sir WILLIAM. Law and Custom of the Constitution. 3 vols. Oxford, 3rd ed. 1897–1900. [192]

AUSTIN, J. The Province of Jurisprudence Determined. London, 1832. [197]

BACON, M. A New Abridgement of the Law. 5 vols. London, 1736–1766. [259]

BALDWIN, J. F. The King's Council in England during the Middle Ages. Oxford, 1913. [28, 341]

BENNETT, H. S. The Pastons and their England. Cambridge, 1922. [231]

BLACKSTONE, Sir WILLIAM. Commentaries on the Laws of England. 4 vols. Oxford, 1765–1769. [126, 211, 291]

BLOCH, M. Les Rois Thaumaturges. Strasbourg, 1924. [8]

BRADY, R. True and Exact History of the Succession of the Crown of England. London, 1681. [19]

BROOKE, Z. N. The English Church and the Papacy from the Conquest to the time of John. Cambridge, 1931. [285]

CAM, H. M. The 'Quo Warranto' Proceedings under Edward I. *History*, x, 1926. [57]

CARLYLE, A. J. and Sir RICHARD. History of Mediaeval Political Theory in the West. 5 vols. Edinburgh and London, 1915– [339]

CARTER, A. T. History of English Legal Institutions. London, 4th ed. 1910. [216]

CHEW, H. The Ecclesiastical Tenants-in-Chief and Writs of Military Summons. *E.H.R.* xli, 1926. [146]

—— The Ecclesiastical Tenants-in-Chief and Knight Service. Oxford, 1932. [146]

CHRIMES, S. B. John, duke of Bedford, his work and policy in England, 1389–1435. *Bull. I.H.R.* vii, 1929. [149]

—— The Pretensions of the duke of Gloucester in 1422. *E.H.R.* xlv, 1930. [37]

—— Note on the Liability of the Lords to contribute to the Wages of the Knights of the Shire. *E.H.R.* xlix, 1934. [155]

CLARKE, M. V. Forfeitures and Treasons in 1388. *T.R.H.S.* xiv, 1931. [160, 252, 266]

CLARKE, M. V. and GALBRAITH, V. H. The Deposition of Richard II. *Bull. J.R.L.* xiv, 1930. [5, 107]

COWELL, J. Law Dictionary. London, 1708. [43, 280]

CRAIES, W. F. A Treatise on Statute Law. London, 3rd ed. 1923. [293]

DAVIES, J. C. The Baronial Opposition to Edward II. Cambridge, 1918. [34]

DAVIES, W. E. The English Law relating to Aliens. London, 1931. [256]

D'ENTRÈVES, A. P. San Tommaso d'Aquine e la Costituzione Inglese nell' opera di Sir John Fortescue. *Atti della Reale Accademia di Scienze di Torino*, lxii, 1927. [203, 339]

DICEY, A. V. Law of the Constitution. London, 8th ed. 1927. [266]

DICTIONARY OF NATIONAL BIOGRAPHY. [204]

DIGBY, Sir KENELM. Introduction to the History of the Law of Real Property. Oxford, 5th ed. 1897. [292]

EDWARDS, J. G. The Parliamentary Committee of 1398. *E.H.R.* xl, 1925. [138]

EDWARDS, J. G. The 'Plena Potestas' of the English Parliamentary Representatives. *Oxford Essays in Mediaeval History presented to H. E. Salter*, Oxford, 1934. [80]

EHRLICH, L. Proceedings against the Crown, 1216–1377. *Oxford Studies in Social and Legal History*, VI, Oxford, 1921. [341]

FIGGIS, J. N. Studies in Political Thought from Gerson to Grotius. Cambridge, 1907. [332]

FOSS, E. The Judges of England. 9 vols. London, 1848–69. [391]

FRAZER, Sir JAMES. Lectures on the Early History of Kingship. London, 1905. [1]

—— Psyche's Task. London, 1909. [69]

GABEL, L. C. Benefit of Clergy in England. *Smith College Studies in History*, XIV, Northampton, Mass. 1929. [287]

GIERKE, O. Das Deutsche Genossenschaftsrecht. 4 vols. Berlin, 1868–1913. [134]

—— Political Theories of the Middle Age. Ed. and trans. F. W. Maitland. Cambridge, 1900. [333]

GNEIST, M. R. VON. History of the English Constitution. Trans. P. A. Ashworth. 2 vols. London, 1866. [83]

—— History of the English Parliament. Trans. A. H. Keane. London, 1889. [82]

GRAY, H. L. The Influence of the Commons on Early Legislation. *Harvard Historical Studies*, XXXIV, Cambridge, Mass. 1932. [71, 73, 74, 160, 163, 218–231, 236–349]

HALLAM, H. View of the State of Europe in the Middle Ages. 3 vols. London, 11th ed. 1855. [81, 132, 271]

—— Constitutional History of England. 3 vols. London, 11th ed. 1866. [33]

HARCOURT, L. W. V. His Grace the Steward and Trial of Peers. London, 1907. [135]

HATSCHEK, J. Englische Verfassungsgeschichte bis zum Regierungsantritt der Königin Victoria. *Handbuch der mittelalterlichen u. neueren Geschichte*, hrsg. G. von Below und F. Meinecke, Abt. 3, 1913. [82]

HEMMANT, M. The Exchequer Chamber, etc. *Bull. I.H.R.* VII, 1929. [46]

— Select Cases in the Exchequer Chamber. *Selden Society*, LI, 1933. [46]

HICKS, J. Passive Obedience Defended. 1683. [339]

HISTORICAL MSS. COMMISSION. 8th Report, 1881. [20, 334, 341]

HOLDSWORTH, Sir WILLIAM. History of English Law. 9 vols. London, 3rd ed. 1923. [10, 57, 75, 134, 154, 155, 192, 204, 214, 272, 292]

—— The Influence of the Legal Profession on the Growth of the English Constitution. Oxford, 1924. [42]

HÜRBIN, J. Peter von Andlau, der Verfasser des ersten deutschen Reichsstaatrechts. Strassburg, 1897. [337]

ILBERT, Sir COURTENAY. Legislative Methods and Forms. Oxford, 1901. [137, 229]

INTERIM REPORT ON HOUSE OF COMMONS PERSONNEL AND POLITICS, 1264–1832. Cmd. 4130, 1932. [136, 334]

JACOB, E. F. Changing Views of the Renaissance. *History*, XVI, 1931. [334]

—— Some English Documents of the Conciliar Movement. *Bull. J.R.L.* xv, 1931. [59, 117, 332, 341]

—— Sir John Fortescue and the Law of Nature. *Bull. J.R.L.* XVIII, 1934. [25, 49, 199, 337]

JACOB, G. Law Dictionary. London, 1744. [126]

JELLINEK, G. Das Recht der Minoritäten. Vienna, 1898. [133]

JENKS, E. Law and Politics in the Middle Ages. London, 2nd ed. 1913. [25]

JOHNSTONE, H. England; Edward I and Edward II, *Cambridge Medieval History*, VII, xiv, 1932. [66]

JOLOWICZ, H. F. Historical Introduction to Roman Law. Cambridge, 1932. [206]

KEIR, D. L. and LAWSON, F. H. Cases in Constitutional Law. Oxford, 2nd ed. 1933. [283]

KERN, F. Gottesgnadentum und Widerstandsrecht im früheren Mittelalter. *Mittelalterlichen Studien*, hrsg. F. Kern, Bd. I, Heft 2, Leipzig, 1914. [8, 254]

—— Recht und Verfassung in Mittelalter. *Historische Zeitschrift*, CXX, 1919. [17, 192, 193]

LAPSLEY, G. T. The County Palatine of Durham. *Harvard Historical Studies*, VIII, Cambridge, Mass. 1900. [55, 267]

—— The Commons and the Statute of York. *E.H.R.* XXVIII, 1913. [92, 160]

—— John de Warenne and 'Quo Warranto' Proceedings in 1279. *Cambridge Historical Journal*, II, 1927. [57]

LAPSLEY, G. T. Review of H. L. Gray's Influence of the Commons on Early Legislation. *E.H.R.* XLVIII, 1933. [236]
—— The Parliamentary Title of Henry IV. *E.H.R.* XLIX, 1934. [5, 8, 23, 26, 34, 62, 106, 108, 157, 160, 266]
LATHAM, L. C. The Collection of the Wages of the Knights of the Shire in the 14th and 15th Centuries. *E.H.R.* XLVIII, 1933. [155]
LIPSON, E. Economic History of England; I, The Middle Ages. London, 4th ed. 1926. [288]
McILWAIN, C. H. The High Court of Parliament. London, 1910. [271, 291]
—— Magna Carta and Common Law. *Magna Carta Commemoration Essays*, London, 1917. [271, 273, 274, 276]
—— The Growth of Political Thought in the West. London, 1932. [135, 193, 324, 338, 339]
MAITLAND, F.W. The Constitutional History of England. Cambridge, 1888. [159]
—— Memoranda de Parliamento. *Rolls Series*, 1893. [83]
—— Wyclif on English and Roman Law, *Law Quarterly Review*, XII, 1896. [194]
—— Domesday Book and Beyond. Cambridge, 1897. [1]
—— Roman Canon Law in the Church of England. Cambridge, 1898. [53, 285, 288]
—— Collected Papers. 3 vols. Cambridge, 1911. [44, 87]
MAXWELL, Sir PETER. On the Interpretation of Statutes. London, 7th ed. 1929. [293, 296]
MAXWELL-LYTE, Sir HENRY. Historical Notes on the Use of the Great Seal. London, 1926. [158, 159]
MEDLEY, D. J. Manual of English Constitutional History. Oxford, 2nd ed. 1898. [161]
MERRIMAN, R. B. Control by National Assemblies of the Repeal of Legislation in the Later Middle Ages. *Mélanges D'Histoire offerts à M. Charles Bémont*, Paris, 1913. [265]
MITCHELL, W. An Essay on the Early History of the Law Merchant. Cambridge, 1904. [288]
MOHL, R. The Three Estates in Medieval and Renaissance Literature. *Columbia University Press*, 1933. [81]
MONTAGUE, F. C. The Elements of English Constitutional History. London, 1923. [159]

404   *Bibliography*

OMAN, C. Warwick the Kingmaker. London, 1891. [28]

PAROW, W. Über die Regierung Englands von Sir John Fortescue. *Sammlung älterer und neuerer Staatswissenschaftlicher Schriften des In- und Auslandes*, x, Berlin, 1897. [340]

PICKTHORN, K. Some Historical Principles of the English Constitution. London, 1925. [xix]

—— Early Tudor Government. 2 vols. Cambridge, 1934. [xviii, 2, 5, 8, 33, 38, 39, 130, 135, 136, 218, 219, 229, 254, 287, 289, 379]

PIKE, L. O. Constitutional History of the House of Lords. London, 1894. [146]

PLUCKNETT, T. F. T. Statutes and their Interpretation in the First Half of the Fourteenth Century. *Cambridge Studies in Legal History*, ed. H. D. Hazeltine, Cambridge, 1922. [25, 49, 250, 252, 272, 283, 284, 290, 291]

—— The Lancastrian Constitution. *Tudor Studies*, ed. R. W. Seton Watson, London, 1924. [xiii, 41, 74, 78, 154]

—— Review of H. L. Gray's The Influence of the Commons on Early Legislation. *Annual Survey of English Law*, 1933. [236]

POLLARD, A. F. The Reign of Henry VII from Contemporary Sources. 3 vols. London, 1914. [379]

—— The Evolution of Parliament. London, 2nd ed. 1926. [81, 85, 119, 154, 340]

—— Review of H. L. Gray's The Influence of the Commons on Early Legislation. *History*, XVIII, 1933. [228, 236, 245]

POLLOCK, Sir FREDERICK. First Book of Jurisprudence. London, 1896. [216]

—— The Expansion of the Common Law. London, 1904. [291]

—— Essays in the Law. London, 1922. [199, 200, 205]

POLLOCK, Sir FREDERICK and MAITLAND, F. W. History of English Law before the time of Edward I. 2 vols. Cambridge, 2nd ed. 1893. [35, 49, 57, 83, 134, 135, 155, 156, 192, 194, 285, 286, 288]

POTTER, H. An Historical Introduction to English Law and its Institutions. London, 1932. [63]

POWICKE, F. M. Mediaeval England. London, 1931. [82]

PRYNNE, W. The Soveragne Power of Parliaments and Kingdomes. London, 1643. [19]

PUTNAM, B. The Enforcement of the Statutes of Labourers. *Columbia Studies in History*, etc., XXXII, New York, 1908. [235]

PUTNAM, B. Early Treatises on the Practice of the Justices of the Peace in the 15th and 16th Centuries. *Oxford Studies in Social and Legal History*, VII, 1924. [7, 14, 16, 47, 130]

RAMSAY, Sir JAMES. Lancaster and York. 2 vols. London, 1892. [36]

—— Dawn of the Constitution. London, 1908. [380]

REDLICH, J. The Procedure of the House of Commons. Trans. A. E. Steinthal. London, 1908. [133, 135, 159]

RICHARDSON, H. G. The Origins of Parliament. *T.R.H.S.* 4th Series, XI, 1928. [80]

RICHARDSON, H. G. and SAYLES, G. O. Early Records of the English Parliaments. *Bull. I.H.R.* VI, 1928. [93]

—— The Early Statutes. *Law Quarterly Review*, L, 1934. [231]

—— Early Coronation Records. *Bull. I.H.R.* XIII, XIV, 1936. [17]

SALMOND, Sir JOHN. Jurisprudence. London, 7th ed. 1924. [211]

SAVIGNY, F. C. VON. System des heutigen römischen Rechts. Berlin, 1840–1851. [206]

SCHUYLER, R. L. Parliament and the British Empire. New York, 1929. [267, 268]

SELDEN, J. Dissertatio ad Fletam, 1647. Ed. D. Ogg. *Cambridge Studies in Legal History*, ed. H. D. Hazeltine, Cambridge, 1925. [341]

SELECT ESSAYS IN ANGLO-AMERICAN LEGAL HISTORY. 2 vols. Cambridge, 1907–1909. [25]

SHARPE, R. R. London and the Kingdom. 3 vols. London, 1895. [147]

SKEEL, C. A. J. The Influence of the Writings of Sir John Fortescue. *T.R.H.S.* X, 1916. [334]

SOHM, R. Institutes of Roman Law. Ed. J. C. Ledlie. Oxford, 2nd ed. 1901. [38]

STOW, J. Annales or a General Chronicle of England. Ed. E. Howes. London, 1631. [63]

STUBBS, W. The Constitutional History of England. 3 vols. Oxford, 5th ed. 1903. [xiv, xv, 3, 19, 24, 71, 82, 83, 99, 159, 271]

TAYLOR, A. The Glory of Regality. London, 1890. [17]

—— Liber Regalis. *Roxburghe Club*, 1890. [17]

THAYER, J. B. A Preliminary Treatise on Evidence at Common Law. London, 1898. [134, 210]

THORNLEY, I. D. The Destruction of Sanctuary. *Tudor Studies*, ed. R. W. Seton Watson, London, 1924. [287]

406   *Bibliography*

Tout, T. F. The Place of the Reign of Edward II in English History. *Manchester Historical Series*, xxi, 1914. [35, 272]
—— France and England: their relations in the Middle Ages and now. *Ibid.* xl. [84]
—— Chapters in Mediaeval Administrative History. 6 vols. *Ibid.* xxxiv, xxxv, xlviii, xlix, lvii, lxiv, 1920–1933. [xviii, 71, 84, 98, 145, 272, 273]
—— Collected Papers. 3 vols. *Ibid.* lxiii, lxiv, lxv, 1932–1934. [66]
Vickers, K. England in the Later Middle Ages. London, 1904. [149]
—— Humphrey, duke of Gloucester. London, 1907. [149, 381]
Viner, C. General Abridgement of Law and Equity. 23 vols. Aldershot, 1741–1753. [250, 259, 260, 285]
Vinogradoff, Sir Paul. Common Sense in Law. London, 1914. [205]
—— Collected Papers. 3 vols. Oxford, 1928. [51, 54, 55, 204, 211, 281]
Wakeman, O. and Hassall, A. Essays introductory to English Constitutional History. London, 1891. [159]
Wallis, J. E. W. English Regnal Years and Titles, etc., *English Time Books*, i, London, 1921. [1]
Waterhous, E. Commentaries on the *De Laudibus* of Sir John Fortescue. London, 1663. [340]
Waugh, W. T. The Great Statute of Praemunire. *E.H.R.* xxxii, 1922: *History*, viii, 1924. [287]
Welch, C. History of the Worshipful Company of Pewterers of the City of London. 2 vols. London, 1902. [126]
Wilkinson, B. The Coronation Oath of Edward II. *Historical Essays in Honour of James Tait*, ed. J. G. Edwards and E. F. Jacob, 1933. [20, 160]
Williams, I. The Sources of Law in the Swiss Civil Code. Oxford, 1923. [198]
Winfield, P. H. Chief Sources of English Legal History. Cambridge, Mass. 1925. [10, 204]
Wylie, J. H. History of England under Henry IV. 4 vols. London, 1884–1898. [26, 35, 118]
Wylie, J. H. and Waugh, W. T. History of England under Henry V. 2 vols. Cambridge, 1914–1929. [118]

INDEX OF SUBJECTS

parliament, 53–55; cannot defeat statute by letters patent, 54; cannot grant away prerogatives, 53, 57–58; cannot grant cognizance of all pleas, 54; cannot join another issue, 45, 53; cannot repeal acts, alter the law, nor tax, without assent of parliament, 59–60; choice of, between statute and common law, 46; dates of reigns of, 33; *de facto* and *de jure*, 33 n. 1, 38, 56; *de facto*, judicial acts of, upheld, 32, 56; demise of, dissolves parliament, 38; discretionary power of, 46–49; dispensing power of, 280–283; divine right of, 33; duties of, 14–20, 38, 333; estate of, 1–62, 91–92: inseparable from the person of, 34–38; goods of mute felons adjudged to, 45; grace of, 8–9; grants by: only with assent of parliament, 58; restricted by previous acts of parliament, 58; subject to restriction, 58 n. 4, 7; officers of: warranted by, 54; restricted, 53, 54; letters patent of, interpreted strictly, 58; limited but uncontrolled, 59–60; need of, for counsel, 39–41; not bound by statute unless named, 45; perjury by, 17; powers of, 39: not diminished by need for assent, 325; prerogative of: cannot be encroached on by the pope, 52–53; inalienable, 35; present in court, 63 n. 1; present in parliament, 63 n. 1; procedural privileges of, 45; proprietary right of, 9–13, 25, 31, 33 n. 1, 34, 56 n. 1; restrained by act of parliament, 53; will of, 8–9

Kingdom, as property, 9–13

Kingship, attributes of, 4–9; as an estate of the realm, 116; of England, in Fortescue, 322–323, 325–328, 340 n. 76; conception of, 3–22; as divine vocation, 20–21; early Germanic notions of, 1; factors in growth of conception of, 1–3; hereditary right to, 25–26; Lancastrian ideas of, 5–6; necessity of, 4; as office, 14; parliamentary title to, 24–25, 29–30; sacrosanctity of, 7; succession to, 22–34; thaumaturgical powers of, 7–8

Lancaster, dukedom of, 35

Lancastrian ideas of kingship, 5–6

Law (*v.* also *sub titt.* God, Nature, Positive), general nature of, 343–344; as custom, 192; as inheritance of the king, 74; making of new, 192–194, 195 n. 1, 250–255, 326–327; sovereignty of, 60; of England, grounds of, 207–213; Merchant, 288–289

Legal right, continuity of, 56

Legislative procedure, 218–231

Legitimism, 25–26, 32–33

Lehnstaat to *Ständestaat*, 82

Letters patent, and statutes, 280–283

Limited monarchy, 302; definition of, 339 n. 68

London, customs of, and statutes, 260 n. 2, 285 n. 4

Lords, house of, 126–130; place of the, in parliament and council, 145–156; spiritual, 102, 105; temporal, 101, 102, 105

Majority rule, principle of, 133–137

Mala prohibita and *mala in se*, 283

Maxims, 210–212

Money grants in parliament, 93, 152

Nature, law of, 196–200, 205, 208, 209, 311; and all creatures, 205 n. 2; in the courts, 198, 214–218

Non obstante clauses, 58 n. 7, 281–283

Novel ley, 250–251

Novellerie, 9, 100

Parliament, general character of, 345–349; as the high court, 70–76, 80–81; as an inheritance of the king, 74; as a representative assembly, 76–80; as the three estates, 115–126; as source of remedies, 75; assent of, necessary to the king, 39, 59–60, 323–325; authority of, 32, 103, 105, 137–140; chancellor's sermons to, 4, 14, 16, 21, 58 n. 3, 69–70, 73, 74, 97, 99, 116, 120, 142–145, 183 n. 2, 196, 197, 253, 305, 332 n. 6, 333 n. 10; texts of, 165–166, 168–191; clerk of, 226 n. 1, 232; consciousness of, 66–67; descriptions of, by analogy, 68–70; dissolved by king's demise, 38; estates in and out of, 32; estates of, 98–100; motives for summons of, 142–145; name of, 66–67; nature of, 66–142; ought not to refuse grants, 39; procedure of, 74–

INDEX OF PERSONS

Exchequer, chief barons and barons of,
  v. sub tit. Justices

Fastolf, Sir John, 120
Faukes, clerk of parliament, 232, 233,
  362
FitzEustace, Philip, prior of St Botolph's,
  118
FitzWalter, lord, 69
Fortescue, lord, of Credan, 331
Furness, abbot of, 214

Glastonbury, abbot of, 54 n. 5, 76, 112
Gloucester, Humphrey, duke of, 37, 53,
  59, 136, 148, 301, 333 n. 10, 380
Gloucester, Thomas of Woodstock, earl
  of, 112
Gratian, 199, 200 n. 1
Grey, Sir Thomas, 112

Hadelow, Edmund, 155
Hazeltine, H. D., 272
Henry I, 64
Henry II, 64
Henry III, 29, 34, 82, 83, 155
Henry IV, 3, 5 n. 1, 7, 8, 9, 16, 40, 63
  n. 1, 67, 91, 106–115, 118, 159; his
  claim to the crown, 23, 29, 65, 111,
  125; as usurper, 31–32; his letter to
  Alexander V, 59, 117, 266, 324
Henry V, 4, 42, 118, 119, 160, 161, 276;
  reply to the Speaker, 100; claim to
  France, 64
Henry VI, 51, 98, 139, 146, 333 n. 7;
  deposition of, 31 n. 3; illness of, 40;
  restoration of, 32 n. 1; minority of, 324
Henry VII, 35, 167; his claim to the
  crown, 32, 33; attainder of, 51
Henry VIII, 18 n. 4
Hereford, Trevenant, John, bishop of,
  107, 109, 113
Heydon, 129
Hobbes, Thomas, 319, 320
Homer, 169
Hooker, Richard, 136

Ikelyngton, Sir John, 159 n. 1
Ireland, Robert de Vere, duke of, 5
Isidore of Seville, 316
Ive, Thomas, 55

James, son of James III, of Scotland,
  167

Jeremiah, 171
Jethro, 172
Josephus, 200
Justices, and chief Justices, including
  barons and chief barons of the exchequer: Arderne, 293; Ascoghe,
  267 n. 7, 356; Ashton, 45, 363;
  Babington, 355; Billing, 16, 215, 368,
  370; Brian, 293, 385, 387; Catesby,
  379; Choke, 44, 47, 49, 261, 262 n.
  1, 265, 294, 365–366, 371, 378;
  Culpepper, 354; Danby, 48, 367;
  Danvers, 50, 220, 235, 388; Fairfax,
  377, 382; Fineux, 234, 283 n. 2, 388,
  390; Fisher, 383; Fortescue, 231–233,
  358–360, 362 (*v.* also Index of Subjects); Fray, 13, 39, 74, 77, 80, 357;
  Frowike, 294, 298, 391, 393; Gascoigne, 352, 353; Hankford, 53, 139,
  353, 354; Hengham, 296; Hill, 76,
  354, 355; Hody (CB), 390; Hody
  (CJ), 77, 139, 263, 266, 356, 357, 358;
  Hussey, 52, 58 n. 4, 375, 380, 382,
  386, 392; Illingworth, 48, 232, 265,
  294, 361, 366; Jenny, 14 n. 3;
  Kingsmill, 393; Littleton, 44, 78, 137,
  257, 365, 372, 373; Markham, 44, 48,
  74, 112, 215, 233, 362, 367, 368;
  Moile, 6, 363; Nedham, 293;
  Newton, 77, 153, 357; Nottingham,
  13, 374; Nottingham, lord, 296;
  Prisot, 233, 263, 363; Radcliffe, 378,
  382; Read, 234, 295, 394; Shareshulle,
  290, 351; Suliard, 381; Thirning, 3,
  112, 114, 355; Thorpe, 76, 155, 156,
  235, 275, 290, 351, 352; Tirwhit,
  75, 353; Townsend, 51, 379, 381;
  Tremaile, 390; Vavasour, 75, 234,
  235, 382, 385, 389, 393; Yelverton,
  58, 198, 215, 216, 265, 294, 368

King's College, Cambridge, provost of,
  78, 234
Kirkby, Thomas, chancery clerk, 154,
  222–224, 232–233, 245, 361, 362
Knut, king, 18 n. 3

Lancaster, Edmund, duke of, 64
Lanfranc, archbishop of Canterbury,
  34
Langley, Thomas, bishop of Durham,
  pro-chancellor, 142
Lastic, John de, 333 n. 7

46393551R00262

Made in the USA
Columbia, SC
26 December 2018